Professional Portal Development
with Open Source Tools: Java™ Portlet API, Lucene, James, Slide

Professional Portal Development with Open Source Tools: Java™ Portlet API, Lucene, James, Slide

W. Clay Richardson
Donald Avondolio
Joe Vitale
Peter Len
Kevin T. Smith

Wiley Technology Publishing

Wiley Publishing, Inc.

Professional Portal Development with Open Source Tools: Java™ Portlet API, Lucene, James, Slide

Published by
Wiley Publishing, Inc.
10475 Crosspoint Boulevard
Indianapolis, IN 46256
www.wiley.com

Published by Wiley Publishing, Inc., Indianapolis, Indiana

Published simultaneously in Canada

For general information on our other products and services please contact our Customer Care Department within the United States at (800) 762-2974, outside the United States at (317) 572-3993 or fax (317) 572-4002.

Wiley also publishes its books in a variety of electronic formats. Some content that appears in print may not be available in electronic books.

Library of Congress Cataloging-in-Publication Data:

Professional portal development with open source tools: Java™ Portlet
API, Lucene, James, Slide (Wrox Press) / by W. Clay Richardson . . . [et al.] . .
    p. cm.
Includes bibliographical references and index.
  ISBN 0-471-46951-3 (PAPER/WEB SITE)
  1. Web site development. 2. Open source software. I. Richardson, W. Clay, 1976-
  TK5105.888P68 2004
  006.7'6--dc22

                        2003023864

Printed in the United States of America

10 9 8 7 6 5 4 3 2

1MA/QZ/QS/QU/IN

Trademark Acknowledgments

About the Authors

W. Clay Richardson

W. Clay Richardson is a software consultant specializing in distributed solutions, particularly portal solutions. He has fielded multiple open-source Web and portal solutions, serving in roles ranging from senior architect to development lead. He is a co-author of *More Java Pitfalls,* also published by Wiley & Sons. As an adjunct professor of computer science for Virginia Tech, he teaches graduate-level coursework in object-oriented development with Java. He holds degrees from Virginia Tech and the Virginia Military Institute.

Donald Avondolio

Donald Avondolio is a software consultant with over seventeen years of experience developing and deploying enterprise applications. He began his career in the aerospace industry developing programs for flight simulators, and later became an independent contractor, crafting healthcare middleware and low-level device drivers for an assortment of mechanical devices. Most recently, he has built e-commerce applications for numerous high-profile companies, including The Home Depot, Federal Computer Week, the U.S. Postal Service, and General Electric. He is currently a technical architect and developer on several portal deployments. Don also serves as an adjunct professor at Virginia Tech, where he teaches progressive object-oriented design and development methodologies, with an emphasis on patterns.

Joe Vitale

Joe Vitale has been working with the latest cutting-edge Java technology intensely. His most recent focus has been on Java portals and object-relational mapping tools. One of these projects was writing a content management system that contained role-based authentication of users and the capability for users to upload, delete, and manage files, and secure resources. The whole system was designed to plug right into a portal's interface and enable the portal to directly communicate with it to obtain its resources. Object-relational mapping technologies have also been a focus, using Apache's Object Relational Bridge (OJB).

Peter Len

Peter Len has over seven years' experience performing Web-based and Java application development in a client-server environment. He has designed, coded, and implemented data and Web site components for each aspect of a three-tier architecture. Mr. Len has been developing with Java for over five years and has recently been involved with portal and Web-service development. He holds a master's degree in both international affairs and computer information systems.

Kevin T. Smith

Kevin T. Smith is a technical director and principal software architect at McDonald Bradley, Inc., where he develops security solutions for Web service–based systems. He has focused his career on building enterprise solutions based on open-source tools. He holds undergraduate and graduate degrees in computer science, software systems engineering, and information security. He has taught undergraduate courses in computer science, given technical presentations on Web services and Java programming at numerous technology conferences, and authored several technical books, including *Essential XUL Programming* (Wiley 2001), *More Java Pitfalls* (Wiley 2003), and *The Semantic Web: A Guide to the Future of XML, Web Services, and Knowledge Management* (Wiley 2003).

Dedication

This book is dedicated to all those who make the daily sacrifices, and especially to those who have made the ultimate sacrifice, to ensure our freedom and security.

Credits

Authors
W. Clay Richardson
Donald Avondolio
Joe Vitale
Peter Len
Kevin T. Smith

Vice President and Executive Group Publisher
Richard Swadley

Vice President and Executive Publisher
Robert Ipsen

Vice President and Publisher
Joseph B. Wikert

Executive Editorial Director
Mary Bednarek

Editorial Manager
Kathryn A. Malm

Executive Editor
Robert Elliott

Senior Production Editor
Fred Bernardi

Development Editor
Eileen Bien Calabro

Production Editor
William A. Barton

Copy Editor
Luann Rouff

Media Development Specialist
Angela Denny

Permissions Editor
Carmen Krikorian

Project Coordinator
April Farling

Graphic and Layout Technicians
Carrie Foster
Jennifer Heleine
Kristin McMullan
Lynsey Osborn

Quality Control Technicians
John Greenough
Andy Hollandbeck
Brian H. Walls

Text Design & Composition
Wiley Composition Services

Proofreading
Henry Lazarek

Indexing
Tom Dinse

Acknowledgments

I would first like to acknowledge Major Todd DeLong, USA, who had the courage and insight to support an open-source portal solution in the face of overwhelming conventional wisdom, and provided inspiration to this book. Those who know him understand that this is a relatively small measure of his courage. Of course, I could not have had any chance of actually getting this book done without the support of my wonderful wife, Alicia, and daughter, Jennifer. I love both of you more than words can describe. Stephanie, we love you and will never forget you. To my fellow authors, Donnie, Joe, Peter, and Kevin, I appreciate the style, class, and integrity you showed during some very difficult times. I am in a much better place now, and sincerely hope that each of you finds a similar situation for yourself. You are all wonderful talents and it was a great pleasure collaborating with you. I would like to thank Bob Elliott and Eileen Bien Calabro for all their hard work and perseverance working with us on this project. To my leadership, Mark Cramer, Joe Duffy, Jim Moorhead, and Tom Eger, it's wonderful to work for guys who don't talk about "core values," but rather just lead by example. I would like to thank my parents, Bill and Kay, my in-laws, Stephen and Elaine Mellman, my sister, Kari, my brother, Morgan, and my stepfather, Dave, for always being there. I would like to acknowledge my grandmothers, Vivian and Sophie, for being what grandmothers should be.

To my technical "posse": Mark "Mojo" Mitchell, Marshall "PAB" Sayen, Mauro "Tre" Marcellino, Scot Schrager, Tom Bachmann, Jon Simasek, Rob Brown, Kim Bell, Kevin McPhilamy, Jon Grasmeder — I look forward to facing more technical challenges with you. To the people I constantly badger for "stuff": Lisa Peters, Chris Reid, Bryan Foster, Steve Tagg, Rick Yard — this has to count for something! Ed, you know how it has to be. I would like to acknowledge those individuals with whom I didn't get to work enough: Arnie Voketaitis, Seth Goldrich, Cliff Toma, Joe Sayen, Kevin Moran, Adam Dean, Ken Pratt, Alex Blakemore, Dave Holberton, Vic Fraenckel, Mike Shea, Jullie Bishop, and many more to whom I will owe a beer for forgetting to mention them. I would like to thank my colleagues at Virginia Tech for their assistance in my career development: Shawn Bohner, Athman Bouguettaya, John Viega, Stephen Edwards, and Tom Sheehan. To Mike Daconta, I appreciate that you gave me my break in writing and that you supported this book, and I can tell now that this lead author thing is harder than it looks! To my duty crew at the Gainesville District VFD: Bob Nowlen, Gary Sprifke, Patrick Vaughn, Marshall Sayen, Gerry Clemente, Javy Lopez, Thomas Mullins, and Brian LaFlamme — we have been through a lot together! Eric Jablow, failing to list you among my mentors in *More Java Pitfalls* was a horrible oversight; I hope I can rectify that here. Matt Tyrrell, despite being a "large cat," you are still like a brother to me. –WCR

I'd also like to thank all of the people I've worked with in the past: Wendong Wang, Arun Singh, Shawn Sherman, Henry Zhang, Bin Li, Feng Peng, Henry Chang., Sanath Shetty, Prabahkar Ramakrishnan, Swati Gupta, Mark Mitchell, Yuanlin Shi, Chiming Huang, Andy Zhang, Chi Luoung, and John Zhang, all of whom I loved working and goofing around with. Additionally, I'd like to thank the members of my current portal development program: Guillermo Suchicital, Susan Hansen, Linda Burchard, Honchal Do, Jae Kim, Johnny Krebs, Steve Brockman, Kevin Mills, Bob Russell, and Arnie Voketaitis. Thanks also to the professors at the Virginia Tech Computer Science/Information Technology Departments: Shawn Bohner, Tarun Sen, Stephen Edwards, John Viega, and all the other dedicated, top-notch staff and instructors.

Acknowledgments

Last, I wish to thank all of the co-authors, who are fun guys to work with and be around: Kevin, Joe, Peter, and Clay. To all of my family: Mom, Dad, Michael, John, Patricia, Jim, Sue, Reenie, Stephen, Emily, Jack, and Gillian, you guys are great. Thanks also to my friends back in New York: the Wieczorek, Devaney, Howard, Pujols, O'Donohoe, and Keane families; and to those in the open source community who have so generously contributed their hard work and time by crafting all of the fantastic tools described in this book, and have created a software culture of trust and collaboration that have allowed so many others to be productive in their programming endeavors. To my wife, Van, who I love more than anything for her easygoing manner and ability to use power tools and golf drivers better than most men. –DJA

To my wife, Jennifer, and my son, Andrew, thank you for all your love and support throughout this process; without you, I would never have found the energy to complete this. I'd also like to thank the following: the rest of my family, but especially my grandfather and grandmother, Carlo and Annette Vitale; my father, Joseph Vitale; my step-mother, Linda Vitale; and my father and mother-in-law, James and Marlaine Moore, for being helpful and offering encouraging advice. Many thanks also to John Carver, Jeff Scanlon, Brandon Vient, and Aron Lee for their great supporting roles as friends. Of course, I would like to thank all of my co-workers at McDonald Bradley Inc., including Kyle Rice, Danny Proko, Michael Daconta, Ken Bartee, Dave Shuping, Joe Cook, Ken Pratt, Adam Dean, Joon Lee, Maurita Soltis, Keith Bohnenberger, Bill Vitucci, Joe Broussard, Joseph Rajkumar, Theodore Wiatrak, Rebecca Smith, Barry Edmond, and many others who have had a significant, positive influence on me throughout the years. Finally, a special thanks goes to my co-authors for all of their hard work and encouragement. Thank you, all! –JV

This book marks my first participation in the development of a technical book. It has been a great challenge and one that has enlightened me in a number of ways. I would first like to thank my co-authors Clay, Donnie, Joe, and Kevin. They are extremely talented developers and thinkers and I truly appreciate their trust in asking me to help author this book. They are always striving to make a difference in their project work and I have benefited greatly from their help and guidance. I would also like to thank the many great people at my company, McDonald Bradley, who have supported my efforts in writing this book and who were willing to help wherever possible. I would especially like to thank Kevin Moran for his editorial efforts as well as the many years of technical mentorship he has so graciously afforded me. Lastly, I would like to thank my lovely fiancée, Ruby, for her editing, patience, support, and guidance during this effort. May she never stop. – PAL

I would like to first thank my co-authors on this project — Clay, Don, Peter, and Joe. I think this book contains some great lessons learned from some of our previous projects. I would also like to express my thanks to Bob Elliott and Eileen Bien Calabro from John Wiley & Sons. Special thanks to Natalie "Bonnie" Schermerhorn for giving me examples for the Llama Web service example. In addition, I can't forget my Southwest Virginia Readability editor, Helen G. Smith, or my Central Virginia Readability editor, Lois G. Schermerhorn. I would also like to recognize the great architecture team on the Virtual Knowledge Base project (as of August 2003): Keith Bohnenberger, Darren Govoni, Eric Monk, Joseph Rajkumar, Joel Sciandra, Maurita Soltis, and Arnie Voketaitis. Mike Daconta, thank you for your support and writing suggestions over the years. To my wife, Gwen, thank you for putting up with me writing on weekends for yet another book project! Last, but not least, I would like to thank God and the following verses, which have affected my life in a powerful way: Philippians 4:4–9 and Romans 8:18–39. Read them — you won't be disappointed. –KTS

Contents

Contents

Contents

Contents

Contents

Contents

Introduction

Portal development projects have become the centerpiece of IT acquisition and development strategy for many organizations. Enterprise integration and Web application developers predictably groan when they hear the word "portal" — nightmares of proprietary APIs, oversold features, and shoddy tool integrations. The authors of this book have been involved in over a dozen production portal efforts over the last several years. In that time, we have dealt with numerous products and frameworks, including some in-house frameworks based on servlets and JSPs. Through all of this, we began to wonder whether these commercial suites were really providing any value. We started to realize that we could put together a framework from open-source products.

We would like to point out that our portal framework is not meant to be an all-or-nothing solution. We present a number of tools that you may use to satisfy your enterprise portal needs, and we demonstrate how to use them, but because portal efforts are largely integration efforts, it would be folly to presume that anyone will drop all of their current systems and pick up our framework.

This book explains a set of tools at the foundation of an open-source portal framework, and demonstrates how to build your own portal using open-source tools. However, before describing the structure of the book, it makes sense to cover some fundamental concepts addressed therein.

What Is a Portal?

"A portal is your enterprise."

"A portal is a single synergistic access to all your enterprise information, and only the appropriate information."

"A portal is a unique IT strategy that allows me to answer the classic "build versus buy" question—yes!"

"A portal is one of those holes in the side of a ship, like they had on the Love Boat!"

All of these are commonly used as definitions of a portal. Obviously, the first two come from people who wish to sell you on your need for a portal. The third is clearly from a CIO who has funded a portal acquisition, and the last is a popular joke (though wrong because, as all *Love Boat* fanatics know, a **port-hole** is what is in the side of a ship).

The Java community decided to come up with a least common denominator agreement on what a portal is by standardizing on a Portlet API. This standard is known as JSR 168: "Portlet Specification." This book views JSR 168 as the bottom line on portals, but understands the youth of this standard and that the disparities among current portal implementations requires considering portals in a more pragmatic sense.

JSR 168 defines a portal as follows:

> *A portal is a Web-based application that commonly provides personalization, single sign-on, and content aggregation from different sources, and it hosts the presentation layer of information systems. Aggregation is the action of integrating content from different sources within a Web page. A portal may have sophisticated personalization features to provide customized content to users. Portal pages may have different sets of portlets creating content for different users. [JSR168]*

Portals are becoming the new foundation of the Web application platform. The proliferation of Web applications has required software to tie these disparate Web applications together into aggregated applications.

Portals are Web-enabled applications that integrate and deliver information. Figure 1 illustrates an overview of an enterprise portal.

Features of a Portal

The following table provides a list of features commonly found in portal products. It should be noted that the fractious portal market has provided a wide spread of features in each product. In fact, JSR 168, like all standards developed by industry committees, only establishes the minimal required set of portal features.

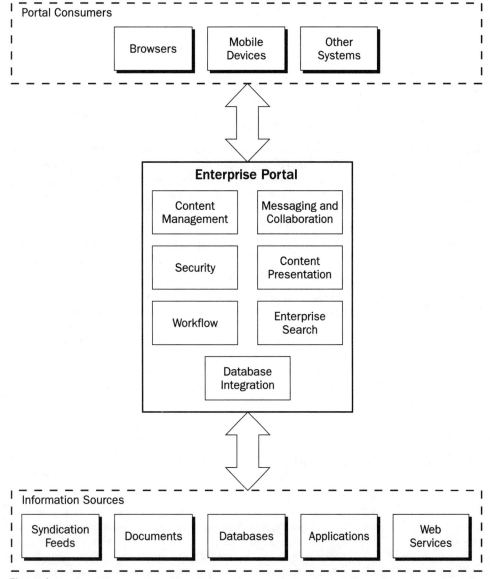

Figure 1

Feature	Description
Aggregation of content	The capability to tie different content fragments into one consistent and interoperating view.
Customized views	Customization commonly refers to having different views based on the role of the person in the organization. For example, HR personnel would have one view, while Finance personnel would have a different one — each customized for their specific job needs.
Personalized content	Personalization takes customization one step further and provides the capability for individual users to customize their view to suit their individual needs. For example, Joe may work in HR, but be specifically responsible for hiring Java developers, so he would want to personalize his view for that task, and perhaps link to content in the Java domain, such as Apache.
Unified security model	Users have an account for their time card application, their HR system, and so on. This provides not only *single sign-on*, but also an enterprise-wide security policy based on role.
Collaboration features	While some portals may provide sophisticated tools for chat, application sharing, common whiteboards, conferencing, and so on, collaboration is mainly about developing communities of interest, whereby people can share common expertise and insight on a particular set of data. For example, a finance user may want to comment on a particular division's report, providing advice or asking questions regarding particular investment decisions.
Localization	Localization involves customizing content to the locale in which it is being presented. This could involve character sets, language, currency exchange, date format, and so on.
Internationalization	Internationalization support enables an application or portal to be developed in such a way that it can be easily localized. Depending on the design of the portal, this can be very hard or very easy.
Workflow	Workflow supports the user's ability to seamlessly move through a set of tasks across multiple data sources and applications. For example, a user may need to pull data from three sources (catalog, inventory, and partner inventory), and update two others (shipping and invoicing) as part of completing a supply chain transaction.
Web services access	Web services have become the latest development in the trend toward interoperability. They provide a strong capability to both access partner systems (business to business) and be consumed by consumer applications (business to consumer). A portal should be able to both consume Web services and provide them.
Self-service	A recent trend in portals, particularly those for external consumption, has been toward users being able to provide self-service. The idea is that it should be easy for a user to provide and access sufficient information to conduct transactions with minimal or no support from other people.

Feature	Description
Client agnostic processing	A portal should be able to service not only many different browsers (all but the most junior Web developers understand how difficult this can be), but also different devices (such as mobile devices) and platforms (such as other applications).

As mentioned before, this table does not encompass all of the features to be found in any portal suite available on the market. Nor is this a minimal set of features expected in any portal. Instead, this list is meant to cut through the buzzwords and provide an understanding of the kind of features that a portal can provide to your enterprise.

Components of a Portal Framework

In addition to having a set of conceptual features, a portal framework also contains a set of commonly found components. Again, this list is neither comprehensive nor limiting, but it provides a solid overview of the kind of components that are available in many portals. The following table describes these common enterprise components:

Enterprise Component	Description
Content management	Content management suites vary greatly in what they do in terms of access control, content markup, presentation, revisioning, and so on. However, most portals maintain some capability to publish and maintain their content.
Syndication access	A newswire provides a good analogy for a syndication feed. Essentially, Web sites produce and update lists of new content. Portals render that content and regularly check for updates from the syndication feed. There are several feed standards, including OCS, RSS 0.9, RSS 1.0, RSS 2.0, and so on. These are usually cached locally on the server for all clients with an interest in that given feed.
Mail	Mail support varies greatly in portals. Almost all provide some support, even if it's only as simple as mailing back user name and password information. More sophisticated implementations enable a Web-based mail client or even e-mail subscriptions to particular content.
Search Engine	While portals go a long way in providing a road map to the information users need to find, users will still need the capability to search through the content sources for things that are too fine-grained for the road map. Portals often exhibit wide disparities in their search engine capabilities, with some having a search tool built into the portal, while others simply support plugging in another tool. This can lead to confusion on the part of developers about which search engine capabilities are actually part of the software they acquired, and which need to be acquired.

Table continued on following page

Enterprise Component	Description
Database Access	Most portals provide a "database browser" portal, which wraps SQL calls into a browsing interface. Others also come with sophisticated object-to-relational mapping suites that can be used to tie databases seamlessly into the portal framework.
Collaboration tools	Threaded, searchable discussion forums are the most common collaboration tools that come with a portal. However, many also include live chat rooms, whiteboard tools, and so on.

This table gives you an appreciation for some of the components commonly found in portal suites. However, we should probably provide you with a formal description of a portlet.

What Is a Portlet?

"Portlets are little windows into your enterprise."

"Portlets are those boxes you see on a Web page."

"Isn't that what they call those portable restrooms you see at construction sites?"

In fact, portlets are reusable user interface Web components that provide a view of an information system. These components provide a markup **fragment,** as they are called by JSR 168, which enables them to be aggregated into larger **portal pages**. This definition, as well as the definition of portal containers and their relationships to servlets and JSP, is covered in detail in Chapter 1.

A Brief History of Enterprise Portals

In the beginning, there were research papers, and those research papers were good. They were expense to print and share, however, so they were shared electronically over the network now called the Internet. The number of users on this network was relatively small, and the places where papers could be found were rather well known, as the users were generally sophisticated.

Tools such as Mosaic and Netscape Navigator were developed to make it even easier for less sophisticated users to browse information online. As the ease of use and publication increased, so did the amount of data. Soon, the Internet was open to commercial ventures, and data of all types (regrettably, in some cases) was soon being shared across this information superhighway.

The User Perspective

It quickly became important to find a way for users to easily find what they were looking for in this storm of information available on the Internet. This imperative resulted in the first generation of **search engines**. Search engines did make it easier to quickly find resources and services on the Internet, but it was still hard to ensure that you got the correct and best data available on a given topic. Effective Web research was still at the mercy of the sophistication of the users.

What if someone who knew the Internet pretty well could put together a road map? Someone did, and called it Yahoo!. It provides a category list through which users can drill down to the information and Web sites that they need. If you want something such as Atlanta Braves statistics, for example, you can find them under a treelike mapping whose topics range from broad to narrow: Directory > Recreation > Sports > Baseball > Major League Baseball (MLB) > Teams > Atlanta Braves. Ultimately, it would provide you with the relevant pages—in this case, links to a number of sports Web sites that maintain an Atlanta Braves page. In addition, you would find a link to sites that enable you to buy tickets at Turner Field. You could have guessed that such sites existed, and you probably could find them eventually, but the search engine enables you to quickly access all of the relevant information (in theory) on the Atlanta Braves. (This shows the ability of a human to have a better understanding of what you are actually seeking than a machine, which gathers its information from a few words and a number of sophisticated algorithms.)

Now, you can bookmark this page and return to it at any time (using the same computer) to find your information on the Atlanta Braves. But what if you want to check the score from last night's game, and get any news from the Braves' clubhouse? Even if you could get that information, you would still want it delivered without asking for it, and many sports sites do have individualized pages for every team in major sports. This is known as **customization**—providing customized content for particular users based on their interest (Braves fan). Moreover, you can get customized information about all of your interests, saving you a tremendous amount of time.

This desire for speed and customization is what fed the development of My Yahoo! It is a portal that enables you to personalize your view with a certain look and feel, with content defined by you—your sports teams, your stocks, your news, and your links. This was clearly a breakthrough in that you could actually cater the Web to your interests, at least as a starting point.

The Business Perspective

It quickly became apparent to businesses that there was real value in getting information to customers, partners, and employees easily and efficiently. The easier the communication became, the quicker the money changed hands. In addition, informational portals began to appear for advertising and subscription purposes. An example of this was ESPN, which provided great sports information. By becoming the preferred place to receive sports information on the Internet, it was able to sell premium content and advertising.

Aside from a being a new media channel, organizations began to recognize an internal value to Web-enabling their applications, databases, and so on. They realized that as their employees became more proficient with the Web browser, training costs for using many of their applications could be decreased, as the company apps would behave similarly to the commercial apps (for example, ordering a book from Amazon). Furthermore, they realized the lower maintenance costs of having one application on the desktop (the Web browser which was standard with the operating system—no statement about the Microsoft lawsuit is implied here) and centrally managing the rest of the application on the server side. This enabled patches, upgrades, and so on to be installed on one machine and affect all of the users. In addition, the test environment of that one machine was much easier to control (because it was easier to match the configuration for only one machine than for one machine per person in your organization). This reduces the number of configuration incompatibilities, and conflicts dramatically wane.

Figure 2 illustrates how organizational applications interacted prior to Web-enabling them.

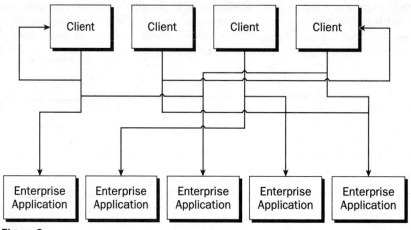

Figure 2

The interdependencies between applications and the subsequent impact of these interdependencies on the organization were quite real, complex, and problematic. However, Figure 3 illustrates what things looked like after Web-enabling the applications.

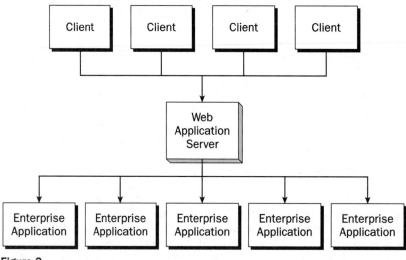

Figure 3

As you can see, Web-enabling the applications cleared up the spaghetti dependency diagram, and the similarities to the portal diagram in Figure 1 are unavoidable.

However, while this appears to be a single, consolidated unit, that is only the illusion of the hardware and network connections. Typically, the integration followed a popular technique at the time — integration by user. Essentially, the user had a front page with links to each of the applications, which the user had to access to find or process a particular piece of information. If users were lucky, they could log in to each of them with the same user name and password, but there was still no concept of a **single sign-on,** or a consistent security model. Furthermore, users were treated as if they were all the same. The data they required and the applications they could access were uniform across the enterprise.

This deficiency led to the development of the enterprise portal, which sought to bring the same concepts to an individual enterprise. Connecting all the apps into one consistent network — available to all of the users based on their role — obviated the need for repetitive data-hunting, and for cutting and pasting information into other applications until that process yielded the appropriate results.

The Technology Perspective

As soon as you identify a need, you will find a software company willing to oversell their product as the solution to that need, including a bunch of needs that you didn't know you had. When the first enterprise portal products came out, they had entirely proprietary APIs, and an interesting mix of feature sets. For example, some had personalization features, others strong content management, while others excelled at enabling workflow. Many had good **enterprise application integration** features. Eventually, though, they all ended up providing a core feature set.

Along the way, J2EE began its meteoric rise through the server-side world. It provided strong enterprise application development and integration features. It also had a substantial impact on Web development activities with the servlet and JSP specifications.

Quickly, though, the portal capabilities became **technical discriminators,** and provided nonstandard extensions to J2EE. These extensions ranged from very close approximations of the standard components, with limited wrappers, to full-blown rewrites of presentation logic code. Some of these extensions even claimed to be predecessors to standard APIs — despite having been released after the standard was widely adopted.

The problem was that the portal implementations were starting to fracture the J2EE application base, which would defeat the driver behind its success — the portability of enterprise applications. IBM recognized the problem and proposed JSR 162, but Sun disagreed with their approach and proposed JSR 167. Ultimately, Sun and IBM agreed to combine their two proposals into JSR 168. JSR 168 evolved slowly as a result of the need to resolve these differences, as well as to compensate for the emerging OASIS standard on Web Services for Remote Portals (WSRP).

> *Web Services for Remote Portals (WSRP) is an OASIS standard that views the portal and Web service interaction from a completely different angle. It conceptualizes what are known as **forward-facing Web services**, which are Web services that are data-centric and provide a specification for how to render that data. These Web services would like a contract to which they can adhere and know how they will be presented to users. This is discussed further in Chapter 10.*

Challenges in Building Portals

Unfortunately, many portal development efforts have been highly fragmented, which has resulted in applications that are difficult to navigate and frustrate users. In fact, the authors of this book first worked together to save a project locked in a textbook example of this phenomenon. Many of these problems occurred because of poor design and improper development strategies that involved the application of proprietary solutions that were difficult to deploy and maintain.

Additionally, improperly designed portal projects have forced organizations to absorb development costs that were disproportionate to the value added. Many of these efforts have resulted in the dilution of a corporation's image and have decreased customer loyalty.

The fact that so many portal failures have occurred should come as no surprise to those who have been involved in portal development programs. Portal application developments are arduous. They require the successful amalgamation of many different technologies and applications that must satisfy a disparate end-user community.

Are Portals Here to Stay?

IDC estimates the market for enterprise portal platforms will reach more than 2.6 billion dollars by 2006. Despite the overall depression in tech spending, Gartner estimates that portal software spending grew 59 percent to $709 million dollars in 2001. Delphi Group estimates that the Portal Market in 2003 will reach $957 million worldwide, and reach $1.14 billion in 2004. Nearly all Web development efforts are being geared toward integration Web portals. This means that a large portion of Java Web developers will be using portal software. Much like JBoss and Tomcat provide open-source options for those who develop Java Web applications, the current portal options have been limited, requiring individual experience in a wide variety of open-source projects.

The money flow clearly indicates that IT investments will continue in portal software. Therefore, developers need to be well versed in this area — not only to provide organizations with the capability to save significant amounts of money by leveraging open-source products, but to keep their own career options open.

What Is Wrong with Web Applications?

There is nothing wrong with conventional Web applications. As a matter of fact, portals are primarily based on them. For a lot of cases, all that needs to be developed is a Web application; done properly, it can easily merge into a portal environment later.

Where developers can run afoul is by ignoring the new portal standards available and writing their own aggregation mechanisms. If, as a developer, you build your own nonstandard portal implementation, you prevent the portability of your application.

However, note that the solution needed is often a simple Web application, which has no requirements for a portal. Suppose, for example, you need a new billing application. You should not assume you need a portal and that, within that portal, you will find the solution to making your application. Instead, you can build the application as necessary, realizing that doing integration-friendly things is good software practice, just as it is good practice to build what customers need, not what you want to give them.

We believe that the concept of the portal as a desktop replacement is still a bit far-fetched and unrealistic, because a Web browser is only *one* of the tools most people use on a daily basis. While centrally managing applications is good, and provides a number of benefits to the distributed office, you lose significant functionality by putting your e-mail and instant messenger into a Web browser. While this is feasible, ultimately it reduces your effectiveness, resulting in a portal that is actually hurting the enterprise. Furthermore, no one has seriously proposed running office automation tools in a Web browser. Heaven forbid they try to do it with a development environment! Therefore, in fact, it is unlikely that the majority of your desktop is anywhere close to being integrated into your Web browser.

Ultimately, a portal can provide good value in presenting an organized view of the data, but it should not feel as if it is an all-encompassing and monolithic desktop replacement. Developers should instead consider user interfaces as appropriate, and leverage other client platforms to provide more sophisticated views, with the portal serving Web services to them.

Why Open Source?

It seems like making the argument for open-source software gets easier every year. This is due in large part to open-source products such as Linux, MySQL, JBoss, Tomcat, and the Apache Web Server (just to name a few), which have been wildly successful. Furthermore, quality software organizations such as the Apache Software Foundation (arguably the best software engineering firm in the world) boast a history of consistent, stable, and successful software deliveries.

The perception of open software being built entirely by hobbyists in their basements with their free time is largely false (although those developers do great work too). Many open-source projects are commercially developed code bases turned over to the open market as a business decision, which is smart because they no longer have to pay to maintain the code. Other open-source developers are students who donate research and products, and still others are top-notch consultants who donate their efforts in part to keep their skills current. Many are people who got into software because they enjoy writing code, and like the idea that they are writing code that others will actually use.

We can't forget the best part about open-source software: it is free. Now, before the GNU people start hunting us down, we should note that *open source* and *free* are not synonymous. Just because most open-source products are free (in fact, we can't think of one that isn't), it doesn't mean that they all are free. All open source means is that you can receive the source in order to identify bugs. However, for the purposes of this book, open source does mean free; that is, you don't pay licensing fees for it.

Of course, these products are not *totally* free, because you generally need slightly more sophisticated people to work with open-source tools. These tools lack a cottage industry that hands out certificates to prove training on a piece of software. That said, many open-source projects are much easier to use than their commercial competitors. If you are still skeptical, try installing JBoss some time.

The greatest thing about capable open-source software is that it solves the classic "build versus buy" engineering dilemma. Software had become so complex that it was simply not practical to choose to build anything. Now, with reliable open-source alternatives, developers can start with the open-source products and build the features sets needed, and avoid trying to interpret the Rosetta Stone of software license pricing.

More important, however, you can choose to invest in your people, not in licenses, which pay for a lot of people who are not interested or even aware of your enterprise. Instead, you can apply your money toward improving your enterprise software directly, with the entire investment going to directly improve mission support, not buying a bloated product with a number of unneeded features, and then needing to hire expensive consultants from that company to come in and make it actually do something for your enterprise — because they are the only ones that know their product.

Consider another advantage. Open-source tools lower barriers to a developer's entry into the market. With open-source products, developers can become proficient with emerging tools and technologies, cultivating an ability to build solutions with them, rather than be tied to a purchasing decision (before they can actually learn hands on or gain new knowledge that can be applied to the next project).

Most important, building a portal is about integrating your enterprise, a process that one cannot take lightly or accomplish easily. Business processes are complex and changing animals. If you could buy the proverbial business adapter, you would have a pretty standard business. Businesses aren't standard, of course, because competitive forces and the ever-shifting variety of people associated with them won't let them be. You are not trying to manufacture a monolithic solution to integrating your enterprise — because you won't — this stuff evolves with your business. You are enabling information movement through your organization. Therefore, it is better to invest in a person, rather than a product that will be outdated in a year. Of course, you can always supplement the effort with outside consultants as necessary. Again, though, you would not be tied to a particular company and their consultants (which are not uniform in quality and availability anyway).

Open-Source Portal Servers

Note an important point about the framework that we are proposing. The principle objective of this book is *not* to provide a monolithic set of tools tied together in one portal suite. Instead, we provide information about a set of products that we find useful in building enterprise portal solutions. This prevents you from saying, "But we already use Microsoft Exchange for our mail server and that will never change, so I can't use your framework!"

Along those lines, we would like to mention a few open-source portal servers currently available.

Apache Jakarta Pluto

Pluto (http://jakarta.apache.org/pluto) was developed by IBM as the reference implementation for the Java Portlet API. Because it is the reference implementation for the Portlet API, which focuses primarily on the portlet container, Pluto can best be described as a portlet container with a rudimentary portal wrapped around it. Pluto is the portlet container for Jakarta's Jetspeed Portal.

Because of the pace of release for Pluto, we chose to cover Pluto in a bonus chapter that will be available on the book's companion Web site.

Apache Jakarta Jetspeed

Jetspeed (http://jakarta.apache.org/jetspeed) was developed at the dawning of the enterprise information portal era in 1999. It has been used extensively and enjoys a large user base. For a long time — in fact, until recently — it was synonymous with open-source portals. It was the only open-source project submitted to the expert group for JSR 168.

Jetspeed 2 is a total redesign based on the Java Portlet API and built around Pluto. It builds upon the success of its earlier 1.4 version, leveraging its considerable development community to achieve a nice project that will surely continue to be successful.

Liferay Enterprise Portal

The Liferay Enterprise Portal (www.liferay.com/home/index.jsp) provides a tremendous amount of value for very little hassle. It supports a wide variety of J2EE application servers and databases. It provides bundled downloads with JBoss and Orion.

Essentially, quickly download, set an environment variable, run a shell script, and you have an enterprise portal. It is set up to quickly provide an easily configurable corporate portal, with such nice features as a Mapquest lookup of your company's address, showing an overview map (with a link to directions).

Extensive portlets come with it, including search, message board, Wiki, journal, news feeds, weather, calendar, stocks, general RSS, instant messaging, SMS messaging, unit conversion, translator, dictionary, and user directory, and that is only about half of them!

The whole framework is built upon Jakarta Struts, which provides a high likelihood that it would be easy to extend. However, extensive documentation is not available. Furthermore, while it seems likely that they will become compliant with the new standard, there is no indication of when this will occur.

(On a side note, the reasons why open-source developers are inspired to do what they do are varied. Check out Liferay's FAQ to see many of these reasons. You might be surprised.)

eXo Portal

The eXo Portal (http://exo.sourceforge.net) is a fascinating portal server that appeared on the open-source scene seemingly out of nowhere. Based on such open-source trendsetters as JBoss, AspectJ, and the Pico Container, it not only provides an independent implementation of JSR 168, but also leverages Java Server Faces in its implementation. It is difficult to determine whether it is more impressive that these leading-edge tools are being provided within a Java Portlet API– compliant portal server or that they can be leveraged so effectively to produce this Java Portlet API portal server. Whether it can supplant the well-established Jetspeed community or the highly refined Liferay product remains to be seen, but it is certainly worth watching.

How This Book Is Organized

This book contains twelve chapters divided into two parts. The first part covers portal concepts and components in our portal framework, and the second part provides information on how to build your own portal using the open-source framework.

Part One: Open-Source Portals

Part One addresses the concepts of portal frameworks, and discusses the tools involved in our open-source portal framework. These chapters help you become acquainted with the toolsets, which are demonstrated in the practical examples of Part Two.

Chapter 1: The Java Portlet API (JSR 168) — This chapter extensively covers the JSR 168 Portlet API. It provides a portlet developer's perspective on how the standard affects them, highlighting important details and pitfalls in the specification. It also demonstrates a simple example.

Chapter 2: Searching with Lucene — Lucene is a great open-source search engine API. This chapter discusses the basics of indexing and searching documents, and includes a useful overview of the Lucene API.

Chapter 3: Messaging with Apache James — Apache James is an open-source e-mail server supporting multiple protocols. Given the central place that collaboration holds in most portal solutions, it makes sense to introduce you to this powerful mail server. This chapter discusses general mail concepts, the JavaMail API, and mailets — a server-side processing framework similar to a servlet.

Chapter 4: Object to Relational Mapping with Apache OJB — The Apache Object Relational Bridge project (OJB) is an interesting framework for object persistence. While this framework is not as "plug and play" as some of the other tools and frameworks covered in this book, it is important in that every portal effort requires the development of some code, and often the most tedious part of Web applications is object-to-relational persistence. Of course, this ends up being the whole purpose of many Web applications, so OJB can be quite a time-saver. In this chapter, we cover OJB and offer insights into how you can use it in your portal applications.

Chapter 5: Content Management with Jakarta's Slide — Slide is a mature content management framework that is used to manage content in various ways — from Internet application portals (such as exolab.org) to distributed file systems via Web browsers. Because content delivery is such a huge part of any portal's work, it is important to understand how to manage the content that is delivered. It must be easy to update your portal with "fresh" and reliable data. Slide provides you a pluggable framework for managing your content. This chapter explores the framework in detail, and describes how to use it.

Chapter 6: Portal Security — The prospect of seamlessly integrating all of your content and applications sounds like a wonderful idea until you begin to fear that you could be giving someone the keys to the company! Not only does one have to worry about troublemakers, but also about inadvertent mistakes. This chapter covers single sign-on, container security, application security, and many other topics that are required to provide a secure portal implementation.

Part Two: How to Build a Portal

In Part Two, we walk you through a how-to on building and operating your own open-source portal. Included here are considerations such as analysis and design of your portal requirements. Many portal projects fail simply because no one understands what to put into the portal. You will cover various development topics and learn how to test and operate your portal.

Chapter 7: Planning for Portal Deployment—Analysis and design of a portal are critical elements in portal development projects. This chapter discusses how to analyze your portal's requirement. We suggest some methodology tips for performing the analysis and development of your portal, and provide a discussion of how this methodology maps to commonly used development methodologies in the industry today. This chapter doesn't seek to invent a new methodology, but rather to illustrate some best practices that can be conducted within the context of any methodology.

Chapter 8: Effective Client-Side Development Using JavaScript—Because of the heavy server-side processing of portals (and Web applications in general), developers often lose sight of techniques that can enable much more effective processing on the client. These techniques are provided to show how, in a multiple-browser environment, you can effectively use technologies such as JavaScript. This chapter is useful not only for portals, but for any Web application development task.

Chapter 9: Developing Applications and Workflow for Your Portal—In this chapter, we demonstrate how to create portlet applications that are compliant with the Java Portlet API. These examples are provided not only for real-life integration, but also to illustrate how you can customize your own implementation.

Chapter 10: Portlet Integration with Web Services—Web services are a large part of the enterprise application integration space, and are providing the interoperability-enabling technology with both client platforms and business partners. This chapter covers the basics of Web services, and provides code examples of integrating with Web services using the Java Portlet API, along with the Axis Web services API. The chapter also demonstrates how to make your portal both a producer and a consumer of Web services, and provides an overview of the Web Services for Remote Portlets (WSRP) specification.

Chapter 11: Performance Testing, Administering, and Monitoring Your Portal—Simply developing your portal is not adequate for a successful portal effort. Portals are evolving things, as much as your business is, so it is important that you consider the methodologies for reducing error while accommodating change. Furthermore, you should prepare your portal to accommodate increasing numbers of users, so you can monitor and manage your portal reliably. This chapter addresses these topics as we explore the continuing adaptation of your business with your portal.

Chapter 12: Unifying the Enterprise Application Space Through Web Start—To a large extent, the appeal of centrally managed applications has driven the "webification" of client/server and desktop applications. It is readily apparent, however, that such Web applications are severely limited in their capabilities, particularly in the areas of asynchronous processing (callbacks) and sophisticated graphical user interfaces (GUIs). This chapter explores a vision for the next-generation portal—the **application portal** centered around Java Web Start.

What Is on the Companion Web Site?

This book has a companion Web site on which you can find the following:

Full source code to examples. Every example presented in the book has working source code available for downloads.

References. You can find interesting links related to open-source software and portlet development.

Errata. This provides corrections to any mistakes that may not have been found during the publishing process.

Bonus chapter. As mentioned previously, because of the timing of the Pluto release, we will be providing a bonus chapter about Pluto as soon as it is available.

How to Use This Book

You can use this book in two primary ways:

As a tutorial. This book covers a wide range of issues on portal development—from development tools to development process, and from project initiation to operational maintenance. It offers techniques and considerations that resulted from the experience of the authors in developing and operating open-source portal implementations. This provides the reader with the ability to learn from our mistakes, as well as to consider our vision.

As a reference. This book has information about a multitude of open-source tools, some of which you may never need and others that may be the perfect fit for your organization. Furthermore, it covers in detail the Portlet API from a portlet developer's perspective. This makes this book invaluable as a desktop reference for portal development.

Source Code

As you work through the examples in this book, you may choose to either type in all the code manually or use the source code files that accompany the book. All of the source code used in this book is available for download at http://www.wrox.com. Once at the site, simply locate the book's title (either through the Search utility or by using one of the title lists) and click the Download Code link on the book's detail page to obtain all the source code for the book. You only need to decompress the file with your favorite compression tool.

Errata

We made every effort to ensure that there are no errors in the text or in the code. However, no one is perfect, and mistakes do occur. If you find an error in one of our books, such as a spelling mistake or a faulty piece of code, we would be very grateful for your feedback. By sending in errata, you may save another developer from hours of frustration, and you will be helping us provide even higher quality information.

Conventions

To help you get the most from the text and keep track of what's happening, we've used a number of conventions throughout the book.

> **Boxes like this one hold important, not-to-be-forgotten information that is directly relevant to the surrounding text.**

This background style is used for asides to the current discussion.

As for styles in the text, we follow these conventions:

- ❑ When we introduce new terms, we **highlight** them in bold.

- ❑ We present code in two different ways, as follows:

```
In code examples, the Code Foreground style shows new, important, pertinent code.
```

```
The Code Background style shows code that's less important in the present context,
or has been shown before.
```

In some cases, we number lines of code in code listings. This is done only when specific lines of code are directly explicated.

[JSR168] is an example of a reference. To see the referenced work, please check the References section at the end of the book.

Contact Us

This book was born out of our interest in building portal solutions with open-source software. It is that spirit of interchange that makes open-source software successful. Therefore, we invite feedback. Please contact us with ideas, suggestions, corrections, new tools, or constructive criticism. One of the most gratifying things about writing is receiving feedback from those who read your work.

You can contact me through e-mail at or through regular mail at the following address:

W. Clay Richardson
c/o Robert Elliot
Wiley Publishing, Inc.
111 River Street
Hoboken, NJ 07030

Hoping you enjoy the book,

Clay Richardson
Haymarket, Virginia

Part 1: Open Source Portals

Chapter 1: The Java Portlet API (JSR 168)

Chapter 2: Searching with Lucene

Chapter 3: Messaging with Apache James

Chapter 4: Object to Relational Mapping with Apache OJB

Chapter 5: Content Management with Jakarta's Slide

Chapter 6: Portal Security

1

The Java Portlet API
(JSR 168)

This chapter discusses the centerpiece of portal development, the Java Portlet API, Java Specification Request 168 (JSR 168). The chapter explains the concepts in the specification, explaining how they fit into portal architectures to enable the developer to be an effective **portal** developer.

Portlet Fundamentals

A **portal** server handles client requests. Much like a Web application server has a Web container to manage running Web components (servlets, JSPs, filters, and so on), a portal has a **portlet container** to manage running portlets. Note that most Web application servers, such as Tomcat, have additional features beyond the Web container (management console, user databases, and so on), including some specialized Web applications (an administration Web application, for example). Portals are expected to follow a similar pattern, providing higher level functionality wrapped around the portlet container that adheres to the specification, enabling portlet applications to be portable, just as Web applications are.

The Portlet API is an extension to the servlet specification, which means that a portlet container is also, by definition, a Web container. Figure 1.1 demonstrates the Portal **stack**, which indicates how the various parts build upon each other to provide a portal server.

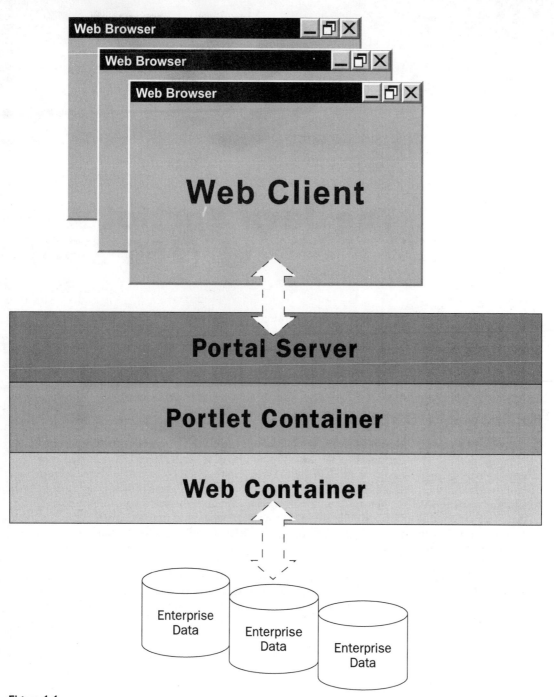

Figure 1.1

As you can see, the servlet container is the basis for any portal, upon which the portlet container extension is built. Likewise, a portal is built on top of that portlet container, which manages the portlets required to handle client requests.

Before describing the relationships between portlets and servlets, we should discuss a few of the fundamental definitions related to the Portlet API.

The following table provides a list of the definitions that are used in this chapter to explain the Portlet API. Of course, many others will be introduced throughout the chapter, but these are the fundamental ones required for an understanding of the chapter.

Term	Definition
Portal	A Web-based application server that aggregates, customizes, and personalizes content to give a presentation layer to enterprise information systems.
Portlet	A pluggable Web component managed by a portlet container; it provides dynamic content as part of an aggregated user interface.
Fragment	The result of executing a portlet, a "chunk" of markup (HTML, XML, and so on) that adheres to certain rules (see the sidebar "Rules for Fragments").
Portlet Container	The runtime environment of a portlet. It manages the life cycle of portlets, and handles requests from the portal by invoking portlets inside the container.

Although this is not an all-encompassing list, it provides the basic terms that are used repeatedly in this chapter.

> **Fragments are not allowed to use certain tags from their respective markup languages. These tags include html, title, head, body, base, frameset, frame, link, meta, and style. Use of these tags will invalidate the entire fragment. This is particularly important to developers (like us!) who have been abusing the forgiving nature of browsers until now.**

Portlets and Servlets

As mentioned before, the Portlet API is an extension to the Servlet API. Therefore, there are both similarities and differences between the components. It is important to understand these distinctions in order to understand why there is a portlet specification (and break habits wrought from using their similar servlet sisters).

The similarities between portlets and servlets are as follows:

❑ Portlets and servlets are both Java 2 Enterprise Edition (J2EE) Web components.

❑ Both are managed by containers, which control their interactions and life cycle.

❑ Each generates dynamic Web content via a request/response paradigm.

The differences between portlets and servlets are as follows:

❑ Portlets generate fragments, whereas servlets generate complete documents.

❑ Unlike servlets, portlets are not bound directly to a URL.

❑ Portlets have a more sophisticated request scheme, with two types of requests: action and render.

❑ Portlets adhere to a standardized set of states and modes that define their operating context and rendering rules.

Portlets are able to do some things that servlets cannot, such as the following:

❑ Portlets have a far more sophisticated mechanism for accessing and persisting configuration information.

❑ Portlets have access to user profile information, beyond the basic user and role information provided in the servlet specification.

❑ Portlets are able to perform portlet rewriting, so as to create links that are independent of the portal server implementation (which have various methods to track session information, and so on).

❑ Portlets have two different session scopes in which to store objects: application wide and portlet private.

Portlets lack some servlet features:

❑ Portlets cannot alter HTTP headers or set the response encoding.

❑ Portlets cannot access the URL that the client used to initiate the request on the portal.

Portlet applications are extended Web applications. Therefore, both types of applications are deployed in Web archive files (WAR) and both contain a Web application deployment descriptor (web.xml). However, a portlet application also contains a portlet application deployment descriptor (portlet.xml).

Because a portlet application is an extension of a Web application, it is logical that it could contain other Web application components. Portlets can use JSPs and servlets to implement their functionality. This capability is discussed later in the chapter.

Portal Interactions

It makes sense to show how a typical portal interaction occurs before diving into details about how portlets can render themselves with JSPs and servlets. Figure 1.2 demonstrates the chain of events that occur inside a portal to manage a typical client request.

Inside a portal is a Portlet API–compliant portlet container that manages the runtime state of portlets. The container evaluates those portlets into fragments, either by making requests of the portlet or by taking a fragment from cache. Then, the container hands the fragments to the portal server that manages aggregating them into portal pages.

Now that you have looked at portals, portlets, and portal containers at a high level, it is time to dig into the specifics about how to build portlets.

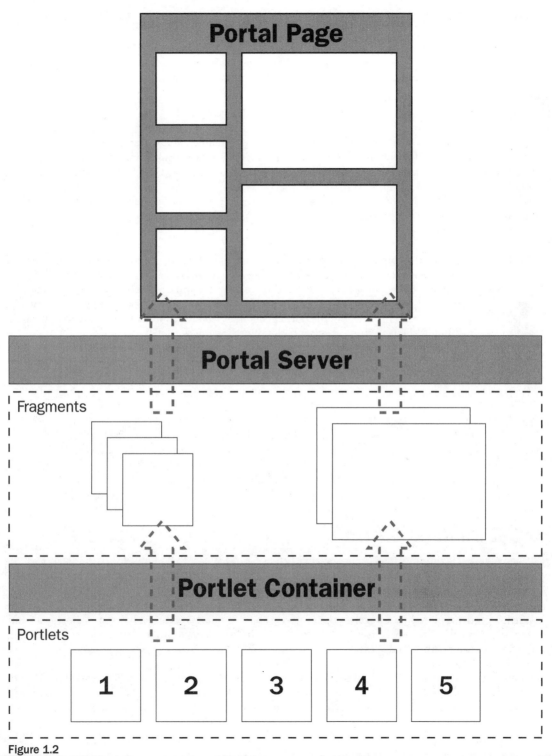

Figure 1.2

The Portlet Interface and the GenericPortlet

The `Portlet` interface defines the behaviors that all portlets must implement. Typically, you would prefer to extend the `GenericPortlet` class to build a portlet, because it provides structures for providing all of the typical portlet implementation methods, not simply the required ones.

Portlet Life Cycle

Much like servlets, a portlet's life cycle is managed by the container, and has an `init` method that is used to manage the initialization requirements (creating resources, configuring, and so on). Portlets are not guaranteed to be loaded until needed, unless you configure the container to load them on startup.

The `init` method takes an object that implements the `PortletConfig` interface, which manages initialization parameters and the portlet's `ResourceBundle`. This object can be used to get a reference to the object that implements the `PortletContext` interface.

Portlet developers don't typically spend a lot of time worrying about the intricacies of portlet container initialization exceptions, because generally they are thrown, and the developer reacts to them (debugging the circumstance that led to the exception and correcting it if appropriate). However, it is worth noting that an `UnavailableException` is able to specify a time for which the portlet will be unavailable. This could be both useful (keeping the portlet container from continuously trying to load the portlet) and aggravating (Why isn't the portlet container reloading my portlet?!) to a developer.

The `destroy` method provides the opportunity to clean up resources that were established in the `init` method. This is analogous to the `destroy` method in a servlet, and is called once when the container disposes of the portlet.

> When an exception is thrown in the portlet **init** method, the **destroy** method is guaranteed not to be called. Therefore, if resources are created in the **init** method prior to the exception being thrown, the developer cannot expect the **destroy** method to clean them up, and must handle them in the exception's catch block.

Portlet Runtime States

When a portlet is running, it has an associated `Preferences` object that allows for customization of the portlet. The initial values of the preferences are those specified in the deployment descriptor, but the portlet has full programmatic access to its preferences.

When a portlet is placed on a page, a `Preferences` object is related to it. The pairing of the portlet and a `Preferences` object on a page is known as a **portlet window**. A page can contain many of the same portlet windows within its display.

Before you start wondering why all of these `Preferences` objects are necessary, realize that this is providing the capability to perform a major features of a portal—customization. While the initial portlet `Preferences` object is great for specifying the configuration and runtime state of the portlet, it is necessary to tweak that state to handle customized views of the portlet. For example, say you have an employee directory portlet. Obviously, it would require certain preferences to get it running. However, when that employee directory portlet is embedded on a "Finance Department" home page, it should not only have a customized look and feel, but also have preferences related to the fact that it is on that page, such as showing only Finance Department employees.

Portlet Request Handling

Two types of requests can be issued against a portlet: action requests and render requests. Not coincidentally, these requests have their accompanying URL types: action URLs and render URLs. An action URL targets the portlet's `processAction` method, while the render URL targets its `render` method.

"There Can Be Only One"

If a client request is an action request, then it can target only one portlet, which must be executed first. No other action requests can be performed on the remaining portlets, only render requests. Figure 1.3 illustrates how a portal container would manage an action request.

As you can see, the portlet container will execute `processAction` on the targeted portlet, waiting until it finishes before it executes `render` on the rest of the portlets on the page. The calling of the `render` method on the remaining portlets can be done in any order, and can be done in parallel.

The `processAction` method is responsible for changing state on the given portlet, while the `render` method is responsible for generating the appropriate presentation content of the portlet. Therefore, it is logical that a user can change only one portlet at a time (you can only click in one box!), and that all portlets would have to call `render` to generate their content again upon the result of the action. However, this is not to say that all portlets are not able to change at a given time.

Consider the following common example: a portal for *The Simpsons*. One of the portlets allows you to select the given Simpson character whose page you would like to view. Other portlets contain character information, recent appearances, greatest quotes, and so on. When you select a new character, you would change the state of that character selector portlet through the `processAction` method. In that method, though, you would edit a given shared attribute that specifies which character's page you are on, which would cause all of the portlets to `render` themselves for that character when you invoked their `render` methods.

> Note one exception to when a portlet's **render** method is called, and that is when the portlet's content is cached. The Portlet API allows containers to choose to use a cached copy of the content, instead of calling **render**. Portlet containers are not required to provide a cache facility, but the spec provides for an expiration cache facility, which is configured in the portlet application deployment descriptor. The deployer provides an expiration-cache element into which the user specifies the number of seconds to cache (or -1 for cache that won't expire).
>
> The cache is per client per portlet, and cannot be shared across client requests. Of course, a developer could implement his or her own portlet managed cache in the **render** method, storing some commonly requested data in the **PortletContext**.

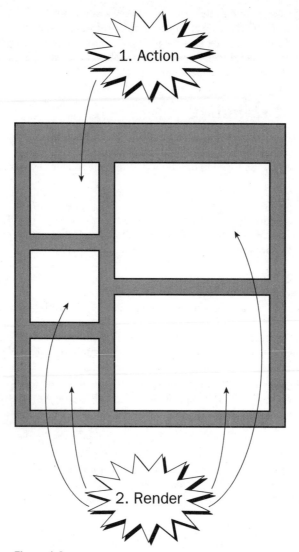

Figure 1.3

ActionRequest

As previously mentioned in the discussion of portlet request handling, action requests handle changing the state of a portlet based on the action request parameters. This is done using the `processAction` method, which takes an `ActionRequest` and `ActionResponse` object as parameters.

The `ActionRequest` object, similar to a `ServletRequest` object, provides the following:

❑   The action request parameters

❑   The portlet mode

❑ The portlet session

❑ The window state

❑ The portlet preferences object

❑ The portal context

To change the portlet mode or window state, you call the appropriate method on the `ActionResponse` object. The change becomes evident when the `render` method is called subsequent to the end of processing in the `processAction` method. You can also pass `render` parameters using the `ActionResponse` object.

RenderRequest

`RenderRequests` generate a fragment from the portlet's current state. The `RenderRequest` object provides access to the following:

❑ The render request parameters

❑ The portlet mode

❑ The portlet session

❑ The window state

❑ The portlet preferences object

There is also an accompanying `RenderResponse` method, which provides the vehicle needed to render content. You can call `getOutputStream` or `getWriter` as you do in a servlet, or you can dispatch the content generation to a servlet or JSP. There is more detail on this technique later in the chapter, in the section "Calling JSPs and Servlets."

> The request and response objects *are not thread-safe*. **This means that a developer should avoid sharing references to them with other threads of execution. Most developers will not run into this problem, but remember this tidbit next time you decide to try something unconventional.**

GenericPortlet

The `GenericPortlet` class is an abstract implementation of the `Portlet` interface. This is the most common way most users will write portlets — by extending this class. The `GenericPortlet` class extends the `render` method by setting the portlet title, and then calling its own `doDispatch` method, which in turn, determines the mode of the Portlet, and calls its appropriate method: `doEdit` for `EDIT`, `doView` for `VIEW`, and so on. There is more discussion on portlet modes later. The following code describes a class that extends `GenericPortlet`:

```
package org.opensourceportals.samples;
import java.io.IOException;
import javax.portlet.ActionRequest;
import javax.portlet.ActionResponse;
```

```
import javax.portlet.GenericPortlet;
import javax.portlet.PortletException;
import javax.portlet.PortletMode;
import javax.portlet.PortletRequestDispatcher;
import javax.portlet.RenderRequest;
import javax.portlet.RenderResponse;
/**
 * @author Clay Richardson
 * ExamplePortlet is a basic example of writing
 * a portlet by extending GenericPortlet
 *
 */
public class ExamplePortlet extends GenericPortlet {
  /*.
   * This method overrides the doEdit of GenericPortlet
   * This is called to provide the markup to be rendered when the
   * portlet mode is PortletMode.EDIT
   * <p>
   * In this case, we will dispatch the method to a JSP
   * located in the portlet root directory called "edit.jsp"
   */
  protected void doEdit(
    RenderRequest request,
    RenderResponse response)
    throws PortletException, IOException {
    PortletRequestDispatcher prd =
      getPortletContext().getRequestDispatcher("/edit.jsp");
    prd.include(request, response);
  }
```

We declare our ExamplePortlet, having it extend GenericPortlet. In here, we also override the doEdit method, which handles rendering when the portlet is in EDIT mode.

```
  /*
   * This method overrides the doHelp of GenericPortlet
   * This is called to provide the markup to be rendered when the
   * portlet mode is PortletMode.HELP
   * <p>
   * In this case, we will dispatch the method to a JSP
   * located in the portlet root directory called "help.jsp"
   */
  protected void doHelp(
    RenderRequest request,
    RenderResponse response)
    throws PortletException, IOException {
    PortletRequestDispatcher prd =
      getPortletContext().getRequestDispatcher("/help.jsp");
    prd.include(request, response);
  }

  /*
   * This method overrides the doEdit of GenericPortlet
   * This is called to provide the markup to be rendered when the
   * portlet mode is PortletMode.VIEW
```

```
     * <p>
     * In this case, we will dispatch the method to a JSP
     * located in the portlet root directory called "view.jsp"
     */
    protected void doView(RenderRequest request,
      RenderResponse response)
      throws PortletException, IOException {
      PortletRequestDispatcher prd =
        getPortletContext().getRequestDispatcher("/view.jsp");
      prd.include(request, response);
    }
```

Similarly, we provide the behavior required to render the portlet when it is in its HELP and VIEW modes.

```
    /* This method was overriden to specify
     * the title programmatically
     * This may be useful if you are going to
     * have parameters in your title like:
     * "News on 9/11/2001"
     */
    protected String getTitle(RenderRequest request) {
      return "Example Portlet";
    }

    /* This method is the meat of the portlet
     * manipulations of the portlet's state are done
     * through this method.
     *
     * For simplicity sake, we will parse a param
     * that indicates the portlet mode to which the
     * portlet should be set.
     *
     */
    public void processAction(ActionRequest request,
      ActionResponse response)
      throws PortletException, IOException {

        PortletMode mode =
          new PortletMode(request.getParameter("mode"));

        response.setPortletMode(mode);
    }

}
```

Finally, we specify overriding the getTitle method, allowing for more complex logic in rendering the title (such as displaying the current date) rather than displaying the static title declared in the deployment descriptor. We also handle the processAction method, which is responsible for the behavior in response to an ActionRequest.

The preceding code shows a basic implementation of a portlet by writing a class that extends Generic Portlet. This portlet doesn't do much beyond dispatch to other JSPs based on its mode (and set its name programmatically), but you see the crux of implementing a portlet.

Other Elements of the Java Portlet API

Now that you have examined the high-level concepts of the Portlet API, this section addresses the lower-level components within the specification, providing a portlet developer's perspective on the internals of the specification, highlighting important concepts and potential pitfalls.

PortletConfig

When a portlet is initialized, it needs access to the initialization parameters and other configuration information. The PortletConfig object provides these. In addition to init parameters, the PortletConfig object can also expose a ResourceBundle for the portlet.

The ResourceBundle contains certain fields required by the specification, including title, short title, and keywords. A ResourceBundle allows for easier localization of your portlet application.

You can specify the ResourceBundle inline in the portlet application deployment descriptor, as follows:

```
<portlet>
  ...
  <portlet-info>
    <title>Homer's D'oh a Day Portlet</title>
    <short-title>doh</short-title>
    <keywords>Simpsons, Homer Simpson, Entertainment</keywords>
  </portlet-info>
  ...
</portlet>
```

Alternatively, you can specify a reference to a ResourceBundle this way:

```
<portlet>
  ...
  <portlet-info>
    <resource-bundle>com.somedomainname.HomerPortlet</resource-bundle>
  </portlet-info>
  ...
</portlet>
```

Whichever method you use (the first is better mostly for applications with minimal localization requirements), the net effect for the developer is the same. These properties are always created in a Resource Bundle and made available through the PortletConfig object.

PortletURL

When building portlet content, it is necessary to build URLs that provide the capability to call the portal. This is the foundation of making the portal interactive. In order to allow for the proper creation of a PortletURL, there are two implementations: ActionURL and RenderURL. Both of these are created from the RequestResponse interface using the createActionURL and createResponseURL methods, respectively. The ActionURL provides the capability to issue action requests on the portal, to do things such as change portlet mode, change window state, submit a form, and so on. The RenderURL provides the capability to skip the portlet's processAction method and merely invoke the render method, passing render parameters to control presentation.

> Portlet developers should use the **PortletURL** objects (or their accompanying tag libraries) instead of directly manipulating HTTP query strings. The corollary to this is that developers should not use **GET** in HTML forms. This is because portals may encode internal state parameters in the **PortletURL**.

You will find several methods of the PortletURL interface interesting:

❑ setSecure — provides the capability to specify whether the URL should use HTTPS or not. If it is not used, it continues with whatever the current request specified. Therefore, you do not have to specify it repeatedly.

❑ setWindowState — enables you to change the window state of the portlet.

❑ addParameter — adds parameters to the URL.

❑ toString — provides a string representation of the URL. Note that it is not guaranteed to be a valid URL, as the portal may use tokens for URL rewriting.

❑ setPortletMode — enables you to set the portlet's mode.

Portlet Modes

A **portlet mode** represents a functional state of a portlet. This is used by the portlet to determine how to manage a render request. That is, depending on the mode, the portlet will render different markup. Portlets are able to change their mode as part of processing action requests. In addition, a portlet can be configured with different modes available and further restrict its availability based on role. The following table describes the standard portlet modes defined in the Portlet API.

Mode	Description
VIEW	Generates markup visualizing the portlet state and properties. Developers implement doView of GenericPortlet to provide this functionality.
EDIT	Produces markup to enable modification of portlet properties. Developers implement doEdit of GenericPortlet to provide this functionality.
HELP	Provides help text for the portlet. Developers implement doHelp of GenericPortlet to provide this functionality.

A portal can also provide custom portlet modes. Note that this is **portal** dependent, not **portlet** dependent. Therefore, if a portlet implements additional portlet modes, they will not be portable between various portlet containers. The portlet needs to override the doDispatch method to call the appropriate render method. For example, if you define a portlet mode called "SPECIAL", the doDispatch method would call its render method, which by convention would be doSpecial. Of course, because you are implementing the method, you could call the method anything you want.

Also note that you can specify which types of markup are available for a given portlet mode. Additional information on configuring portal modes is presented in a later section, "Portlet Application Deployment Descriptor."

Window States

The **window state** indicates to the portlet how much space is being allocated to it. This enables the portlet to modify its rendering to suit that window state. The following table contains the window states specified by the Portlet API.

State	Definition
NORMAL	The portlet will share the screen with other portlets. This means that the portlet should limit its markup.
MINIMIZED	The portlet should provide little or no output.
MAXIMIZED	The portlet doesn't share the screen with other portlets; thus, the portlet is not limited in its markup.

Much like portlet modes, a portal can define custom window states, which must also be configured in the portlet deployment descriptor.

Portlet Context

`PortletContext` is a wrapper object for your portlet application. There is one `PortletContext` object per portlet application. The `PortletContext` provides the following:

- ❑ Accesses initialization variables
- ❑ Gets and sets context attributes
- ❑ Logs events
- ❑ Gets application resources (such as images, XML files, and so on)
- ❑ Obtains a request dispatcher to leverage servlets and JSPs in the portlet

Portal Context

A portlet can get a reference to the portal in which it is running through the `PortalContext` object. Calling the `getPortalContext` method of the `PortletRequest` object will return the `PortalContext`.

The `PortalContext` provides the following:

- ❑ The name of the portal, through `getPortalInfo`
- ❑ Portal properties, through `getProperty` and `getPropertyNames`
- ❑ The supported portlet modes, through `getSupportedPortletModes`
- ❑ The supported window states, through `getSupportedWindowStates`

Portlet Preferences

In order to perform customization or personalization of your portlet, you need some way to vary certain parameters of the portlet. These are called **portlet preferences**. The classic portlet example is the weather portlet, and following that example, you could have a preference called "cities," with values representing the zip codes of the cities for which you want the weather. Note that preferences are only meant for configuring the portlet, so maintaining the list of all cities available in a preference would be an inappropriate use of preferences. Thinking of them in an object-oriented programming sense, they would be attributes of the portlet itself.

Preferences are manipulated through an object that implements PortletPreferences. All preference values are stored as String arrays, so you would not have the capability to store complex objects as you do with request or session attributes, nor do you have the advantage of declaring the type, as you would with environment entries. Therefore, if you are storing numbers as preferences, you will need to do conversions yourself.

Specifically, the PortletPreferences interface provides the following:

❑　getNames — This returns an Enumeration of the names of the available preferences.

❑　getValue — You pass it the name of the preference you are looking for, along with a default value (in case it isn't found), and it returns the first element of the array of that preference's values.

❑　getValues — You pass it the name of the preference you want and a String array of default values and it returns a String array of its values.

❑　setValue — You pass it the name of the preference and the value of that preference, and it sets it to a single-element String array containing that value. This method throws an UnmodifiableException if the preference cannot be modified.

❑　setValues — You pass it the name of the preference and a String array representing the values for that name, and it sets the preference values. This method throws an UnmodifiableException if the preference cannot be modified.

❑　isReadOnly — You pass it the name of a preference and it returns a Boolean indicating whether the preference can be modified.

❑　reset — You pass it the name of the preference and it will restore the default; if there is no default, it will delete the preference.

❑　store — This stores the preferences. Because this can only be done from within processAction, it will throw an IllegalStateException if it is done from within a render invocation. The method will also throw a ValidatorException if it fails validation.

❑　getMap — This returns a Map of the preferences. The Map consists of String keys and a String[] for values. This map is also immutable (cannot be changed).

> Note two important things to understand about the **store** method. First, it is an atomic transaction. Therefore, all of the changes must succeed or none of them will succeed. This is critical to understand if you have an enormous preference list for your portlet and you don't do a tremendous amount of validation of the input. Second, you could get stung by concurrent writes to the preference store. The critical message here is that you should view your preferences as one distinct entity and not a collection of independent parameters accessible through a common interface.

The following code is an example of retrieving and setting preferences:

```
    try {
    PortletPreferences myPrefs = request.getPreferences();
    String [] cities =
      myPrefs.getValues("cities",
                         new String[] {"20112","90210"});
    for (int i=0; i < cities.length; i++) {
      System.out.println(cities[i]);
    }
    String [] newCities = new String[] {"20169","22124"};
    myPrefs.setValues("cities",newCities);
    myPrefs.store();
    } catch (ValidatorException ve) {
    System.out.println("Preferences did not validate.");
    } catch (UnmodifiableException ume) {
    System.out.println("The preference is not modifiable");
    } catch (IllegalStateException ise) {
    System.out.println("You cannot be in render!");
    }
```

Developers can define custom classes to provide validation of preferences. These classes implement the PreferencesValidator interface and must provide their validation capability in a thread-safe manner. Implementing a PreferencesValidator is very simple: There is only one method, validate, which takes a PortletPreferences object and returns nothing. Simply throw a ValidatorException if any of the values doesn't meet the logic you define.

Sessions

Because portals are built upon the request-response paradigm (and predominantly upon HTTP), there has to be some mechanism available to maintain state across invocations. For example, it isn't sensible to authenticate users with every request. There are several techniques to manage sessions, with cookies and URL rewriting being two of the most popular in Web applications (cookies are used under the hood by many servlet containers to implement the HTTPSession).

Sessions are critical to portlet development, but there are many ways to implement them, so the Portlet API provides the PortletSession interface. When a client makes a request, the server sends a session identifier in the response. If the client wants to join the session, the client provides that session identifier with their next request.

The PortletSession can be used to hold attributes. PortletSession operates much like HTTPSession in this regard, providing the capability to store key-value pairs, with arbitrary objects. There is one major difference. The PortletSession has two different scopes:

❑   APPLICATION_SCOPE is very similar to the HTTPSession scope. An object placed in this scope is available to all the portlets within the session.

❑   PORTLET_SCOPE refers to when an object is available to only that portlet.

PORTLET_SCOPE is unique in that it provides a namespace for the given attribute. For example, an attribute called city.name would be stored in javax.portlet.p.47?city.name. ("47" is an internally assigned identification number). This attribute name prevents namespace collision with other portlets storing their session variables with similar names.

Despite having a special system for naming its attributes, PORTLET_SCOPE doesn't protect its attributes from other Web components. In addition, the namespace application is done completely under the hood. You just call getAttribute and setAttribute specifying PORTLET_SCOPE and the namespace conversion is done by the PortletSession object. To make it even more convenient, other Web components can receive this feature through the PortletSessionUtil.decodeAttribute method by passing the simple attribute name, such as "city.name".

Calling JSPs and Servlets

Because portlet applications are a complementary extension to Web applications, there must be a mechanism to include Java Server Pages and servlets in a portlet. Upon first examination of the GenericPortlet class, many Web developers cringe and think, "Oh, no! We are back to the old servlet days of embedding markup!" However, much like servlet developers found using a RequestDispatcher helpful in avoiding the "all your eggs in one basket" problem of placing all of your markup in your servlet, or all of your Java code in a JSP, a portlet developer can use a PortletRequestDispatcher.

When implementing the render method of the Portlet interface or, more likely, implementing one of the "do" methods of the GenericPortlet class (for example, doView, doEdit, and so on), the developer can use a PortletRequestDispatcher as follows:

```
String reqPath = "/calView.jsp";
PortletRequestDispatcher prd =   portContext.getRequestDispatcher(reqPath);
prd.include(req, resp);
```

In this case, we have specified our JSP, calView.jsp, which is located in the root of the portlet application, which we refer to with a leading slash. You must always start the path with a leading slash, and provide a path from the PortletContext root (usually the root directory of your portlet application). From there, you get a PortletRequestDispatcher (prd) from your PortletContext (portContext). Then you pass your RenderRequest (req) and your RenderResponse (resp) as parameters to the include method of the PortletRequestDispatcher (prd).

Similarly, we can call a servlet by its declared name (in the Web application deployment descriptor, also known as web.xml). For example, we might have specified a servlet such as the following in the web.xml:

```
<servlet>
  <servlet-name>chart</servlet-name>
  <servlet-class>org.opensourceportals.ChartServlet</servlet-class>
  <load-on-startup>0</load-on-startup>
</servlet>
```

Because we have named our servlet "chart," we can specify it as follows:

```
String reqName = "chart";
PortletRequestDispatcher prd = portContext.getNamedDispatcher(reqName);
prd.include(req, resp);
```

This time we used the getNamedDispatcher method with the name of our servlet in order to get a PortletRequestDispatcher. This is another important point to consider if you choose to do the following:

```
String reqPath = "/calView.jsp?user=Jennifer";
PortletRequestDispatcher prd = portContext.getRequestDispatcher(reqPath);
prd.include(req, resp);
```

Because the parameter user is specified in the query string, it will take precedence over any other render parameters named user being passed to the JSP. You probably will not encounter this problem, but it is something to keep in the back of your mind in case you run into crazy behaviors: specifying a query string takes precedence over other parameters.

There are restrictions on the use of HttpServletRequest. These methods are not available to the included servlet or JSP:

❑   getProtocol

❑   getRemoteAddr

❑   getRemoteHost

❑   getRealPath

❑   getRequestURL

❑   getCharacterEncoding

❑   setCharacterEncoding

❑   getContentType

❑   getInputStream

❑   getReader

❑   getContentLength

These methods will all return null (getContentLength returns zero) if invoked from a servlet or JSP that has been included by a PortletRequestDispatcher. Depending on how you create your PortletRequestDispatcher, you may not have access to other methods. These additional methods are not available to servlets or JSPs accessed from a PortletRequestDispatcher created by calling getNamedDispatcher:

❑   getPathInfo

❑   getPathTranslated

❑   getServletPath

❑   getRequestURI

❑   getQueryString

The reason why the preceding methods would be unavailable through getNamedDispatcher is pretty simple: Because you didn't use a path for your request, there is no data with which these fields can be populated. Likewise, `HttpServletResponse` has restrictions on what is accessible. The unavailable methods of `HttpServletResponse` are:

- ❑ `encodeRedirectURL`
- ❑ `encodeRedirectUrl`
- ❑ `setContentType`
- ❑ `setContentLength`
- ❑ `setLocale`
- ❑ `sendRedirect`
- ❑ `sendError`
- ❑ `addCookie`
- ❑ `setDateHeader`
- ❑ `addDateHeader`
- ❑ `setHeader`
- ❑ `addHeader`
- ❑ `setIntHeader`
- ❑ `addIntHeader`
- ❑ `setStatus`
- ❑ `containsHeader`

The encode methods always return null, and `containsHeader` always returns false, but the remainder will simply do nothing. This could be a source of great frustration if you are not careful as a developer, because it simply will not work and will provide no notice.

> *The Java Portlet Specification recommends against using the forward method of the **RequestDispatcher** of an included servlet or JSP. While this doesn't seem like a big deal, note that Apache's Struts Framework uses the **RequestDispatcher** forward method in its **ActionServlet**. Given the popularity of Struts as a Web application framework, this could make a significant impact on portal integration in many enterprises. This is not to say that it may not work anyway, but it is non-deterministic and should be carefully examined in your circumstance and tested with your portal implementation.*

Portlet Application Structure

Portlet applications are structured just like Web applications in that they have the following features:

- ❑ Can contain servlets, JSPs, Java classes, Java archives (JAR files) and other static files
- ❑ Are self-contained; all things in the Web application are packaged together in a common root
- ❑ Have a WEB-INF/classes directory to store standalone classes to be loaded by the application `classloader`
- ❑ Have a WEB-INF/lib directory to store Java Archives (JAR files) to be loaded by the application `classloader`

❑ Have a Web application deployment descriptor located at `WEB-INF/web.xml`

❑ Are packaged as Web archives (WAR files)

In addition to these features, the portlet application contains a portlet application deployment descriptor, located at `WEB-INF/portlet.xml`. This file is described in detail later in this chapter, in the section "Portlet Application Deployment Descriptor."

Security

Because security is a bigger matter than simply the requirements of the Portlet API, we defer the discussion on security in the Portlet API to Chapter 6.

CSS Style Definitions

In order to achieve a common and pluggable look and feel for portlets, the Java Portlet API defines a set of Cascading Stylesheets (CSS) styles that portlets should use in rendering their markup. By using a standard set of styles, portals can support *skins,* customized colors and fonts. These styles are meant to coincide with the OASIS Web Services for Remote Portlets standard.

In order to be complete, these style definitions are presented in the following table, as specified in Appendix C of the JSR 168 (Java Portlet API).

Attribute Name	Description
`portlet-font`	This is for normal, unaccented text used in a portlet. Size can be overridden using the `style` attribute with something such as "font-size:large".
`portlet-font-dim`	This is for suppressed text, essentially text that has been grayed out.
`portlet-msg-status`	This is used to represent text that is providing the current state of an operation in project, such as *"Please wait while data loads..."*
`portlet-msg-info`	Use this for informational text such as "Reminder: your username is your e-mail address."
`portlet-msg-error`	This styles messages such as "An unexpected error occurred, please contact the administrator."
`portlet-msg-alert`	This is for warnings, such as "Could not get open database connection, please try again in a couple of minutes."
`portlet-msg-success`	This relays messages when the submission was successful, such as "Your request was submitted."
`portlet-section-header`	Use this to render the table or section header.
`portlet-section-body`	This is to style the internals of a table cell.
`portlet-section-alternate`	When using a technique called *banding,* in which you provide alternate styles in between alternate rows, this style provides that capability.

Attribute Name	Description
`portlet-section-selected`	This style is used for highlighting a particular set of cells for the user.
`portlet-section-subheader`	If you have subheadings in your table that you need to distinguish from your table header, you use this style.
`portlet-section-footer`	If you include a footer to your table, this style would be used for those cells.
`portlet-section-text`	This style is used for things that do not fit in the other style definitions.
`portlet-form-label`	This is to style the label for the whole form, such as "User Registration Form."
`portlet-form-input-field`	This is for the text that a user enters into an input field.
`portlet-form-button`	This is for the text that appears on the face of a button.
`portlet-icon-label`	This styles text next to an application-specific icon, such as "Export."
`portlet-dlg-icon-label`	This styles text next to a standard icon, such as "Cancel."
`portlet-form-field-label`	This styles text that separates form fields (such as radio buttons).
`portlet-form-field`	This is used for labels of checkboxes, but not for input fields.
`portlet-menu`	This styles the menu itself (e.g., color).
`portlet-menu-item`	Use this to style an ordinary menu item that is not selected.
`portlet-menu-item-selected`	This is used to style an item that has been selected.
`portlet-menu-item-hover`	Use this to style an ordinary menu item when the mouse hovers over it.
`portlet-menu-item-hover-selected`	This is used to style a selected item when the mouse hovers over it.
`portlet-menu-cascade-item`	Use this to style an unselected menu item that has menu items nested underneath it.
`portlet-menu-cascade-item-selected`	Use this to style a selected menu item that has menu items nested underneath it.
`portlet-menu-description`	This styles text that is used to describe the menu.
`portlet-menu-caption`	This is used for the menu caption.

By using these styles, portlet developers ensure that their portlets can be reused in many portlet applications, and be consistent with WSRP. In addition, it enables developers to apply "skins" from other portlet applications to their portlet.

User Information Attributes

User attributes are used to create a profile for a user. They are meant to be standardized on the World Wide Web Consortium's (W3C) Platform for Privacy Preferences (P3P) 1.0 (www.w3.org/TR/P3P/). These attributes are also consistent with the efforts of the OASIS Web Services for Remote Portals standard. The following table lists the user attributes and their descriptions.

Attribute Name	Description
user.bdate	The user's birth date, expressed in milliseconds from January 1, 1970 at 00:00:00 Greenwich Mean Time
user.gender	The sex of the user
user.employer	The name of the user's employer
user.department	The department in which the user works
user.jobtitle	The user's job title
user.name.prefix	The prefix of the user's name (Mr., Mrs., Dr., etc.)
user.name.given	The user's given name (Jennifer, Alicia, etc.)
user.name.family	The user's last name (Richardson, Smith, Avondolio, etc.)
user.name.middle	The user's middle name (Anne, Clay, Trent, etc.)
user.name.suffix	The suffix following a user's name (Sr., Jr., III, etc.)
user.name.nickname	A user's nickname (Mojo, PAB, BP, etc.)
user.home-info.postal. name	The name that should appear at the top of a home address (for example, The Richardsons or William C. Richardson)
user.home-info.postal. street	The street address of the user's home (1600 Pennsylvania Avenue or 742 Evergreen Terrace)
user.home-info.postal. city	The postal city of the user's home (Haymarket, Manassas, etc.)
user.home-info.postal. stateprov	The state or province used in the user's home address (Virginia, British Columbia, etc.)
user.home-info.postal. postalcode	The user's home zip code (90210, etc.)
user.home-info.postal. country	The user's home country (United States of America, Canada, etc.)
user.home-info.postal. organization	A subheading in the address block, like "Finance Department," which doesn't make a lot of sense for a home address, but is included for completeness
user.home-info.telecom. telephone.intcode	The international access code for the user's home telephone (for example, 44 for the United Kingdom and 1 for the United States).
user.home-info.telecom. telephone.loccode	The user's home telephone area code (for example, 703, 818, etc.)

Attribute Name	Description
`user.home-info.telecom.` `telephone.number`	The user's home telephone local number (for example, 555-1111, etc.)
`user.home-info.telecom.` `telephone.ext`	The user's home telephone extension, if they have one (for example, 745, 2918, etc.)
`user.home-info.telecom.` `telephone.comment`	Comments about the user's home telephone (optional)
`user.home-info.telecom.` `fax.intcode`	The international access code for the user's home fax (for example, 44 for the United Kingdom and 1 for the United States)
`user.home-info.telecom.` `fax.loccode`	The user's home fax area code 703, 818, etc.)
`user.home-info.telecom.` `fax.number`	The user's home fax local number (555-1111, etc.)
`user.home-info.telecom.` `fax.ext`	The user's home fax extension, if they have one (745, 2918, etc.)
`user.home-info.telecom.` `fax.comment`	Comments about the user's home fax (optional)
`user.home-info.telecom.` `mobile.intcode`	The international access code for the user's home mobile telephone (for example, 44 for the United Kingdom and 1 for the United States)
`user.home-info.telecom.` `mobile.loccode`	The user's home mobile telephone area code (for example, 703, 818, etc.)
`user.home-info.telecom.` `mobile.number`	The user's home mobile telephone local number (555-1111, etc.)
`user.home-info.telecom.` `mobile.ext`	The user's home mobile telephone extension, if they have one (for example, 745, 2918, etc.)
`user.home-info.telecom.` `mobile.comment`	Comments about the user's home mobile telephone (optional)
`user.home-info.telecom.` `pager.intcode`	The international access code for the user's home pager (for example, 44 for the United Kingdom and 1 for the United States)
`user.home-info.telecom.` `pager.loccode`	The user's home pager area code (for example, 703, 818, etc.)
`user.home-info.telecom.` `pager.number`	The user's home pager local number (for example, 555-1111, etc.)
`user.home-info.telecom.` `pager.ext`	The user's home pager extension, if they have one (for example, 745, 2918, etc.)
`user.home-info.telecom.` `pager.comment`	Comments about the user's home pager (optional)

Table continued on following page

Attribute Name	Description
`user.home-info.online.email`	The user's home e-mail address
`user.home-info.online.uri`	The user's home Web page
`user.business-info.` `postal.name`	The name that should appear at the top of a work address (for example, Sun Microsystems or XYZ, Inc., etc.)
`user.business-info.` `postal.street`	The street address of the user's work (for example, 1600 Pennsylvania Avenue or 742 Evergreen Terrace)
`user.business-info.` `postal.city`	The postal city of the user's work (for example, Haymarket, Manassas, etc.)
`user.business-info.` `postal.stateprov`	The state or province used in the user's work address (for example, Virginia, British Columbia, etc.)
`user.business-info.` `postal.postalcode`	The user's work zip code (for example, 90210)
`user.business-info.` `postal.country`	The user's work country (for example, United States of America, Canada, etc.)
`user.business-info.` `postal.organization`	A subheading in the address block, like "Finance Department"
`user.business-info.` `telecom.telephone.intcode`	The international access code for the user's work telephone (for example, 44 for the United Kingdom and 1 for the United States)
`user.business-info.` `telecom.telephone.loccode`	The user's work telephone area code (for example, 703, 818, etc.)
`user.business-info.` `telecom.telephone.number`	The user's work telephone local number (555-1111, etc.)
`user.business-info.` `telecom.telephone.ext`	The user's work telephone extension, if they have one (for example, 745, 2918, etc.)
`user.business-info.` `telecom.telephone.comment`	Comments about the user's work telephone (optional)
`user.business-info.` `telecom.fax.intcode`	The international access code for the user's work fax (for example, 44 for the United Kingdom and 1 for the United States)
`user.business-info.` `telecom.fax.loccode`	The user's work fax area code (for example, 703, 818, etc.)
`user.business-info.` `telecom.fax.number`	The user's work fax local number (for example, 555-1111, etc.)
`user.business-info.` `telecom.fax.ext`	The user's work fax extension, if they have one (for example, 745, 2918, etc.)
`user.business-info.` `telecom.fax.comment`	Comments about the user's work fax (optional)

Attribute Name	Description
user.business-info. telecom.mobile.intcode	The international access code for the user's work mobile telephone (for example, 44 for the United Kingdom and 1 for the United States)
user.business-info. telecom.mobile.loccode	The user's work mobile telephone area code (for example, 703, 818, etc.)
user.business-info. telecom.mobile.number	The user's work mobile telephone local number (555-1111, etc.)
user.business-info. telecom.mobile.ext	The user's work mobile telephone extension, if they have one (for example, 745, 2918, etc.)
user.business-info. telecom.mobile.comment	Comments about the user's work mobile telephone (optional)
user.business-info. telecom.pager.intcode	The international access code for the user's work pager (for example, 44 for the United Kingdom and 1 for the United States)
user.business-info. telecom.pager.loccode	The user's work pager area code (for example, 703, 818, etc.)
user.business-info. telecom.pager.number	The user's work pager local number (for example, 555-1111, etc.)
user.business-info. telecom.pager.ext	The user's work pager extension, if they have one (for example, 745, 2918, etc.)
user.business-info. telecom.pager.comment	Comments about the user's work pager (optional)
user.business-info. online.email	The user's work e-mail address
user.business-info. online.uri	The user's work Web page

As you can see, the attributes are a bit repetitive, but offer a breadth of options to you as a developer in terms of which user attributes you need to use for your portlet application.

However, it is not sufficient just to use these in your application. Your deployment descriptor must declare which of these are used by a portlet application, and the deployer needs to map them against the related ones available in the targeted portal server. This is where using the standard attributes comes in handy, as it will greatly reduce, if not eliminate, the amount of mapping necessary to deploy your application.

Presuming you have done all of the appropriate mappings (and the section "Portlet Application Deployment Descriptor" discusses how to do this in your portlet.xml), you can gain access to user attributes such as the following:

```
Map userdata = (Map) request.getAttribute(PortletRequest.USER_INFO);
String workEmail =
(String) request.getAttribute("user.business-info.online.email");
```

You grab a Map of the deployed user attributes by getting that attribute from the `PortletRequest`. Then, you simply look up the appropriate value; in this case, the user's work e-mail (stored under "user.business-info.online.email").

User attributes are very important in deploying personalized portlet solutions. Be sure to familiarize yourself with these attributes.

Portlet Tag Library

The Portlet JSP Tag Library gives developers the capability to reference Portal components from within a JSP page. The following table explains the tags:

Tag Name	Purpose
defineObjects	This tag declares three objects within the JSP page: RenderRequest renderRequest, RenderResponse renderResponse, and PortletConfig portletConfig.
actionURL	This tag builds action URLs that point to the current portlet. This tag is nested with param tags in order to pass the appropriate parameters in the action URL.
renderURL	This tag builds render URLs. It also is nested with param tags.
namespace	This tag provides a unique name based on the current portlet in order to avoid conflicts in variable and function names when all of the portlet fragments are consolidated into a portal page.
param	This tag gives the name and value of a parameter. It is nested inside either the actionURL or renderURL tags.

Portlet Deployment

This section describes the portlet application deployment descriptor (`portlet.xml`), by dissecting a sample and explaining the various sections of the descriptor piece by piece.

Portlet Application Deployment Descriptor

In order to understand the portlet application deployment descriptor well, you should examine each part.

If you have used XML very much, you will find this first section unremarkable. The only thing worth noting here is that the `version` attribute is required to determine which version of the specification is in effect.

```xml
<?xml version="1.0" encoding="UTF-8"?>
<portlet-app  xmlns="http://java.sun.com/xml/ns/portlet"
  version="1.0" xmlns:xsi="http://www.w3.org/2001/XMLSchema-instance"
xsi:noNamespaceSchemaLocation="http://java.sun.com/xml/ns/portlet-app_1_0.xsd">
```

Portlet Declarations

This is the first part of the declaration of one portlet. In this, we give it a description, a local name, a display name, and a class name. The description and display name are meant to make it more human-friendly, while the local name and the class actually provide the nuts and bolts required to programmatically load and reference the portlet. The local name must, of course, be unique within the portlet application.

```
<portlet>
   <description>Example of creating a portlet</description>
   <portlet-name>ExamplePortlet</portlet-name>
   <display-name>Example Portlet</display-name>
   <portlet-class>org.opensourceportals.samples.ExamplePortlet</portlet-class>
```

The `expiration-cache` tag represents the number of seconds a portlet is kept in cache. The expiration cache value of `-1` means that the portlet will always be kept in cache. If the value were zero, it would be just the opposite — never cached.

```
<expiration-cache>-1</expiration-cache>
```

This next section declares the supported portlet modes and mime types. For each mime type, the supported portlet modes are listed. Wild cards (*) are acceptable in describing a mime type. For example, all text-based mime types could be specified as `text/*`, and all mime types could be expressed as `*/*`. In this case, the portlet supports traditional HTML with three different modes available: VIEW, EDIT, and HELP. However, it supports the VIEW mode only when the content type is the Wireless Markup Language (WML). Each of these definitions must be unique — that is, you cannot define multiple supports blocks for the same MIME type.

```
<supports>
   <mime-type>text/html</mime-type>
   <portlet-mode>view</portlet-mode>
   <portlet-mode>edit</portlet-mode>
   <portlet-mode>help</portlet-mode>
</supports>
<supports>
   <mime-type>text/wml</mime-type>
   <portlet-mode>view</portlet-mode>
</supports>
```

This portlet provides only one `Locale`, English, for its internationalization support. It could support many locales, and it would list them all here. For more information, examine Java's internationalization support.

```
<supported-locale>EN</supported-locale>
```

This element (`<portlet-info>`) provides the metadata about the portlet. The title element represents the title that will be displayed on the portlet. The short title provides an abbreviated way of referencing the portlet, such as in a management console. Similarly, the keywords are meant to provide context about the subject of the portlet. This portlet information could have also been referenced in a `ResourceBundle`, with only the name of the `ResourceBundle` specified here.

```
<portlet-info>
  <title>Pre-configured title</title>
  <short-title>Example</short-title>
  <keywords>JSR 168, Portlet API, Example, Simple</keywords>
</portlet-info>
```

This section shows the portlet preferences. Of course, the preferences you define must be unique. The index-location preference is read-only, so it cannot be changed programmatically; instead, it must be changed here. The second preference, sites-to-crawl, shows how multiple values can be specified for a preference. The last preference, crawl-depth represents a number that must be converted through Integer.parseInt, because preferences are all retrieved as either a String or a String array. The preferences-validator element specifies a class that is used to validate these portlet-preferences. In this case, the validator would confirm that the sites-to-crawl are valid and that the crawl-depth is less than five (to keep the crawling time down).

```
<portlet-preferences>
  <preference>
    <name>index-location</name>
    <value>/opt/lucene/index</value>
    <read-only>true</read-only>
  </preference>
  <preference>
    <name>sites-to-crawl</name>
    <value>http://jakarta.apache.org</value>
    <value>http://java.sun.com</value>
    <value>http://onjava.com</value>
  </preference>
  <preference>
    <name>crawl-depth</name>
    <value>2</value>
  </preference>
  <preferences-validator>
    com.opensourceportals.validator.CrawlValidator
  </preferences-validator>
</portlet-preferences>
```

Here we have the relevant security references for the portlet. The role-name element specifies the parameter that should be passed to the request.isUserInRole(String roleName) method. The role-link is the role, defined in the portlet application's web.xml, into which the user should be mapped.

```
<security-role-ref>
  <role-name>ADMIN</role-name>
  <role-link>administrator</role-link>
</security-role-ref>
```

This closes the definition of the portlet. This can be repeated as many times as necessary to define all of the portlets within your portlet application. Of course, each of your portlets must have a unique name within this portlet application.

```
</portlet>
```

Portlet Customization Declarations

This defines a custom portlet mode called MY_MODE. Of course, whenever an application defines a custom portlet mode, it must not only be available through the targeted portal server, but also needs to have portlets that actually use the mode (while programming defensively enough to avoid breaking in unsupported portal servers).

```
<custom-portlet-mode>
    <description xml:lang="EN">Custom portlet mode MY_MODE</description>
    <portlet-mode>MY_MODE</portlet-mode>
</custom-portlet-mode>
```

LEFT-SIDE is defined here as a custom window state. Just as with custom portlet modes, custom window states can cause problems with your application's portability. In addition, like custom portlet modes, you can define multiples in the same application, but they must have unique names.

```
<custom-window-state>
    <description xml:lang="EN">Docked into the left side</description>
    <window-state>LEFT-SIDE</window-state>
</custom-window-state>
```

User Attributes and Security Constraints

The following code defines a user attribute called user.business-info.online.email that refers to a user's business e-mail address. Typically, these attributes are mapping from the portal server's personalization database, which is why using standard names can ease the integration of user attributes. Developers should use user attributes from the W3C P3P standard, as specified in the Portlet API. This should ensure that they are unique (as required in the XML Schema for the portlet.xml) and reusable (standards-compliant).

```
<user-attribute>
    <description>P3P attribute for work e-mail address</description>
    <name>user.business-info.online.email</name>
</user-attribute>
```

This is the security constraint for this portlet application. It lists the name of the portlet, ExamplePortlet, and also specifies a user data constraint of INTEGRAL. User data constraints define the guarantees specifying how the portlet communicates with the user. Three values are allowed here: NONE, INTEGRAL, and CONFIDENTIAL. NONE means that there are no guarantees about the transmission of data between the portlet application and the user. INTEGRAL specifies that the data must be checked to ensure that it has not been manipulated (no added or removed information from the message). CONFIDENTIAL requires that the data cannot be read by anyone other than the user. Typically, Secure Sockets Layer (SSL) is used to provide both INTEGRAL and CONFIDENTIAL constraints.

```
<security-constraint>
    <portlet-collection>
        <portlet-name>ExamplePortlet</portlet-name>
    </portlet-collection>
    <user-data-constraint>
        <transport-guarantee>INTEGRAL</transport-guarantee>
    </user-data-constraint>
</security-constraint>
```

This defines the end of the portlet application.

```
</portlet-app>
```

Building a Portlet

Now, let's work through a complete example of a portlet. This portlet is a little more complex than our previous example, but it is not as involved as the portlets found in Chapter 9, which covers building portlet applications.

The first thing to do in building the portlet is to build the portlet class. Most portlet classes simply extend GenericPortlet, as shown in the following code:

```
/*
 * This class demonstrates a basic search portlet
 * using the Jakarta Lucene search API.
 *
 */
package org.opensourceportals.samples;
import java.io.IOException;
import javax.portlet.ActionRequest;
import javax.portlet.ActionResponse;
import javax.portlet.GenericPortlet;
import javax.portlet.PortletException;
import javax.portlet.PortletMode;
import javax.portlet.PortletPreferences;
import javax.portlet.PortletRequestDispatcher;
import javax.portlet.RenderRequest;
import javax.portlet.RenderResponse;
import javax.portlet.ValidatorException;
import org.apache.lucene.analysis.Analyzer;
import org.apache.lucene.analysis.standard.StandardAnalyzer;
import org.apache.lucene.queryParser.ParseException;
import org.apache.lucene.queryParser.QueryParser;
import org.apache.lucene.search.Hits;
import org.apache.lucene.search.IndexSearcher;
import org.apache.lucene.search.Query;
import org.apache.lucene.search.Searcher;
/**
 * @author Clay Richardson
 *
 */
public class LucenePortlet extends GenericPortlet {
    /*
     * This method overrides the doEdit of GenericPortlet
     * This is called to provide the markup to be rendered when the
     * portlet mode is PortletMode.EDIT
     * <p>
     * This mode should always show a form to change the indexPath
     * preference, indicating where the index is stored.
     */
    protected void doEdit(
```

```
    RenderRequest request,
    RenderResponse response)
    throws PortletException, IOException {
    PortletRequestDispatcher prd =
      getPortletContext().getRequestDispatcher("/searchEdit.jsp");
    prd.include(request, response);
  }
```

We declare our `LucenePortlet`, which extends `GenericPortlet`. When we are in EDIT mode, we display the `searchEdit.jsp`.

```
  /*
   * This method overrides the doHelp of GenericPortlet
   * This is called to provide the markup to be rendered when the
   * portlet mode is PortletMode.HELP
   * <p>
   * This method provides help information by dispatching
   * the request to "help.jsp"
   */
  protected void doHelp(
    RenderRequest request,
    RenderResponse response)
    throws PortletException, IOException {
    PortletRequestDispatcher prd =
      getPortletContext().getRequestDispatcher("/help.jsp");
    prd.include(request, response);
  }
```

And when we are in HELP mode, we display `help.jsp`.

```
  /*
   * This method overrides the doEdit of GenericPortlet
   * This is called to provide the markup to be rendered when the
   * portlet mode is PortletMode.VIEW
   * <p>
   * In this case, we will dispatch the method to a JSP
   * located in the portlet root directory called "view.jsp"
   */
  protected void doView(
    RenderRequest request,
    RenderResponse response)
    throws PortletException, IOException {
    String queryMode = request.getParameter("queryMode");
    String forwardString = "/searchView.jsp";
    if (queryMode != null) {
      forwardString = "/searchResults.jsp";
    }
    PortletRequestDispatcher prd =
      getPortletContext().getRequestDispatcher(forwardString);
    prd.include(request, response);
  }
```

Rendering the VIEW mode depends on whether we passed in a query mode RenderRequest parameter. If there is a queryMode parameter, we display the results; if not, we display the search box.

```
/* This method is overriden to specify
 * the title programmatically
 */
protected String getTitle(RenderRequest request) {
  return "Lucene Portlet";
}
/* This method is the meat of the portlet
 * manipulations of the portlet's state are done
 * through this method.
 * <p>
 * There are really two types of actions for this portlet
 * depending on which mode we are in.  In the VIEW mode,
 * we have an action that searches a Lucene Index and then
 * places the hits in a request attribute.  In the EDIT mode,
 * we allow users to change the location of the Lucene
 * index.
 *
 */
public void processAction(ActionRequest aReq, ActionResponse aRes)
  throws PortletException, IOException {
  PortletMode mode = new PortletMode(aReq.getParameter("mode"));
  aRes.setPortletMode(mode);
  if (mode.equals(PortletMode.VIEW)) {
    PortletPreferences prefs = aReq.getPreferences();
    String indexPath = prefs.getValue("indexPath", null);
    Searcher searcher = new IndexSearcher(indexPath);
    Analyzer analyzer = new StandardAnalyzer();
    StringBuffer queryBuffer = new StringBuffer();
    String searchString = aReq.getParameter("searchString");
    if (searchString != null) {
      queryBuffer.append(searchString);
      String line = queryBuffer.toString();
      try {
        Query query = QueryParser.parse(line, "contents", analyzer);
        Hits hits = searcher.search(query);
        aReq.setAttribute("hits", hits);
      } catch (ParseException pe) {
        pe.printStackTrace();
      }
    } else {
      aRes.setRenderParameter("queryMode", "begin");
    }
```

Our processAction behavior depends on the portlet's mode. If we have a searchString object, then we use it to query Lucene. If not, we set a render parameter.

```
  } else if (mode.equals(PortletMode.EDIT)) {
    /**
     * If the Submit button is passed as a parameter, then we
```

```
    * know it came from a form.
    */
   if (aReq.getParameter("Submit") != null) {
     PortletPreferences prefs = aReq.getPreferences();
     String indexPath = aReq.getParameter("indexPath");
     prefs.setValue("indexPath", indexPath);

     try {
       prefs.store();
       aRes.setRenderParameter(
         "success",
         "The update was successful.");
     } catch (ValidatorException ve) {
       System.out.println("Preferences did not validate.");
       aRes.setRenderParameter(
         "success",
         "The preferences did not validate.");
     }

     aRes.setRenderParameter(
       "index",
       prefs.getValue("indexPath", ""));
   /**
    * Otherwise, we want to pull the preference, and pass it
    * as a render parameter to our portlet.
    */
   } else {
     PortletPreferences prefs = aReq.getPreferences();
     aRes.setRenderParameter(
       "index",
       prefs.getValue("indexPath", ""));
   }
 }
}
}
```

In EDIT mode, we set the "index" portlet preference based on the parameters submitted from the searchEdit.jsp. If there is no "Submit" parameter, we know that it is the initial view of the EDIT page, and therefore, we want to retrieve the "index" preference.

The LucenePortlet uses a common method of building portlets in that it delegates its user interface rendering to JSPs through a PortletRequestDispatcher. Two major actions are processed by the portlet. One, in VIEW mode, handles searching the Lucene index; and the other, in EDIT mode, allows modification of the Lucene index location, through a portlet preference called indexPath.

We want to determine whether the indexPath preference is actually pointed at a Lucene index, so we will implement our own PreferencesValidator, called LuceneValidator, which is shown in the following code:

```
/*
 * This class demonstrates a basic validator.
 *
 */
```

```
package org.opensourceportals.validator;
import java.io.File;
import java.util.ArrayList;
import java.util.List;
import javax.portlet.PortletPreferences;
import javax.portlet.PreferencesValidator;
import javax.portlet.ValidatorException;
/**
 * @author Clay Richardson
 */
public class LuceneValidator implements PreferencesValidator {
  /*
   * In order to create a validator, we implement the
   * javax.portlet.PreferencesValidator interface.
   *
   * If it fails validation, we throw a ValidatorException.
   *
   */
```

We declare our `LuceneValidator` by extending `PreferencesValidator`.

```
public void validate(PortletPreferences preferences)
  throws ValidatorException {
  List problems = new ArrayList();
  String indexPath = preferences.getValue("indexPath", null);

  //Does the preference even exist?
  if (indexPath == null) {
    problems.add("indexPath");
    throw new ValidatorException(
      "indexPath preference doesn't exist",
      problems);
  } else {

    //Let's check to see if the index is actually there
    //The segments file is a good file to key off of...
    File index = new File(indexPath, "segments");
    if (!index.exists()) {
      problems.add("indexPath");
      throw new ValidatorException(
        "The index doesn't exist",
        problems);
    }
  }
}
}
```

The `LuceneValidator` checks first to see if the `indexPath` preference is actually set to some value. If it is set, then it determines whether the specified directory contains a "segments" file, which would indicate the presence of a Lucene search engine index. This is a perfect example of how you would want to use a validator as a mechanism to check a condition that is more complicated than simply "present" or "not present." If either of these conditions is false, then the `LuceneValidator` will throw a `ValidatorException`.

Now that we have managed the major logical parts of the `LucenePortlet`, we will review the presentation aspects of the portlet. The following code shows `search_view.jsp`, which presents a user interface for searching:

```
<%@ page import="javax.portlet.PortletURL" %>
<%@ taglib uri="http://java.sun.com/portlet" prefix="portlet" %>
<portlet:defineObjects/>
<table width="100%" border="0" cellspacing="0" cellpadding="0">
  <tr>
    <th>SEARCH</th>
  </tr>
  <tr>
    <td>
      <FORM action="<portlet:actionURL />" method="POST">
        <input type="text" name="searchString"/>
        <INPUT type="submit" name="Submit" value="Go"/>
      </FORM>
    </td>
  </tr>
</table>
```

In this JSP, we see the first use of the Portlet Tag Library. These tags provide access to the portlet from within a JSP. The most interesting use here is the `actionURL` tag, which is the proper way of creating links within a portlet application. Creating them as was traditionally done in Web applications, by appending parameters to an HTTP query string, is not correct, as it may omit portal-specific references that should be included in the URL.

Logically, we now need a page to view the results of our search. The following code provides a search results page:

```
<%@ page import="java.util.*,org.apache.lucene.search.*,java.text.*" %>
<%@ page import="org.apache.lucene.document.*" %>
<jsp:useBean id="hits" scope="request" type="org.apache.lucene.search.Hits"/>
<%
String shaded = "silver";
DecimalFormat form = new DecimalFormat("#");
%>
<p>
<i><b><%=hits.length()%></b></i> Documents match your request.
<p>
<center>
<table width="100%">
<%
    for (int i = 0; i < 25; i++) {
            Document doc = hits.doc(i);
            if (i % 2 == 0) {
                shaded = "silver";
```

```
            } else {
                shaded = "white";
            }
%>
        <tr bgcolor="<%=shaded%>">
            <td>
            <%=(i+1+startRow)%>.  (<font color="red">
            <%=form.format((hits.score(i)*100))%>%</font>)
                    <a href="<%=doc.get("url")%>"><%=doc.get("title")%></a><br>
            <%=doc.get("summary")%>
            </td>
        </tr>
    </tr>
<%          }  %>
</table>
</center>
```

As you can see, this is a simplistic search result page, providing only twenty-five search results, and no paging capability.

Finally, the following code provides the portlet application deployment descriptor, also known as the `portlet.xml` file:

```xml
<?xml version="1.0" encoding="UTF-8"?>
<portlet-app>
    <portlet id="LucenePortlet">
        <portlet-name>LucenePortlet</portlet-name>
        <display-name>Example Search Portlet with Lucene</display-name>
        <portlet-class>org.opensourceportals.samples.LucenePortlet</portlet-class>
        <expiration-cache>-1</expiration-cache>
        <supports>
            <mime-type>text/html</mime-type>
            <portlet-mode>EDIT</portlet-mode>
            <portlet-mode>VIEW</portlet-mode>
            <portlet-mode>HELP</portlet-mode>
        </supports>
        <portlet-info>
            <title>Example Search Portlet with Lucene</title>
            <short-title>Lucene Search</short-title>
            <keywords>Search, Lucene</keywords>
        </portlet-info>
        <portlet-preferences>
            <preference>
                <name>indexPath</name>
                <value>C:\lucene\index</value>
            </preference>
            <preferences-
validator>org.opensourceportals.validator.LuceneValidator</preferences-validator>
        </portlet-preferences>
    </portlet>
</portlet-app>
```

The `portlet.xml` file is very basic, just like the portlet we just wrote. It provides three modes, and specifies a validator for its preferences.

Summary

This chapter focused on explaining the Java Portlet API. It provided a basic end-to-end example of a portlet to demonstrate the API in a practical use. However, for a more comprehensive chapter on building portlet applications, see Chapter 9.

2

Searching with Lucene

Lucene is an open-source search API that was originally built by Doug Cutting and is now maintained by the Apache Software Foundation's Jakarta Project. The Lucene project Web site is located at http://jakarta.apache.org/lucene.

Note that Lucene is a search engine **API** and not a search engine **application**. Of course, this causes you to say, "What?! I have been robbed. I want a search engine, not an API to write my own search engine!" Now, we will not even discuss the "value proposition" of open-source software, which is well understood to all but a few concerned vendors, but it should be noted that making Lucene an API gives you the flexibility to use it in your application. Having worked with a few search engine applications, we can assuredly say that it is better to implement interfaces yourself than write tortured adapters to relatively closed APIs. By the time you are done reading this chapter, you will see how easy it really is.

This chapter explains the concepts behind search engine applications, describing how they are implemented in Lucene, and showing you how to use the Lucene API to build search applications.

Understanding Search Engine Concepts

What is a search engine? The simple answer, and the one that most people offer without much thought, is that it is a text box into which you type text, after which you press a Submit button. From there, it returns a set of documents that contain your selected words. Now, all of us that have done extensive Web research understand that it is more complicated than just returning particular documents that contain the "magic words." We know that search engines that simply do text matching are horribly ineffective.

When we talk about the effectiveness of a search engine, we are talking about two concepts:

❑ **Accuracy** — What percentage of all the documents available for the particular query issued were actually returned?

❑ **Precision** — What percentage of the documents returned are actually about the particular query?

Figure 2.1 illustrates the concept of accuracy. The large circle on the bottom represents all of the possible documents available on a given topic. The smaller circle above represents the documents returned from a search. The overlap in the middle represents the accurate documents. In a perfectly accurate search, the top circle would completely cover the bottom circle.

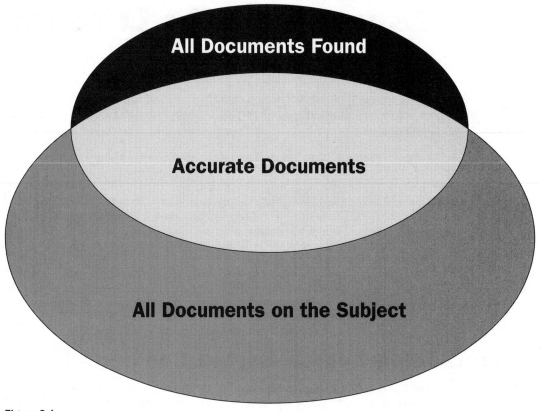

Figure 2.1

Figure 2.2 demonstrates the concept of precision. The large circle on the bottom represents the documents returned from a search. The smaller circle above represents the returned documents that are really about the search topic. The overlap in the middle represents the precise documents. In a perfectly precise search, the top circle would completely cover the bottom circle.

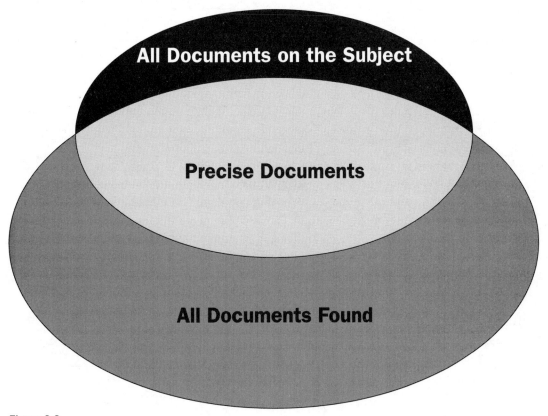

Figure 2.2

Basically, the idea is to find an optimal point at which you receive as many of the documents that are relevant as possible while minimizing documents that should not be retrieved.

The Anatomy of a Search Engine

So, how exactly does a search engine work? The simple answer is that it sucks in a bunch of documents and organizes them into an index. That index is then used to return answers to queries in rank order. Figure 2.3 illustrates this concept.

Figure 2.3 demonstrates the two paths through the search engine. The first path shows how the index gets filled with documents. The documents are fed to an analyzer that then transforms them into the appropriate **weighted terms** (or scores) and passes them to the IndexWriter. The second path through the search engine shows how the index is queried for documents. The same analyzer is used to derive a user-defined set of terms that are, in turn, passed to the IndexSearcher to perform the search of the index. Because indexes rarely ever hold the entire document verbatim, a set of Hits are returned, with each hit representing what is retained about the document within the index.

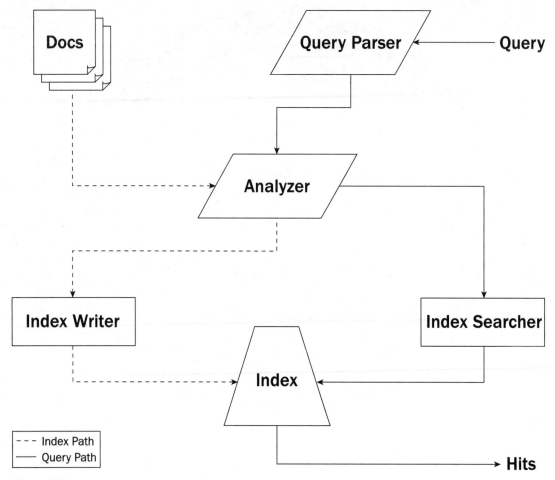

Figure 2.3

As you can see, the central part of a search engine is its indexes. How these indexes are built is remarkably similar amongst all search engines. An algorithm builds a list of entries, with each of the entries containing a document identifier and a **scored term**. For example, a page from the American Kennel Club scores the term "dog" at 9.03. While the number really depends on the scoring system chosen by the algorithm, it essentially represents the confidence of the search engine that this document is relevant to the term "dog." When a query is sent to a search engine, the same algorithm is used to score what the query means (in these weighted terms), which then allows us to compare it with the weighted terms of the indexed documents.

These algorithms vary, but some of the typical facets of search engines are represented in the following table.

Technique	Description
Stop Words	Certain words, such as "the," "a," "and," and so on have very little use or meaning in indexing documents (they appear on every page).
Stemming	This technique chops off parts of a word to get to the root word; for example, the word "cats" becomes "cat."
META tags	META tags provide a way for developers to suggest keywords for a given page. This can be used to increase the score for certain words in the document. Unfortunately, they often bias the index for a document regardless of the actual relational relevance to the document. For example, in the early days of the Internet, Web developers would use "explicit words" as keywords, hoping to increase traffic to their unrelated site—and it worked. Therefore, many search tools ignore the suggested keywords either somewhat or entirely, preferring to allow their indexing algorithm to ascertain the document content.
Page ranking	Page ranking turns Web surfers into editorial assistants. By allowing the users of a search engine to rank the applicability of a given document to their search, the index gets "smarter."
Page linkages	Page linkages operate on the premise that if your page is a good reference about something, chances are good that someone has linked to it, particularly if it is related. Therefore, a linkage from a highly relevant document could lend itself to a higher ranking. Of course, sometimes links are not very relevant to the current page. For example, our home page may have links to http://www.nationalreview.com, which tells you some things about us, but doesn't really tell you much about that page (other than maybe its popularity). Of course, popularity is useful in a search engine until you realize that the most popular sites are generally well known and more generic—and search engines like to find specific things.
Parts of Speech	Often, considering the part of speech of a word can define its value. Furthermore, if you consider its grammatical function, then you can weigh it more heavily. For example, is the word the subject of a sentence?
Term Proximity	Term proximity relates to how close two words are in a sentence, with the premise that they are closely related if they are close together.
Semantic Nets/ Bayesian Nets	This principle is a far more sophisticated example of the previous one. Essentially, what it seeks to do is group together like words into "concepts." For example, the concept "Butcher of Baghdad" seems to always be related to "Saddam Hussein," so essentially these nets organize words into statistical proximities and perform very complex matching algorithms to determine how closely related one net is to another. The advantage of this strategy is that the more data you feed it, the more statistical evidence it gathers and hence the "smarter" it becomes.
Term Expansion	This takes a term and runs it through a thesaurus to add more terms to gain a better understanding of the words surrounding the original term.

Which of these techniques are used and to what extent a given search engine uses each is dependent on the search engine. Usually, this is a closely guarded proprietary secret, wrapped in a shroud of marketing materials. What about Lucene? The answer depends on how you decide to build your analyzers.

Before describing the anatomy of Lucene, take a look at an example of these indexing strategies at work. Figure 2.4 shows a paragraph to be indexed.

> My name is Clay. I have been programming with Java since 1996. In addition to working as a Java Architect, I write books on Java and teach a course on Java for Virginia Tech. In my free time, I am a volunteer firefighter.

Figure 2.4

This sample is a typical example of a paragraph that search engines process every day. For simplicity's sake, we have left it as a very small passage and have given it a broad scope to demonstrate how a document can be about numerous things. Of course, we will also simulate a very simplistic (and probably not very effective) algorithm, for the sake of covering the basics.

One of the first things done in processing a given piece of text is to remove all of the superfluous garbage that is not very useful in terms of indexing a document. Remember that the central point in indexing a document is to find the words that describe what the document is about (accuracy), and not add too much garbage (precision). Therefore, we should remove the things that are common to the vast majority of documents. The first thing to remove is the punctuation, as it is not helpful in distinguishing documents. Then, we remove words that are so common in the English language that we would find them in virtually every document. These words are called **stop words** in Lucene speak, as you want to stop them from being indexed (because they will kill your precision). Typical examples are articles (such as "a," "an," and "the"), prepositions (such as "of," "for," and "to"), and conjunctions (such as "but," "if," and "then"). A good stop words list will contain many words that you would not instantly recognize as frequently overused. There are people who study the use of the English language extensively, and they produce lists of words that are so frequently used that they seem to lose any discernable meaning when analyzing text, such as "everything," "anyone," and "nobody." These words are so widely used in many contexts that it is hard to derive any meaning from their use in a given piece of text. Figure 2.5 shows how our sample is processed to eliminate the punctuation and stop words.

> ~~My name is~~ Clay. ~~I have been~~ programming ~~with~~ Java ~~since~~ 1996. ~~In~~ addition ~~to~~ working ~~as a~~ Java Architect, ~~I~~ write books ~~on~~ Java ~~and~~ teach ~~a~~ course ~~on~~ Java ~~for~~ Virginia Tech. ~~In my~~ free time, ~~I am~~ a volunteer firefighter.

Figure 2.5

Notice how this cuts a significant amount of data out of the paragraph, as many of the words we employ are used to "glue together" our sentences. You can see how the remaining words, taken individually, seem more meaningful.

Another technique involved in processing text is to provide stemming. This is a very simplistic stemming algorithm, but Figure 2.6 shows how stemming reduces three of the words to their more meaningful roots.

Clay programming Java 1996 addition working Java Architect
write books Java teach course Java Virginia Tech free time
volunteer firefighter

Figure 2.6

Some words are more readily related by using their root form — "work," "works," and "working" all demonstrably mean the same thing. Notice also that stemming the word "addition" is not necessarily a good thing, as "add" is not exactly the same concept. This shows you the inexact science of stemming, which is frequently the issue in indexing algorithms. The more you manipulate the text, the more likely you are to introduce error and uncertainty.

Figure 2.7 shows the next step in our simple algorithmic processing. This relates to grouping and ranking terms by parts of speech (or a more specifically grammatical role).

Java
Clay
program
1996
add
work
Java Architect
write
book
teach
course
Virginia Tech
volunteer
firefighter
free
time

Figure 2.7

Notice how our algorithm has preserved the proper names for both the title of "Java Architect" and the university "Virginia Tech." This approach recognizes that names often have a lot of significance (which is why we have them), and therefore creates combined terms. Some search engines do this type of processing and others do not. Note that the Standard Analyzer for Lucene, by reducing everything to lowercase, would make such processing practically impossible. However, it is introduced here in order to give you an idea of numerous ways that one can look at a piece of text and process it for meaning.

Figure 2.8 shows the final index entries. Note that most search engines, for speed purposes, store their data in what is known as an **inverted index**. Therefore, you actually list the terms and then the documents that contain those terms. This is much like the index of this book, except that the terms in the index are not weighted. For our example, we will weight them.

```
Java
<336, 0.99>
<356, 0.87>
<378, 0.76>
<236, 0.67>
<386, 0.56>
<598, 0.44>
Java Architect
<336, 0.89>
<226, 0.67>
<278, 0.56>
<236, 0.47>
```

Figure 2.8

In this example, two terms have been pulled from our index. Below each of the terms is a list of document identifiers, along with a weighting of that document for that term. In our example, our document was given identifier 336, and we have arbitrarily given it a high rating on both ends (normally, these ratings would be ascertained from a number of weighting algorithms).

Now that you have looked at the general concepts of indexing, it is time to examine how Lucene works.

The Anatomy of Lucene

Lucene is a very straightforward and modular API. It involves a set of classes that you implement, or you can choose to use some of the demo classes included with the Lucene distribution.

To index documents using Lucene, you write a method (or a utility class) that performs the following steps:

1. Gathers a list of files to be indexed.

2. Creates an instance of a Document object to handle an InputStream to each file. This could be an instance of FileDocument or HTMLDocument — both included as part of the Lucene demo.

3. Creates an instance of Analyzer. This could be the included StandardAnalyzer or one as sophisticated as you can make it.

4. Creates an IndexWriter with the following: a location of where to locate (place) the index, the instance of Analyzer just created, and a flag to tell it whether to create the index or not (if it is missing).

5. Adds the Document objects to the IndexWriter using the addDocument method.

As you can see, the process is very straightforward. In fact, Lucene deploys with two demonstrations of how to do exactly this; furthermore, the Javadoc is very good at explaining how things work. The following basic code example performs the task:

```
/*
 * BasicIndex.java
 *
```

```
 * in
 *
 * org.opensourceportals.lucene
 *
 */
package org.opensourceportals.lucene;
import org.apache.lucene.index.*;
import org.apache.lucene.document.*;
import org.apache.lucene.analysis.standard.*;
import java.io.*;
import java.util.*;
/**
 * @author Clay
 */
public class BasicIndex {
  public static void main(String[] args) {
    if (args.length == 0) {
      System.out.println(
        "Usage: java BasicIndex <index-path> [files]");
    }
    String indexPath = args[0];
    IndexWriter writer;
    try {
      writer =
        new IndexWriter(indexPath, new StandardAnalyzer(), false);
      for (int i = 1; i < args.length; i++) {
        System.out.println("Indexing: " + args[i]);
        File indexFile = new File(args[i]);
        InputStream fis = new FileInputStream(indexFile);
```

We have created a basic application that shows how to index a document. We created an IndexWriter based on the location of the index given in the first argument, and then we iterated through the remaining arguments to get the locations of the files that we need to process.

```
        /*
         * We use a Document with four fields:
         * the file path, the last modified date
         * the length of the file
         * and the file's contents.
         */
        Document doc = new Document();
        doc.add(Field.UnIndexed("path", indexFile.getPath()));
        doc.add(
          Field.UnIndexed(
            "length",
            Long.toString(indexFile.length())));
        doc.add(
          Field.UnIndexed(
            "modified",
            new Date(indexFile.lastModified()).toString()));
        doc.add(
          Field.Text("text", (Reader) new InputStreamReader(fis)));
```

```
            writer.addDocument(doc);
            fis.close();
        }
        writer.close();
    } catch (IOException ioe) {
        System.out.println(ioe);
    }
    }
}
```

Now, we create the Document object that we are going to index and define a set of fields that are relevant metadata to store in our index. In this case, we decide to store the file path, the file length, the file's last modified date, and the contents of the file. (Of course, we would want to limit storing the whole file if we had large files.) Then we write the document to the `IndexWriter`.

Of course, only placing documents in an index is pointless if they cannot be queried, so the following steps walk you through how that is accomplished:

1. Create a `QueryParser` by passing in the default field to search (as a String) and an instance of `Analyzer` (important: make sure you use the same type of `Analyzer` that was used to build the index).

2. Call `parse` on `QueryParser` to return a `Query` object.

3. Initialize an `IndexSearcher` with the location of the index you wish to search.

4. Pass the `Query` object into the `search` method of `IndexSearcher`, which will return a `Hits` object.

5. Because the `Hits` object is just a ranked list of `Document` objects, you then parse that data and present it as you wish.

Once again, this is a pretty straightforward process to search a document. Furthermore, a demo Web application included with Lucene does precisely this. The following code is a very simple example of how to show the process in code:

```
/*
 * BasicSearch.java
 *
 * in
 *
 * org.opensourceportals.lucene
 *
 */
package org.opensourceportals.lucene;
import org.apache.lucene.search.*;
import org.apache.lucene.queryParser.*;
import org.apache.lucene.analysis.standard.*;
import org.apache.lucene.queryParser.*;
/**
 * @author Clay
 */
public class BasicSearch {
    public static void main(String[] args) {
```

```
if (args.length == 0) {
  System.out.println(
    "Usage: java BasicSearch <index-path> \"search string\"");
}
String indexPath = args[0];
String searchString = args[1];
try {
  Searcher searcher = new IndexSearcher(indexPath);
  Query query =
    QueryParser.parse(
      searchString,
      "text",
      new StandardAnalyzer());
```

We create an IndexSearcher from our first argument and a Query based on our second argument. Notice our choice of a StandardAnalyzer and how it coincides with the analyzer used to create the index. This is important because the document and the query need to be analyzed using the same algorithm to get accurate results.

```
Hits hits = searcher.search(query);
for (int i = 0; i < hits.length(); i++) {
  System.out.println(
    hits.doc(i).get("path")
      + "; Size: "
      + hits.doc(i).get("length")
      + " bytes; Last Modified: "
      + hits.doc(i).get("modified")
      + "; Rating: "
      + hits.score(i));
  }
} catch (Exception ioe) {
  System.out.println(ioe);
}
}
```

Now, we pass our Query into our IndexSearcher which returns a Hits object. We iterate through that Hits object, retrieving each of its Document objects. For each of those, we print out three of its fields ("path", "length", and "modified") and its relative score.

Both of these basic examples overlook the most advantageous thing about the Lucene search API. Because it is not a tool, but rather an API, the interfaces are very clean. Therefore, while no tool would use such simplistic mechanisms to index and search documents, Lucene can provide similar capabilities. Furthermore, it can provide real value in being extensible and customizable. In order to determine how to provide these capabilities, it is important to examine a number of these specialized objects.

Analyzer

Much of the early part of this chapter was devoted to describing how search engines analyze text. This is because it is the central activity and purpose of a search engine. The great thing about Lucene is that you can write your own Analyzer to accommodate the sophistication desired for your particular application. Next is an example of how a custom Analyzer looks.

```java
/*
 * CustomAnalyzer.java
 *
 * in
 *
 * org.opensourceportals.lucene
 *
 */
package org.opensourceportals.lucene;
import org.apache.lucene.analysis.*;
import java.io.*;
import java.util.*;
/**
 * @author Clay
 *
 * This is an example of how to build a basic Analyzer
 */
public class CustomAnalyzer extends Analyzer {
  private static Hashtable stopWords;
  /**
   * An array containing some common English words
   * that are usually not useful for searching.
   */
  public static final String[] STOPWORDS = {
        "about", "after", "all", "also", "an", "and",
        "another", "any", "are", "as", "at", "be",
        "because", "been", "before", "being", "between",
        "both", "but", "by", "came", "can", "come",
        "could", "did", "do", "does", "each", "else",
        "for", "from", "get", "got", "has", "had",
        "he", "have", "her", "here", "him", "himself",
        "his", "how", "if", "in", "into", "is", "it",
        "its", "just", "like", "make", "many", "me",
        "might", "more", "most", "much", "must", "my",
        "never", "now", "of", "on", "only", "or",
        "other", "our", "out", "over", "re", "said",
        "same", "see", "should", "since", "so", "some",
        "still", "such", "take", "than", "that", "the",
        "their", "them", "then", "there", "these",
        "they", "this", "those", "through", "to", "too",
        "under", "up", "use", "very", "want", "was",
        "way", "we", "well", "were", "what", "when",
        "where", "which", "while", "who", "will",
        "with", "would", "you", "your", "0", "1", "2",
        "3", "4", "5", "6", "7", "8", "9", "000", "$",
        "a", "b", "c", "d", "e", "f", "g", "h", "i",
        "j", "k", "l", "m", "n", "o", "p", "q", "r",
        "s", "t", "u", "v", "w", "x", "y", "z"
  };
  /**
   * Constructor for our CustomAnalyzer.
   * We take the opportunity to make a hash table for the
   * stop words - to be used in the tokenStream method.
   */
  public CustomAnalyzer() {
    stopWords = StopFilter.makeStopTable(STOPWORDS);
  }
```

We declared our stop words and override the default constructor to populate a `Hashtable` of those stop words using the `StopFilter` object's `makeStopTable` method.

```
/**
 * The critical method to override in order to perform Analysis
 *
 * The String is used so that an Analyzer can be passed a field
 * name and thus use a set of strategies for analysis depending
 * on the field that was passed in.  We don't need such a
 * capability
 */
public TokenStream tokenStream(
  String doesNothing,
  Reader reader) {
  return new StopFilter(
    new LowerCaseTokenizer(reader),
    stopWords);
}
}
```

`CustomAnalyser` does little more than change everything to lowercase and filter out stop words, but it provides a basic example of how to write an Analyzer. Note that the `tokenStream` method takes a String; this is new from previous releases of Lucene, which took only a `Reader`. The rationale behind this is that you could want to use a different strategy for analyzing the text based on the field. We didn't use that feature here, but it provides the capability, if desired, for a more sophisticated implementation.

Document

In designing your indexing solution, you must first consider how to create your `Document` objects. Because a document is essentially a record in your index, you can think of this as developing the schema for your index. It becomes particularly important in determining which fields can be searched, which are tokenized, and which are available for displaying results. The following table discusses the types of fields.

Method	Indexed	Tokenized	Stored	Example Usage
`Field.Text(String name, String value)`	True	True	True	The document summary
`Field.Text(String name, Reader value)`	True	True	False	A large document summary (worth storing but too big to hold verbatim)
`Field.Keyword(String name, String value)`	False	True	True	The keywords or document title (the searchable metadata fields)
`Field.UnIndexed(String name, String value)`	False	False	True	The modification date (not searched but returned)
`Field.UnStored(String name, String value)`	True	True	False	The document's full text

As you can see, there is a bit of overlap among the field types. Essentially, you should ask yourself whether this field needs to be searched, whether it needs to be displayed, and whether it is too big to be stored. Those questions will help guide your selection of what field types to use.

Directory

The `Directory` object is an abstraction of the underlying storage of indexes. There are two existing implementations of the abstract `Directory` class: `FSDirectory` for file systems, and `RAMDirectory` for in-memory storage. In theory, you can implement your own `Directory` object to store your indexes in numerous underlying storage mechanisms such as databases or document management systems. Unfortunately, the `Directory` class adopts a file-based paradigm, which makes it tougher to understand how to implement the interface.

Understanding the Lucene Query Syntax

Lucene provides the flexibility for you to write your own query language. However, this flexibility has already provided a strong query language to use right out of the box. A good reference for this is available online at http://jakarta.apache.org/lucene/docs/queryparsersyntax.html. The following sections explain the syntax.

Terms

Terms are generally like your conventional search engine. Each word, separated by a space, is a term unless you place them in quotes:

```
members "vast right wing conspiracy"
```

In this case, there are two terms: "members" and "vast right wing conspiracy." Clearly, you do not want the terms vast, right, wing, or conspiracy by themselves. They are combined to be a meaningful term.

Fields

Our previous search will search against the default field that you specified when you initialized your `QueryParser`. However, sometimes you would like to search against another of the fields in your index:

```
site:www.rnc.org "vast right wing conspiracy"
```

In this case, you are specifying that you want to search for "www.rnc.org" in the site field (which you created) in your index. The "vast right wing conspiracy" term is still being run against the default field.

Term Modifiers

There are a number of ways that you can modify a term within your search. The following table demonstrates a list of these modifiers.

Technique	Example	Description
Single Character Wildcard	to?t	Matches any character in that one position. For example, "toot" or "tort" would be valid matches.
Multiple Character Wildcard	to*t	Matches any number of characters in that position. In this case, the word "toast" would also be valid.
Fuzzy	Usama~	Placing a tilde (~) at the end of the word provides fuzzy logic using the Levenshtein Distance algorithm. In this case, this would return "Osama" as a valid term. This is useful when you believe you may be a character off on a spelling. This technique implicitly boosts the term by 0.2 also.
Boosting	UML^5 tools	Increases the relevance of a search term. In this case, it means that "UML" is five times more relevant than "tools." The boost factor must be positive, but can be a decimal (for example, 0.5).
Proximity	"Microsoft Java"~7	This will return results where the words "Microsoft" and "Java" are within seven words of each other. This can provide a basic conceptual search capability by indicating how certain key words can be closely related.

You cannot use wildcards at the beginning of a search term.

Boolean Operators, Grouping, and Escaping

Lucene supports the common Boolean operators found in almost all search engines:

❑ AND indicates that two terms must be present together in a given document, but in no particular order, such as a phrase term (for example, "cold war"). For another example, Homer AND Simpson will return pages that contain both terms, even if they are not next to each other.

❑ OR will return pages that contain either of the terms indicated. This is helpful when you have alternate ways of describing a particular term. "Bull Run" OR Manassas would return pages that contain either of the names used to describe the first battle of the American Civil War.

❑ + means that a term must exist on a given page. If you use +Wrox Java, it would return only pages that had "Wrox" on them.

❑ - means that a term cannot appear on a given page. If you wanted to look at all pages related to Wrox that don't pertain to Microsoft, you could use Wrox -Microsoft.

❑ NOT behaves much like the "-" command. If you were looking for documents about the Bundy family, but you didn't want to be bogged down by all the documents about Ted Bundy, you would use Bundy NOT Ted.

Grouping is another powerful capability that also exists in Lucene. Usually, if you are going to use Boolean conditions, you need a mechanism to group together conditions. Consider the following example:

```
("order of battle" AND "casualty figures") at the First Battle of ("Bull Run" OR
Manassas)
```

In this case, you want pages that contain the order of battle and the casualty figures for the first battle of what is known as either "Bull Run" or Manassas. This shows a perfect example of using grouping and Boolean operators to make sophisticated queries.

Of course, to support this expansive query syntax, Lucene uses a number of special characters, listed here:

```
+ - && || ! ( ) { } [ ] ^ " ~ * ? : \
```

Therefore, for you to search for a TV show called "Showdown: Iraq," you would need to escape the colon in the query as follows: `"Showdown\: Iraq"`. Notice how this is just like the escape sequence in Java, so it should be easy to remember.

While you have seen the power of the Lucene Query Syntax, and how useful it can be in creating sophisticated searches, it is very important to consider the sophistication of the users of your system. While most developers, and particularly open source developers, are strong Web researchers, most users of your system will not have a strong understanding of Lucene's searching capabilities. Therefore, it becomes very important to provide a good user interface to enable users to maximize the benefits of searching with Lucene.

Figure 2.9 provides an example of an Advanced Search page meant to leverage these advanced capabilities.

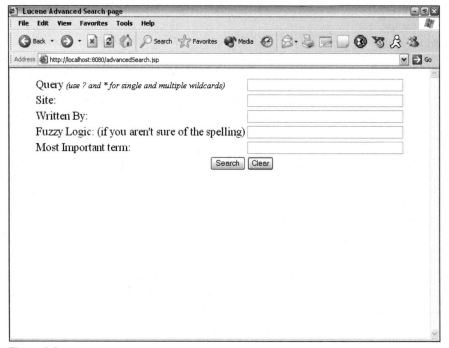

Figure 2.9

Optimizing Lucene's Performance

In order to understand the performance considerations of Lucene, first consider how Lucene creates its indexes. Lucene creates segments that hold a certain number of files in them. It is easy to think of a segment as an **index part**. Lucene holds its index in memory until it reaches the allowed capacity, and then it writes it to a segment on the disk. Once a certain number of segments have been written, Lucene merges the segments into bigger segments.

To determine how often to write and merge the indexes to disk, the `IndexWriter` has a member variable known as the `mergeFactor`. The `mergeFactor` specifies how many files are stored before writing a segment. In addition, it controls how many segments are written before they are merged together. Raising the merge factor increases the speed of your indexing activity, because more is being kept in memory and fewer file reorganization manipulations are being conducted. However, note two obvious problems here. First, your machine is limited in the amount of memory it has (a small fraction of the disk space), and second, the operating system can often limit the number of files you can have open at one time.

You also need to know that `IndexWriter` has a member variable called `maxMergeDocs`. This variable sets the limit on the number of files that can be contained in one segment.

Of course, the more files you have, and the less merging you do, the slower your searching will be. However, anticipating this problem, `IndexWriter` has a method known as `optimize` that will combine the segments on the disk (and reduce the number of files). Note that optimization can slow down indexing tremendously, so a strong consideration would be to limit the use of `optimize` in indexing-intensive applications, and use it extensively in searching-intensive applications.

Summary

Lucene is a powerful search engine API. It is written in a very modular fashion, which allows you, as a developer, a tremendous amount of freedom in how you decide to use it to solve your problems. Because it is an API, it could be very effectively used to index your e-mail Inbox, a database, or a set of news feeds. The applications are limited only by how you choose to use them.

This chapter covered the basics of search engines. Then we showed the techniques that search engines use to analyze text. From there, we described the internals of the Lucene API, providing some examples of how to do the major tasks required of an application developer who implements a solution with this API. We described the query syntax as a means of helping developers understand the toolset available for searching, and to encourage them to develop more sophisticated GUIs to leverage it.

Part II of this book describes how to build your own portal. It provides practical examples of how you can add Lucene to your enterprise portal solution.

3

Messaging with Apache James

The **Java Apache Mail Enterprise Server (James)** is an open-source Java mail server that is part of the Apache Software Foundation's Jakarta project. It is a 100 percent pure Java mail server that was designed to be a powerful, portable, and robust enterprise solution for e-mail and e-mail-related services. Part of its strength comes from the fact that it is based on current and **open protocols**. James is comprised of several different components and can be configured in different ways to offer a fully flexible and customizable framework. It is currently built on top of the Apache Avalon application framework (http://avalon.apache.org), which is also part of the Jakarta project. This framework encompasses good development practices and provides a solid foundation to host the James mail server.

This chapter explores various concepts of the James server. It explains how to obtain, install, and configure the James server, and describes the various components that provide for the total e-mail solution. The chapter concludes with an introduction to the **JavaMail Application Programming Interface (API)**, a small example application for sending and receiving e-mail using JavaMail and the James e-mail server, and an example of how James can be used as part of a portal application. This chapter covers many aspects of the James mail server, but for a more in-depth discussion and explanation of all of the components that comprise the James framework, visit its primary Web site at http://james.apache.org.

Introducing James

James was designed to be a complete enterprise mail solution. It can serve as a core component in an overall portal solution. The James server has many design objectives that are implemented in a number of features, including the following:

❑ **Server Portability** — Apache James is a 100 percent pure Java application that is based on the Java 2 platform and the JavaMail API.

❑ **Complete Solution** — The James mail server can handle the transport and storage of mail messages on a single server. It does not require any other server or another associated application.

❑ **Protocol Abstraction** — James views the various mail protocols as simply communication languages that tie the mail client to the mail server. It does not depend on any particular protocol, but rather follows an abstracted server design.

❑ **Mailet Support** — A mailet is a discrete piece of mail processing logic that is incorporated into the processing of a mail-compliant mail server. Apache James is such a server and supports the Apache Mailet API. Mailets are easy to write and enable developers to build highly customized and powerful mail applications.

❑ **Resource Abstraction** — Apache James abstracts its resources and accesses them through defined interfaces, much like the e-mail protocols are used. These resources include features such as JavaMail, used for mail transport, the Mailet API, and Java DataBase Connectivity (JDBC), for message and user data storage. James is highly modular and packages its components in a very flexible manner.

❑ **Secure and Multi-Threaded Design** — Apache James has a careful, security-oriented, fully multi-threaded design, allowing enhanced performance, scalability, and mission-critical use. This approach is based on the technology developed for the Apache JServ servlet engine.

James also introduces several concepts that are at the core of how it manages to operate as a mail server, from both a production and administrative point of view. We will first describe them in a little more detail so that you get a better idea of how they work. How to configure these items in the James server is described in the section "Configuring James."

Working with Mailets and Matchers

As mentioned earlier, a **mailet** is a discrete piece of mail processing logic that is incorporated into the processing of a mail server. James operates as a mailet-compliant mail server, which means that it understands how to process the Java code that uses the Mailet API. A mailet can do several things when processing a mail message. It can generate an automatic reply, build a message archive, update a database, or any other thing a developer would like to do with a mail message. James uses **matchers** to help determine whether a mailet should process a given e-mail message that just arrived. If a match is found, James invokes that particular mailet.

The Mailet API is a simple API used to build mail processing instructions for the James server. Because James is a mailet container, administrators of the mail server can deploy mailets. These mailets can either be prepackaged or custom built. In the default mode, James uses several mailets to carry out a variety of server tasks. Other mailets can be created to serve other purposes. The current Mailet API defines interfaces for both matchers and mailets. Because the API is public, developers using the James mail server can write their own custom matchers and mailets.

Writing mailets and matchers is a relatively simple process. For mailets, you typically implement the `Mailet` interface through the `org.apache.mailet.GenericMailet` class. This class has several methods, but in order to write a generic mailet, you only have to override the `service` method:

```
abstract void service(Mail mail)
```

Writing a matcher is just as simple. Simply use the `org.apache.mailet.GenericMatcher` class and override the `match` method:

```
abstract Collection match(Mail mail)
```

Matchers, as identified earlier, are used to match mail messages against a set of conditions. If a match is met, it returns a set of the recipients of that message. Matchers do not modify any part of the message during this evaluation. Mailets, on the other hand, are responsible for processing the message and can alter the content of the message or pass it on to some other component. James comes bundled with several mailets and matchers in its distribution. The following sections describe the various mailets and matchers that are bundled with the James server.

Bundled Matchers

The matchers that are bundled with James were identified by members of the user and developer communities because they were found useful in their own configurations. Following is a list of the specific matchers. More information on these matchers, including configuration information, can be found at http://james.apache.org/provided_matchers_2_1.html.

❑ `All` — A generic matcher that matches all mail messages being processed.

❑ `CommandForListserv` — This matcher is used as a simple filter to recognize mail messages that are list server commands. It matches messages that are addressed to the list server host as well as any message that is addressed to a user named <prefix>-on or <prefix>-off on any host.

❑ `FetchedFrom` — This matcher is used with the James `FetchPOP` server. `FetchPOP` is a component in James that allows an administrator to retrieve mail messages from multiple POP3 servers and deliver them to the local spool. This process is useful for consolidating mail residing in accounts on different machines to a single account. The `FetchedFrom` matcher is used to match a custom header set by the `FetchPOP` server.

❑ `HasAttachment` — Matches mail messages with the MIME type multipart/mixed.

❑ `HasHabeasWarrantMark` — Matches all mail messages that have the Habeas Warrant. A Habeas mark indicates that the message is not a spam message even though it may look like spam to the e-mail server. Information on these messages can be found at www.habeas.com.

❑ `HasHeader` — Matches mail messages with the specified message header.

❑ `HostIs` — Matches mail messages that are sent to a recipient on a host listed in a James configuration list.

❑ `HostIsLocal` — Matches mail messages sent to addresses on local hosts.

❑ `InSpammerBlacklist` — Checks whether the mail message is from a listed IP address tracked on mail-abuse.org.

❑ `IsSingleRecipient` — Matches mail messages that are sent to a single recipient.

❑ `NESSpamCheck` — This is a matcher derived from a spam filter on a Netscape mail server. It detects headers that indicate if it is a spam message.

❑ `Recipients` — Matches mail messages that are sent to a recipient listed in a specified list.

❑ `RecipientsIsLocal` — Matches mail messages that are sent to recipients on local hosts with users that have local accounts.

❏ RelayLimit — This matcher counts the number of headers in a mail message to see if the number equals or exceeds a specified limit.

❏ RemoteAddrInNetwork — Checks the remote address from the e-mail message against a configuration list of IP addresses and domain names. The matcher will consider it a match if the address appears in the list.

❏ RemoteAddrNotInNetwork — Checks the remote address from the e-mail message against a configuration list of IP addresses and domain names. The matcher will consider it a match if the address is not in the list.

❏ SenderInFakeDomain — Matches mail messages in which the host name in the address of the sender cannot be resolved.

❏ SenderIs — Matches mail messages that are sent by a user who is part of a specific list.

❏ SizeGreaterThan — Matches mail messages that have a total size greater than a specified amount.

❏ SubjectIs — Matches mail messages with a specified subject.

❏ SubjectStartsWith — Matches mail messages with a subject that begins with a specified value.

❏ UserIs — Matches mail messages that are sent to addresses that have user IDs listed in a configuration list.

Bundled Mailets

The bundled mailets, like the matchers, are commonly used by members of the user and development community. More information on the following mailets, including configuration information, can be found at http://james.apache.org/provided_mailets_2_1.html:

❏ AddFooter — Adds a text footer to the mail message.

❏ AddHabeasWarrantMark — Adds a Habeas warrant mark to the mail message.

❏ AddHeader — Adds a text header to the mail message.

❏ AvalonListserv — Provides functionality for a basic list server. It implements some basic filtering for mail messages sent to the list.

❏ AvalonListservManager — Processes list management commands of the form <list-name>-on @ <host> and <list-name>-off @ <host>, where <list-name> and <host> are arbitrary.

❏ Forward — Forwards the mail message to the recipient(s).

❏ JDBCAlias — Performs alias translations for e-mail addresses stored in a database table.

❏ JDBCVirtualUserTable — Performs more complex translations than the JDBCAlias mailet.

❏ LocalDelivery — Delivers mail messages to local mailboxes.

❏ NotifyPostmaster — Forwards the mail message to the James postmaster as an attachment.

❏ NotifySender — Forwards the mail message to the original sender as an attachment.

❏ Null — Completes the processing of a mail message.

- PostmasterAlias — Intercepts all mail messages that are addressed to postmaster@<domain>, where <domain> is one of the domains managed by the James server. It then substitutes the configured James postmaster address for the original one.

- Redirect — Provides configurable redirection services.

- RemoteDelivery — Manages the delivery of mail messages to recipients located on remote SMTP hosts.

- ServerTime — Sends a message to the sender of the original mail message with a timestamp.

- ToProcessor — Redirects processing of the mail message to the specified processor.

- ToRepository — Places a copy of the mail message in the specified directory.

- UseHeaderRecipients — Inserts a new message into the queue with recipients from the MimeMessage header. It ignores recipients associated with the JavaMail interface.

Understanding SpoolManager

As a mail server, James uses POP3 and SMTP services to receive and send e-mail messages. What James does with a message once it receives it, however, is up to the SpoolManager. James separates the services that are used to deliver the mail messages from the service that it uses to process a piece of mail once it is received. The SpoolManager is a mailet and is the service component that James uses for its mail processing engine. As previously described, it is a combination of matchers and mailets that actually carry out the mail processing.

The SpoolManager continues to check the spool repository for any new mail messages. Mail can be placed in the spool repository from any number of sources. These include the POP3 or SMTP services. The SpoolManager contains a series of processors. Each one will indicate what state the mail message is in as it is processed in the SpoolManager. When a piece of mail is found in the repository, it is first sent to the root, or first, processor. Besides holding newly arrived mail messages, the spool repository also holds messages as they transit from one processor to another. Mail messages continue through the various processors until they are finally marked as completed by a mailet.

The SpoolManager can be configured to address many needs that an administrator may have. Processes to perform operations such as filtering and sorting can easily be created through custom matchers and mailets that are used by the SpoolManager component. A large part of the James mail server's flexibility lies in the power of the SpoolManager.

Understanding Repositories

James uses repositories to store mail and user information. There are several different types of repositories and each serves a different purpose. The **user repository** is used to store information about users of the mail server. This may include user names, passwords, and aliases. The **mail repository** is used to store mail messages that have been delivered. **Spool repositories** will in turn store messages that are currently being processed. Last is the **news repository**, which is used to store news messages. Aside from having different types of repositories, James can also use different types of storage for these repositories. These storage types include File, Database, and DBFile. Each of these is briefly described next.

File Repositories

File-based repositories store their data on the computer's file system. This type of repository is very easy to configure and in fact is the default repository storage type for the James mail server. Each of the four types of repositories (user, mail, spool, and news) has a file-based repository storage capability. Using a file repository, however, comes with its faults. There may be performance issues when compared with the other storage types and it is not recommended for use if the mail server is used for large amounts of mail processing.

Database Repositories

Repositories that use a database to store their data take a little more effort to configure than the file-based repositories. Instructions on how to configure James to use a database as a repository can be found in the James configuration file. In order to use a database, the administrator must know how to set up the JDBC connection using the appropriate JDBC driver. This will include furnishing the JDBC driver class, the Uniform Resource Locator (URL) to connect to the database, and a valid user name/password combination. The James configuration already comes with a driver for the MySQL database. If another database, such as Sybase or Oracle, is used, the appropriate Java Archive (JAR) or ZIP file containing the driver classes must be added to the James lib subdirectory. The user, mail, and spool repository types have JDBC-based implementations.

DBFile Repositories

The DBFile repository is a special storage mechanism that is used only for the mail repository type. As the name indicates, the DBFile repository uses both the file system and a database to store data. The file system is used to store the body of a mail message, while the message's headers are stored in a database. This configuration is used to take advantage of the performance of a database and the ease of using a file system. It also splits the work between the two storage types so that neither one is overtaxed.

Working with RemoteManager

The RemoteManager is used for administrative purposes. It operates through a simple telnet-based interface once the James server is started. Once logged into the RemoteManager, the administrator can perform such operations as creating or removing users, configuring user aliases, and shutting down the server. Information on how to start the RemoteManager is described in the README file located in the base directory of the James install.

Implementing James

Now that we have introduced several concepts regarding Internet mail and the James server itself, let's download, install, and configure the James server to see how it operates. Once we have the James server up and running, we can then start to write some application code that will be used to send and receive mail messages. That is described in the next section. For now, let's run through the necessary steps that are used to deploy the James mail server.

Downloading James

To download the James mail server, simply go to http://jakarta.apache.org/builds/jakarta-james. From there, you will have a choice to obtain the latest build or one of the nightly builds. The nightly builds, however, are typically a little less stable that the latest builds because they have not been tested as thoroughly. You may also choose to obtain an earlier version of James. In each of the directories, you will also have the option of downloading the binary or source code. The quickest option to get things started is to go to http://jakarta.apache.org/builds/jakarta-james/latest/bin/ and download the file in the format of your choosing.

Installing James

Prior to using the James server, a few items must be in place. To run James, the Java Runtime Environment (JRE) of Java version 1.3 (or later) must already be installed on the computer that will run the James server. The environment variable JAVA_HOME must also be set to the location of the JRE's home directory and $JAVA_HOME/bin must be in the PATH variable. Users who want to deploy James on a Unix server should also note that the root user is needed to access ports that are below 1024. By default, the James mail and news services (POP3, SMTP, and NNTP) all run on ports below 1024. Because of this, the root user may have to be used when starting James. There may be ways around this however.

After downloading the file, unpack the file so that the James directory structure is expanded and visible. Once the James archive is unpacked, it is still not possible to obtain access to the main configuration files. Due to the current configuration of the Avalon Phoenix container that is used to run James, the server must first be started in order for the full distribution to be unpacked. After you have initially unpacked the James archive file (ZIP or JAR), go to the bin subdirectory under the James installation directory and execute the appropriate "run" script (run.sh for Unix platforms and run.bat for Windows). This will start the James server. Once started, shut it down. Once the server is shut down, the configuration files can be found and edited.

The main configuration file is the config.xml file. In the James 2.1.2 version, this file is located in the apps/james/SAR-INF subdirectory of the main James installation directory. The README.html file, however, lists the file in the apps/james/conf subdirectory, which is incorrect. Other versions of James may have the file in another location. See the installation instructions for your version to determine where the config.xml file is located.

The default configuration that comes with James will work out-of-the-box, but will not be sufficient for a production mail server. In the next section, "Configuring James," we describe how to configure some of the items in James, as well as how to use the RemoteManager to perform some administrative tasks such as creating users. As mentioned earlier, the mail and news services are already configured with default ports. When James is started, the port numbers for the POP3, SMTP, and NNTP services are displayed. The default ports used are 110 (POP3), 25 (SMTP), and 119 (NNTP). If, by chance, any of these ports is currently in use by some other program on the computer, the error "java.net.BindException: Address already in use: JVM_Bind" will be displayed. The error message will also be listed in the log file. Other parts of the error message should give an indication as to which port it is referring to. If this happens, you must modify the config.xml file and change the default port to some other port number and try to restart James.

Additional information concerning installing James can be found at http://james.apache.org/installation_instructions_2_1.html (the current version) or in the README.html file located in the James installation directory.

Configuring James

As mentioned earlier, you can operate James as a local mail server without modifying the default configuration. All you need to do is create some user accounts and then create an application using the JavaMail

API to send and receive mail messages. Both of these items are discussed in the sections "Creating User Accounts" and "JavaMail in Practice." This local out-of-the-box configuration, however, is really only good for testing purposes. In order to use James in a production enterprise system, several items must be configured by modifying the `config.xml` mentioned earlier. These items are briefly described in the following sections. Further information on configuration items can be found at http://james.apache.org/documentation_2_1.html (the current version).

DNS Server Configuration

A Domain Name Server (DNS) is used to locate another server on the network. This is important when sending mail messages because if the recipient's e-mail address is not known by the local server, a check must be made on a DNS server to determine where to transport the message. By default, the James configuration assumes that a DNS server can be found on the localhost. The wrapper tag in the configuration file that encloses the relevant DNS references is the `<dnsserver>` tag. Enclosed in this tag are one or more `<server>` tags that each hold a single DNS IP (Internet Protocol) address. There is also an `<authoritative>` tag that is used to specify whether authoritative DNS records are required. By default, this is set to false, and should only be changed if you are familiar with its meaning. The following example illustrates what this may look like in the configuration file:

```
<dnsserver>
    <server>127.0.0.1</server>
    <server>159.247.45.67</server>
    <authoritative>false</authoritative>
</dnsserver>
```

POP3 Server Configuration

The POP3 configuration settings are controlled by the `<pop3server>` tag. This tag has the attribute `enabled` to indicate whether the POP3 server is enabled. By default, the attribute is set to true. This tag contains several child elements, including the following:

❏ `<port>` — This denotes the port on which the POP3 server will run. If this tag is omitted, the default port will be 110.

❏ `<bind>` — This is an optional tag used to describe the IP address to which the POP3 service should be bound.

❏ `<useTLS>` — This is an optional tag with a Boolean value that is used to denote which server socket factory to use.

❏ `<handler>` — This tag is only used to provide backward capability and will no longer appear in future versions of James.

There are also a few optional child tags that are used with advanced configurations. These tags include `<serverSocketFactory>`, `<threadGroup>`, and `<connectionLimit>`.

SMTP Server Configuration

The SMTP configuration tag `<smtpserver>` is used in much the same manner as the `<pop3server>` tag. It contains the same attribute and children element tags along with the same definitions for their use. The default port for the SMTP server is 25.

NNTP Server Configuration

The NNTP service is controlled by two different configuration blocks. The first is the `<nntpserver>` tag. It contains the same tag attribute and child elements as the `<pop3server>` and `<smtpserver>` tags. The NNTP server, by default, will run on port 119. The other configuration block is controlled by the `<nntp-repository>` tag. This tag relates to the server-side NNTP article repository and contains the following child element tags:

❑ `<readOnly>` — This is a required tag that takes a Boolean value. If the value is true, then posting messages to the NNTP server will not be permitted.

❑ `<rootPath>` — This is a required tag that takes a String value and must be in the form of a URL that begins with a `file:` prefix. This value will specify the root directory of the NNTP repository. An example of this tag's use may look like the following:

```
<rootPath>file:/opt/apps/ntp/groups</rootpath>
```

❑ `<tempPath>` — Similar to the `<rootPath>` tag, this denotes the directory in which the NNTP server will store any posted articles before they are sent to the spool.

❑ `<articleIDPath>` — Similar to the `<rootPath>` tag, this denotes the directory in which the NNTP server will store the mappings between the article ID and the groups that contain the article.

❑ `<articleIDDomainSuffix>` — This is a required tag that represents the suffix that is appended to all article IDs generated by the NNTP server.

❑ `<newsgroups>` — This tag is a wrapper for one or more `<newsgroup>` tags. The value of each `<newsgroup>` tag is the name of a newsgroup.

FetchPOP Configuration

Configuration of the `FetchPOP` service is controlled by the `<fetchpop>` tag. It contains the single attribute `enabled`, which has a default value of false. This attribute is used to denote whether or not the service is enabled. The `<fetchpop>` tag has only one valid type of child element tag: the `<fetch>` tag. There can be multiple `<fetch>` tags, but each tag can denote only a single `FetchPOP` task. Each `<fetch>` tag contains the single required attribute `name`. The value of this attribute must be unique in relation to any other `<fetch>` tag's attribute value. In addition to the one attribute tag, several child element tags are used:

❑ `<host>` — Denotes the hostname or IP address of a POP3 server hosting the mail that will be fetched.

❑ `<user>` — Denotes the user name of the mail account to be fetched.

❑ `<password>` — Denotes the password for the listed user.

❑ `<interval>` — Denotes the time, in milliseconds, between fetch requests.

With `FetchPOP`, there are also various considerations to take into account. Issues such as how to handle a subset of mail or how to catch undeliverable mail must be addressed. These and other items are described in more detail in the James `FetchPOP` configuration documentation.

RemoteManager Configuration

The RemoteManager configuration is controlled by the <remotemanager> tag. As mentioned earlier, the RemoteManager is used for administrative tasks such as adding and deleting users, setting up aliases, and shutting down the server. It contains the same attribute and child element tags as the <pop3server> tag. By default, the RemoteManager runs on port 4555.

Repository Configuration

In the earlier section "Understanding Repositories," it was mentioned that James has four different repository types (user, mail, spool, and news) and three different repository storage types (File, Database, DBFile). By default, James is configured to use the file storage type for each of the repository types. You can easily configure James to use these different storage devices. The configuration file uses various top-level tags such as <mailstore>, <user-store>, and <database-connections> to perform such configurations. The configuration file itself has explanations and examples concerning the use of these tags.

SpoolManager Configuration

Configuration of the SpoolManager is controlled by the <spoolmanager> tag. This tag contains several general child element tags, including the following:

- ❑ <threads> — This specifies the number of threads that the SpoolManager will use to process messages in the spool. The value of this tag can have an impact on the performance of the James server.

- ❑ <mailetpackages> — This is a required tag that contains one or more <mailetpackage> tags. The value of the <mailetpackage> tag will contain a Java package name that contains classes that can be instantiated as mailets.

- ❑ <matcherpackages> — This is a required tag that contains one or more <matcherpackage> tags. The value of the <matcherpackage> tag will contain a Java package name that contains classes that can be instantiated as matchers.

- ❑ <processor> — This is used to define the processor tree for the SpoolManager. The <spoolmanager> tag can contain several of these tags. Each <processor> tag contains the required attribute name, and its value must be unique in relation to any other <processor> tag attribute value. The value of the name attribute is significant to the SpoolManager because it creates a linkage between a processor name and the state of a mail message as defined in the Mailet API. Some processor names, such as root and error, are required.

Each <processor> tag may contain zero or more <mailet> tags. The order of each <mailet> tag is also important because it indicates the order in which each matcher/mailet pair will be traversed by the processor. The <mailet> tag, in turn, has two required attributes: match and class. The match attribute will contain the name of a specific Matcher class to be instantiated; the class attribute will contain the name of the Mailet class.

Global Server Configuration

James contains several global configuration items that do not fit into any of the other categories. They have a global impact across the entire James server.

James Block

The `<James>` tag (notice the uppercase) contains several child element tags that should be checked and modified if necessary upon installation:

- ❏ `<postmaster>` — This tag denotes the address it will use as its postmaster address.

- ❏ `<usernames>` — This tag contains only the three attributes `ignoreCase`, `enabledAliases`, and `enableFowarding`. Each attribute takes a Boolean value of true or false.

- ❏ `<servernames>` — This tag determines which mail domains and IP addresses the server will treat as local. It has two Boolean attributes: `autodetect` and `autodetectIP`. A value of true for these attributes causes the server to attempt to determine its own host name and IP address so that it can add it to the list of local mail domains. It also may contain zero or more `<servername>` tags. The value for this tag is a single hostname or IP address that should also be added to the list as a local mail domain.

- ❏ `<inboxRepository>` — This tag acts as a container for the single tag `<repository>`. The `<repository>` tag is used to define the mail repository that will be used to store locally delivered mail.

Connectionmanager Block

This block uses the `<connection>` tag to control general connection management. It contains two child elements:

- ❏ `<idle-timeout>` — The value for this element represents the number of milliseconds that it takes for an idle client connection to be marked as timed out by the connection manager. The default is five (5) minutes.

- ❏ `<max-connections>` — The value for this element represents the maximum number of client connections that the connection manager will allow per managed server socket. The default value is 30. If a value of 0 (zero) is given, then there is no limit imposed by the connection manager.

Objectstorage Block

This block controls the low-level file repository-to-file mapping. This block should remain unchanged.

Socketmanager Block

This block controls the socket types that are available in the James server. It should not be modified unless you intend to enable SSL.

Threadmanager Block

This block controls the thread pooling in the James server. It should be modified only by administrators who are familiar with its implications.

Creating User Accounts

User accounts created in James are shared across all of the services. Once a user account and password are generated, the account can be used for POP3, SMTP, and NNTP. Once the James server is started, user accounts can be created through the `RemoteManager`. By default, user account information is stored in files on the file system. If you want to use a different repository type, make sure the configuration file is changed accordingly before users are added. If a change is made after user accounts have been created, that data may be lost.

Once James is started, you can access the `RemoteManager` through a telnet session. To create a user once the server has started, perform the following steps:

1. Telnet to the `RemoteManager` by using the host and port on which it is listening. By default, the host is localhost and the port is 4555. The command should read **telnet localhost 4555**. These items can be modified in the configuration file.

2. You will then be prompted for the administrator's user name and password. By default, the administrator's user name is root and the password is root. These two items can also be changed by modifying the configuration file.

3. Once logged in, you can create your first user by typing **adduser <username> <password>**. The user name should only contain the name of the user and not the complete e-mail address. Once a user is created, the full e-mail address will be a combination of the user name followed by the @ symbol and any domain name that is listed in one of the configuration file's `<servername>` tags.

Simply follow Step 3 to add any other user. To see other commands that can be run in the `RemoteManager`, type in the word **help**.

Introducing JavaMail API

The JavaMail API is a package of Java classes that is used for reading, writing, and sending electronic messages. JavaMail is used to create Mail User Agent (MUA) programs. User agents represent a mail client that sends, receives, and displays mail messages to a user. Note that the purpose of a MUA is not for transporting, delivering, or forwarding e-mail messages. That is the job of a Mail Transfer Agent (MTA). In essence, an MUA relies on the MTA to deliver the mail that it creates. In order to use JavaMail, you will need to install a few items first:

❑ Install the Java 1.2 (or later) Java Development Kit (JDK).

❑ Obtain the latest JavaMail API. This can be found at http://java.sun.com/products/javamail/index.html. Once you have downloaded and unbundled the appropriate file, simply add the `mail.jar` file in your local CLASSPATH. This is really the only file you need from the downloaded package. It contains classes needed to perform POP3, SMTP, and IMAP4 services. The installed Java JDK contains any other classes that are needed.

❑ The JavaMail API requires the Javabeans Activation Framework (JAF) API in order to function properly. This package is used for basic MIME-type support. The JAF API can be downloaded at http://java.sun.com/products/javabeans/glasgow/jaf.html. Once you have downloaded and unbundled the appropriate file, simply add the `activation.jar` file to your local CLASSPATH.

Once you have accomplished the previous three steps, you will be ready to write the code necessary to send and receive e-mail messages. Before starting, however, it will be necessary to review the JavaMail API to ensure an understanding of how it works. Seven core classes make up the JavaMail API: `Session`, `Message`, `Address`, `Authentication`, `Transport`, `Store`, and `Folder`. Understanding these core classes is key to performing nearly all the operations needed for sending and receiving messages. The following sections describe each of these core classes.

The Session Class

The `Session` class defines a basic mail session. Virtually everything depends on this session. Its most commonly used methods provide the capability to load the classes that represent the Service Provider Implementation (SPI) for various mail protocols. The `Session` object uses the Java `Properties` (`java.util.Properties`) object to obtain information such as the user's name, password, and mail server. There are two ways of obtaining a `Session` object. The first is the default `Session`, which can be shared across the entire application:

```
Properties props = new Properties();
Session session = Session.getDefaultInstance(props, null);
```

The second is to obtain a unique `Session` object:

```
Properties props = new Properties();
Session session = Session.getInstance(props, null);
```

In both cases, the `Properties` object is used to store information, and the `null` argument is used in the place of an `Authenticator` object, which is described shortly.

Message Class

After creating a `Session` object, you will need to create a `Message` object. A `Message` object is used to represent everything that relates to a message. The `Message` class is an abstract class, so you have to work with a message subclass. This can typically be either `javax.mail.internet.MimeMessage` or `javax.mail.internet.SMTPMessage`. To create a `Message` object, you need to pass your `Session` object to its constructor:

```
SMTPMessage message = new SMTPMessage(session);
```

Once the `Message` object is created, you can then start to add content to the message. With typical text-based messages, you will not have to set the MIME-type that describes the content of the message because the default is text/plain. If, however, you want to send a different type of e-mail message (such as an HTML message), you must specify the MIME-type. The following is an example of how to set this:

```
String htmlData = "<h1>Hello There</h1>";
message.setContent(htmlData, "text/html");
```

If you use the default type, you can use the method `setText` to set the content. You will then use other methods to set additional message data, such as the subject and the recipient address:

```
message.setText("Hello There");
message.setSubject("Read This Email");
message.addRecipient(Message.RecipientType.TO, new
                                InternetAddress("peter@localhost");
```

Notice two things about setting the recipient. The first argument sets the type of recipient. Three options can be used:

- ❏   RecipientType.TO

- ❏   RecipientType.CC

- ❏   RecipientType.BCC

The second argument deals with the actual user account information for the recipient. Instead of a simple String value, it uses an InternetAddress object. The InternetAddress object is a subclass of the third core class of the JavaMail API, Address.

Address Class

When creating a message to send, you must assign the message to one or more recipients. Like the Message class, the Address class is abstract. In order to create an address, you must use the Internet Address (javax.mail.internet.InternetAddress) class. There are two ways to create an address. One requires only an e-mail address, and the other adds a person's name to which the e-mail address should be associated:

```
Address address = new InternetAddress("peter@localhost");
Address address = new InternetAddress("peter@localhost", "Peter A. Len");
```

Once an address is created, you can use it to set either the **From** or the **To** address. It is also possible to set multiple addresses for each type:

```
// Setting one 'From' address
message.setFrom(address);
// Setting multiple 'From' addresses
Address address[] = ...;
message.addFrom(address);
// Setting recipients
message.addRecipient(Message.RecipientType.TO, address2);
message.addRecipient(Message.RecipientType.CC, address3);
```

Authenticator Class

The Authenticator class is used to access protected resources in the mail server. When getting mail messages from the server, for example, you need to provide a user name and password. The Authenticator class can be used to set up a mechanism whereby the user is presented with a logon window prior to accessing any mail messages. In order to use this mechanism, you must create a class that extends Authenticator and have a method with the signature public PasswordAuthentication getPasswordAuthentication(). You must then register your subclass with the Session object. It will then be notified when authentication is necessary. An example may look like the following:

```
Properties props = new Properties();
Authenticator auth = new MyAuthenticator();
Session session  = Session.getDefaultInstance(props, auth);
class MyAuthenticator extends Authenticator() {
    public PasswordAuthentication getPasswordAuthentication() {
        // Perform some operation to retrieve the user's name and password,
        // such as with Java Swing.
        String username = ...;
        String password = ...;
        return new PasswordAuthentication(username, password);
    }
}
```

Transport Class

The last step necessary in composing a message is to be able to send it. This is done through the `Transport` class, which is another abstract class. It works in a similar fashion to that of the `Session` class. There are two methods for using, or obtaining, the `Transport` class. The first is to use the default version of the class by making a call to its static method `send`:

```
Transport.send(message);
```

The other way is to get an instance of the class from the session for the protocol you want to use. With this method, you can also pass in information such as a user name and password. You must then explicitly close the connection. An example may look like the following:

```
Transport transport = session.getTransport("smtp");
transport.connect(host, username, password);
transport.sendMessage(message, message.getAllRecipients());
transport.close();
```

You will notice in the second example that you can get a reference to a `Transport` object by simply supplying the name of the protocol—in this case, SMTP. JavaMail already has pre-built implementations of these protocols so you do not have to build your own. Both ways work fine, but the latter method may be more efficient if you are sending multiple messages. This is because you can send each message with the same `Transport` object, as it remains active until it is closed. Using the `send` method in the first example will create a new connection to the mail server each time it is called.

Store and Folder

Both the `Store` and `Folder` objects work together in obtaining a message. Just as with sending a message, the `Session` class is used to receive mail messages. Once you get a handle to the session, you will connect to a `Store` object. Similar to the `Transport` object, you indicate what protocol to use and possibly specify user information. An example may look like the following:

```
Store store = session.getStore("pop3");
store.connect(host, username, password);
```

Once you have made the connection to the `Store`, you must then obtain a `Folder` object and open it before any messages can be read. When using the POP3 protocol, the only folder available is the INBOX folder. If you are using the IMAP protocol, there may be other folders that are available. An example may look like the following:

```
Folder folder = store.getFolder("INBOX");
Folder.open(Folder.READ_WRITE);
Messages messages[] = folder.getMessages();
```

In the preceding example, we opened the folder with `Folder.READ_WRITE`. This is used to indicate that the contents of the folder can be modified. Another option to use is `Folder.READ_ONLY`, which states that the contents of the folder can only be read. Once you have a `Message` object to read, you can do any number of things with it, such as obtaining the recipients of the message, getting the subject line, or getting the message's content. You can also send a reply or forward the message to someone else. Examples of how to do these various tasks are described in the next section, "JavaMail in Practice." After you are finished with the messages in the folder, both the folder and the session must be closed:

```
folder.close(boolean);
session.close();
```

The Boolean value used when closing the folder indicates whether or not to update the contents of the folder by removing messages that have been marked for deletion.

JavaMail in Practice

So far, we have explained how to obtain, install, and run the James mail server, as well as some general concepts of the mail server and the JavaMail API. In this section, we combine both of these aspects to illustrate how JavaMail can be used to connect to the James server in order to send and receive mail messages. In general, speaking in terms of *sending* and *receiving* mail messages is a bit simplistic. Many different functions within each of these concepts can be performed. They can also present technical challenges when it comes to building a full-scale e-mail application for use in something like an enterprise portal. We have already briefly described some of these actions, but the following sections present more detail and examples.

Sending Messages

In order to send an e-mail message, you need a mail server (James), an API for writing code to perform the action (JavaMail), and an application that the user interacts with to generate the message. Typically, this application is some sort of Graphical User Interface, or GUI, which contains fields into which the user can enter the information. In the following example, we will create the code necessary to perform such actions. The example uses a Java Server Page (JSP) to render the HTML needed for the GUI, as well as the Java code to obtain the data and use the JavaMail API to connect to the James mail server. Figure 3.1 shows the interface used for the user to create a message.

The following listing shows the code used for generating this interface as well as sending the message data and image attachment to the James mail server.

Figure 3.1

Listing 3.1: Code For Sending E-mail

```
001  <%@page import="java.util.*" %>
002  <%@page import="javax.mail.*" %>
003  <%@page import="javax.mail.internet.*" %>
004  <%@page import="javax.activation.*" %>
005  <%@page import="com.sun.mail.smtp.*" %>
006
007  <%
008      String action = request.getParameter("action");
009      String from = request.getParameter("from");
010      String to = request.getParameter("to");
011      String cc = request.getParameter("cc");
012      String subject = request.getParameter("subject");
013      String msgText = request.getParameter("message");
014      String file = request.getParameter("attachment");
```

The first few lines are used to import the Java classes necessary to send the message. Lines 8–14 are used to retrieve the data that was sent when the user submitted the form. A check is then made to see if a null value was sent and, if so, reassigns an empty value. Typically, you would also want to ensure that certain fields had values.

```
015
016      if (action == null) { action = ""; }
017      if (from == null) { from = ""; }
018      if (to == null) { to = ""; }
019      if (cc == null) { cc = ""; }
020      if (subject == null) { subject = ""; }
021      if (msgText == null) { msgText = ""; }
```

```
022     if (file == null) { file = ""; }
023
024     String status = "";
025  %>
026  <% try { %>
027  <% if (action.equals("send")) { %>
028     <%
029         // Create a Properties object.
030         Properties props = System.getProperties();
031         props.put("mail.smtp.host", "localhost");
032
033         // Get a handle to the Session.
034         // because that has already been defined in the JSP.
035         Session mySession = Session.getDefaultInstance(props, null);
036
037         // Create a Messsage.
038         SMTPMessage message = new SMTPMessage(mySession);
039
040         // Set the 'from' address.
041         message.setFrom(new InternetAddress(from));
042
043         // Set the 'to' and 'cc' addresses.
044         StringTokenizer tokensTo = new StringTokenizer(to, ";");
045         String         addr = "";
046         while (tokensTo.hasMoreTokens()) {
047             addr = tokensTo.nextToken();
048             message.addRecipient(Message.RecipientType.TO,
049                                         new InternetAddress(addr));
050         }
051         StringTokenizer tokensCC = new StringTokenizer(cc, ";");
052         while (tokensCC.hasMoreTokens()) {
053             addr = tokensCC.nextToken();
054             message.addRecipient(Message.RecipientType.CC,
055                                         new InternetAddress(addr));
056         }
057
058         // Set the 'subject'.
059         message.setSubject(subject);
060
061         // Set the date the message would be sent.
062         message.setSentDate(new Date());
```

Lines 35–62 are used to obtain a handle to the session, create a Message object, and then fill the message with certain attributes, such as the subject, the date, and the recipients.

```
063
064         // Handle the attachment, if there is one.
065         if (!file.equals("")) {
066
067             // Set the 'text' as the first body part.
068             BodyPart mbp = new MimeBodyPart();
069             mbp.setText(msgText);
070             Multipart mp = new MimeMultipart();
```

```
071            mp.addBodyPart(mbp);
072
073            mbp = new MimeBodyPart();
074            String imgName = file.substring(file.lastIndexOf("\\")+1);
075            DataSource src = new FileDataSource(file);
076            mbp.setDataHandler(new DataHandler(src));
077            mbp.setFileName(imgName);
078            mp.addBodyPart(mbp);
079            message.setContent(mp);
080
081        }else {
082            // Use the default method if no attachment.
083            message.setText(msgText);
084        }
085
```

When sending an attachment, you must generate the content of the message as a `Multipart` object (line 70), which consists of multiple parts. In this example, the text of the message is the first part and the image attachment is the second part. To attach the image, you must load the image through a `DataSource` object (line 75) and assign it to a `DataHandler` object. On line 79, the `Multipart` object is then set as the content of the message. Line 87 then sends the message on its way.

Starting on line 94 and continuing to line 164, we simply write the HTML code that is used to present the user with the interface to enter the data in the browser.

```
086    // Send it.
087    SMTPTransport.send(message);
088
089    status = "Message Sent";
090    %>
091
092 <% } %>
093
094    <html>
095    <body>
096    <form action="mailsend.jsp" method="post">
097    <input type="hidden" name="action" value="send">
098    <center>
099      <font color="red"><b><%=status%></b></font><br>
100      <h1>Send Mail</h1>
101
102      <table>
103       <tr>
104        <td align="left">
105          <font face='monotype corsiva' size="+2">From:</font>
106        </td>
107        <td align="left">
108          <input type="text" name="from" size="30">
109        </td>
110       </tr>
111       <tr>
112        <td align="left">
113          <font face='monotype corsiva' size="+2">To:</font>
```

```
114          </td>
115          <td align="left">
116            <input type="text" name="to" size="50">
117            <small>Separate addresses with a semicolon (;)</small>
118          </td>
119        </tr>
120        <tr>
121          <td align="left">
122            <font face='monotype corsiva' size="+2">CC:</font>
123          </td>
124          <td align="left">
125            <input type="text" name="cc" size="50">
126            <small>Separate addresses with a semicolon (;)</small>
127          </td>
128        </tr>
129        <tr><td> <p></td></tr>
130        <tr>
131          <td align="left">
132            <font face='monotype corsiva' size="+2">Subject:</font>
133          </td>
134          <td align="left">
135            <input type="text" name="subject" size="70">
136          </td>
137        </tr>
138        <tr>
139          <td align="left" valign="top">
140            <font face='monotype corsiva' size="+2">Message:</font>
141          </td>
142          <td align="left">
143            <textarea name="message" rows="10" cols="50"></textarea>
144          </td>
145        </tr>
146        <tr>
147          <td align="left">
148            <font face='monotype corsiva' size="+2">Attachment:</font>
149          </td>
150          <td align="left">
151            <input type="file" name="attachment">
152          </td>
153        </tr>
154        <tr><td> <p></td></tr>
155        <tr>
156          <td align="center" colspan="2">
157            <input type="submit" value="Send">
158          </td>
159        </tr>
160      </table>
161    </center>
162    </form>
163    </body>
164    </html>
165
166 <% }catch (Exception e) { %>
167    Error: <%=e%>
168 <% } %>
```

Lines 166 to 168 are simply used to catch any errors that may occur when the page is loaded and will present the user with the error message. As shown in Figure 3.1, all of the recipients are associated with the host *localhost*. This is the host name for the James mail server running on the local server. Line 31 in Listing 3.1 sets *localhost* as the SMTP mail host in the `Properties` object. This indicates that all of the recipients are users associated with the James mail server that we are using. If any of the recipients used a different host name (e.g., johndoe@yahoo.com), the James server would need the IP address of a DNS server that can map the host name to its location on another server. The identification of DNS servers is listed in the James configuration file.

Receiving Messages

Now that we have successfully generated and sent an e-mail message, we must now retrieve the message from the mail server. Typically, an interface is used to obtain information from a user for authentication purposes. An example may look like what is shown in Figure 3.2.

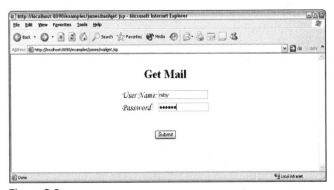

Figure 3.2

Once authenticated, the mail server knows which mail messages it can send back to the user, as shown in Figure 3.3.

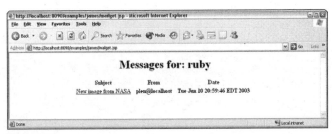

Figure 3.3

Once users are presented with a list of messages from their inbox, they should be able to then view the entire contents of any messages. Different mail interfaces perform the operation in different ways. Figure 3.4 shows one example of how this may look.

Figure 3.4

Similar to sending the message, our example for retrieving mail uses a JSP. The code necessary to perform the authentication and retrieve the message data from the mail server is shown in the following listing. Some of the code is similar to that of the previous listing and so is not described here.

Listing 3.2: Code For Receiving E-mail

```
001   <%@page import="java.util.*" %>
002   <%@page import="java.io.*" %>
003   <%@page import="javax.mail.*" %>
004   <%@page import="javax.mail.internet.*" %>
005   <%@page import="javax.activation.*" %>
006   <%@page import="com.sun.mail.smtp.*" %>
007
008   <%
009      String action = request.getParameter("action");
010      String msgnum = request.getParameter("msgnum");
011      String username = request.getParameter("username");
012      String password = request.getParameter("password");
013
014      if (action == null) { action = ""; }
015      if (msgnum == null) { msgnum = ""; }
016      if (username == null) { username = ""; }
017      if (password == null) { password = ""; }
018
019      String status = "";
020      String defaultDir = "C:\\tomcat-4112\\webapps\\examples\\";
021   %>
022   <% try { %>
023   <% if (action.equals("get")) { %>
024      <%
025      String  host = "localhost";
026      int     port = 111;
```

Line 20 lists the directory in which the attachment will be saved. In a production application, this is normally read in from something such as a property file. Line 26 specifies the POP3 port number as 111.

If the POP3 port is something other than the default port or 110, it must be stated when the connection to the store is made (see line 36).

```
027
028       // Get a handle to the Properties.
029       Properties props = System.getProperties();
030
031       // Get a handle to the Session object.
032       Session mySession = Session.getDefaultInstance(props, null);
033
034       // Connect to the Store.
035       Store store = mySession.getStore("pop3");
036       store.connect(host, port, username, password);
037
038       // Obtain a handle to the inbox.
039       Folder folder = store.getFolder("INBOX");
040       folder.open(Folder.READ_WRITE);
041
042       // Obtain the messages.
043       Message messages[] = folder.getMessages();
044
045       Message  msg;
046       String   from = "";
047       String   subject = "";
048       String   date = "";
049
050       %>
051       <html> <body> <form>
052       <center>
053       <h1>Messages for: <%=username%></h1>
054       <table>
055       <th>Subject</th> <th></th> <th>From</th> <th></th>
056       <th>Date</th> <th></th>
057       <%
058       for (int i=0; i<messages.length; i++) {
059         msg = messages[i];
060         date = msg.getSentDate().toString();
061         subject = msg.getSubject();
062         from = ((msg.getFrom())[0]).toString();
063       %>
064       <tr>
065        <td align="left">
066         <a href="mailget.jsp?action=get&msgnum=<%=i%>&username=
067                            <%=username%>&password=<%=password%>">
068         <b><%=subject%></b>
069         </a>
070        </td>
071        <td>  </td>
072        <td align="left"> <b><%=from%></b> </td>
073        <td>  </td>
074        <td align="left"> <b><%=date%></b> </td>
075        <td>  </td>
076       </tr>
077       <%
```

```
078        }
079        %> </table> <%
080
081        if (!msgnum.equals("")) {
082
083          %> <p><hr><p> <%
084
085          BodyPart        part;
086          MimeMultipart   mime;
087
088          int       messageNumber = (new Integer(msgnum)).intValue();
089          Object    obj;
090          Class     cls;
091          Class     strCls= Class.forName("java.lang.String");
092          Class     mimeCls = Class.forName(
093                               "javax.mail.internet.MimeMultipart");
094          File      file = null;
095          String    filepath = "";
096
097          for (int i=0; i<messages.length; i++) {
098            if (i == messageNumber) {
099              msg = messages[i];
100              date = msg.getSentDate().toString();
101              subject = msg.getSubject();
102              from = ((msg.getFrom())[0]).toString();
103
104              //msg.setFlag(Flags.Flag.DELETED, true);
```

Line 58 starts a loop for each message, which will be used to display the information to the user. Typically, the user name and password are not handled in the manner shown in this example (see the `href` on line 66). Line 104 is commented out. If you would like to have messages deleted from the mail server after they are retrieved, simply uncomment the line.

```
105
106          %>
107          <center> <table>
108            <tr>
109              <td align="right"><b>Subject:</b>
110              </td><td><%=subject%></td>
111            </tr>
112            <tr>
113              <td align="right"><b>Date:</b> </td><td><%=date%></td>
114            </tr>
115            <tr>
116              <td align="right"><b>From:</b> </td><td><%=from%></td>
117            </tr>
118            <%
119
120            Address[] to = msg.getRecipients(Message.RecipientType.TO);
121            if (to != null) {
122              for (int t=0; t<to.length; t++) {
```

```
123          if (t == 0) {
124            %>
125            <tr>
126             <td align="right"><b>To:</b> </td><td><%=to[t]%></td>
127            <tr>
128            <%
129          }else {
130            %> <tr><td> </td><td><%=to[t]%></td><tr> <%
131          }
132        }
133      }
134
135      Address[] cc = msg.getRecipients(Message.RecipientType.CC);
136      if (cc != null) {
137        for (int c=0; c<cc.length; c++) {
138          if (c == 0) {
139            %>
140            <tr>
141             <td align="right"><b>CC:</b> </td><td><%=cc[c]%></td>
142            </tr>
143            <%
144          }else {
145            %> <tr><td> </td><td><%=cc[c]%></td></tr> <%
146          }
147        }
148      }
149
150      obj = ((MimeMessage) messages[i]).getContent();
151      cls = obj.getClass();
```

Lines 120–148 are used to obtain and display each recipient name from the two recipient types used in the example. On lines 150 and 151, we receive the content of the message as an object and then compare the `object` class with either the `String` class or the `MimeMultipart` class. This is done because the content may have been added to the message in different ways (see lines 79 and 83 from Listing 3.1).

```
152        if (cls == mimeCls) {
153          mime = (MimeMultipart) obj;
154          for (int j=0; j<mime.getCount(); j++) {
155            part = mime.getBodyPart(j);
156            if (part.isMimeType("text/plain")) {
157              // Should be the message text.
158              %>
159              <tr>
160               <td align="right"><b>Message:</b> </td>
161               <td><%=part.getContent()%></td>
162              </tr>
163              <%
164            }else if (part.getDisposition().equals(
165                                        Part.ATTACHMENT)) {
166              filepath = defaultDir + part.getFileName();
167              file = new File(filepath);
168
169              int    chunk = 1000;
```

```
170                    byte[] buffer = new byte[chunk];
171                    int    length;
172
173                    InputStream is = part.getInputStream();
174                    FileOutputStream os = new FileOutputStream(file);
175                    while ((length = is.read(buffer)) != -1) {
176                        os.write(buffer, 0, length);
177                    }
178                    is.close();
179                    os.close();
180
```

Lines 166–180 are used to transfer the data from the attachment part to the file through the use of input and output streams. These streams are then closed in lines 178 and 179.

```
181                    %>
182                    <tr>
183                    <td align="right" valign="top">
184                       <b>Attachment:</b>
185                    </td>
186                    <td><img src="<%=filepath%>"></td>
187                    </tr>
188                    <%
189
190                }else {
191                    // Handle other types here.
192                }
193              }
194
195           }else {
196             %>
197             <tr>
198              <td align="right"><b>Message:</b> </td><td><%=obj%></td>
199             </tr>
200             <%
201            }
202
203          %> </center> </table> <%
204          break;
205        }
206      }
207    }
208
209    folder.close(true);
210    store.close();
211    %>
212
```

Both the `Folder` and `Store` objects are closed on lines 209 and 210. The Boolean value sent when closing the folder is used to indicate whether files flagged for deletion should be removed from the server (see line 104). The code example then finishes up (starting on line 215) by generating the HTML needed for the browser interface.

```
213   <% }else { %>
214
215     <html>
216     <body>
217     <form action="mailget.jsp" method="post">
218     <input type="hidden" name="action" value="get">
219     <center>
220      <font color="red"><b><%=status%></b></font><br>
221      <h1>Get Mail</h1>
222
223      <table>
224       <tr>
225        <td align="left">
226          <font face='monotype corsiva' size="+2">User Name:</font>
227        </td>
228        <td align="left">
229          <input type="text" name="username" size="20">
230        </td>
231       </tr>
232       <tr>
233        <td align="left">
234          <font face='monotype corsiva' size="+2">Password:</font>
235        </td>
236        <td align="left">
237          <input type="password" name="password" size="20">
238        </td>
239       </tr>
240       <tr>
241        <td> <p></td>
242       </tr>
243       <tr>
244        <td align="center" colspan="2">
245          <input type="submit" value="Submit">
246        </td>
247       </tr>
248      </table>
249     </center>
250     </form>
251     </body>
252     </html>
253   <% } %>
254
255   <% }catch (Exception e) { %>
256     Error: <%=e%>
257   <% } %>
```

The preceding examples of sending and receiving e-mail messages are used here as one possible scenario for implementing an e-mail client. There are obviously other ways to both develop the client interface and utilize the JavaMail API. It is really up to the developer to decide how it is built. In addition, the two examples are shown as individual components only. This is done to keep the examples simple. In reality, both components may be part of a larger enterprise system such as a portal application.

Summary

The Apache James mail server is a powerful tool that can be used as a core component in the framework of a larger enterprise system. It is not only very flexible, powerful, and easy to configure, it can also give you total control over how e-mail or news messages are used and processed in your overall application framework. This may become very important if the mail server plays a significant role in your overall architecture and you do not want to rely on someone else's server for reliable service.

In this chapter, we explained some general concepts about Internet mail and the James server. We then described the various components and configuration parameters of the server and provided an introduction to the JavaMail API, which can be used to send and receive mail. We finished the chapter by providing two fairly basic, but comprehensive, examples of how to send and receive mail messages using a JSP page, the JavaMail API, and the James mail server.

Although we did not describe at length every aspect of the James server, you should now have a good understanding of how to configure and deploy it, as well as how it can be used in an overall mail solution.

4

Object to Relational
Mapping with Apache OJB

Object Relational Bridge (http://db.apache.org/ojb), or OJB, is an open-source object relational mapping tool that is used to store Java objects in relational databases. It is currently maintained by the Apache Software Foundation's DB project. Persistent objects (objects that exist past the lifetime of an application) are a large part of today's software development tasks, and OJB provides all the necessary functionality to meet the most complex object-to-relational mapping needs.

OJB is a very flexible object-to-relational tool and supports such industry standards as ODMG (Object Database Management Group) and JDO (Java Data Objects).

This chapter covers object relational mapping concepts, OJB API layers, the development of a message board sample application using OJB, and OJB extras.

Exploring Object-to-Relational Mapping Concepts

Object-to-relational (O/R) mapping tools enable you to use an object-oriented (OO) programming approach to developing powerful applications by leveraging the capabilities of OO programming languages with relational databases. This type of developing enables you to think in a more OO way, rather than the standard "I have data, let me store it directly to a database" way. With O/R, you are free to think in terms of storing, manipulating, and retrieving objects from a relational data source, instead of just data. This sheds an entirely new light on how the data relates, where it was derived from, and what state it was in when the user decided to save it.

A term you will see often used in O/R mapping is **transparent persistence**. Simply stated, this is the ability to alter data that is stored in a relational database through means of an object-oriented programming language. The alternative to using transparent persistence would be to use embedded SQL statements or an interface such as JDBC to manipulate the data. The disparity between using the two is actually very significant. Using transparent persistence not only saves you development time, it can also improve the overall performance of your application.

Object-to-relational mapping tools save you development time because the number of lines of code that you have to write is significantly less than when you implement a JDBC or embedded SQL solution. O/R mapping tools such as OJB are sophisticated, and have a very robust feature set, eliminating the headache of creating transaction management code, checking data types, mapping tables to objects, and ensuring data integrity, all of which is taken care of for you. In addition, OJB adheres to all the latest industry standards, which relieves you from the pressure of developing your own approach that follows those standards.

Performance can increase substantially when using OJB as the main focus for an O/R mapping solution because OJB incorporates a caching system. **Caching** is the capability to maintain data in the calling application's memory, to reduce the strain on network traffic or the storage data source. The implementation of a caching system has the following benefits:

❑ **Enables a significant reduction in the amount of database look-ups** — The O/R tool does not have to perform a SELECT from the database every time a query for data is issued by the application if that query has already been performed.

❑ **Keeps track of objects and reduces the amount of duplicate objects contained in memory** — This is very beneficial because it decreases the amount of memory the application needs — by keeping track of objects that exist and not creating new ones that have the same ID.

❑ **Prevents non-terminating loops from occurring when performing circular look-ups** — The cache system of OJB is also very flexible, enabling you to create your own subsystem based on the one provided by OJB. Therefore, very complex caching systems can be developed to fit your needs.

Understanding OJB Technology Features

OJB has an extremely robust feature set and supports two industry standards: ODMG (Object Database Management Group) and JDO (Java Data Objects). The main features of OJB can be categorized into three sections: flexibility, scalability, and functionality. These features are described in the following tables.

The flexibility features enable you to determine which API would best suit your needs and to build your own API. For example, if you needed to build your own API, you could take the existing PersistenceBroker API as a basis and expand on it to develop a specific API to fit your requirements.

Feature	Description
ODMG API	OJB has a fully functional set of APIs that are compliant with ODMG 3.0.
JDO API	OJB currently uses a plug-in to support JDO 1.0. A full implementation of JDO is expected in the 2.0 release of OJB.
OTM Layer	The Object Transactional Manager layer contains all the common functionality of JDO and ODMG.

Feature	Description
PersistenceBroker API	This is essentially the "kernel" API layer for OJB, and is what all the other technologies use as their foundation.

Scalability is one of the more impressive features of OJB. Few O/R mapping tools in the industry support load balancing across multiple physical machines.

Feature	Description
Stand-Alone Mode	This is the default mode for OJB and signifies the usage of a single PersistenceBroker server existing in the same Java Virtual Machine instance as the client application.
Client/Server Mode	This is used for load balancing when you need the capability to have multiple PersistenceBroker servers running in multiple Java Virtual Machines on different computers.

OJB has a vast array of functional features to choose from when developing your applications. The following table lists the main features that you are most likely to use during the development process.

Feature	Description
Object Caching	OJB incorporates a caching system that caches previously accessed or stored objects.
Transaction Management	Transaction Management is also built into OJB. Therefore, if an execution of a command were to go awry during a persistent store procedure, the transaction management system would be able to roll back any changes that had occurred.
JNDI Lookup	OJB supports the capability to look up data sources via JNDI, allowing for smooth integration with J2EE architectures.
Lock Manager	Manages current transactions on objects.
1:1, 1:N, M:Ns mappings	OJB contains a very robust mapping feature set that supports one-to-one, one-to-many, and many-to-many relational mappings.
Sequence Manager	The Sequence Manager takes care of creating unique IDs for newly created objects automatically.
XML mapping	All of the mappings created by OJB are stored in XML documents.

Using OJB API Layers

This section describes the three main API layers contained in OJB. It also goes through some of the queries associated with each API. The three main APIs are the PersistenceBroker, ODMG, and JDO. ODMG and JDO are built using the PersistenceBroker API as their foundation. They were implemented to enable OJB to adhere to their individual standards. You can build an application that leverages all the valuable functionality of OJB without ever needing the JDO or ODMG APIs. Figure 4.1 shows a diagram of how these different APIs are related to each other.

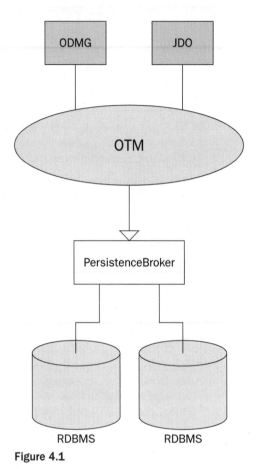

Figure 4.1

Figure 4.1 indicates that ODMG and JDO both make use of the Object Transaction Manager (OTM). The PersistenceBroker API, however, does not use the OTM and therefore cannot keep track of object state. Therefore, if transaction management is a requirement of your application, then you would need to choose either the ODMG API or the JDO API, unless of course you wanted to build your own OTM for the PersistenceBroker API.

Developing with the PersistenceBroker API

The PersistenceBroker API (PBAPI) is the "kernel" of OJB. All other APIs use the PBAPI as a foundation. The PBAPI is great for building simple applications and familiarizing yourself with OJB concepts. It is not recommended for use with applications that require a robust feature set.

The PBAPI consists of the following capabilities:

- ❑ Object-Relational mapping
- ❑ Basic RDBMS query capabilities that allow the retrieval of objects
- ❑ Removing objects from an RDBMS
- ❑ Inserting objects into an RDBMS
- ❑ Updating objects that are currently stored in the RDBMS

The PBAPI *does not* do any of the following:

- ❑ Store any information about object transactional state
- ❑ Have any type of lock management capabilities
- ❑ Have an advance object query language

The following example will aid you in understanding PBAPI and how it appears in the context of a fully functional deployed Web application. The example chosen is a message board Web application that enables the user to do the following:

- ❑ Post articles to the message board
- ❑ View stored articles
- ❑ Delete stored articles

The information is accessed and stored via the PBAPI into a relational Sybase ASA database. We could have chosen any OJB-supported relational database to use as our data store. For more information on supported databases, see the "OJB Extras" section of this chapter. The diagram shown in Figure 4.2 provides a high-level overview of where all the components of the sample exist and how they generally interact.

This example uses two classes that are mapped to the database through the PBAPI: the `Message` class and the `Viewer` class. The `Message` class is used to store new articles that the user posts. It is also used when viewing and deleting messages from the database. The `Viewer` class functions as an access log, which stores user information when a message is viewed. We have incorporated both classes for the purpose of exploiting OJB's ability to perform 1:N mappings of objects.

OJB maps the two classes together in the `repository.xml` file under a tag called `<collection-descriptor/>`. The common attribute in the two classes that links them together is the message ID, `protected int m_nID`. Before we go any further, let's take a look at all the individual components of the sample application and their uses. These components are described in both the following table and the sections that follow.

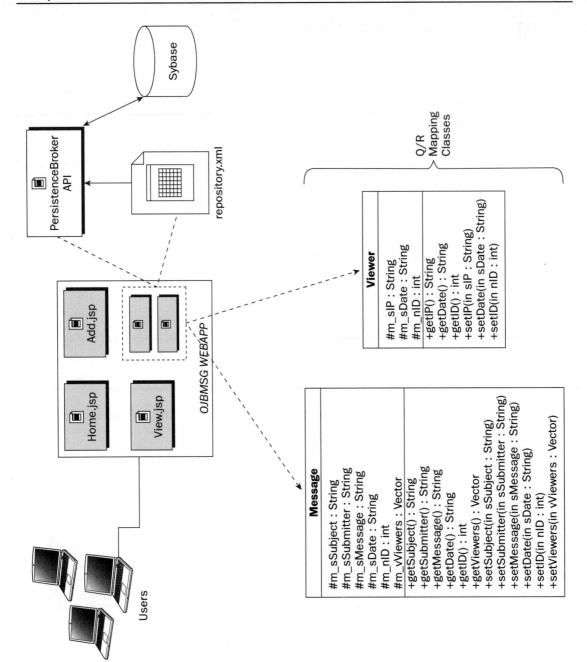

Figure 4.2

Component	Description
Home.jsp	This is the default page that will be displayed to users when they access the message board Web application. It displays a summary list of messages that currently exist in the database.
Add.jsp	This file provides an interface for submitting a new article to the message board.
View.jsp	Accessed from Home.jsp when a user clicks on a message, View.jsp will be invoked, displaying the full message to the user.
Message Class	The Message class is the main O/R class that is used for querying messages, deleting messages, and submitting messages to the data source.
Viewer Class	The Viewer class keeps track of the last user to view a specific message and is used in conjunction with the Message class. This example uses both classes to demonstrate OJB's 1:N capabilities.
repository.xml	This file is the resource repository that OJB uses when creating a new PersistenceBroker. It also contains pointers to three other XML files that describe database connections, class mappings, and internal mappings.
repository_database.xml	This file contains a list of JDBC connections that can be used to access relational databases. In our example, we will be using one connection to a Sybase database.
repository_user.xml	This is where the user-defined class mappings are stored — for example, Message and Viewer.
repository_internal.xml	OJB's internal mappings are stored here. OJB uses them to provide functionality such as lock and sequence management.
web.xml	This file stores configuration information about the example message board Web application.

The Message Class

The Message class is the most frequently used class in the message board example. It is very simple in design, and its core purpose is to contain information about a message that is going to be stored in the database, retrieved from the database, or deleted from the database. OJB utilizes this class and understands its contents through the mapping of the class in the repository_user.xml file. In order for a class to be mapped in the OJB metadata repository, it must adhere to the OJB guidelines.

The OJB guidelines for the classes you will write are basic and adhere to the design of transparent persistence. All you have to remember is to include a public no-argument constructor in your class. We also recommend implementing the java.io.Serializable interface in your class. Although this interface is not required, we have found that you will run into fewer errors if you ensure that your class can be serialized. The following code shows the Message class, taken directly from the message board example:

```
/*
 * Created in 2003
 *
 * Message.java
 *
 */
package com.ojbmsg.test;
import java.io.*;
import java.net.*;
import java.util.*;
/**
 * @author Vitale
 */
public class Message implements java.io.Serializable {
    protected String m_sSubject;
    protected String m_sSubmitter;
    protected String m_sMessage;
    protected String m_sDate;

    protected int m_nID;
    protected Vector m_vViewers;

    public Message() {
        // Initialize member variables
        m_nID = 0;
        m_sSubject   = "";
        m_sSubmitter = "";
        m_sMessage   = "";
        m_sDate      = "";
        m_vViewers = new Vector();
    }
```

The Get and Set methods presented in the code example to follow simply set the protected variables in this class. The variables that the methods manipulate are directly linked to the data source's table columns, which are mapped in the repository_user.xml file. So when the variables' data changes, the data source whose table columns are linked to those variables are also changed automatically by OJB.

```
    // Get Methods
    public String getSubject() {
        return m_sSubject;
    }
    public String getSubmitter() {
        return m_sSubmitter;
    }
    public String getMessage() {
        return m_sMessage;
    }
    public String getDate() {
        return m_sDate;
    }
    public int getID() {
        return m_nID;
    }
```

```
            public Vector getViewers() {
                return m_vViewers;
            }
            // Set methods
            public void setSubject(String sSubject) {
                m_sSubject = sSubject;
            }
            public void setSubmitter(String sSubmitter) {
                m_sSubmitter = sSubmitter;
            }
            public void setMessage(String sMessage) {
                m_sMessage = sMessage;
            }
            public void setDate(String sDate) {
                m_sDate = sDate;
            }
            public void setID(int nID) {
                m_nID = nID;
            }
            public void setViewers(Vector vViewers) {
                m_vViewers = vViewers;
            }
```

The Message class is extremely straightforward, but you are probably wondering what the repository mapping entries are going to look like. The mapping entries offer a lot of flexibility, and can give the impression of being more complex than they really are. The following XML illustrates the mapping entries for the Message class:

```
<class-descriptor
        class="com.ojbmsg.test.Message"
        table="tblMESSAGE"
>
    <field-descriptor id="1"
        name="m_nID"
        column="ID"
        jdbc-type="INTEGER"
        primarykey="true"
        autoincrement="true"
    />
    <field-descriptor id="2"
        name="m_sSubmitter"
        column="SUBMITTER"
        jdbc-type="VARCHAR"
    />
    <field-descriptor id="3"
        name="m_sSubject"
        column="SUBJECT"
        jdbc-type="VARCHAR"
    />
    <field-descriptor id="4"
        name="m_sMessage"
        column="MYMESSAGE"
        jdbc-type="VARCHAR"
```

```
          />
          <field-descriptor id="5"
               name="m_sDate"
               column="MYDATE"
               jdbc-type="VARCHAR"
          />

          <collection-descriptor
               name="m_vViewers"
               element-class-ref="com.ojbmsg.test.Viewer"
               orderby="ID"
               sort="DESC"
               auto-retrieve="true"
       auto-update="true"
       auto-delete="true"
          >
               <inverse-foreignkey field-id-ref="1"/>
          </collection-descriptor>
     </class-descriptor>
```

The mapping entries can be broken down into three key elements:

❑   The <class-descriptor> defines the class to which the object entry is mapped and what table in the database it is mapped to.

❑   The <field-descriptor> maps a member variable of the class that you are mapping to a column of the table mapped in the <class-descriptor>.

❑   The <collection-descriptor> is the most complex part of the mapping entries. It creates the 1:N relationship between the Message class and the Viewer class.

The <class-descriptor> contains two elements that you must set up: the **class element,** used for mapping the entry to your Java class, and the **table element,** which must point to a table in the data source to which you will be connecting. In this example, we are mapping the class element to com.ojbmsg.test .Message and the table element to tblMESSAGE.

The <field-descriptor> has three elements, with an optional fourth. The ID element is optional and enables you to assign a specific ID to each field-descriptor. The **name** element must point to a member variable in the class specified in the <class-descriptor> element. The **column** element references a column name in the relational database you are using. The final element is the **jdbc-type,** which is used to specify the type of data that will be mapped. All the supported JDBC types are described later in this chapter in the section "Supported JDBC Data Types."

The <collection-descriptor> has multiple elements that can be used to fit your needs. The elements used in this example consist of the following:

❑   The **name,** which points to a vector of Viewer classes.

❑   The **element-class-ref,** which references the type of class that is in the name element. In this case, the class is the Viewer class.

❑   The **orderby** element, which tells OJB how to organize the Collection class objects.

❑ The **sort** element, which is used to sort the `Collection` class objects in ascending or descending order.

❑ The **auto-retrieve** element, which instructs OJB to automatically incorporate the `Collection` class objects when performing any operations on the parent classes (in this case, the `Message` class).

❑ The **auto-update** element, which forces OJB to automatically update the `Collection` class objects when the parent class is being operated on.

❑ The **auto-delete** element, which enables OJB to perform deletes on the `Collection` class objects without asking for permission when the parent class is being deleted. This prevents the desynchronization of related `Collection` class objects.

The `Viewer` class's primary goal is to demonstrate the one-to-many mapping capabilities of OJB. OJB also supports many-to-many mappings, but that is beyond the scope of this example. For more information on many-to-many mappings, please visit the OJB Web site at http://db.apache.org/ojb and read the "Advanced O/R" tutorial. The `Viewer` class keeps track of users who have viewed messages. It records the user's IP address and the date they viewed the message. The following code illustrates the code for the `Viewer` class:

```
/*
 * Created in 2003
 *
 * Viewer.java
 *
 */
package com.ojbmsg.test;
import java.io.*;
import java.net.*;
import java.util.*;
/**
 * @author Vitale
 */
public class Viewer implements java.io.Serializable {
    protected String  m_sIP;
    protected String  m_sDate;
    protected int     m_nID;

    public Viewer() {
        // initialization of member variables
        m_nID   = 0;
        m_sIP   = "";
        m_sDate = "";
    }
```

The `Get` and `Set` methods in this class alter the protected class variables while OJB makes use of the mappings in the `repository_user.xml` file to transfer the variables' values to the mapped data source:

```
// Get Methods
public String getIP() {
    return m_sIP;
}
```

```
    public String getDate() {
        return m_sDate;
    }
    public int getID() {
        return m_nID;
    }
    // Set methods
    public void setIP(String sIP) {
        m_sIP = sIP;
    }
    public void setDate(String sDate) {
        m_sDate = sDate;
    }
    public void setID(int nID) {
        m_nID = nID;
    }
}
```

The Viewer class is straightforward in design compared to the Message class. It does not have a direct relationship with any classes. Nor does it need to know that the Message class has a 1:N association with it in order to function properly. This is depicted in the following code:

```
<class-descriptor
        class="com.ojbmsg.test.Viewer"
        table="tblVIEWER"
>
    <field-descriptor id="1"
        name="m_nID"
        column="ID"
        jdbc-type="INTEGER"
        primarykey="true"
        autoincrement="true"
    />
    <field-descriptor id="2"
        name="m_sIP"
        column="IP"
        jdbc-type="VARCHAR"
    />
    <field-descriptor id="3"
        name="m_sDate"
        column="VIEWDATE"
        jdbc-type="VARCHAR"
    />
</class-descriptor>
```

In the preceding code, you can see that the Viewer class mapping entries have no ties to the Message class. If you recall from previous code, the Message class had a <collection-descriptor>, which referenced the Viewer class. The Viewer class mapping entries do not have such a descriptor and therefore the class stands alone.

JDBC Connection Mapping

The final XML entries that must be inserted into the OJB metadata repository are the JDBC connections that you need OJB to make in order to operate correctly. The following code illustrates a JDBC connection to a Sybase ASA server:

```
<jdbc-connection-descriptor
     jcd-alias="Sybase"
     default-connection="true"
     platform="Sybase"
     jdbc-level="1.0"
     driver="com.sybase.jdbc2.jdbc.SybDriver"
     protocol="jdbc"
     subprotocol="sybase:Tds:localhost"
     dbalias="2638"
     username="DBA"
     password="SQL"
     batch-mode="false"
     useAutoCommit="1"
     ignoreAutoCommitExceptions="false"
/>
```

You can have multiple JDBC connection descriptors in your mapping file, which would provide your application with the capability to connect to multiple databases at any given time. Specific information about the elements of the `<jdbc-connection-descriptor>` is described in the following table.

Element	Description
jcd-alias	A JDBC description alias. You can specify any alias name you wish that will aid you in identifying the JDBC connection.
default-connection	If set to true, this is the default connection that OJB will use if none is specified when creating a PersistenceBroker.
platform	OJB supports over ten relational database platforms. You can find more about this in the "OJB Extras" section of this chapter.
jdbc-level	Specifies the JDBC protocol version to use.
driver	Specifies the driver to use to connect to the database.
protocol	Protocol part of the connection string to use via JDBC.
subprotocol	Sub protocol of the connection string.
dbalias	Alias name of the database to connect to. Our example just uses the port and no database name. Therefore, the default database of the connection is used.
username	Specifies the user name to use when connecting to the database.
password	Specifies the password to use when connecting to the database.

Table continued on following page

Element	Description
batch-mode	Batch-mode is used only if a database supports it. Each implementation of the mode is database-dependent. Batch-mode can be changed at run-time using the `PersistenceBroker.serviceConnectionManager` `.setBatchMode(...)`
useAutoCommit	Affects the way OJB uses the auto-commit mode. There are three modes; the default mode is 1. 0 — turns auto-commit off. 1 — sets auto-commit explicitly to true when a connection is created, and temporarily sets it to false when necessary (default). 2 — sets auto-commit explicitly to false when a connection is created.
ignoreAutoCommit Exceptions	If set to false, OJB will ignore any exceptions that are thrown from the use of auto-commit.

Home.jsp

This is the default page that is displayed to users when they access the message board sample Web application. When this page is displayed, a list of currently existing messages is shown to the user. This page also provides links to the user to enable the viewing of a specific message in greater detail or to delete a specific message from the database. The code to perform all this functionality is embedded within Home.jsp.

In order to retrieve the messages and display them to the user, you need to know how many messages exist in the database first. If none are available, then there is no need to waste your time trying to iterate through non-existent messages. The following code shows how to use the `PersistenceBroker` API to retrieve the number of messages that exist in the database:

```java
PersistenceBroker broker;
public int getCount() {

    try {
        // Create a PersistenceBroker object using the
        // PersistenceBrokerFactory.
        broker = PersistenceBrokerFactory.defaultPersistenceBroker();

        // Construct a query to be issued
        Query query = new QueryByCriteria(Message.class, null);

        // Ask the broker to retrieve the extent collection
        Collection allMessages = broker.getCollectionByQuery(query);

        // If there are messages then return the number of messages
        if (allMessages != null) {
            broker.close();
            PersistenceBrokerFactory.releaseAllInstances();
            return allMessages.size();
        } else {
```

```
                broker.close();
                PersistenceBrokerFactory.releaseAllInstances();
                return 0;
            }
        } catch (Exception e) {
            System.out.println(e);
            e.printStackTrace();
            broker.close();
            PersistenceBrokerFactory.releaseAllInstances();
        }
        return 0;
    }
```

Once you have the number of messages that exist in the database, you can then retrieve each one independently to exhibit to the user. You need to use getMessage to retrieve the specified message from the server. The getMessage method is shown in the following code:

```
public Message getMessage(String sIndex, String sUserIP) {
    Message msgFound = null;
    try {
        // Create a PersistenceBroker object using the
        // PersistenceBrokerFactory
        broker = PersistenceBrokerFactory.defaultPersistenceBroker();

        // Construct a query to be issued
        Query query = new QueryByCriteria(Message.class, null);

        // Ask the broker to retrieve the extent collection
        Collection allMessages = broker.getCollectionByQuery(query);

        // Now iterate through the results
        java.util.Iterator iter = allMessages.iterator();
        int nIndex = Integer.parseInt(sIndex);
        int i = 0;

        // Search for the message we are looking for
        while (iter.hasNext()) {
            i++;

            // If we found our message exit the loop
            if (i == nIndex) {
                msgFound = (Message) iter.next();
                break;
            } else {
                iter.next();
            }
        }
```

Once you have found a message, you need to create a Viewer object that will let the message know that it has been viewed. The new Viewer object is then saved to the Message object, which is in turn saved to the data source using the store method of the broker object:

```
        // If we have a message, return it
        if (msgFound != null) {
            // Construct a viewer object to show that this message has
            // been accessed
            Vector tmpvVwrs = msgFound.getViewers();
            Viewer tmpView = new Viewer();

            Calendar clNow = Calendar.getInstance();

            tmpView.setIP(sUserIP);
            tmpView.setDate(
                Integer.toString((clNow.get(Calendar.MONTH) + 1)) + "/" +
                Integer.toString(clNow.get(Calendar.DAY_OF_MONTH)) + "/" +
                Integer.toString(clNow.get(Calendar.YEAR))
            );

            tmpView.setID(msgFound.getID());
            tmpvVwrs.add(tmpView);

            // Save the new Viewer to the Message class
            msgFound.setViewers(tmpvVwrs);

            try {
                // Begin transaction
                broker.beginTransaction();

                // Store the new persistent making it persistent
                broker.store(msgFound);

                // Finally commit the transaction
                broker.commitTransaction();
            } catch (PersistenceBrokerException ex) {
                // Rollback on error
                broker.abortTransaction();
                System.out.println(ex.getMessage());
                ex.printStackTrace();

                broker.close();
                PersistenceBrokerFactory.releaseAllInstances();
            }
            broker.close();
            PersistenceBrokerFactory.releaseAllInstances();
        } else {
            broker.close();
            PersistenceBrokerFactory.releaseAllInstances();
        }
    } catch (Exception e) {
        System.out.println(e);
        e.printStackTrace();

        broker.close();
        PersistenceBrokerFactory.releaseAllInstances();
    }
    return msgFound;
}
```

From the `getCount` and `getMessage` examples, you can perceive that there is a systematic approach to issuing queries using the `PersistenceBroker` API. The following sequence shows the generic steps in issuing a query utilizing the PBAPI:

1. Obtain a `PersistenceBroker` by using the `PersistenceBrokerFactory` `defaultPersistenceBroker` method:

```
broker = PersistenceBrokerFactory.defaultPersistenceBroker();
```

2. Construct a query using a class that is mapped in the OJB metadata repository:

```
Query query = new QueryByCriteria(Message.class, null);
```

3. Ask the broker to retrieve a collection of objects based on the query statement:

```
Collection allMessages = broker.getCollectionByQuery(query);
```

4. Iterate through the collection results and manipulate the objects you want to change:

```
java.util.Iterator iter = allMessages.iterator();
```

5. After changing the objects, you then need to store them back in the database. This requires you to issue a `transaction` method and a `store` method:

```
broker.beginTransaction();
broker.store(msgObject);
broker.commitTransaction();
```

6. Finally, you need to close the broker and release any instances that you created from the broker pool:

```
broker.close();
PersistenceBrokerFactory.releaseAllInstances();
```

To delete a message, you would use the same general code that was depicted in the `getMessage` method, but rather than store the object with the `broker.store` function, you would execute a `delete` on the object:

```
    try {
        broker.beginTransaction();
        broker.delete(msgObject); // Delete the Message
        broker.commitTransaction();
        etc.
```

In the preceding code, you now have all the necessary functionality to execute the Home.JSP program and see the results. Figure 4.3 shows what the OJB message board looks like after it has retrieved all the messages that exist in a database.

The Home.jsp code is now complete and functioning. The following section describes how to add a message to a database using the `PersistenceBroker` API. Add.jsp will demonstrate this functionality.

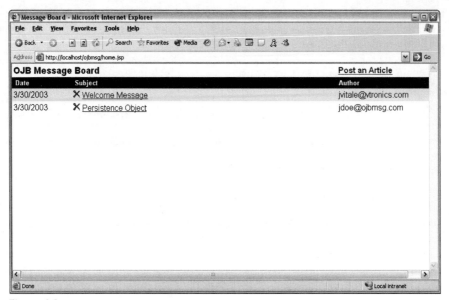

Figure 4.3

Add.jsp

This page is accessed when the user wants to submit a new article to the message board. A form is shown to the user requiring them to enter information in several fields. Once the user has filled out the form and pressed the Submit button, the information is actually submitted to the same Add.jsp page, which displays an embedded note to the user informing them that their article has been submitted to the message board.

The majority of the code is similar to the code in previous examples; the main exception is that you need to construct the Message object and fill it with data before you can persistently store it. Another point to note here is that when the objects are stored, the PersistenceBroker API will automatically create a unique ID for the object(s) and store it in the database. Figure 4.4 exemplifies the Add.jsp article submission form.

The addMessage method is called when the user clicks the Submit button. The addMessage method processes the form data, converts it into a Message object, and then uses the PBAPI to store the object in the database. The following code displays the addMessage code:

```
public Message addMessage(
    String sSubmitter, String sSubject, String sMessage) {
    Message msgToStore = null;

    try {
        broker = PersistenceBrokerFactory.defaultPersistenceBroker();

        // Create Message to store
        msgToStore = new Message();
```

```
                // Add submitter to message
                msgToStore.setSubmitter(sSubmitter);

                // Add subject to message
                msgToStore.setSubject(sSubject);

                // Add article to message
                msgToStore.setMessage(sMessage);

                Calendar clNow = Calendar.getInstance();

                // Set the date
                msgToStore.setDate(
                  Integer.toString((clNow.get(Calendar.MONTH) + 1)) + "/" +
                  Integer.toString(clNow.get(Calendar.DAY_OF_MONTH)) + "/" +
                  Integer.toString(clNow.get(Calendar.YEAR)));
```

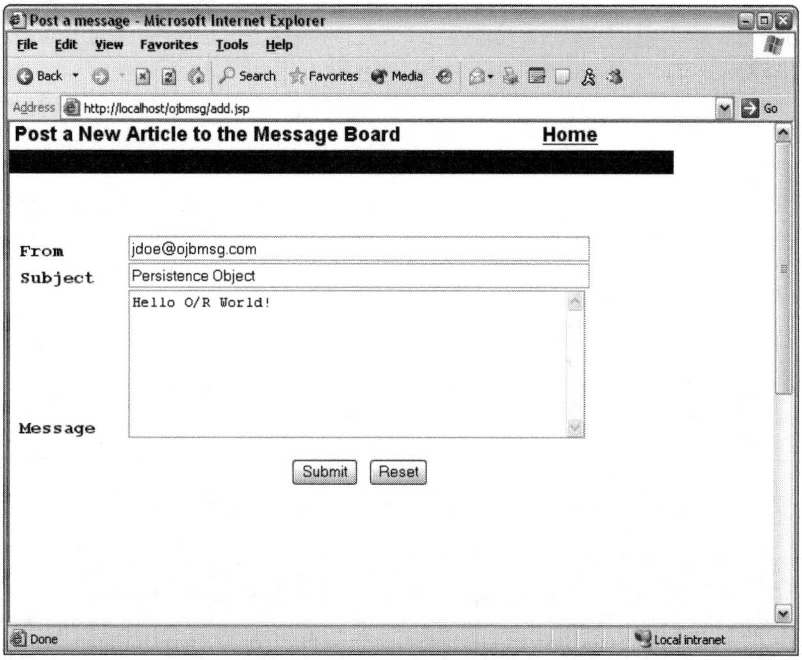

Figure 4.4

The broker.store method performs the actual persisting of the Message object, msgToStore, to the data source:

```
                // now perform persistence operations
                try {
                    broker.beginTransaction();
```

```
            // Store the new object
            broker.store(msgToStore);

            broker.commitTransaction();
        } catch (PersistenceBrokerException ex) {
            broker.abortTransaction();
            System.out.println(ex.getMessage());
            ex.printStackTrace();

            broker.close();
            PersistenceBrokerFactory.releaseAllInstances();
        }
        broker.close();
        PersistenceBrokerFactory.releaseAllInstances();
    } catch(Exception e) {
      System.out.println(e);

      broker.close();
      PersistenceBrokerFactory.releaseAllInstances();
    }
    return msgToStore;
}
```

View.jsp

This is the final JSP in the message board example. It does not introduce any new code and utilizes the same getMessage method found in Home.jsp. What it does differently is display the full contents of a specific message to the user. Figure 4.5 is a screenshot of what the user would see when a message is accessed with View.jsp.

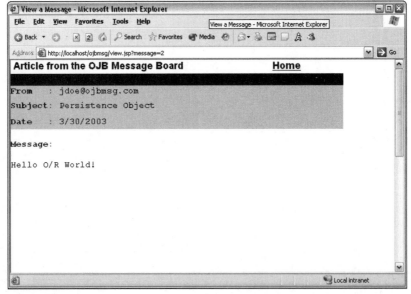

Figure 4.5

Developing with the ODMG API

This section briefly describes how to develop OJB applications using the ODMG API. OJB has created its own implementation of the ODMG APIs, which it stores in the package org.apache.ojb.odmg. In order to use the vast feature set of ODMG, you have to deal directly with an object that acts as the main entry point of the ODMG APIs. This object is distinguished by the interface org.odmg.Implementation, which enables you to obtain OQL objects, database objects, persistent collection objects, and transaction objects. The good news is that if you have used ODMG before with non-OJB applications, the code will be very similar to what you have created in the past, as all vendors must implement the org.odmg.Implementation interface. The main difference is learning how OJB provides you access to the ODMG object.

The examples that follow are based on creating the same type of functionality seen in the PersistenceBroker API message board example, but utilizing ODMG instead. The core functionality covered here includes opening a database, deleting and retrieving objects, and updating and storing objects.

Opening a Database

As stated earlier, OJB has its own specific implementation of the org.odmg.Implementation interface; this is simply org.apache.ojb.odmg.OJB. Now we need to obtain an instance of this class using the static factory method getInstance. Using this instance, we can now open or create an ODMG database (org.odmg.Database). The complete code follows:

```
import org.apache.ojb.odmg.OJB;
import org.odmg.Database;
import org.odmg.Implementation;
import org.odmg.ODMGException;
public Database open() {
    // Obtain an ODMG object of type org.odmg.Implementation
    Implementation odmgObject = OJB.getInstance();

    Database odmgDB = odmgObject.newDatabase();

    //open database
    try {
        odmgDB.open("repository.xml", Database.OPEN_READ_WRITE);
    } catch (ODMGException e) {
        e.printStackTrace();
    }

    return odmgDB;
}
```

Retrieving Objects

Obtaining objects using ODMG is quite a bit different than using the PersistenceBroker API. You need to use the Object Query Language (OQL) designated by ODMG and set up query statements, which are very similar to SQL statements. With the PBAPI, you issue queries directly on the objects with QueryByCriteria methods. You need to obtain an OQLQuery object first, and then create a query statement and execute it. This returns the Message objects in a DList, which you can later iterate through when you are ready to process them. The following example shows the complete code for retrieving objects using ODMG:

```
import org.apache.ojb.odmg.OJB;
import org.odmg.DList;
public DList getAllMessages() {

    try {
        // Begin a transaction
        Transaction trans = odmgObject.newTransaction();
        trans.begin();

        // Obtain an OQLQuery object
        OQLQuery query = odmgObject.newOQLQuery();

        // Create the OQL select statement
        query.create("select allmessages from " +
             Message.class.getName());

        // Execute the query
        DList allMessages = (DList) query.execute();

        // Commit the transaction
        trans.commit();

        // Return the DList of messages
        return allMessages;
    }
    catch (Exception e) {
        System.out.println(e);
        e.printStackTrace();
    }
    return null;
}
```

Storing Objects

Storing objects is extremely easy with the ODMG API. All you need to do is start a new transaction, create a write lock on the object to store, and then commit the transaction. The following example demonstrates the code to store objects with ODMG:

```
public void storeObject(Message msg) {

    Transaction trans = null;
    try {
        // Obtain a new transaction object
        trans = odmgObject.newTransaction();
        trans.begin();

        // We need to write lock the new object
        trans.lock(msg, Transaction.WRITE);

        // Now we commit the transaction
        trans.commit();
    } catch( Exception e ) {
        System.out.println(e);
        e.printStackTrace(System.out);
    }
}
```

Updating Objects

Updating objects requires more interaction than storing objects. In order to update an existing object, you have to execute a query that can find the specific object that you are looking for. Once the object is obtained, you then invoke a write lock on the object. The final steps are to update the necessary data contained in the object and then commit the transaction. Following is the complete code needed for updating objects using ODMG:

```java
public void update(Message msg)
{
    Transaction trans = null;

    // Create a query to find a message with the specific ID
    String oqlQuery = "select * from " + Message.class.getName() +
                        " where id = " + msg.getID();

    // Get the current database
    Database odmgDB = odmgObject.getDatabase(null);

    try {
        trans = odmgObject.newTransaction();
        trans.begin();
        OQLQuery query = odmgObject.newOQLQuery();
        query.create(oqlQuery);

        // Execute the query
        DList dlMessages = (DList) query.execute();

        // Retrieve the message
        Message msgFound = (Message) dlMessages.get(0);

        // Set write lock
        trans.lock(msgFound, Transaction.WRITE);

        // Edit message subject line
        msgFound.setSubject("The subject has been edited");

        // Commit transaction
        trans.commit();
    } catch (Exception e) {
        // RollBack
        trans.abort();

        System.out.println(e);
        e.printStackTrace(System.out);
    }
}
```

Deleting Objects

Deleting objects with ODMG API requires the same methods as updating objects. First, you have to obtain the object you want to delete. Second, you need to mark it for deletion with `Database.deletePersistent(Object)`. Third, you simply commit the transaction and the `delete` operation is carried out. The following example displays the code for deleting objects:

```java
public void delete(Message msg){

    Transaction trans = null;

    // Get the current database
    Database odmgDB = odmgObject.getDatabase(null);

    // Create the OQL query
    String oqlQuery = "select * from " + Message.class.getName() +
                        " where id = " + msg.getID();

    try {
        trans = odmgObject.newTransaction();

        // Begin Transaction
        trans.begin();

        OQLQuery query = odmgObject.newOQLQuery();

        query.create(oqlQuery);

        // Execute query
        DList dlMessage = (DList) query.execute();

        Message msgFound = (Message) dlMessage.get(0);

        // Mark message for deletion
        odmgDB.deletePersistent(msgFound);

        // Commit the transaction
        trans.commit();
    } catch (Exception e) {
        // RollBack
        trans.abort();

        System.out.println(e);
        e.printStackTrace(System.out);
    }
}
```

Developing with the JDO API

OJB does not currently have its own implementation of JDO. OJB uses a plug-in called **OJBStore,** located in the package `org.apache.ojb.jdori.sql`. A full JDO implementation is scheduled for the 2.0 release of OJB, and so is currently beyond the scope of this book.

OJB Extras

This section contains various information that you should find helpful when using OJB. It covers the following: the steps that should be taken to verify an OJB installation; the database platforms that OJB can be successfully used with; the JDBC types that OJB enables for your use when developing your applications; how to correctly deploy an OJB application; and, finally, some special performance notes regarding OJB.

Verifying an OJB Installation

Regardless of what API layer you chose to develop with, it is imperative that you make sure that OJB is properly installed on your machine. The OJB development team makes this process extremely easy using JUnit and Ant. You want to make sure that you have JDK 1.2 or later installed before proceeding with the following tests.

1. Ensure that the JAVA_HOME environment variable points to the root directory of the Java SDK installation.

2. Make sure that you have downloaded the latest binary or source distribution of OJB.

3. From the base directory of your new installation of OJB, execute **bin\build junit** for win32 machines or **bin/build.sh junit** for Unix machines.

These steps should initiate a chain of regression tests that can take several minutes to complete. After all the tests have completed, a summary of the results will be displayed in the console. Make sure that no tests failed. A typical output from these tests is as follows:

```
junit-no-compile-no-prepare:
    [junit] Running org.apache.ojb.broker.AllTests
    [junit] Tests run: 187, Failures: 0, Errors: 0, Time elapsed: 26.228 sec
    [junit] Running org.apache.ojb.odmg.AllTests
```

A common error that can occur during the beginning of the tests is that the Ant script will not be able to locate the j2ee.jar file. A simple solution is to put a copy of the file in the OJB_BASE\lib directory. The other option is to edit the build script to point to the location of the j2ee.jar.

Supported Database Platforms

OJB currently supports a large array of database platforms that can be used with OJB persistent object development. Each database system requires its own JDBC driver to enable access to it. The currently supported database platforms are as follows:

- ❑ Db2
- ❑ Hsqldb
- ❑ Informix
- ❑ MS Access
- ❑ MS SQL Server
- ❑ MySQL
- ❑ Oracle
- ❑ PostgreSQL
- ❑ SybaseASA
- ❑ SybaseASE
- ❑ Sapdb
- ❑ Firebird

❑   Axion

❑   NonstopSQL

Supported JDBC Data Types

OJB supports the most common JDBC data types that applications use today. The following describes the supported JDBC data types and their Java equivalent.

JDBC Type	Java Equivalent
CHAR	String
VARCHAR	String
LONGVARCHAR	String
NUMERIC	java.math.BigDecimal
DECIMAL	java.math.BigDecimal
BIT	boolean
TINYINT	byte
SMALLINT	short
INTEGER	int
BIGINT	long
REAL	float
DOUBLE	double
FLOAT	double
BINARY	byte[]
VARBINARY	byte[]
LONGVARBINARY	byte[]
DATE	java.sql.Date
TIME	java.sql.Time
TIMESTAMP	java.sql.Timestamp
CLOB	Clob
BLOB	Blob
ARRAY	Array
DISTINCT	mapping underlying type
STRUCT	Struct
REF	Ref
JAVA_OBJECT	Java class

Deploying OJB Applications

Deploying OJB applications requires specific knowledge of the OJB resources and configuration files that are needed to run an OJB-supported application. This section describes the resources and configurations and explains how each fits into the OJB framework.

Jar Files

The following table is a list of Jar files supplied with OJB in the `ojb_root/lib` directory. The files with an asterisk next to their name are required for OJB to run. The other files are used for building purposes only.

Jar File	Version
db-ojb-xxx.jar*	Latest release
ant-1.5.jar	1.5
antlr-2.7.1.jar	2.7.1
commons-beanutils-1.4-dev.jar*	1.4-dev
commons-collections-2.0.jar*	2.0
commons-dbcp-1.0.jar*	1.0
commons-lang-1.0-b1.1.jar*	1.0-b1.1
commons-logging-1.0.1.jar*	1.0.1
commons-pool-1.0.1.jar*	1.0.1
crossdb.jar	1.0 RC1
ejb.jar	1.0
hsqldb-1.7.1.jar*	1.7.1
jakarta-regexp-1.2.jar	1.2
jcs-1.0-dev.jar*	1.0-dev
jta-1.0.1.jar*	1.0.1
junit-3.8.jar	3.8
log4j-1.2.6.jar*	1.2.6
p6spy-1.0.jar*	1.0
servletapi-2.2.jar	2.2
torque-3.0.jar	1.3
xalan-2.4.jar	2.4
xerces-2.0.2.jar*	2.0.2

Metadata Files

Two main files are needed in order for OJB to run correctly:

❑ The `repository.xml` file and any resources it points to are needed for deployment.

❑ The `ojb.properties` file is also need for runtime configurations.

These files must also be stored in the CLASSPATH because OJB will attempt to load them via the `ClassLoader` resource look-up.

JDBC Drivers

The JDBC drivers that you use for your specific application must be included when deploying the application, and they must also be referenced in the CLASSPATH.

CLASSPATH Settings

For a standalone application, you must have the following files in your CLASSPATH:

❑ db-ojb-xxx.jar

❑ OJB.properties

❑ repository.xml

❑ JDBC drivers

❑ Any additional Jars your application may require

OJB Performance

OJB calls will be obviously slower than issuing direct JDBC queries because OJB introduces an extra layer between the RDBMS and the actual business logic that is used. However, this does not mean that the OJB team has not taken steps to ensure the best possible performance. The OJB team has rewritten the reflection classes that are used to access the persistent objects for optimal performance.

OJB provides an API layer that makes it easy for developers to create O/R mapping applications. You basically just need to weigh the options of capability, convenience, and rapid development time versus the best possible performance solution. OJB also provides built-in object caching features, which enhance query times drastically.

The bottom line is that the performance hit you may encounter using OJB versus straight queries is minor in comparison to the amazing feature set and functionality that is built in to OJB. It is also important to note that all O/R mapping tools are slower than straight queries; this is not exclusive to OJB.

Summary

Object Relational Bridge (OJB) is a powerful, flexible, and exciting object-to-relational mapping tool that contains a vast array of functionality for incorporating persistent objects into your application designs. OJB takes all of the guesswork out of O/R mapping and is truly a transparent persistence O/R mapping tool.

This chapter described Object-to-Relational mapping and then explained the main features of OJB. Next, it covered how to use OJB's API layers and demonstrated a complete message board application that utilizes OJB's features. You saw fully functional code that exploited the PersistenceBroker API and ODMG API. Finally, you examined the configurations needed in order to deploy OJB in your own applications.

The next chapter describes content management with Jakarta's Slide.

5

Content Management with Jakarta's Slide

Jakarta's Slide (http://jakarta.apache.org/slide) is an open-source content management and integration system. It provides a robust API and a low-level content management framework, which can be used as a foundation for building your own, more complex content management systems. Slide is currently maintained by the Apache Software Foundation and was originally developed by Remy Maucherat.

Slide manages binary content from distributed data sources and organizes it in a hierarchical fashion. It also provides many additional features that can be used to manage the data sources, such as versioning, indexing, searching, locking, and security. These are known as **helpers** in the Slide world.

Slide also supports Web Distributed Authoring and Versioning (WebDAV) capabilities, which are implemented via a servlet. WebDAV is a very popular protocol that is an extension of the HTTP protocol. It is used for editing and managing Web-based content on remote Web servers. It is also an Internet Engineering Task Force (IETF) standard and is supported by many popular software companies (Microsoft, IBM, Novell, and more).

In this chapter, we explain the Slide architecture—specifically, namespaces, domains, and APIs; provide information on the setup and configuration of Slide; discuss WebDAV and Slide; and show examples of Slide using a WebDAV-supported client.

Slide Architecture

The architecture of Slide's features and services were developed from a modular and pluggable design consisting of high-level and low-level services, with a concentration on security, versioning, locking, and structure. The high-level services have strong dependencies on each other in order to keep the security of Slide's components intact. The low-level services are not concerned with security and are more related to functionality. These services are all designed to be pluggable, meaning you can add or remove services as needed. This pluggable design of low-level services makes Slide extremely flexible and readily adaptable to a wide variety of content management needs.

You should understand the five main architectural concepts of Slide:

- ❑ External architecture
- ❑ Internal architecture
- ❑ Transaction management architecture
- ❑ Namespace
- ❑ Domain

External Architecture

The external architecture (EA), shown in Figure 5.1, is the highest-level architecture perspective.

There are two simplistic layers in the EA: the **client layer** and the **server layer**.

The client layer contains three components, which are used to communicate with the server. The first component is the **WebDAV client**. The WebDAV client is an application that supports and understands the WebDAV protocol from a client perspective. The WebDAV client connects to the WebDAV servlet and communicates its requests to the WebDAV servlet. Many WebDAV client tools are available, but two of the most common are DAV Explorer and the Microsoft Windows Operating System (O/S). Windows has WebDAV capabilities built right into the O/S. You will see examples of using Windows to issue WebDAV operations later in this chapter, in the section, "WebDAV and Slide." DAV Explorer is a standalone Java application developed by the University of California, Irvine. DAV Explorer looks very similar to Windows Explorer and it supports most of the functionality specified in RFC 2518, which is the WebDAV Distributed Authoring Protocol specification. You can download DAV Explorer from www.ics.uci.edu/~Webdav/.

The second component is the **HTTP client**, which is an application that communicates with the Slide server via the HTTP protocol. An example application could be any Web browser. With the HTTP client, the content management system can be managed easily through a Web-based interface. This falls right into play with portal development and is probably the best approach for administering content from a portal perspective.

The final component of the client layer is a **Java Application Client.** A Java Application Client can be created to utilize Slide's API layer directly without going through the WebDAV servlet layer. This is definitely a plus when performance is a factor in the development task you are presented with.

From a portal development standpoint, you would most likely choose either the HTTP client approach or the WebDAV approach for managing content, as both lend themselves to easy remote management capabilities. The standalone Java application approach requires more configurations in order to get the application up and running. If you want a portable standalone Java application as your approach for managing content, then using Java Web Start (JWS) technology would be a great option. Java Web Start enables you to download an application from the World Wide Web via a Web browser by simply clicking on a hyperlink. The only configuration requirement of the machine that is downloading the program is that it has Java Web Start installed. Added benefits of using JWS are the extra security and versioning features built into its protocol. You can always be sure that administrators are using the latest copy of an application and that the software is legitimate, as certificates and digital signatures are used. Please see Chapter 12 for more in-depth information on Java Web Start.

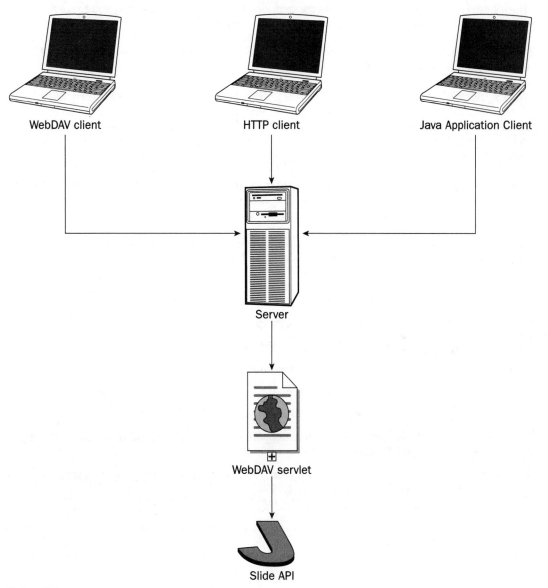

Figure 5.1

The server layer enables the client layer to communicate with it through one of two methods. One method is to use the WebDAV servlet for communication. WebDAV clients and HTTP clients use this approach. The second method is for the client to communicate directly with the Slide API. Standalone Java applications are the prime candidates for using the Slide API for communication.

Internal Architecture

The internal architecture digs deeper into the component realm of Slide, enabling you to see the individual pluggable interfaces that exist. Figure 5.2 depicts the internal architecture.

The internal architecture can be depicted with four layers: The **Application layer**, the **Slide API layer**, the **Helper layer**, and the **Data Store layer**.

The Application layer provides the means by which clients can access the Slide API. There are two methods for doing this. One is to use the WebDAV servlet for communication. As described in the preceding section, the WebDAV client and HTTP client interface with the WebDAV servlet for communication purposes. The second method is to use a standalone Java application that will directly access the Slide API layer.

The Slide API layer provides access to the content management Java classes called **helpers**, and acts as a bridge between the Application layer and the Helper layer. The Slide API accepts operation requests from the Application layer and executes the requests accordingly.

The Helper layer encapsulates all the functionality to which an application would need access. The helpers that currently exist in Slide are described in the following table.

Helper	Description
Structure	Provides access to the namespace tree
Lock	Enables data-locking capabilities
Security	Provides access to security functionality
Content	Enables the management of content, revisions, and metadata
Macro	Provides high-level object management functionality
Index	Currently not implemented, this helper will provide indexing and searching capabilities.
Process	Currently not implemented, this helper will handle approvals, confirmations, and notifications.

The Data Store layer is where all the data is housed and managed. Also available is transaction management support for managing user data transactions.

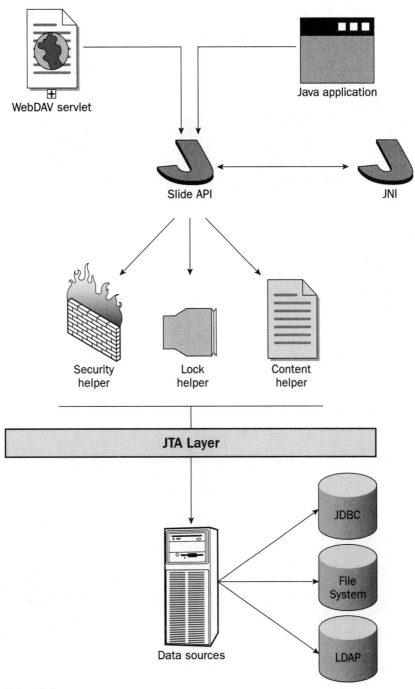

WebDAV servlet

Java application

Slide API

JNI

Security
helper

Lock
helper

Content
helper

JTA Layer

Data sources

JDBC

File
System

LDAP

Figure 5.2

Transaction Management

Slide implements a very robust transaction management system. Transaction management is very important when dealing with content management, especially in a system that is accessed by multiple users at any given time. This is definitely the case when building Java portals. The transaction management architecture is shown in Figure 5.3.

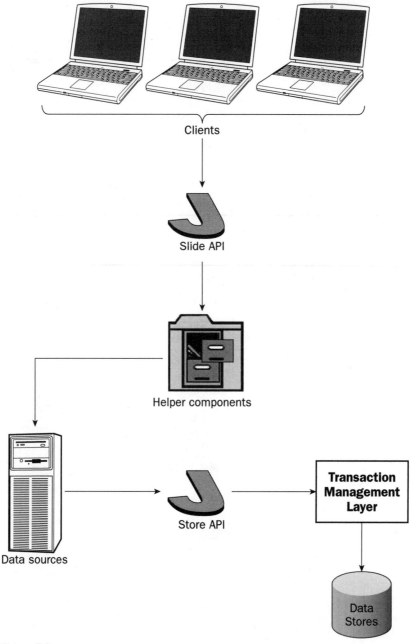

Figure 5.3

Transaction management is key to a successful content management framework — without it, data can easily become corrupted or out of sync. Slide uses Java transaction management as a basis for its transaction management system. The following sections take a little deeper look into what this entails, explaining what transactions are and how they are managed in the Slide architecture.

Transactions

A **transaction** is defined as a compilation of tasks that must be performed. They can consist of several operations executing different functionalities in a given order or without order at all. These tasks have to be managed individually in order to preserve data integrity. In addition to ensuring that data isn't corrupted, data integrity management also encompasses the following:

- ❑ **Security** — limits who has access to the specific data

- ❑ **Versioning** — keeps track of the latest version of the data

- ❑ **Locking** — ensures that only one user is altering the data at one time

- ❑ **Replication** — persists the new data updates to other stores that contain the same data

Transaction Attributes

You have probably heard of the acronym **ACID** before. All transactions share the same attributes, and they are easily remembered with the ACID acronym: atomicity, consistency, isolation, and durability.

- ❑ **Atomicity** — This describes any operation that is indivisible, which simply means that the operation will either complete fully or will fail completely and be rejected by the managing system. In other words, an operation either passes or fails; there is no middle ground or partial completion.

- ❑ **Consistency** — A transaction must manage its data in an all-or-nothing manner. When a transaction has completed, the data must be stored fully in the data store. However, if a transaction fails, the data that was in the process of being persisted to the data store must be removed, and the original data that exists in the data store must be returned to its previous state. This follows the guidelines of data integrity.

- ❑ **Isolation** — In theory, several transactions can occur at the same given time. However, the transactions should not conflict with each other. Therefore, the management system has to keep track of who has already committed a transaction and in what order the transactions were committed, in order to avoid conflicts. From an individual transaction standpoint, a transaction that is being executed should be isolated from all other transactions that are occurring, meaning that other transactions should appear as if they have completed either before it or after it, in a sequential manner.

- ❑ **Durability** — Sometimes errors occur after transactions are committed and changes are persisted to the data store. In this case, the transaction management system needs to be durable enough to recognize that the errors occurred after the data was persisted and the transaction was complete. Therefore, the data should not be rolled back to the previous state; rather, it should still reflect the most recently persisted data.

Transactions end in a very simplistic manner even if the underlying details are a bear to manage. In short, a transaction will both be successful and save its new changes or it will fail and roll back all changes it may have made to the data store.

Slide's use of Java's transaction management system provides you with an elegant way to manage transactions at the programming level. This is definitely a plus when you need to develop a very robust content management system.

Namespaces

A **namespace** is a conglomerate of files, directories, actions, and security policies, all contained in a hierarchical information tree structure. One namespace per application is the general rule. All the information in the namespace is independent of other existing namespaces. One namespace cannot reference another namespace or include links to other namespaces. This type of rule structure isolates application data and security from other applications with different namespaces.

Namespaces also include actions and subjects that are, generally speaking, security policies that have been created for a specific application. **Actions** control user permissions to content by defining read/write constraints for individual users and groups. **Subjects** are the users and groups that are defined for the application.

Given that the data is stored in a hierarchical information tree, there needs to be a standard way to access the information in the tree. Slide uses Uniform Resources Identifier (URI) technology to do this. URIs are simply strings that are used to identify resources. The string syntax is reminiscent of the Unix file system, starting with a forward slash (/) as the root of system. When you need access to a specific node in the hierarchical information tree, you simply specify a path as you would in a Unix file system to locate the resource—for example, `/bin/conf/server.xml`.

If you need to make sure that your URIs are adhering to the W3 specification for addressing, please check out the following Web site for further information on URI addressing: www.w3.org/addressing.

Helpers

Slide contains seven individual helpers that enable the management of objects in a namespace. You were briefly introduced to these helpers in the table that appears in the section "Internal Architecture" of this chapter. The following sections now describe each of these helpers: Structure, Security, Lock, Content, Macro, Index/Search, and Process.

Helpers are also referred to as high-level services in the Slide world. In order to access information nodes regardless of where the information is located or what form it is stored in, applications must use these helper objects.

Structure Helper

The structure helper provides the necessary functionality for applications to access the hierarchical information tree of a namespace. The structure package for navigating and manipulating a namespace is contained in the package `org.apache.slide.structure`. Besides the structure interface, six classes are also contained within the package. They are defined in the following table.

Class	Description
ActionNode	This class is used to define actions on available Slide objects. Actions can dynamically be added to a namespace in order create a new security policy.
GroupNode	A GroupNode defines a group of nodes. These defined groups of nodes are generally users.

Class	Description
LinkNode	A LinkNode is a node that links to another node in the system.
ObjectNode	The ObjectNode is an abstract data type and can represent any kind of object node that exists in the system.
StructureImpl	This class is the default implementation of the Structure interface.
SubjectNode	The SubjectNode is the most commonly occurring type of node in a namespace. It is used to store Slide information and can reference a file, a directory, or a principal.

To access and manipulate the node hierarchy of a namespace, you must acquire a structure object. In order to obtain a structure object, you need to call the method NamespaceAccessToken.getStructureHelper(). This method call will return a structure object that will provide you with all the necessary methods for manipulating a namespace.

Security Helper

Slide's security helper provides a role-based, hierarchical security system that has a tremendous amount of functionality that you can use immediately in your content management application fairly easily. The security helper provides a layer between calls coming from users and the content contained in the system. When a user or client tries to execute an operation on data, Slide will perform a security check on the user to make sure that the user has the right permissions to perform the operation. Additional permissions can be added dynamically through the security helper from client applications that have access to do so. The security helper is contained in the package org.apache.slide.security. Only two classes are associated with this package: the NodePermission class and the SecurityImpl class.

Slide does use role-based access and it is similar to general role-based access systems, but with an added twist of assigning roles to nodes. The roles are not necessarily focused on users, but rather on individual nodes in the namespace. This is a different way of thinking, but it makes sense when using a content management system. Therefore, the main framework for role-based access is individual nodes. If you do not specify a role for a particular node, it will default to the role of nobody.

Roles are assigned to individual nodes in a namespace through the use of Java interfaces. You can leave these interfaces empty if you wish or you can extend the functionality. In order to assign a particular role to a node, the node must first meet a few expectations. First, the node has to extend the SubjectNode class. Second, the node must also implement the role interface. Finally, the node must have a default constructor. If all three of these requirements are met by the node, a role can then be associated with it. Figure 5.4 illustrates the principles of security within Slide.

Permissions on child nodes are inherited from their parent nodes. If you had a URI such as /father and then created a sub node called son, "/father/son", son would inherit all the permissions that /father had automatically. These behavior principles apply throughout the hierarchical tree. Therefore, if /users had a new child called /users/joe, /users/joe would inherit all the permissions assigned to /users.

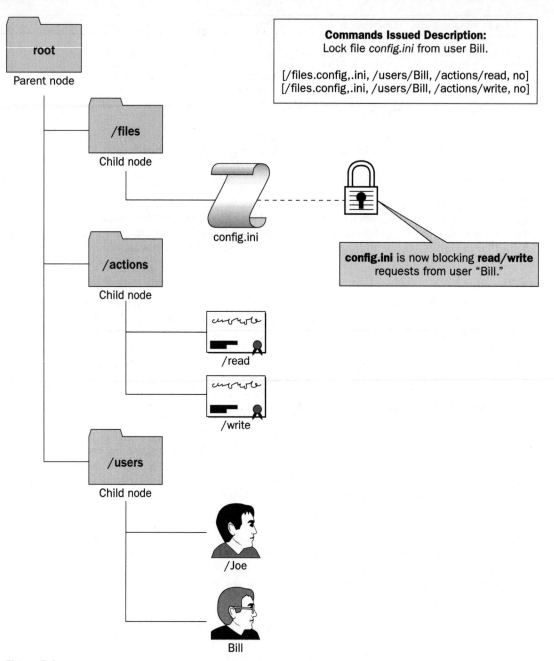

Figure 5.4

`ObjectNodes` have permissions associated with them in the form of quintuples, and use the following format:

```
[Target Subject, Executing Subject, Action, Inheritance]
```

Referring to Figure 5.4, if you wanted to give /users/joe the /actions/read capabilities on a particular node, you would use the following syntax:

```
[/files, /users/joe, /actions/read, yes]
```

You can also explicitly define the file to which you want to give a node access, as shown in the following example:

```
[/files/whatever.txt, /users/joe, /actions/read, yes]
```

Slide keeps track of all the permissions for you and performs all the necessary security checks when a user tries to access a particular node. If a security check were to fail, you would immediately be sent an `AccessDeniedException` stating that an exception was thrown when such and such a user tried to perform the given command. Once you understand the behavior of the security system, it is fairly simple to use. Action types in Slide can be user-defined. Once they are created, any number of security checks can be performed. Following are the default actions built into Slide:

❑ Read object

❑ Create object

❑ Remove object

❑ Grant permission

❑ Revoke permission

❑ Read permissions

❑ Lock object

❑ Kill lock

❑ Read locks

❑ Read revision metadata

❑ Create revision metadata

❑ Modify revision metadata

❑ Remove revision metadata

❑ Read revision content

❑ Create revision content

❑ Modify revision content

❑ Remove revision content

As discussed earlier, two main classes are associated with the `org.apache.slide.security` package: the `SecurityImpl` class and the `NodePermission` class. However, the package contains other classes that provide useful information. The following table provides a complete description of the classes associated with the security package.

CLASS	DESCRIPTION
Security	This is the security helper interface.
NodePermission	This class is used to impose security constraints on nodes within the hierarchical tree, and provides all the necessary methods to manage the security constraints.
SecurityImpl	This is the implementation class for the security helper interface described earlier. This class provides the capability to check permissions, revoke permissions, iterate through a permission list, grant permissions, and deny permissions.
AccessDeniedException	This class represents an access denied exception and will occur when access to a specific node is denied. The exception will contain information about the object on which the exception occurred, the subject URI, and the action that was attempted.
SecurityException	This class is a generic exception class that is used when no other exception class fits the criteria of the security exception.

Lock Helper

The lock helper provides the Slide content management system with the capability to enable a user to prevent a particular action from occurring on a resource for a duration specified by the user. For example, if an application wanted exclusive read and write access to a file, the application could use the lock helper to block other users from performing read or write actions on that file.

The lock helpers also provide the client application with the capability to check resources for locks and determine whether the resource is accessible and lockable. It also provides the user with information about how long the lock is for and who is locking it.

In the event that you try to perform a lock on a particular object and it fails, an `ObjectLockedException` will be returned to you indicating that your operation failed. You can use the `ObjectLockedException` to obtain more information about why the exception occurred.

To lock a `SubjectNode`, the following information must be provided: **[target subject, owner subject, locked action, duration, inheritance]**.

For instance, if you wanted to lock the `/files` node, you could use the following information to do so: **[/files, /users/joe, /actions/write, 20m, yes]**.

This would prevent the `/files` node from being written to for the duration of time specified by the user Joe. In addition, any sub nodes under `/files` would also be locked, as you explicitly told the lock helper to use inheritance. As you can see, Slide lock helper architecture is very similar to the security helper architecture in the sense that child nodes inherit locks placed upon their parent nodes. Figure 5.5 illustrates the lock architecture in action.

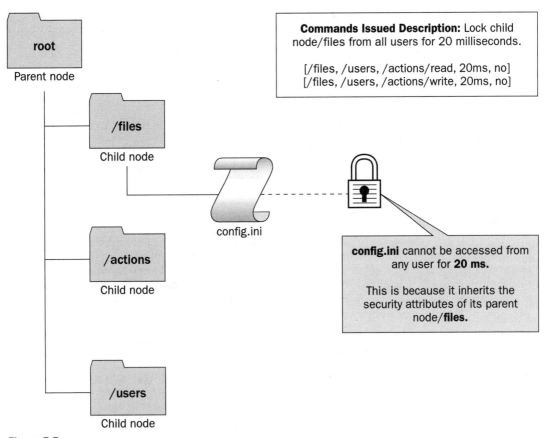

Commands Issued Description: Lock child node/files from all users for 20 milliseconds.

[/files, /users, /actions/read, 20ms, no]
[/files, /users, /actions/write, 20ms, no]

config.ini

config.ini cannot be accessed from any user for **20 ms.**

This is because it inherits the security attributes of its parent node/**files.**

Figure 5.5

The lock helper is contained in the package org.apache.slide.lock. Although several classes are included in the package, two main classes are important when managing locks: LockImpl and NodeLock. These two classes, as well as the other classes present in the lock helper package, are described in the following table.

CLASS	DESCRIPTION
Lock	This is the Lock interface.
LockImpl	This class implements the lock interface and provides applications with the capability to check locks, enumerate through locks, kill locks, renew locks, create a lock, and unlock a lock.
NodeLock	This class enables you to lock a node through the use of its many methods. It also provides the capability to get the expiration date of a lock, determine whether the lock has expired, set an expiration date, set an owner, find out who the owner is, set the inheritance property of the node, and validate that the lock is still active.

Table continued on following page

CLASS	DESCRIPTION
LockException	The default exception class. It is thrown in cases that don't fall into the other three exception ranges.
LockTokenNotFound Exception	This exception is thrown if the token for the lock cannot be found.
ObjectIsAlready LockedException	This exception is thrown if an object is already locked.
ObjectLockedException	If an object is already locked, this exception will be thrown if a user tries to lock the object again.

Content Helper

The content helper's classes are contained in the package org.apache.slide.content. These classes provide the functionality for accessing and altering content, metadata, and revisions of nodes. Slide automatically separates different versions of content that it manages and provides mechanisms for branching and custom version control. The metadata that is associated with each content object node is maintained by Slide as well. The following table describes the classes associated with the org.apache.slide.content package.

CLASS	DESCRIPTION
Content	This is the Content interface for the helper class that will be implemented by ContentImpl.
ContentImpl	This is the implementation of the Content interface. This class enables you to create a new revision, create a branch, merge two branches, remove a revision, retrieve a revision descriptor, and store the contents of an updated revision.
NodeProperty	The NodeProperty class is all about accessing and manipulating the properties of a node. With it, you can add permissions, enumerate permissions, get the name of the namespace, set a namespace, and remove permissions.
NodeRevision Content	This class encapsulates the content of a revision and provides methods for interfacing directly with the content, such as reading the content, setting the content, validating the content, and streaming the content.
NodeRevision Descriptor	This class enables you to manipulate the metadata of a particular node.
NodeRevision Descriptors	This class enables access to all the branches and revisions that have been created and stored.
NodeRevisionNumber	This class is simply used for creating a revision version number.
BranchNotFound Exception	When trying to access a branch that does not exist, this exception will be thrown.

CLASS	DESCRIPTION
ContentException	This is a general exception for the content helper package. Any exceptions that occur that do not fit into any of the ones previously listed default to this exception.
NodeNotVersioned Exception	This exception is thrown when an error occurs during the attempt to access version information from a node that does not contain any.
RevisionAlready ExistsException	If a user tries to store the same revision, a conflict will occur and this exception will be thrown, indicating that the revision stated already exists.
RevisionContentNot FoundException	If a user tries to retrieve the revision content of a node that doesn't contain any, this exception is thrown.
RevisionDescriptor NotFoundException	If a user tries to retrieve the revision descriptor of a node that doesn't contain any, this exception is thrown.
RevisionNotFound Exception	This generic exception is thrown when a user tries to access revision data and an error occurs.

Macro Helper

The macro helper contains an assortment of classes that make complex namespace management operations easier to perform. Performing a recursive copy, move, or delete operation can be a nightmare to code; luckily, these macro helpers assist in achieving such functionality. All of the macro helper classes are contained in the org.apache.slide.macro package. The following table describes the classes contained in the package.

Class	Description
Macro	This is the Macro Interface that is implemented by MacroImpl.
MacroImpl	This class is the actual implementation of the Macro class. This class enables you to perform copies, deletes, and moves, and to perform each recursively within a given namespace.
MacroParameters	This is just a parameter class that is passed when using the macros in the MacroImpl class.
ConflictException	Anytime a conflict occurs during a macro operation, this exception is thrown. For example, if a conflict happens during a copy/move operation, this exception would be thrown.
CopyMacroException	This exception is thrown when errors occur during a copy process.
DeleteMacroException	This exception is thrown when errors occur during a delete process.
ForbiddenException	This exception is thrown when an operation is forbidden. For example, if you tried to do a copy and a move operation and specified the same location for both the original location and the destination location, this exception would be thrown.
MacroException	This is the default generic exception class of this package.

Index/Search and Process Helpers

These helpers are planned for the future and have not yet been implemented by the Slide development team.

Stores

Stores in Slide are used for saving content and metadata about objects. Low-level services can be created to extend Slide's storing capabilities. Store repositories can range from relational databases to file systems, so the need for low-level services that can handle the needs of various objects is required. All services, however, fit into two types of services: **descriptors store** and **content store**.

The **descriptors store** services are responsible for storing metadata, managing locks, storing structures, and managing security. The **content store** services are solely responsible for managing, storing, accessing, and manipulating content.

The reason to have different types of repositories is simple: Different types of content are stored. Certain repositories are better at dealing with large amounts of data, whereas others are better at creating meanings and relationships for the data. Every object defined in Slide could potentially have a different type of low-level service associated with it. Therefore, even though a namespace cannot access or reference other namespaces, it doesn't mean that the namespace cannot distribute its data across multiple content stores.

The Slide configuration file determines how the low-level services map to individual nodes. Therefore, it is up to the administrator to set up the different configurations for various objects. As with everything else in a namespace, if you do something to a parent node, it affects the child nodes. When an administrator assigns low-level services to specific nodes, the child nodes of that parent node will also be assigned to the low-level services, unless otherwise specified. Figure 5.6 illustrates the use of multiple content stores in a single namespace.

Figure 5.6 uses three different service mappings to store different content. The **/files** nodes of this example is stored in a file system. Obviously, this makes sense for the type of content—in this case, files—that is being stored. The **/actions** nodes are stored via JDBC to a relational database or system that supports JDBC connections. Finally, the **/users** nodes are stored in an LDAP server. From this diagram, you can see that only one namespace exists, but that the content is distributed among multiple data stores.

Domain

A domain can contain one or more registered namespaces. The domain controls access to the registered namespaces and performs initialization and connection management of the namespaces. There can be only one domain per Java Virtual Machine (JVM), which is maintained by the domain administrators. The domain administrators manage everything about a domain, including what namespaces are contained in the domain and how they are initialized; the creation and mapping of low-level services; the structure of the domain; and access and security.

The domain is initialized when Slide is first started. The initialization of the domain is based on a domain configuration file, which is set up by the domain administrator prior to starting Slide. The `slide.properties` file contains the path to the configuration file. The path can also be obtained via the `org.apache.slide.domain` object at runtime. The domain initialization can be called again at runtime through the static method `Domain.init,` though this is not the recommended approach.

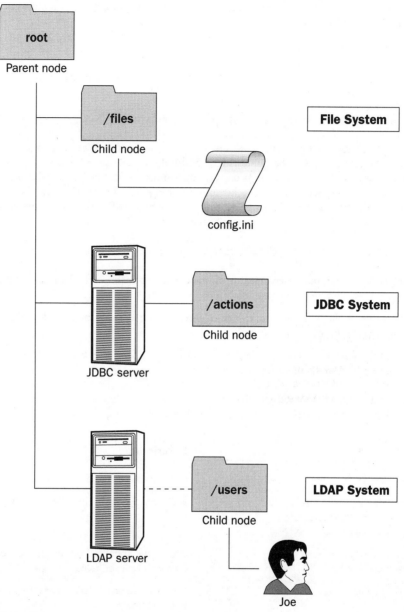

Figure 5.6

One important point not mentioned yet is that the only object you have access to when developing for Slide from a client perspective is the `Domain` object. Using the `Domain` object, you can gain access to namespace objects and retrieve information about namespaces contained in the domain. If the initialization of the domain was successful, you can use the following two methods to gain access to the domain:

❏　If the method `Domain.accessNamespace` is successful, it will grant the user access to the specified namespace, as follows:

```
Domain.accessNamespace(SecurityToken securityObject, String namespace)
```

❏　The method `Domain.accessDomain` enables the user to enumerate through the available namespaces contained in the domain, as follows:

```
Domain.accessDomain(SecurityToken securityObject)
```

All of the aspects described in previous sections, such as helper functions, transaction management, and security, come into play here. When you use the method `Domain.accessNamespace`, a security object is passed in to the method. This object is used by the domain to determine if it should grant permission to the requested namespace. Therefore, a key point to remember here is that even if a user has access to the Slide APIs, that user cannot do anything unless granted specific access to a namespace. If access is granted, the domain gives the user a `NamespaceAccessToken`.

This `NamespaceAccessToken` object serves three main purposes:

❏　It conceals the namespace object from the client application and controls the methods that are performed on the namespace.

❏　It enables a client application to obtain access to the helper functions described in-depth in previous sections of this chapter.

❏　It implements the `UserTransaction` interface, enabling clients to support, use, and control transaction management functionality.

The static `Domain` class is contained in the package `org.apache.slide.common.Domain`. The following table describes key static methods that you may find useful.

Method	Description
`accessDomain(SecurityToken token)`	Provides access to the domain
`accessNamespace(SecurityToken token, java.lang.String namespaceName)`	Provides access to the specified namespace based off the security token
`closeNamespace(NamespaceAccess Token token)`	Closes the specified namespace based on the `NamespaceAccessToken`
`enumerateNamespaces`	Provides an enumeration of namespaces contained in the domain
`getDefaultNamespace`	Returns a string representation of the default namespace for this domain
`getDomainFileName`	Returns the configuration filename that the administrator can use to configure the domain
`log(java.lang.Object data, int level)`	A log method for inserting information into the domain's log file

Slide API Layer

The final component of the Slide architecture is a component that should already be familiar to you from previous discussions. The Slide API layer (SLAPIL) is intertwined throughout the external, internal, transactional, domain, and namespace architecture components. The SLAPIL mainly consists of the seven helper classes described in the section "Slide Architecture."

Another important API layer to mention is the WebDAV API layer, which Slide integrates into its architecture. The APIs for the WebDAV library are located in the package `org.apache.Webdav.lib`. Slide also integrates a WebDAV administration tool for configuring and administrating WebDAV capabilities. The integration of WebDAV enables clients to access Slide remotely using its protocol. You learn more about WebDAV and how to use it in the "WebDAV and Slide" section of this chapter.

Setting Up and Configuring Slide

This section explains the necessary steps involved in getting Slide up and running on your machine. It focuses on setting up Slide on a Windows system, but also addresses a few Unix configuration specifics where appropriate. For the most part, both types of configurations should be extremely similar, as Slide is written in Java.

Installing and Running Slide

You can download two types of installation files from the Slide Web site: the **source file bundle** and the **binary file bundle**. The authors recommend downloading both and extracting each bundle to the same directory, starting with the source bundle first and then extracting the binary bundle. If you download both bundles, you won't have to worry about compiling the source files if you chose to download only the source bundle. On the flip side, if you just download the binary files, you will not be able to inspect the Slide source files. Having the code and the binary files helps you understand the architecture of the system and enables you to dig into certain components and see what they are doing under the hood.

Once you have extracted the bundles, Slide is actually ready to go. Of course, you will need to perform specific configurations in order to use certain features of Slide (such as the administration portion and WebDAV portion), but to get an initial look at Slide, it will run as is upon extraction. The first step to perform before configuring or running anything is to set up an environmental variable called SLIDE_HOME. Set the SLIDE_HOME variable to point to the base installation directory into which you installed Slide — for example, SLIDE_HOME = D:\jakarta\jakarta-slide-1.0.16.

This is not a requirement of Slide, but rather a convenience factor when accessing different directories from Slide's home directory.

In order to run the Slide standalone server, you need to bring up a console window and change directory to the SLIDE_HOME\server directory. From here, depending on whether you are on Windows or Unix, you would issue one of the following commands:

- ❑ **Windows**: bin\startup
- ❑ **Unix**: ./bin/startup.sh

Once the server has started up, all you have to do now is bring up a Web browser and enter **http://localhost:8080** to view the Slide welcome page. In addition to the configuration options described in this section, the welcome page contains additional information about how to configure Slide appropriately. Figure 5.7 shows the Slide welcome page.

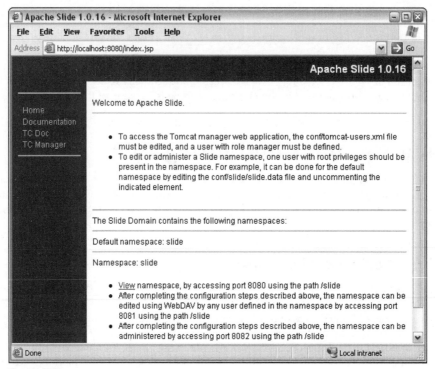

Figure 5.7

If you were able to bring up the Slide welcome screen, then everything is configured correctly up to this point. Let's proceed to apply the configurations suggested on the welcome screen.

Tomcat Manager

The Tomcat Manager enables you to manage the Web applications running on your server. In order to gain access to the Tomcat Manager, you need to set up a Tomcat user in the `tomcat-users.xml` file. The file is located in your `SLIDE_HOME/server/conf/` directory. In order to edit the file, you need to open the file in your favorite text editor. The contents of the file will look similar to the following:

```
<tomcat-users>
   <user name="tomcat" password="tomcat" roles="tomcat" />
   <user name="role1"  password="tomcat" roles="role1"  />
   <user name="both"   password="tomcat" roles="tomcat,role1" />
</tomcat-users>
```

You now need to insert a new user who is part of the manager role. You should also grant this user access to the root role for now. It will be used later when you try to access other components of Slide. Therefore, add the following line, but feel free to use your own user name and password:

```
<user name="jvitale" password="password" roles="manager,root" />
```

In order for the changes to take effect, you need to restart the standalone server. This can be accomplished from a console window by changing to the SLIDE_HOME\server directory and then executing the next two steps:

1. At the console window, execute the shutdown shell command. If you are on Windows, it is **bin\shutdown.** On Unix, use **./bin/shutdown.sh.**

2. Once the server has shut down, simply restart it with the aforementioned startup commands:

- ❑ **Windows:** bin\startup
- ❑ **Unix:** ./bin/startup.sh

When the server has finished executing, you can navigate back to the Slide welcome screen and click the TC Manager link on the left side. It will instruct you for a user name and a password. Enter the user name and password that you set up for the manager and click OK. This brings up the Tomcat Manager screen, as shown in Figure 5.8. This screen enables you to add and remove Web applications to your virtual host on the fly.

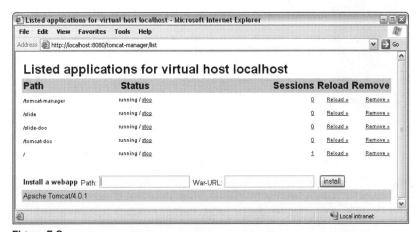

Figure 5.8

The final configuration step we must perform before we can move on is to edit the SLIDE_HOME/conf/slide/slide.data file. It contains a section that is commented out that needs to be uncommented and configured to grant a user root privileges in order to edit or administer a Slide namespace. Therefore, bring the file up in your favorite text editor. Locate the section that is commented out containing the following data:

```
<objectnode etc.>
    <revision>
      <property name="password"
namespace="http://jakarta.apache.org/slide/">password</property>
    </revision>
</objectnode>
```

The key to configuring this correctly is to uncomment the revision element and supply a password. Once this step is completed, you need to restart the server again. Then, you should be able to access the Slide Administration tool via the following URL: http://localhost:8082/slide

You will be required to enter a user name and password. The password should be the password that was just entered in the revision section, and the user name is the same user name that was used to configure the Tomcat Manager. The screenshot in Figure 5.9 shows the Slide Administration tool in action.

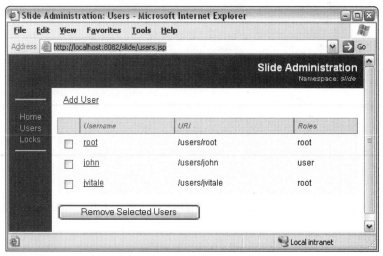

Figure 5.9

Congratulations! All of the user configuration and initial configurations are complete. You should now have access to all of the components contained in Slide, including the WebDAV components, which are covered in the section "WebDAV and Slide."

The Slide Server

The Slide server is a fully functional content management system that includes an embedded Tomcat 4.0.1 server. You don't have to download any extra components or integrate Slide with any servers in order to have a fully integrated content management system. It is all included in the Slide binary bundle for you. The server is started and configured the same way that a normal Tomcat server is. A few additional directory structures are added by Slide, but for the most part, the Tomcat server functions the same as any Tomcat server would function. For more specific information about Tomcat, please see their documentation, which is located on the Jakarta Web site at http://jakarta.apache.org/tomcat.

The Slide-specific files that need to be managed are the Slide domain file, called `slide.xml`, which resides in the `SLIDE_HOME/server/conf` directory, and the `Domain.xml` file, which resides in a Web application. The Slide server also has three main concentration points, called **views**. These views are referred to as the client view, the editor view, and the admin view. Each view serves a separate purpose and may reside on a different port.

Client View

The client view is accessed via the default Tomcat port, which is generally 8080. The client view is simply the normal Tomcat environment without virtual hosting. Instead, Slide manages the virtual hosting of different Web applications added to the Slide domain itself. When a new namespace is defined in the Slide domain, a Web application context will automatically be created for the servlet container.

Standard Java Web applications should work fine without any added configuration as long as they don't access the files contained in the Web application using direct file system access. In order for Web applications to avoid using direct file system access to manipulate their files, all they have to do is replace their file system calls with `ServletContext.getResource` methods. This call uses a conceptual file system access model.

Admin View

There are currently two admin views. One is the Tomcat Manager described earlier in the chapter. It requires that a user who is in the "manager" role be created in the `conf/tomcat-users.xml` file. It resides on port 8080 and enables an administrator to start, stop, and reload views, contexts, and active sessions. The other admin view resides on port 8082 and is actually shown in Figure 5.9. This is a Slide Web application that is a work in progress and will eventually enable administrators to manage all aspects of their specific namespaces.

Editor View

The editor view can be accessed via the 8081 port, which is used mainly for WebDAV access. Users that log in to the editor view can access, edit, and view content only if they are granted access based on their permissions. The root user must have a password set in the `Domain.xml` file in order for the root user to be successfully authenticated.

All clients that support the WebDAV protocol can be used to manage content. This includes the client that comes with Slide. It is a command-based tool but will provide a free tool for becoming familiar with the WebDAV protocol and Slide.

WebDAV and Slide

Slide supports Web-based Distributed Authoring and Versioning (WebDAV) capabilities, which are implemented via a servlet. WebDAV is a very popular protocol that is an extension of the HTTP protocol. It is used for editing and managing Web-based content on remote Web servers. It is also an Internet Engineering Task Force (IETF) standard and is supported by many popular software companies, including Microsoft, IBM, and Novell. For further reading on the WebDAV protocol, check out the WebDAV resource page located at www.webdav.org.

Slide's WebDAV servlet resides on port 8081 and can be accessed by any client that supports the WebDAV protocol. Windows contains Web folders that offer built-in support for the WebDAV protocol. The following section demonstrates how to use Window's WebDAV support to manage content in the Slide server.

Windows XP WebDAV Example

In Windows XP, we need to use the **map a network drive utility**, which is located on the Tools menu in Windows Explorer, in order to show the WebDAV capabilities of Slide. Figure 5.10 shows the Map Network Drive screen.

Figure 5.10

From the Map Network Drive screen, choose the link titled "Sign up for online storage or connect to a network server." Proceed through the wizard until you come to a screen that asks where you want to create this network place. Make sure that you select "Choose another network location. Specify the address of a Web site, network location or FTP site."

After the preceding steps have been executed, the screen in Figure 5.11 will appear, asking you for an address of the network place to which you wish to connect. In the text field provided, type in the address of the Slide server and specify the WebDAV port, which by default is 8081.

Once you enter the address, click Next to proceed to the next screen. Windows will try to connect to the Slide WebDAV servlet at this point. If an error occurs, verify that the address specified is correct and that a valid root user exists. The steps for setting up a root user are covered in the "Tomcat Manager" section of this chapter. You can also log into the WebDAV servlet area through a Web browser to test connectivity. You won't be able to edit any of the content, but you can see the node structure. To test the WebDAV servlet, point your browser to http://localhost:8081/slide and log in. If the login fails, then you know that the issues you are having are related to user permissions.

If you were able to successfully log in to the WebDAV servlet, the screen shown in Figure 5.12 will be displayed, asking you to specify a name for your new network place. The name doesn't matter; you can specify any name you wish.

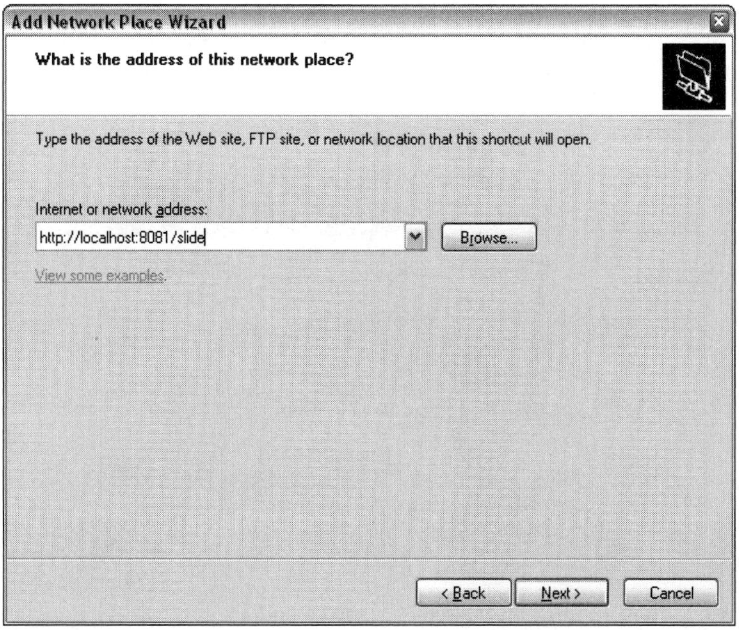

Figure 5.11

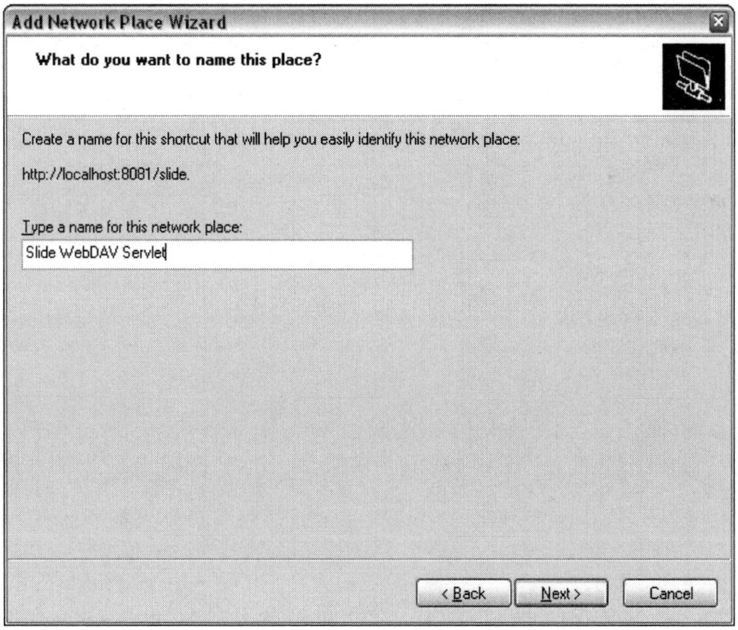

Figure 5.12

After you name your network place and click Next, you will be prompted to log in again to the server. Use the same user name and password as you did before. The login screen is displayed in Figure 5.13; notice how the name of the server is Slide DAV Server. This is the correct server to which you want to connect.

Figure 5.13

When you finish logging into the Slide WebDAV server and are successful, you will be immediately shown a screen that contains the root nodes of the default namespace you are logged into. In this case, the default namespace is Slide. Figure 5.14 shows the root nodes that should be displayed to you now.

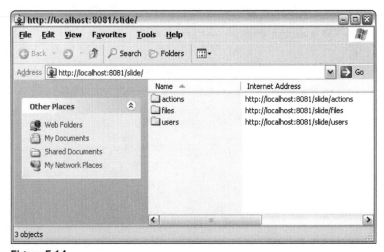

Figure 5.14

Listed are the root nodes: /actions, /files, /users. If you want to add a file to the /files section, you can perform standard Windows Explorer commands to accomplish the task, even drag and drop will work. If you want to see what kind of actions have been established in this namespace, you can change to the /actions section and see a list of action nodes, as shown in Figure 5.15.

In this case, three action nodes have been implemented. From this example, you can see how simple it is to use WebDAV to manage the content in the content management system, as well as how sophisticated

WebDAV technology is. Using Slide as your content management system provides you with access to a wealth of tools that should more than fit your needs, and whatever is lacking you can always create yourself.

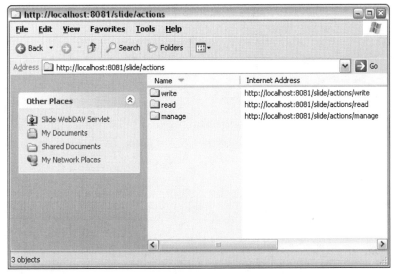

Figure 5.15

Summary

Jakarta's Slide is a powerful open-source content management and integration system that provides the developer with a rich framework to create their own sophisticated content management systems.

In this chapter, you have seen the power of the Slide architecture, consisting of numerous components and APIs called helpers, which enable client applications to access the most intricate parts of the content management system, thus providing the ultimate in flexibility.

Slide's use of domains and namespaces provides intense security, right down to the node level. Not only can Slide manage binary content that exists on the namespace's server, it can also manage content that is distributed in multiple data stores across different locations.

Slide provides a useful Web-based interface for managing namespaces, users, Web applications, and security. However, Slide really excels through its support of the Web-based Distributed Authoring and Versioning (WebDAV) protocol.

Slide's flexibility, scalability, and attention to security make it a great choice as a content management system, especially where Web applications are needed. Therefore, it fits perfectly into the scope of a Java Portal system.

The next chapter focuses on Portal security and its associated technologies.

6

Portal Security

Over the past few years, an increasing number of companies have been creating portals to allow their partners, customers, and employees access to critical and sensitive information. Most portal developers have faced incredible security challenges in this regard. Many vendors have created proprietary "stove-piped" solutions for some of the security requirements, tying developers to a particular product. This often works well until the product doesn't work, the software is no longer supported, or you need to rescale your architecture. If you are a developer who has been in that boat, we feel your pain because we've been there. How can portal developers meet their security challenges with a standards-based, open-source security solution? This chapter answers that question — first by introducing you to essential security concepts, and then by showing you standards, open-source tools, and techniques that you can use to secure your portal solution.

Core Security Concepts

In order to appropriately discuss security issues, concerns, and solutions in the scope of portal development, it is necessary to define a few terms: **authentication, authorization, Single Sign-On (SSO), confidentiality, integrity,** and **non-repudiation**. Because you can find entire texts dedicated to these concepts, this section provides only a simple introduction, focusing on the scope of what the portal developer and designer need to know. The terms defined in this section are important for your understanding of achieving the security goals of your portal when you read the implementation section in the middle of the chapter, "Building Security Solutions for Your Portal."

Authentication

Authentication is the first step in providing access control, and it involves validating the identity of a user. In a portal environment, authentication may be achieved via user name/password login, validation of a user's client certificate, or identity validation with a smart card or biometric device.

Developing a solution for authentication usually means providing a repository for validating these identities and integrating it with your system. **Mutual authentication** means proving the identity of both parties involved in communication, and this is done using special security protocols, such as SSL/TLS. **Message origin authentication** is used to ensure that the message was sent by the expected sender, and that it was not replayed.

In the implementation section, this chapter focuses on how to provide authentication services in your portal. Authentication at the portal level is one of the most important aspects to providing security—it will dictate how your application interacts with other enterprise applications and Web services.

Authorization

Once a user's identity is validated, it is important to know what the user has permission to do. The separation of access control into two distinct mechanisms, authentication and authorization, enables a logical separation of first validating identity, and then validating what resources that identity has access to consume or produce. Authorization determines a user's permissions, roles, or other credentials that are used to provide access to certain services that your portal provides. Role-Based Access Control (RBAC) is an important access control strategy, especially because the capability is prevalent in J2EE architectures. Because it has become a key focus of the security of portal development, it is a primary focus of this chapter.

Extensive use of RBAC as a successful framework for the management of authorization credentials exists in many commercial Web-based systems, relational databases, and portals. A key component of RBAC is to map roles to permissions, and to map users to roles, as shown in Figure 6.1. In RBAC, access to resources is controlled by security roles, which is very helpful for authorization management.

Figure 6.1 also shows views of some of the traditional access control authorization mechanisms—using Access Control Lists (ACLs). In the past, large and complex ACLs mapped users to permissions, and restricted access to resources by permissions and users. Abstracting the user—and the resources—from low-level permissions is very helpful in authorization management. Because the number of permissions is usually extremely high, keeping access control lists for discretionary access in an ever-changing environment can be difficult with subject-to-object mappings. Instead, mapping these permissions to never-changing roles can happen at one time, and users can be assigned and unassigned to these roles throughout the lifetime of the individual in that organization. This makes the management of access control easier.

What is the most difficult part of setting up a role-based access control system? An organization must define its roles based on the business process, not just the organization chart. The technical part of the solution is usually the easiest part. The schema must be flexible, and it must be able to withstand the rigors of reorganization. NIST's "Introduction to Role-Based Access Control" provides a good explanation: "With role-based access control, access decisions are based on the roles that individual users have as part of an organization. Users take on assigned roles (such as doctor, nurse, teller, manager). The process of defining roles should be based on a thorough analysis of how an organization operates and should include input from a wide spectrum of users in an organization." [NIST]

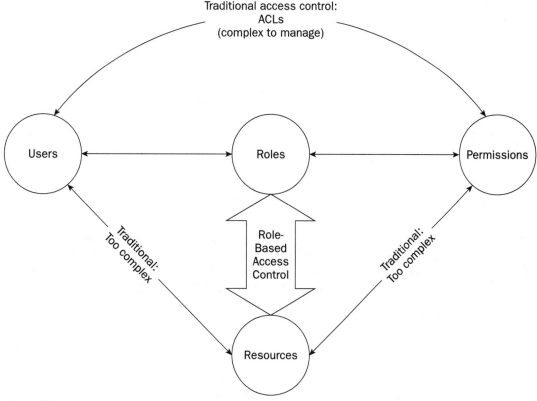

Figure 6.1

The role-definition process is very important. However, as this book is geared toward programmers and developers, we will leave that part to the process people; later, this chapter delves into how you can set up role-based access for your portal. For more information on RBAC and role management, we invite you to visit http://csrc.nist.gov/rbac/.

Single Sign-On (SSO)

Single Sign-On (SSO) is a popular feature. This useful functionality enables the user to authenticate only once to his or her client, so that the user does not have to memorize many user names and passwords for other Web sites, Web services, and server applications. In a portal scenario, it is important to realize that portlets, shared between many portals, may communicate with enterprise applications that have identity and authorization security constraints. Furthermore, beyond the portal, Web services may be distributed, and may talk to other Web services, which may need the original user's credentials. Figure 6.2 shows the dilemma that we face as we attempt to create Single Sign-On solutions.

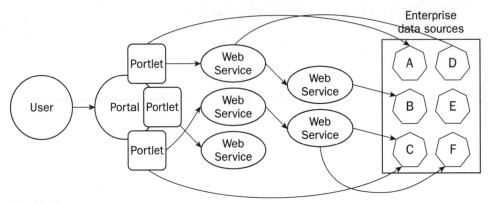

Figure 6.2

Looking at Figure 6.2, note the numerous challenges. The user initially authenticates to the portal, and the portal determines the user's authorization credentials, but the portal contains portlets that communicate with Web services. To make the situation more complex, these Web services may communicate with other Web services, which communicate with back-end databases and enterprise applications. Because of all of the points between the user and the eventual back-end data source, we face considerable security challenges. In looking at Figure 6.2, consider the following questions:

❑ How do the eventual data sources (A–F) have assurance that the user actually authenticated, or what the user's roles are?

❑ If the data sources A–F and the Web services in the diagram use different authentication mechanisms and data stores, how can that be handled in a portal solution?

❑ If the data sources A–F and the Web services in the diagram have different user names and passwords for each user, how can we provide authentication without forcing the user to "log in" six times? For example, what if user "Kevin Smith" has many user names and passwords, in addition to a personal digital certificate? For data source A, he may be required to use "kevintsmith," and for the others, he might be required to use user names "ksmith04," "kevinsmith," ksmith," and "ktsmith." This is a common dilemma that portal designers face.

These questions are valid concerns that you should keep in mind, because you, as an enterprise architect, may be required to answer them. Once the user has authenticated and the authorization credentials have been validated by the portal, technology **enablers** are used to pass these credentials throughout the life cycle of the message, regardless of how many points and nodes are involved between the portal and the eventual data source. This concept is usually referred to as **deep authentication**, because authentication credentials are passed from the portal to the portlets to the back-end Web services and data sources. [SMITHK] Several architectural solutions can provide this functionality in a standard way. You can find many technology enablers for SSO, including Kerberos, SAML (Secure Assertion Markup Language), and other cryptographic protocols. The implementation section focuses on some of these solutions and how you might build such a solution when you build your portal.

Confidentiality

When sensitive information is transmitted, it is important to keep it secret. Confidentiality is the security goal for hiding sensitive information, and we can provide confidentiality solutions with **encryption**. With encryption, a plaintext message is jumbled with a cryptographic algorithm to produce a ciphertext message. Using a key (or shared secret), the intended recipient can decrypt the data. Many different cryptographic algorithms, symmetric (secret-key) algorithms, and asymmetric (public key) algorithms can be used to provide different levels of protection for your data. In creating a solution to satisfy confidentiality requirements, many things need to be considered — key management for distributing keys, ciphers to use, and cryptographic protocols that provide these services.

Many higher-level protocols, such as Secure Sockets Layer (SSL) and its later version, Transport Layer Security (TLS), provide bulk encryption between two points. In these higher-level protocols, the cipher is determined, and key negotiation is achieved, at the beginning of the protocol, in order to establish a "shared secret" that both sides can understand. It is important to understand that SSL is a point-to-point protocol, and can be used for mutual or one-way authentication between two points only. In environments with a simple client and server, such a session may be enough to protect the confidentiality of the data in the transmission. Although SSL does well at protecting data between two points, its benefits fall short when protecting transmissions connecting multiple points, such as the scenario shown in Figure 6.2. Although SSL and TLS resolve one piece of the security puzzle, other technologies may be required to meet the security goals of Web services, depending on your requirements.

Luckily, as a portal developer, you probably won't have to worry about the low-level details of cryptography. You will have to provide it, and know how to satisfy your confidentiality requirements with known open-source tools. Referring back to Figure 6.2, we are still faced with another challenge. Because there may be a distance (many nodes) between your portal and your eventual data source, you will have to ask yourself (and your customers) the following questions:

- ❑ **Is there a requirement for encryption at all?** If there are no confidentiality requirements, don't worry about it. Note that there is a trade-off between encryption operations and speed of performance. If you have a confidentiality requirement, the portal should be able to accommodate the requirements of confidentiality, but the portal architect should realize that the cryptographic mechanisms involved will have an impact on performance

- ❑ **Does encryption between the user and the portal satisfy the requirements?** If so, a simple SSL/TLS connection between the user and the portal may suffice. If that doesn't satisfy the requirements, does there need to be bulk encryption between the user, the portal, and all of the Web services, nodes, and enterprise applications in the solution? If so, the solution becomes a bit more difficult.

- ❑ **Does the encryption need to be directly between the portal and the eventual data source, even though other Web services pass that information along?** That is, do you need to keep some data a "secret" from the Web services? If so, you will need a shared secret between the portal and the eventual data source, and not just bulk encryption between the nodes. XML Encryption, a W3C standard, is quite useful for this purpose.

The implementation section of this chapter describes solutions for some of these challenges. Key enabling technologies and standards that help provide confidentiality solutions are XML Encryption, SSL/TLS, XKMS, and OASIS Web Services Security (WSS).

Data Integrity

In a network, it is important to ensure that data is not altered in transit. Validating a message's integrity means using techniques that prove that data has not been altered in transit. Because it is possible that message injection, IP spoofing, and packet tampering can occur on TCP/IP networks, many applications may require the use of digital signatures, MAC (Message Authentication Codes), or hash algorithms to validate the integrity of the data.

A portal architecture presents integrity challenges between the user and the portal, as well as between the portal, the Web services, and the eventual enterprise data sources. Based on your requirements, SSL/TLS may provide the necessary message integrity between the user and the portal. When there is the requirement that the body of SOAP messages passed to Web services have built-in integrity checks, other standards can be used to achieve integrity. XML Signature, a W3C standard, provides message integrity in addition to non-repudiation (discussed in the next section). The OASIS Web Services Security specification provides mechanisms that achieve such a solution for Web services. The implementation section of this chapter describes solutions and tools for achieving integrity.

Non-repudiation

Non-repudiation is the side effect of digitally signing a message, and it is a security service that can be used in legally proving that a user has performed a transaction or sent a message. In many business-to-business (B2B) systems whereby thousands of expensive transactions take place, non-repudiation is often an essential requirement. Because digital signatures are based on public key cryptography, the sender of the signed message cannot successfully *repudiate* the fact that he signed the message—it can be mathematically proven by a third party that the sender indeed signed the message with his or her private key.

Although we often discuss non-repudiation in the context of a user signing something, the discussion can be tied to an enterprise with portals, applications, and Web services. A portal may sign a portion of its message to a Web service, and a Web service may sign a portion of its messages. A side effect of digitally signing a document is also **integrity**. Because the signed message is actually the signature of the hash of the message used for proving integrity, many simply view non-repudiation as very strong integrity. XML Signature is a W3C standard used for providing non-repudiation, and is used in other standards, such as the WS-Security standard. The following section describes such standards.

Key Security Standards

The following security standards are playing—and will continue to play—a significant role in the development of portals. This section provides a very brief overview of what you, as a portal developer, need to know.

SSL and TLS

SSL stands for Secure Sockets Layer, and TLS stands for Transport Layer Security. SSL was created by Netscape, and it was enhanced by the IETF (Internet Engineering Task Force) in 1996 to become TLS. As a result, they are similar, and the terms are still used interchangeably. Both are higher-level cryptographic protocols that are used to achieve confidentiality and data integrity between two points. Optionally, they can be used for mutual authentication when both parties have digital certificates. Because TLS is based on SSL, they are very similar. There are subtle differences between the two protocols, but they will not interoperate. Frankly, the non-cryptographer layperson usually interchanges the two because they achieve the same goal. For the purposes of this book, we simply refer to both protocols as SSL. People refer to using SSL with HTTP as **HTTPS Sessions,** a process providing confidential Web transmissions. From a portal developer's perspective, an SSL session can protect confidentiality and data integrity between the user and the portal, and between the portal and its next layer of communication. This is usually a server configuration issue, the details of which are discussed in the section "Building Security Solutions for Your Portal."

XML Encryption

XML Encryption is a W3C standard that handles XML documents and XML element-level confidentiality — it can be used to encrypt elements of an XML document. XML encryption can be used with key exchange algorithms and public key encryption to encrypt documents (and elements of XML documents) to different parties. Unlike SSL, a point-to-point protocol that is decrypted at each point, XML encryption can be used in solutions where there are multiple network nodes between the portal and the end data source. Apache's XML Security package, Verisign's open-source TSIK (Trust Services Integration Kit) package, as well as many others provide XML Encryption functionality.

XML Signature

XML Signature is a W3C standard that provides a way to prove message integrity and non-repudiation of XML documents and elements of XML document. Any part of an XML document can be digitally signed — becoming self-validating when the document recipient has the signer's public key. XML Signature, sometimes called XML-DSIG or XML-SIG, relies on public key technology in which the hash (or message digest) of a message is cryptographically signed — thus providing both integrity and non-refutable proof (non-repudiation) that the signer indeed signed the elements. In situations where portals need to communicate with Web services, XML Signature plays an important role. Because a signed document can be self-validating, credentials of the end user can be passed on in SOAP messages beyond the portal. Apache's XML Security package, Verisign's open-source TSIK (Trust Services Integration Kit) package, as well as many others, provide XML signature capability.

SAML

SAML, the Security Assertion Markup Language, is an OASIS standard that is used for passing authentication and authorization information between parties, and it is one of the building blocks for Single Sign-On (SSO). In a portal environment, a portal can *assert* that it authenticated a user, and that the user has certain security credentials. A SAML assertion can be digitally signed using XML Signature. Because signed SAML can travel between platforms and organizations, regardless of how many points it crosses, it has the potential to solve significant challenges in Web services security. [SMITHK] In Figure 6.3, for example, if the portal authenticates the user "Alice" and knows that Alice has the "Power Users" security role for RBAC, has access to the "Master Portlet," and can access the "M2" data source, the portal application can create a SAML assertion, sign it, and pass it on. Because SAML can be signed with XML Signature, it is self-validating: Anyone trusting the signer will trust the credential.

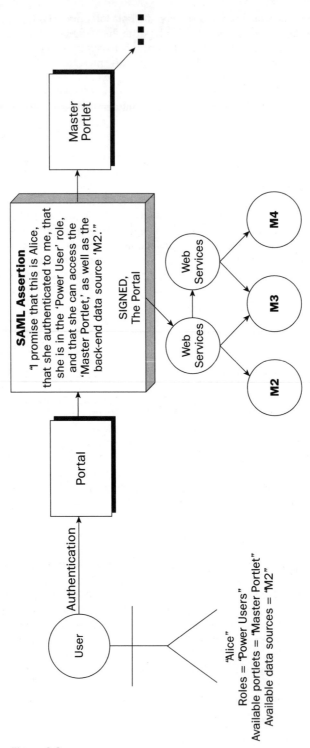

Figure 6.3

SAML is an important standard, and many open-source toolkits are available, including those by vendors Netegrity and Verisign, as well as the open-source project OpenSAML. JSR 155, entitled "Web Services Security Assertions," will provide the standard Java API for SAML assertions.

OASIS Web Services Security (WSS)

Web Services Security is in the standards process at OASIS, and is managed by the OASIS Web Services Security Technical Committee. The specification will, without a doubt, play a key role in the security of Web services. Relying on the well-accepted standards of SOAP, XML Encryption and XML Signature, the specification was released in April 2002 by Microsoft, IBM, and Verisign as "WS-Security," and is a specification that describes enhancements to SOAP-based Web services to provide protection through integrity, confidentiality, and message authentication. The OASIS Web Services Security Technical Committee has released three specifications: "Web Services Security: SOAP Message Security," "Web Services Security: Username Token Profile," and "Web Services Security: X.509 Token Profile." Together, these specifications provide a rich framework and a high-level security standard that will work with Web services. WSS will certainly play a role in portal development when portals communicate with Web services. The development of WSS continues, including work involving SAML. Over the next year, many implementations of WSS will be available for use when building security solutions for Web Services.

Building Security Solutions for Your Portal

Now that you are familiar with the security vocabulary, it is time to describe how to build security services into your portal. This section explains the basic security services that were defined in the preceding sections, and will help you understand how to easily achieve them as your security requirements dictate.

Figure 6.4 shows a diagram of the portal-centric enterprise. Note the five main areas: a core enterprise infrastructure, the Web container, the portal, Web services, and enterprise applications. The portal itself is composed of a portlet container, which manages a number of portlets and adheres to the Java Portlet Specification (JSR 168). This portlet container leverages the security services of your Servlet 2.3–compliant Web container (that is, a Web server), which provides security services. Much of the security of the Web container depends on the security infrastructure of your enterprise, which is the infrastructure portion of Figure 6.4. Finally, the portlets of your portal communicate with Web services, which talk to enterprise applications.

The significance of Figure 6.4 is that the security of each area has dependencies: Just as the security of the Web container on which your portal relies depends on the security infrastructure of your enterprise, so will the security of your enterprise applications depend on the security of your Web services. Because you, as a portal designer and developer, will have to focus on configuring the Web container, the portlet container, and communicating back-end enterprise applications, the following sections provide instructions and guidelines for securing those aspects.

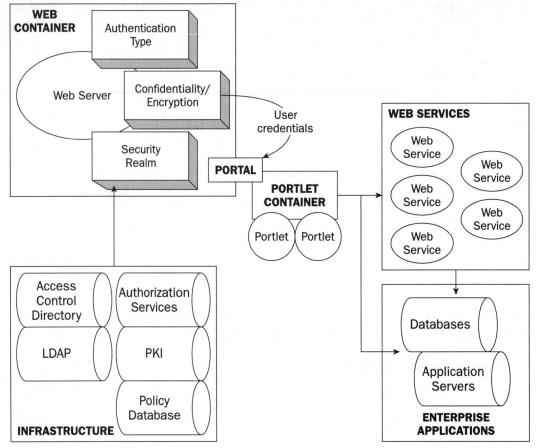

Figure 6.4

Web Container Security — Apache Tomcat

As the engine of your portal will be your Web server, many security services are provided by your Web container. With the emergence of the Servlet 2.3 specification in late 2000, the concept of **container-managed security** became a powerful means to delegate responsibility of access control and authorization to the Web server in a standard way. The Servlet 2.3 specification enables the portal designer to specify many security mechanisms in a Web application's deployment descriptor, and also enables the application, written in JSPs or servlets, to access security information pertaining to users and roles in a standard way. The Apache Tomcat Web container became one of the first Web servers to use the security mechanisms of the Servlet 2.3 specification, using **security realms**. Based on the Servlet specification, the Web container can provide the security services of authentication and authorization, as well as data integrity and confidentiality between the user and the portal.

Container-managed security is an important concept for portal developers to understand. The Java Portlet Specification 1.0 relies on the security of the container, and states that "the portal should leverage the authentication mechanisms provided by the underlying servlet container." [JSR168] The section "Security of the Portlet Container" addresses some of these issues.

For now, this section presents a high-level but fairly detailed view of some of the security features of Apache Tomcat. Much of the discussion of the configuration of Tomcat and development using these security features can be applied to any Servlet 2.3–compatible Web container. Here, we discuss **server configuration,** where much of your security can be dictated at server configuration time, **Web application configuration,** where security can be dictated at application configuration time, and **programmatic security,** where security can be dictated at compile time with JSPs and servlets. For additional information, you can consult the Tomcat documentation at http://jakarta.apache.org/tomcat/.

Server Configuration

Many security features in Apache Tomcat can be configured in your server's `server.xml` file, located in the `conf` directory of your Tomcat distribution. By modifying this file, you can specify your own access control directory by using security realms; set up encryption HTTP sessions (HTTPS) with SSL/TLS to achieve confidentiality; and log events at granular levels. The next two sections focus on two very important features that can be configured: security realms and SSL.

Security Realms

In the section "Core Security Concepts," we briefly defined and discussed authentication and authorization. In Tomcat (and other Servlet 2.3 and later standard containers), these can be achieved by using a **security realm.** The Apache Tomcat project defines a realm as "a 'database' of usernames and passwords that identify valid users of a Web application (or set of Web applications), plus an enumeration of the list of **roles** associated with each valid user." [REALMHOWTO] The Web container can control access to resources via roles to achieve RBAC, and given the realm configuration, users can have any number of roles associated with their user name.

Using realms, the mapping of users to roles and the collection of passwords associated with a user is done outside of the Web server — usually in a database or an LDAP directory server. Tomcat defines a Java interface (`org.apache.catalina.Realm`) to provide this connection. Java developers may implement this interface to create their own realm, or you can simply configure your Web server to use the available realms. Three primary types are used in production: a DataSource realm, a JDBC realm, and a JNDI realm. A DataSource realm accesses its information from a relational database using a JNDI DataSource, a JDBC realm accesses its information from a relational database using a JDBC connection, and a JNDI realm accesses its information from an LDAP directory server, using a JNDI connection. Tomcat additionally provides a MemoryRealm, which simply uses a local XML file for authentication and authorization credentials. Given the realm configuration, the Web server can authenticate users and authorize users into specific pages, or dynamic content, based on their role or their identity. Using this standard mechanism for container-managed security, the Web application developer can determine the user's identity and the user's security role, and can, based on application configuration, control with any given granularity what the user can access or do.

> It is possible to test your system by using a MemoryRealm in Tomcat, controlled by an XML file of users and roles, but it is not recommended for production use. In using that solution, all of your user information is loaded into memory. If you have numerous users, this puts an intensive load on your system. Moreover, in order to change user-role mappings and add users, you will have to either restart your Web server or somehow force a reload of the file. You're better off with a database or directory-based realm when you go into production.

Setting up such a realm is only a configuration task, and configuration is easy and flexible, depending on your needs. In Tomcat, the `<Realm>` XML tag of your server's main configuration file controls how your Web container gets those credentials. This tag can be contained by three possible elements in your server's configuration file: the <Engine> element, the <Host> element, and the <Context> element. Most of the time, your realm is contained by the <Engine> element; and in this case it is shared across all of the applications of your Web server unless it is overridden by another <Realm> element in a subordinate <Host> or <Context> element. If it is inside a <Host> element, it is shared across all Web applications for that virtual host. If it is placed inside a <Context> element, the realm will be used only for that particular Web application. The following code illustrates examples of the <Realm> tag in action with Apache Tomcat — two examples that use a MySQL database for authentication and authorization, and an example in which an LDAP database is used for authentication and authorization.

```xml
<!--
    These are three examples of how the <Realm> tag in Apache Tomcat
    May be configured to provide authentication and authorization.
-->

<!-- 1) Example of how a simple MySQL Database Realm can be
     Configured
-->
<Realm   className="org.apache.catalina.realm.JDBCRealm"
         debug="99"
         driverName="org.gjt.mm.mysql.Driver"
         connectionURL="jdbc:mysql://foo.com/authority?user=t;password=t"
         userTable="users" userNameCol="user_name"
         userCredCol="user_pass"
         userRoleTable="user_roles" roleNameCol="role_name" />
<!-- 2) The same database, configured as a DataSource -->
<Realm className="org.apache.catalina.realm.DataSourceRealm"
         datasourceName="java:/comp/env/jdbc/realmdb"
         userTable="users" userNameCol="user_name"
         userCredCol="user_pass"
         userRoleTable="user_roles" roleNameCol="role_name" />
<!-- 3) Example of how a JNDI Realm can Be Configured -->
         <Realm className="org.apache.catalina.realm.JNDIRealm"
                debug="99"
                connectionName="cn=Directory Manager"
                connectionPassword="Isabella_was_born_during_edits"
                connectionURL="ldap://maloryfox.trumantruck.com:389"
                digest="MD5"
                roleBase="dc=roles,dc=trumantruck,dc=com"
                roleName="cn"
                roleSearch="(uniqueMember={0})"
                roleSubtree="false"
                userPassword="userPassword"
                userPattern="cn={0},dc=trumantruck,dc=com"/>
```

The first realm example in the preceding code uses a MySQL database server as a JDBC realm as part of the infrastructure for identification and authorization of users. Setting the driverName, connectionURL, userTable, userCredCol, userRoleTable, and roleNameCol attributes configures the server to authenticate a user. The second example shows the same database used by the Web server as a DataSource realm, passing in the JNDI name of the DataSource in the datasourceName attribute, and using the appropriate org.apache.catalina.realm.DataSourceRealm class. Finally, the third example shows an example of configuring a JNDI realm to use an iPlanet Directory Server for authentication and authorization. In that example, the attributes connectionName, connectionPassword, `connectionURL, digest, roleBase, roleName, roleSearch, roleSubtree, userPassword,` and `userPattern` specify the connection details.

Because the documentation on Tomcat Realms is excellent, and because we do not want to regurgitate the "REALM HOWTO" document provided with Tomcat, we will only provide a detailed example of setting up a JDBC database realm, and give you an example of creating your own security realm when necessary. The following table lists the available attributes for the JDBC realm type. Certain attributes, such as `connectionName` and `connectionPassword`, are used only if you need to authenticate to your database to get to the credentials.

Hint: If you are going to the trouble to set up an access control database, you probably want to password-protect it!

Attribute	Description	Required?
className	The name of the class to use. JDBC realms must use apache.`catalina`. realm.JDBCRealm	Yes
connectionName	The database user name used to connect to the database to get credential information	If connection requires a password
connectionPassword	The database password used to connect to the database to get credential information	If connection requires a password
connectionURL	The JDBC URL	Yes
debug	Level of debugging (0..99) used to write to the associated Tomcat Logger. The higher the number, the greater amount of logging information written to file.	No
digest	The digest algorithm used to store passwords in digested formats for this data source. This is a popular method of password storage, and an alternative to storing your passwords in the clear. Note that if you use this, you must use the standard types in `java.security.MessageDigest` (MD5, etc.), and you must remember to digest your passwords before you insert them into your database!	No
driverName	The name of the JDBC driver	Yes
roleNameCol	The column in the `userRoleTable` containing the names of your security roles for RBAC	Yes
userCredCol	The column in the `userTable` containing the names of user passwords for RBAC	Yes
userNameCol	The column in the `userTable` and the `userRoleTable` that contains the names of your users	Yes

Table continued on following page

157

Attribute	Description	Required?
userRoleTable	The table that contains a user name and a role for RBAC authorization	Yes
userTable	The table that contains users and their passwords for RBAC authentication	Yes

The following code shows a very simple example of using the JDBC-ODBC bridge to connect to a database. In this case, we set up a simple Microsoft Access Database (just so we could visually show you what it looks like).

```
01:     <Realm  className="org.apache.catalina.realm.JDBCRealm" debug="99"
02:         driverName="sun.jdbc.odbc.JdbcOdbcDriver"
03:         connectionURL="jdbc:odbc:Realm" digest="MD5"
04:         userTable="users" userNameCol="user_name"
05:         userCredCol="user_pass"
06:         userRoleTable="user_roles"
07:         roleNameCol="role_name" />
```

As you can see from Figure 6.5, our user table is users, and our table that does the user-role mappings is user_roles. Another thing to notice is that we used the MD5 digest algorithm to store the password in digested format. However, note that with most digest algorithms, the same plaintext (cleartext passwords) produces the same ciphertext (the way it looks in the database shown in Figure 6.5).

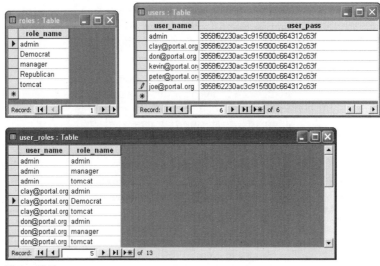

Figure 6.5

Of course, creating a DataSource realm is quite similar, and so is setting up a JNDI realm for accessing LDAP directories.

Finally, you may create your own realm — the following example shows some code that was written to handle the way that MD5 passwords are used in iPlanet/Netscape Directory servers. As you can see, the class is a subclass of the `org.apache.catalina.realm.JNDIRealm` class. In this particular code listing, the method `getHexValue()` was used to avoid problems. In some implementations of Netscape Directory Servers and the iPlanet directory server, the hex value in the `userPassword` field is often found with the name of the algorithm in curly braces (for example, {MD5}), and is encoded with base64 encoding. This is sometimes a problem when you are setting up authentication on a JNDI security realm, because this is something that other directory servers do not do. The following code solves that problem, with the `getHexValue()` method and calls to it in the methods `getUserDN()` and `getPassword()`.

We have broken up this listing to walk you through this example. In the beginning of the code listing, we have overridden `getUserDN()`, which returns the distinguished name of a successfully authenticated user. To make certain that we can authenticate the user successfully, we need to be able to compare a digest of the password with the hex value of the string in the `userPassword` field.

```java
import org.apache.catalina.realm.*;
import org.apache.catalina.util.*;
import javax.naming.*;
import javax.naming.directory.*;
import java.security.Principal;
public class iPlanetRealm extends JNDIRealm
{
  protected static final String info =
  "org.apache.catalina.realm.iPlanetRealm/1.0";
  protected static final String name = "Our iPlanet Realm";
  /**
   * Return the distinguished name of an authenticated user
   * (if successful)
   * or <code>null</code> if authentication is unsuccessful.
   *
   * @param context The directory context we are accessing
   * @param username Username to be authenticated
   * @param credentials Authentication credentials
   *
   * @exception NamingException if a directory server error occurs
   */
  protected String getUserDN(DirContext context,
                             String username, String credentials)
  throws NamingException
  {
    if (debug >= 2)
      log("getUserDN(" + username + ")");
    if (username == null)
      return(null);
    if ((userFormat == null) || (userPassword == null))
      return(null);
    // Retrieve the user password attribute for this user
    String dn = userFormat.format(new String[] { username});
    if (debug >= 3)
      log("  dn=" + dn);
    Attributes attrs = null;
    try
```

```
  {
    attrs = context.getAttributes(dn, userPassword);
  } catch (NameNotFoundException e)
  {
    return(null);
  }
  if (attrs == null)
    return(null);
  if (debug >= 3)
    log("  retrieving attribute " + userPassword[0]);
  Attribute attr = attrs.get(userPassword[0]);
  if (attr == null)
    return(null);
  if (debug >= 3)
    log("  retrieving value");
  Object value = attr.get();
  if (value == null)
    return(null);
  String valueString = null;
  if (value instanceof byte[])
    valueString = new String((byte[]) value);
  else
    valueString = value.toString();

  valueString = getHexValue(valueString);

  // Validate the credentials specified by the user
  if (debug >= 3)
    log("  validating credentials");
  boolean validated = false;
  if (hasMessageDigest())
  {
    // Hex hashes should be compared case-insensitive
    validated = (digest(credentials).equalsIgnoreCase(valueString));
  }
  else
    validated = (digest(credentials).equals(valueString));
  if (validated == false)
  {
    //just in case we do our own digests
    validated = credentials.equals(valueString);
  }
  if (debug >= 2)
  {
    log(" our digest of the credentials=" + digest(credentials));
  }
  if (validated)
  {
    if (debug >= 2)
      log(sm.getString("jndiRealm.authenticateSuccess",
                        username));
  }
  else
  {
```

```
      if (debug >= 2)
        log(sm.getString("jndiRealm.authenticateFailure",
                          username));
      return(null);
    }
    return(dn);
  }
```

To compute the hexadecimal value of the message digest in the directory server, we call our own method, `getHexValue()`, which does the conversion. The next few methods in the class override other methods in JNDIRealm. In order to have the `getPassword()` method return the correctly encoded password, we need to be able to do our conversion again with our `getHexValue()` method. The following listing shows the overridden `getName()` method, the `getPassword()` method, and the `getPrincipal()` method:

```
public String getName()
{
  return("MyIPlanetRealm");
}
public String getPassword(String username)
{
  String valueString = null;
  try
  {
    log("getPassword has been called...");
    if (username == null)
      return(null);
    if ((userFormat == null) || (userPassword == null))
      return(null);
    // Retrieve the user password attribute for this user
    String dn = userFormat.format(new String[] { username});
    if (debug >= 3)
      log("  dn=" + dn);
    Attributes attrs = null;
    try
    {
      attrs = context.getAttributes(dn, userPassword);
    } catch (NameNotFoundException e)
    {
      return(null);
    }
    if (attrs == null)
      return(null);
    if (debug >= 3)
      log("  retrieving attribute " + userPassword[0]);
    Attribute attr = attrs.get(userPassword[0]);
    if (attr == null)
      return(null);
    if (debug >= 3)
      log("  retrieving value");
    Object value = attr.get();
    if (value == null)
      return(null);
    if (value instanceof byte[])
```

```
            valueString = new String((byte[]) value);
        else
            valueString = value.toString();
        valueString = getHexValue(valueString);
        // Validate the credentials specified by the user
    }
    catch (Exception e)
    {
        e.printStackTrace();
    }
    return(valueString);
}
public Principal getPrincipal(String username)
{
    System.out.println("calling authenticate on " +
                        username + ","
                        + getPassword(username));
    return(authenticate(username, getPassword(username)));
}
```

Finally, the key to our custom realm is shown in the next example. In order to correctly authenticate a user, we need to use this method to convert a base64-encoded message digest with preceding brackets to a hexadecimal digest. The following listing shows just how we do it.

```
private String getHexValue(String iplanetEncodedPassword)
{
    //get rid of the {algorithm} that is in front of the digested
    //user password
    String hexval = iplanetEncodedPassword;
    log(" iPlanet String=" + iplanetEncodedPassword);
    if (iplanetEncodedPassword.startsWith("{"))
    {
        String base64val =
            iplanetEncodedPassword.substring(
                iplanetEncodedPassword.indexOf('}')+1
        );

        hexval =
            HexUtils.convert(Base64.decode(base64val.getBytes()));
        if (debug >= 2)
        {
            log(" Hex value of iPlanet String=" + hexval);
        }
        System.out.println("hex value is " + hexval);
    }
    else
    {
        log("It seems to be hex-encoded already.. returning..");
    }

    return(hexval);
}
}
```

It should be noted that you will rarely have to create your own custom security realms—by default, Tomcat comes with realms that can easily communicate with your directory servers and databases with authentication and authorization credentials. It is good to know that if you absolutely have to do it, you can inherit from classes in the `org.apache.catalina.realm` package.

Finally, creating a utility to manage your authentication and authorization credentials in a Tomcat realm is something that you have to do on your own. In the past, we have created Web applications that parse the `<Realm>` tag in the `server.xml` file to find out how to manage the users, and the user-role mappings, for our security realms.

A Single Sign-On strategy for your portal can be achieved by using security realms that are shared across Web applications. Setting up a realm—and a storage mechanism for your realm (LDAP or database)— is a very important part of your portal's security strategy.

For more information on setting up Tomcat security realms, and specifically setting up DataSource and JDBC realms, please visit http://jakarta.apache.org/tomcat/tomcat-5.0-doc/realm-howto.html.

SSL for Confidentiality

If you need the security service of confidentiality when presenting sensitive data to your users in your portal, you will probably need to configure your Web container to use SSL. TLS is actually the more up-to-date term for this service, but because many people continue to use SSL to describe it, we will too.

In building your portal, realize that when you are providing the service of confidentiality, your server is doing encryption and decryption, which is computationally expensive performance-wise. For that reason, wisely choose the areas of your portal that will actually need encryption. Some pages, such as the login page, can be configured to use SSL-based authentication with HTTPS, whereas your user's session information can be carried from that page over to the other regular HTTP pages.

Setting up SSL/TLS in Tomcat to protect confidentiality of your user's sessions and integrity of the end-to-end data is an easy task. The key steps to set this up are as follows:

❑ Download JSSE (Java Secure Socket Extension), which contains the code for setting up the secure connection if you don't have JDK 1.4 or later on your machine. (If you do have JDK 1.4 or later, it's built in.)

❑ Either generate a self-signed RSA-based digital certificate or have one issued to you by a trusted authority.

❑ Load the certificate in your keystore, and then you can configure Tomcat to use it.

If you are going to generate a self-signed certificate, simply use the keytool utility that comes with your JDK in your `$JAVA_HOME/bin` directory. An example of such a session is shown in the following code.

```
C:\>keytool -genkey -alias tomcat -keyalg RSA -keystore c:/keystore
Enter keystore password:  omgykkyb
What is your first and last name?
  [Unknown]:  Joe Portal
What is the name of your organizational unit?
  [Unknown]:  BuildingOpenSourcePortalsWithJava
What is the name of your organization?
  [Unknown]:  Wiley
```

```
What is the name of your City or Locality?
  [Unknown]:  Mechanicsville
What is the name of your State or Province?
  [Unknown]:  Virginia
What is the two-letter country code for this unit?
  [Unknown]:  US
Is CN=Joe Portal, OU=BuildingOpenSourcePortalsWithJava, O=Wiley,
  L=Mechanicsville, ST=Virginia, C=US correct?
  [no]:  y
Enter key password for <tomcat>
        (RETURN if same as keystore password):
```

The preceding code shows the generation of the self-signed certificate and storing it in the keystore located on the filesystem at `C:\keystore`. Next, it's time to configure your server to use it. Luckily for us, there is a commented-out example in Tomcat's `server.xml` file. After making a few changes to the SSL connector's `Factory` class, the following code shows the resulting configuration options that enable an encrypted channel between the browsers and the server hosting our portal.

```
01: <!— Define a SSL Coyote HTTP/1.1 Connector on port 8443 —>
02: <Connector
        className="org.apache.coyote.tomcat4.CoyoteConnector"
03:            port="8443" minProcessors="5" maxProcessors="75"
04:            enableLookups="true"
05:            acceptCount="100" debug="0" scheme="https"
               secure="true"
06:            useURIValidationHack="false"
               disableUploadTimeout="true">
07: <Factory
08:      className="org.apache.coyote.tomcat4.CoyoteServerSocketFactory"
09:   keystoreFile="C:/keystore" keystorePass="omgykkyb"
10:   clientAuth="false" protocol="TLS" />
11: </Connector>
```

The important things for us to add in this listing are on line 9. Because we specified a keystore (and did not use the default), we needed to use the `keystoreFile` and `keystorePass` attributes of `Factory` to specify how Tomcat can access the certificate. Note that in line 10, a `clientAuth` attribute is set to false. If it had been set to true, only clients using certificate authentication could gain access to the site.

Now that we have configured Tomcat to use SSL, we can go to https://localhost:8443/ to test it. The alert shown in Figure 6.6 (or something like it) should warn the user that the site is untrusted. Because we generated the certificate ourselves, we get this message. Of course, SSL will still work on your site if the user chooses to proceed, but in order to avoid warnings like this, there is another step that you can take.

Because most browsers by default trust certificate authorities such as Verisign and Thawte, you may get those authorities to sign your certificate. In order for that to happen, you need to generate a Certificate Signing Request (CSR) to allow such a certificate authority to sign your public key, generating an X.509 certificate and therefore authenticating your identity so that your site can be trusted. The certificate authority of your choice will have detailed instructions for this process. Luckily, your Java keytool utility can generate such a request by executing the following:

```
keytool -certreq -keyalg RSA -alias tomcat -file certreq.csr
        -keystore c:/keystore
```

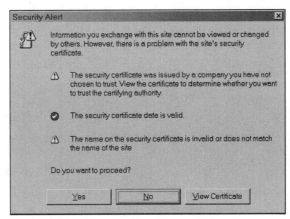

Figure 6.6

By executing that command, the keytool utility creates a file called `certreq.csr` that you will need to send to your certificate authority. They will send you their certificate and give you instructions for downloading their certificate chain. Once you get your certificate and download their certificate chain of trust, you can import these back into your keystore, and Tomcat will use this as your new certificate.

For more information on configuring Tomcat to use SSL, see http://jakarta.apache.org/tomcat/tomcat-5.0-doc/ssl-howto.html.

Application Configuration

From the Tomcat application level (meaning your application's `web.xml` file descriptors), you can configure authentication and levels of authorization at the Web-page level. Tomcat has three types of authentication: BASIC (in which it pops up a user name/password window), DIGEST (in which the hash of the password is passed to the server), and FORM (in which you can create a customized form for authentication).

The following code shows an example of setting BASIC authentication and RBAC to a group of pages. In lines 11–19, we set a security constraint on a collection of pages (in this case, one page specified by the `foo.html` URL pattern on line 14). The authorization constraint listed on lines 16–18 specifies that the end-user must have the manager role. Finally, lines 21–24 force the user to log in to the portal using BASIC authentication when he or she attempts to access the protected resource collection.

```
01: <?xml version="1.0"?>
02:
03:<web-app>
04: <display-name>Authentication Test</display-name>
05:    <description>Authentication Test</description>
06:
07: <welcome-file-list>
08:        <welcome-file>home.jsp</welcome-file>
09: </welcome-file-list>
10:
11: <security-constraint>
12:    <web-resource-collection>
```

```
13:        <web-resource-name>REALM Test</web-resource-name>
14:        <url-pattern>foo.html</url-pattern>
15:    </web-resource-collection>
16:    <auth-constraint>
17:        <role-name>manager</role-name>
18:    </auth-constraint>
19: </security-constraint>
20: <login-config>
21:    <auth-method>BASIC</auth-method>
22:    <realm-name>My Portal</realm-name>
23: </login-config>
24: </web-app>
```

The preceding code is a simple test for setting up BASIC authentication using the `<login-config>` tag. The following code provides an example of FORM authentication, which also utilizes the `<login-config>` tag, but specifies custom pages for the authentication and error screens.

```
01:<login-config>
02: <auth-method>FORM</auth-method>
03: <realm-name>Authentication</realm-name>
04: <form-login-config>
05:     <form-login-page>/login.jsp</form-login-page>
06:     <form-error-page>/error.jsp</form-error-page>
07: </form-login-config>
08:</login-config>
```

To use FORM-based authentication, you need to now create a login page, which is shown in the following code. It is important to know that the mandatory items in this example are the `form` action (`j_security_check`), the `username` attribute (`j_username`), and the `password` attribute (`j_password`).

```
01: <title>Login Page</title>
02: <CENTER>
03: <body bgcolor="white">
04: <form method="POST"
05:     action='<%= response.encodeURL("j_security_check") %>' >
06:     <table border="0" cellspacing="5">
07:         <tr>
08:             <th align="right">Username:</th>
09:             <td align="left">
10:                 <input type="text" name="j_username">
11:             </td>
12:         </tr>
13:         <tr>
14:             <th align="right">Password:</th>
15:             <td align="left">
16:                 <input type="password" name="j_password">
17:             </td>
18:         </tr>
19:         <tr>
20:             <td align="right">
21:                 <input type="submit" value="Log In">
22:             </td>
23:             <td align="left">
```

```
24:                      <input type="reset">
25:              </td>
26:          </tr>
27:      </table>
28: </form>
```

Finally, the following code shows the configuration for digest authentication, which is very similar to BASIC authentication.

```
<login-config>
    <auth-method>DIGEST</auth-method>
    <realm-name>Digest Authentication Example</realm-name>
</login-config>
```

Many developers choose to use the DIGEST authentication method when they are worried about user names and passwords traveling in the clear, but are not concerned enough to use encryption. With DIGEST authentication, when the user authenticates, the browser sends the hash value of the password, and the server compares that value with the hash value of the password taken from its security realm for the user. It should be noted that DIGEST authentication does not offer security comparable to SSL. Computing hash values is a simple computational task, and the ciphers used with the SSL/TLS algorithms offer much stronger security.

Programmatic Security Access with JSPs and Servlets

Any Servlet 2.3 container offers methods on the `ServletRequest` object that enable the developer to restrict access within a JSP or servlet, depending on the user's identity or role. This provides a fine-grained level of access that can be embedded in the logic of your portal or portlet. The following table shows the methods of the `ServletRequest` object that can be used by the portal developer in assigning role-based access and fine-grained access to a user.

Method	Description
`boolean isUserInRole(String role)`	If the user is in the role passed in as the argument, this will return true; otherwise, it returns false.
`String getRemoteUser()`	Returns the name the client used for authentication. If there was no authentication, it will return `null`.
`java.security.Principal getUserPrincipal()`	Returns a principal object for the user

The following code shows an example of a JSP that provides such fine-grained access. In line 3, the JSP takes the user's user ID from the `ServletRequest` object, and uses it for customization on line 3 if that user ID is not null. On line 20, the JSP provides an administrator's menu if the user belongs to the administrator's role.

```
01: <H1>Welcome to this test page</H1>
02: <%
03:   String username = request.getRemoteUser();
04:   if (username != null)
05:   {
```

```
06: %>
07:      Hello there, <%=username%> .
08:
09: <% } %>
10:
11: <HR>
12:  <H2>Resources</H2>
13:  <TABLE>
14:    <TR><TD><B>Default Menu</B></TD></TR>
15:    <TR>
16:      <TD><A HREF="superportal.jsp">Super Portal</A></TD>
17:      <TD><A HREF="http://www.trumantruck.com/">Kevin's truck</A></TD>
18:    </TR>
19:  </TABLE>
20: <% if (request.isUserInRole("administrators")) { %>
21:  <TABLE>
22:    <TR>
23:      <TD><B><I>Administrator's menu</I></B></TD>
24:    </TR>
25:  <TR>
26:   <TD><A HREF="del_link.jsp">Delete Link</A>
27:      <TD><A HREF="realmadmin.jsp">User/Role Administration</FONT></A>
28:    </TR>
29:  </TABLE>
30: <% } %>
```

The following code snippet shows another example of security at the JSP level by forcing logout and redirection of a user. Using the `invalidate()` method of the `HttpSession` object, a portal can force a user logout, and by using the `sendRedirect()` method of the `ServletResponse` object, we can redirect the user to another page. By using a simple JSP page, such as shown in the following code, we can program simple logout functionality in our portal.

```
<%
session.invalidate();
String url = response.encodeURL("home.jsp");
response.sendRedirect(url);
return;
%>
```

As we have shown, many security features are present in your Web container, and if you take advantage of them, you can apply these features to the security of your portal.

Security of the Portlet Container

Because portlets can be accessed by so many users, and because portlets often have connections to back-end data stores that contain sensitive data, many will have security requirements. As a result, the portlet container must leverage the security of the Web container covered in the last section. Because it is the responsibility of the Web container to authenticate users and determine the security roles for users, it must also convey a user's identity and role information to the portlet container so that portlets will have access to this information. Luckily, the Java Portlet API is very similar to the Java Servlet API, and maintains the same concepts of security roles. Just like Web servers, portlets control security via descriptors, and control access by using programmatic security.

Programmatic Security

The programmatic security in portlets is quite simple, and is very similar to the security provided by Java servlets. A good example of the similarities between Java servlet security and Java portlet security can be seen in the `PortletRequest` interface, with its security-related methods, listed in the following table.

Method	Description
`boolean isUserInRole (String role)`	If the user is in the role passed in as the argument, this will return true; otherwise, it returns false.
`String getRemoteUser()`	Returns the name the client used for authentication. If there was no authentication, it will return `null`.
`java.security.Principal getUserPrincipal()`	Returns a principal object for the user
`getAuthType()`	Returns the authentication method. The possible return values are `PortletRequest.BASIC_AUTH`, `PortletRequest.CERT_AUTH`, `PortletRequest.DIGEST_AUTH`, `PortletRequest.FORM_AUTH`, or `null` if there was no authentication.
`isSecure()`	Returns a Boolean indicating whether this request was made using a secure channel between the client and the portal, such as HTTPS

Much like the `ServletRequest` object's security methods shown in the last table, this table shows that a portlet may call the `getRemoteUser()` method to get the authenticated user's name, `isUserInRole()` to determine whether a user is in a specific security role, `getUserPrincipal()` to get the principal object for a user, `getAuthType()` to find the authentication method, and `isSecure()` to determine whether the connection between the user and the portal is encrypted.

The following code shows an example of the portlet accessing this interface. Here, the portlet calls these methods on the `RenderRequest` object, which realizes the `PortletRequest` interface.

```java
import javax.portlet.*;
import java.io.*;
public class SnobbyPortlet extends GenericPortlet
{

  public void doView(RenderRequest request,RenderResponse response) throws
PortletException, IOException
  {
    Writer writer = response.getWriter() ;
    if (request.isUserInRole("VIP"))
    {
      writer.write(
        "<p class='portlet-msg-info'>Okay, you are a VIP!</p>"
      );
      writer.write("<p class='portlet-font'>Welcome, mister VIP!</p>");
    }
    else
```

```
    {
      writer.write("<p class='portlet-font'>" +
        "Since this is a snobby portlet, and you are not a VIP," +
        "you are a nobody. Wipe your feet on the way out.</p>");
    }

  }
}
```

In addition to calling methods such as isUserInRole() in portlets such as this, a portlet may throw a PortletSecurityException if there is a security violation, and this will be handled by the container.

Portlet Descriptor-Configured Security

Security constraints of the portlets themselves can be described in a portlet descriptor. Each portlet may define the roles required, the role mappings, and other constraints, in the portlet.xml descriptor, as shown in the following example.

```
<portlet-app>
  ...
    <portlet>
      ...
      <security-role-ref>
        <role-name>PortalManager</role-name>
        <role-link>PortletManager</role-link>
      </security-role-ref>
      <security-constraint>
        <display-name>Secure Portlets</display-name>
        <portlet-collection>
          <portlet-name>accountSummary</portlet-name>
        </portlet-collection>
        <user-data-constraint>
          <transport-guarantee>CONFIDENTIAL</transport-guarantee>
        </user-data-constraint>
      </security-constraint>
      ...
    </portlet>
  ...
</portlet-app>
```

In the preceding code, you can see the portlet descriptor addressing a few security issues:

❑ **The portlet descriptor is mapping security roles using the `<security-role-ref>` tag.** Here, we map the main Web container's security role, PortalManager, to a new role, PortletManager. This can be done when you want to do role mappings between the Web container and the portlet container.

❑   The portlet descriptor defines a transport guarantee with the `<transport-guarantee>` tag. This guarantee revolves around connection. If the element's value is CONFIDENTIAL, this means that the data transmitted must be encrypted (usually with SSL).

For more information on configuring security aspects of your portlets, visit Jakarta Pluto (the reference implementation of the Java Portlet Specification) at http://jakarta.apache.org/pluto/.

Beyond the Portal — Secure Back-End Communication

An important aspect that many developers and managers often miss is security beyond the portal — security of the back-end communication between your portal and the back-end applications that feed it. Sometimes, it is acceptable for the portal to connect to a back-end database with its own user name and password, and the tunnel can be protected with SSL. In a J2EE architecture, user and role information is passed from the Web container layer to the J2EE layer, and access to EJBs can be controlled by RBAC security roles at the bean method level of granularity. In other situations, where trust is not propagated (see the "Single Sign-On [SSO]" section at the beginning of this chapter), the back-end application would like the portal to authenticate on behalf of the user. It is the latter scenario — usually involving Web services — that is the most challenging.

Luckily, it is possible to use open-source tools to provide propagation of trust, Single Sign-On, and non-repudiation of a user's initial authentication by leveraging some of the Web service standards (for example, XML Signature or SAML) discussed earlier in this chapter. By passing a signed SAML attribute assertion that lists the user's authentication means, identity, and other credentials, you can provide proof of the end-user's identity and his authorization levels. An open-source API providing the necessary cryptography, combined with any open-source Web service toolkit, can be used to validate signed SAML placed in the SOAP header of Web service messages. Using Apache Axis, for example, you can create an Axis Handler that validates the digital signature of a signed SAML assertion using the Apache XML Security package, and you can control access to Web services by comparing the credentials in the SAML assertion to the Web service's access control policy.

Figure 6.7 shows an example security architecture that provides such a security solution. In this architecture, the user authenticates to the portal, the portal retrieves information from its standard Servlet 2.3 security realm to get the user's credentials, the portal creates and signs a timestamped and signed SAML assertion based on that user's identity and roles, and this is passed on to the back-end data sources. The hash of the SOAP body should also be placed in the SAML assertion as a SAML attribute so that the mapping of the end-user to the end-user's request should not be lost. Of course, some processing must be done on the Web service side (with servlet filters or handlers) to handle signature validation and access control.

An architecture similar to the one shown in Figure 6.7 can provide end-to-end security for the portal enterprise.

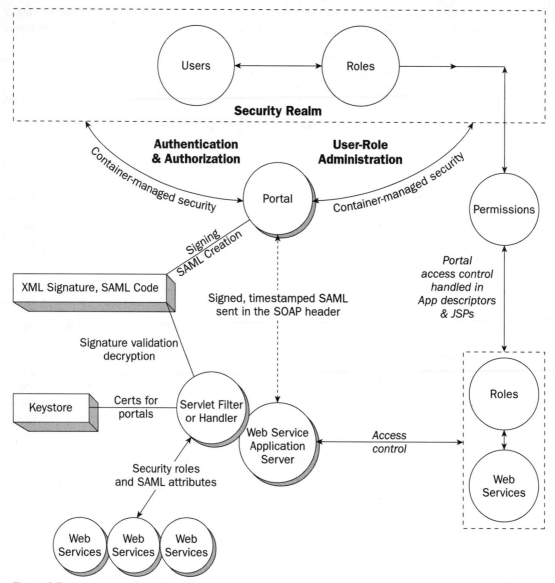

Figure 6.7

Summary

This chapter introduced you to information security concepts and techniques that you can use when developing portals with security requirements. In the chapter, we defined a security vocabulary, briefly introduced relevant security standards, and provided an overview of how to configure and develop security solutions as a portal developer. Focusing on accepted standards and open-source technologies, this chapter provided you with some entry points into developing security services for open-source portals.

Part 2: How to Build a Portal

7

Planning for Portal Deployment

Writing about portal deployment planning is a little like those heady philosophical discussions one has in high school about Existentialism, and the struggle to make rational decisions in an irrational universe. A lot of that type of debate relates to the building of portals, particularly the need to make choices and then commitments to them. The difficult aspect of this decision making is that portal design involves the task of aggregating disparate subsystems into a single interface that has to satisfy a contradictory set of users and their needs. Additional factors that make this decision-making process so difficult are the rapid changes in data and technologies, organizational issues, and, last but not least, ignorance.

Portal plans often start out innocently as a means of collaboratively sharing information among a common user base. Questions like "Who will use the portal?"; "What synergy among our disparate user groups will this portal bring?"; and, perhaps, "What self-service features can we expect from this portal?" will have been addressed in broad terms at the onset of a program, so that the monies needed for development and deployment start flowing. But what happens next? One word comes to mind: chaos.

To overcome this chaos, pre-emptive measures need to be made at the onset of portal development to ensure that technical surprises don't surface during the latter stages of development. The application of iterative modeling procedures such as the Unified Process (UP) or Extreme Programming (XP) will increase your chances of avoiding those surprises.

When planning a portal deployment, many concerns need to be addressed, but the two most important modeling determinations are the management of Web content data and the user communities that will be exposed to that data. Accommodations must be made to ensure that portlet content is not rendered improperly to the disparate user base, which could compromise an individual's privacy. User profiles should be established so that content can be shown in proper user communities. This chapter addresses these matters. Across all portal applications, content is exposed to its users in many forms, but the most prevalent forms of exposure include message boards, calendars, weather forecasts, news, and search utilities. For portals to retain and increase their user bases, they need to maintain lucid navigation flows so that end-users know where they are and where they are going to go next. If a design does not provide a proper navigation model, users may become confused, lose interest, and ultimately browse somewhere else.

The illustration in Figure 7.1 defines a portal in very simple terms. Generally, a file cabinet is a place where multitudes of related and unrelated data are stored for office use. The file cabinet analogy can be applied to portals because they warehouse unrelated data for business operations. With file cabinets, individual folders are tabbed to indicate the content they keep. With portals, portlet applications emulate folders in that they represent individual subsystems of data.

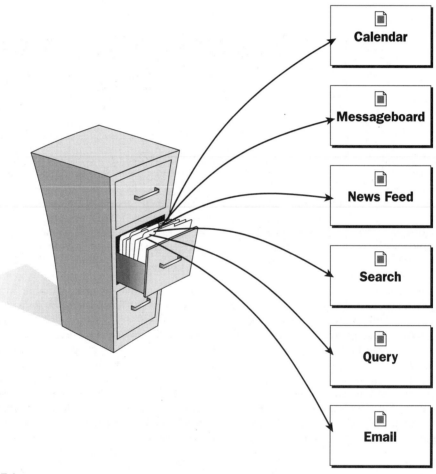

Figure 7.1

This chapter explains some requirement-capturing techniques to begin your portal planning activities. It will also help you with other design decision techniques that you should consider when building your portal, so you can mitigate the chaos that naturally ensues during the inception phase of development.

You'll also be looking at requirement considerations and some tools to ensure that requirements are managed and adhered to properly. In addition, this chapter covers software design methodologies, design decisions, search and content management tools, design pattern considerations, client/server processing, Web services for remote portals, portal navigation, and portlet integration planning.

System Requirements

Typically, a requirement is considered a specific characteristic or functionality that the system must perform on a problem domain from a customer's perspective. If a requirement is established but does not affect a stakeholder, it should be considered a design or implementation decision.

To gather requirements for a portal project, development, testing, and design teams should sit down with all of the program's stakeholders who are responsible for all of the different subsystems and/or portlets to determine the features that are needed for the successful deployment of your system. The exclusion of partners who are expected to contribute content to the portal usually ends up hurting your program in the long run. Similarly, the inclusion of extraneous portal participants in your development/design meetings could also be a distraction. A compromise must be drawn that allows for the limited participation of each portlet subsystem's team with members who possess technological and problem domain expertise of their application. Those members must then be allowed to report back to their team about the details of those meetings. Last, all concerned parties should be prepared to negotiate trade-offs in each other's deployments. Requirements come in many flavors, but the following sections describe some typical requirements that portal applications might consider capturing during their design activities, along with definitions and questions you should ask.

Interface Requirements

Interface requirements address the basic flow of content into and out of the portal through its portlets. To properly describe and address these requirements, a design team might pose the following questions:

- ❑ What is the input/output?
- ❑ How will the portal data be handled?
- ❑ How will the portal data be formatted?

Decisions need to be made up front as to what interfaces will be developed and provided so that portal developers can render and persist portal data content. Once a determination has been made about the input sources, then requirements need to be captured regarding how that data will be handled and formatted. For SOAP implementations, XML parsers or XSL transform stylesheets might be selected, along with their associated library files. If Java Data Objects (JDO) components are being developed, then XML-mappings used to abstract database interfaces will have to be decided upon.

Operational Requirements

Operational requirements focus on 24 x 7 portal uptime so that user operations and maintenance activities do not conflict. Some questions that your design team might consider when capturing these requirements are as follows:

Chapter 7

❑   What does the system do?

❑   What are your performance constraints and expectations?

❑   How often and when will new content be made available to users?

❑   When and what maintenance activities are needed to service the portal community?

Operational requirements for a portal indicate what activities the individual portlet components will perform inside the larger portal view. Constraints and user expectations need to be delineated by the stakeholders to ensure that the portlet subsystems play together properly in the portal sandbox. Additionally, rules need to be established to ensure that Web content updates and maintenance operations do not halt operations.

Data Requirements

There are many data requirements, too many to list here, but with portal implementations, care should be taken during requirements analysis to consider the content delivery mechanism used to publish data. One issue that might be considered when gathering requirements that address data delivery is whether your system will implement **push** or **pull** operations.

The traditional model of content delivery on the Web reflects the latter strategy — users search repeatedly, or "pull" data in a random manner, which can become tedious and frustrating when the information they are seeking does not measure up to their needs. Because of this dilemma, technologies were developed to "push" content to user desktops. Push technology works by having end users fill out profiles in which they specify particular types of data they want "pushed" to their applications; in our case, it could be a portlet. This profile acts like a filter for content and is stored on either the client's machine or on some content provider's server.

Unfortunately, latency issues can become a problem with the implementation of push technology. Networks can become overloaded and filters can allow significant amounts of unwanted content to be propagated to a system if the filters are not properly configured. Typically, profiles work well for simple queries such as stock quotations and weather forecasts and can overwhelm a system when complex alert systems are implemented.

Additionally, consideration needs to be given to how your portal system will persist data during transactional activities. Will a relational database or an XML file suffice as data-persistence mechanisms? Are your data operations atomic, and can they be rolled back if they are not properly processed? Should data abstraction layers be implemented, like Java Data Objects (JDO) or other Object/Relational Mapping (ORM) tools? These are just a few of the issues that your portal team should deliberate on during data-requirements analyses.

Security Requirements

Security is usually one of the biggest concerns for any portal deployment process. Relevant data needs to be exposed to users of a portal based on profile information that might be stored in an LDAP directory server or some other persistent data store for retrieval. User communities need to be established so that Web content can be targeted properly to the portal audience. Some questions that might be used to capture common security requirements are as follows:

❑   Will declarative or programmatic security be implemented?

❑   What type of a Security realm is needed for deployment?

❑   Will security features propagate properly among all of the disparate portlets?

Compromised data on a portal application, or any Web application for that matter, negatively impacts the user community that will use and support that application. Any single incident can severely damage the reputation of a company that deploys a portal, which will impair its ability to effectively conduct future operations. Because of this, portal applications must address the threat of a security breach or the compromising of delicate user profiles, by implementing security operating policies that can help improve user trust.

Many portal frameworks roll their own proprietary security APIs, but in many instances, consideration should be given to the adherence to open security standards. When addressing security in a portal, architects need to consider the use of programmatic security when ascribing responsibilities to portlet containers because the individual portlets need to be certain of the roles of the user who is accessing them. The JSR-168 specification indicates that the portlet container will share the same Servlet 2.3 security APIs that implement the `Request` interface methods to perform programmatic security. That should prove beneficial for servlet applications that use these features and now can be wrapped fairly easily with the new portlet wrappers available in portals that are JSR-168–compliant.

Quality Assurance Requirements

Quality assurance measures are needed on all software development projects to propagate best practices, and to ensure that code baselines remain intact and that developer modifications remain in sync. Two important questions that must be asked when determining quality assurance requirements are

❑   How will deployed software be refactored ?

❑   How will software be migrated from one system to another?

Quality assurance processes control system differences to manage risk and error propagation. The establishment of processes is needed to ensure systematic patterns of action that provide evidence that the portal program adheres to defined technical requirements.

After defining these processes, such as those shown in Figure 7-16, later in this chapter, tools need to be identified to achieve a program's stated quality assurance goals. Additionally, standards and conventions need to be established so that best practices can be distributed across the development spectrum.

Adherence to some quality assurance requirements can be facilitated with open-source applications and continuous integration activities using CVS, ANT, and CheckStyle; unit and load testing with JUnit and JMeter; and Scarab, for bug tracking. The following sections describe these activities.

Software Configuration Management

Software **configuration management** requires that source code and design artifact be managed properly so that deployment goals can be attained. Open-source configuration management tools such as CVS and Subversion control source code versions and their modifications so that development teams can stay in sync, minimizing delivery risks.

A configuration management plan should be established at the onset of a program to describe all of the configuration management operations that will be implemented during a project's life cycle. This plan should detail resources and activity schedules, and the personnel responsible for these operations.

Jakarta's ANT

ANT is an open-source build application that is written in Java and uses XML tags to target a broad range of configuration management activities. ANT's utility lies in its ability to extend build functionality with XML file structures and the Java programming language. An ample number of core tasks and external tasks have been developed for ANT to meet and surpass many source code management and deployment operations.

With all portal development efforts, quality assurance activities are paramount because changes to its design are inevitable due to their dynamic nature. ANT allows for the automation of database scripts, CVS activities, and source code compilation, build and deploy tasks that can be run on different platforms.

A simple but effective task that can be useful in ensuring that your code base adheres to a set of programming guideline is CheckStyle. CheckStyle (http://checkstyle.sourceforge.net/) automates the checking of source code so that developers can continue to work on developing code while ANT script with CheckStyle targets ensure that standards are being adhered to.

CheckStyle is a time-saving development tool that helps programmers write Java code that adheres to a coding standard. It automates the process of checking Java code to spare humans this boring (but important) task. This makes it ideal for projects that want to enforce a coding standard.

CheckStyle is highly configurable and can be used to support almost any coding standard. Supplied with CheckStyle is an example configuration file that supports the Sun Code Conventions. In addition, other sample configuration files are supplied for other well-known conventions, as shown in Figure 7.2.

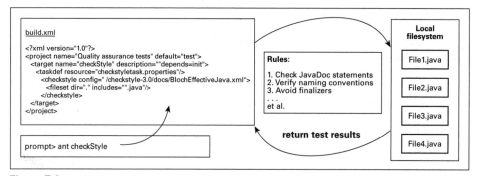

Figure 7.2

Unit and Load Testing

When building portlet applications in your portal, it is always important to generate test applications along with the source code. Perhaps that seems trivial, but the time savings are invaluable when you've been told that your code is no longer working several months after you checked it into a source code repository. With these tests, you can jog your memory in an easy fashion to recollect how your code worked, and determine what new bugs were introduced to undermine your software. Several open-source offerings can be used to perform unit testing (JUnit) and load testing activities (JMeter). Chapter 11 addresses this subject in greater depth.

Bug Tracking

Bugs are an unavoidable aspect of software development. The key to dealing with them is ensuring that they are tracked and fixed, and that someone corroborates that they are properly corrected. Web-based defect tracking systems provide program stakeholders with the capability to remotely ascertain the feature requests, bug fix details, and problem resolution. Scarab (http://scarab.tigris.org/) is an open-source tool that you can implement to meet your bug defect tracking needs.

Continuous Integration

Continuous integration is a concept championed by Martin Fowler that emphasizes an Extreme Programming practice of testing your software baseline through automated procedures to ensure that bugs reveal themselves quickly rather than propagating through your system and revealing themselves in the latter stages of development, which could cripple your deployment plans.

Requirements Summary

Clearly, requirements are important in that they capture what the stakeholders of a system expect their system to do. In order for these requirements to be considered valid, they need to be correct, realistic, and traceable. Portal component developers must be vigilant in their requirements-capturing undertakings because scope creep or mismanaged requirements handling can undermine the efforts of all the dependent groups that are responsible for its release.

For example, it makes no sense to establish a requirement that your target run on a Solaris platform when you've been told that the application you're developing can only run on Windows. System performance always tests the stated criterion that your requirements should be realistic. Sure, you can state that your content queries should return results in less than five seconds, but is that always realistic? Sometimes more difficult queries can deliver results after five seconds; does that mean that your requirement is unrealistic? Perhaps, but it is always important to set realistic requirement goals that apply to reasonable requests that occur in a consistent manner. As far as traceable requirements are concerned, make sure that system features can be verified against a requirements specification, that errors can be identified, and that changes in your system can be managed.

It is extremely helpful for portal architects to experiment with iterative measures to achieve resonance in their processes as they're working through their portal development. Additionally, it is very important to be cognizant of all of the different perspectives of the portlet integrators so that teams can work toward a consensus during operations.

Software Design Methodologies

The initial activity for every program is to capture requirements. This is a tricky proposition, however, because the requirements you elicit at the beginning of your task invariably change by the end of the task. This phenomenon is not unique to portals; it happens on all software programs, but can be exacerbated when disparate systems are all aggregated on a single view, as they are on portals. Because of this inevitability, it's always important to maintain a good relationship with your stakeholders to ensure that some give-and-take can be achieved when these modifications occur, as well as with your portal development and integration teams, which need to ensure that modifications on one subsystem do not sabotage other portlets that reside in the enterprise portal. To communicate changes and to facilitate future amendments, all changes need to be captured in a **portlet integration plan**, as described in the latter section of this chapter.

The Unified Process (UP)

The Unified Process (UP), which is an amalgamation of processes by Booch, Jacobsen, and Rumbaugh, is a popular modeling process that emphasizes **iterative development**. Each iteration includes its own requirements analysis, design, implementation, and testing activities. The UP consists of four phases that can be used to define a system's requirements and to perform object-oriented analysis and design operations. These four phases are **inception, elaboration, construction,** and **transition**. During these phases, your program scope is understood, your architecture risks are mitigated, and your releasable system is crafted and deployed so that maintenance can manage your implementation. Further elaboration on the Unified Process can be found in Craig Larman's excellent book *Applying UML and Patterns*. This chapter describes artifact generation for two of those phases, inception and elaboration, and how they can be applied to portal design. The inception phase generally scopes out a program's vision, and forms a case for the development of a system from a conceptual view. UP documents that are crafted in this phase are **use cases** and **use-case models**. Elaboration clarifies the vision established in the inception phase and provides more concrete predictions of the overall project — specifically, the stakeholder requirements.

Figure 7.3 shows a simple use-case model for a portal application. In the portal system, the actor known as the **Portal User** interacts with the calendaring, search, and query activities. The **Portal Administrator** participates in the spidering and monitoring scenarios.

Use cases are generally simple narratives that describe the goals of a system. Figure 7.4 illustrates a use case scenario for adding a message to a message board application.

Use cases are created to capture text descriptions of requirements that outline system functionalities that are expected when a system is deployed. Figure 7.4 demonstrates some high-level aspects that might be included in your use case, ones that are not necessarily required for publication. These concepts include the actors of the system, a description of the use case, the pre- and post-conditions of the scenario being described, and a linear sequence of the scenario, including alternative variations and perhaps some requirements that are warranted for its implementation. A very nice Web site that contains some use case templates can be found at www.usecases.org.

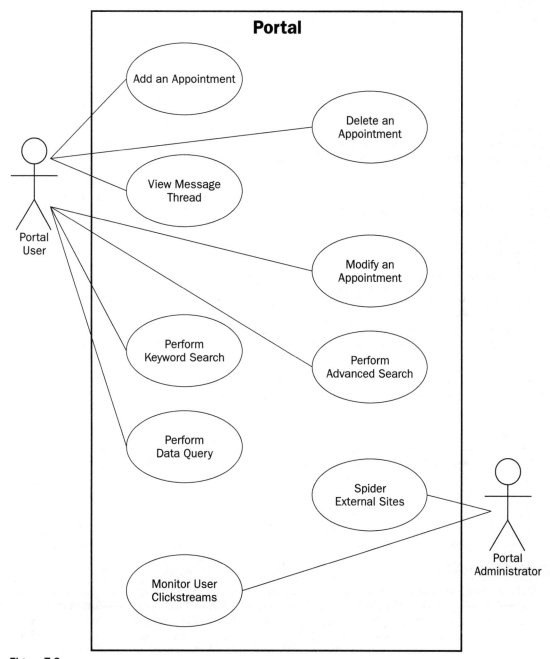

Figure 7.3

Use Case UC1: Add Messages to Messageboard Portlet

Primary Actor: Portal users

Stakeholders and Interest:
• Portal User: Desires the ability to add/delete/modify comments to the Messageboard portlet
• Portal Administrator: Desires the ability to add comments to existing Messageboard entries

Brief Description:
Add messages to the Messageboard portlet. Portlet users with Administrative privileges can append comments to individual user comments.

Pre-Conditions:
PORTLETMESSAGES and PORTLETMSGTHREAD tables are deployed on a MySQL database. user profiles have been established in a Netscape Directory Server to delineate user roles and privileges.

Success Guarantee (Post-Conditions):
None specified for this case

Main Success Scenario (or Basic Flow):
1. Portal User: invokes the Demo portal
2. Portal User: logs in with individual user name/password
3. Portal User: clicks on message link in Messageboard portlet
4. Portal User: adds comments to Messageboard form and clicks Submit button
5. Portlet indicates a proper message has been entered and renders message links on Messageboard portlet.

Extensions (or Alternate Flows):
2a. Portal Administrator: logs in with user name/password
2b. Portal Administrator: logs in with improper user name/password
3a. Portal Administrator: appends comments to existing user comments
3b. Portlet detects error and prompts user to enter a proper user name/password.
4a. Portal User: does not fill out all required form items needed for proper submission
5a. Portlet detects errors and prompts user to fill out all required forms for proper submission.

Special Requirements:
None specified for this use case

Figure 7.4

Domain Model

The development of **domain models**, which are part of the Unified Process and are elaborated on in Larman's book [LARMAN], can be useful in determining individual concept classes for future construction. This type of object modeling enables developers to conceptualize ideas about what classes are needed for construction and their responsibilities among other components. This is performed by breaking down your target system into conceptual models or abstracted elements, as shown in Figure 7.5.

Construction of a domain model for a portal would start with breaking down the system into conceptual classes for the problem domain for all of the individual portlets. All of the scenarios crafted for the portlets are used to determine the classes needed for construction. Noun-phrase identification is a good starting point for this. Say that for your message board scenario you have the action flow depicted in Figure 7.5.

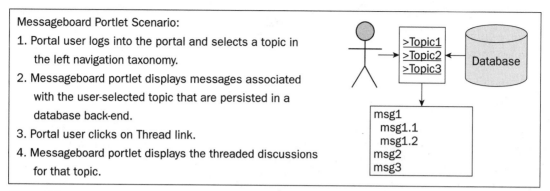

Messageboard Portlet Scenario:

1. Portal user logs into the portal and selects a topic in the left navigation taxonomy.
2. Messageboard portlet displays messages associated with the user-selected topic that are persisted in a database back-end.
3. Portal user clicks on Thread link.
4. Messageboard portlet displays the threaded discussions for that topic.

Figure 7.5

The candidate classes that can be drawn from the scenario flow depicted in Figure 7.5 are as follows: `Portal User`, `Topic`, `Messageboard`, and `MessageThread`. A domain model that might be drawn for these conceptual classes is shown in the following table.

Conceptual Class Category	Examples
Physical or tangible objects	Messageboard, portalUser, Topic
Transactions	messageAdd, messageDelete
Roles of people	portalUser, portalAdministrator
Processes	ViewingThread

A simple **association checklist,** demonstrated in the following table, would define relationships between the conceptual classes.

Category	System
A is a member of B	Topic – Messageboard
	threadedDiscussion – Messageboard
A communicates with B	threadedDiscussion – Messageboard
A uses or manages B	Portal – Portlet
	Portlet – Messageboard
	Messageboard - threadedDiscussion

The example provided in the preceding table is obviously simplistic, but it does make clear how you should approach the creation of conceptual classes for your portal effort. This association checklist should be created for all of your subsystems, or portlets, to capture all of the classes that will be needed for deployment. The next step is to draw a domain model diagram with your new conceptual classes, like the one shown in Figure 7.6.

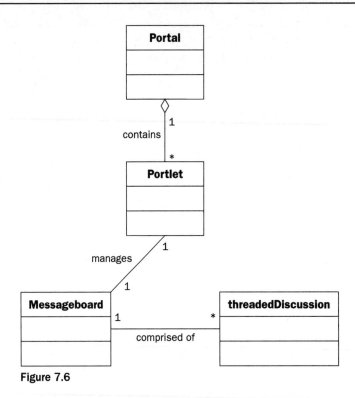

Figure 7.6

As demonstrated in the preceding examples, domain modeling is an excellent business modeling technique, but unfortunately this process can become quite cumbersome and time-intensive for complex portal applications that handle many subsystems in their portlet applications. The idea is to conceptualize what your portal system will do in a visual manner so that, going forward, you can better appreciate and complete your development tasks.

Software Architecture Document (SAD)

The Software Architecture Document (SAD) is part of the elaboration design phase and serves as a pertinent learning tool to provide a high-level view of a system and its interfaces. A SAD encapsulates a general architectural summary of a system, using several different views to illustrate all of the aspects of the system.

A SAD commonly is partitioned into several overviews that describe conceptual understandings of a potential system deployment. An example SAD is shown in Figure 7.7. All of its components (Introduction, Architecture Goals, Use Case View, Logical View, Data Flow, Deployment Flow, Data Views, and Requirements Matrix) serve as a guide for architectural analysis so that anyone reading it can gain an understanding of the overall system at a glance.

The Introduction section of the SAD elucidates all of the different terminologies that will be used in the paper, and describes the scope of the program from a conceptual perspective. With many portal deployments, this section might describe J2EE technologies targeted for implementation, provide an illustration of the enterprise portal, and describe briefly how the target system will manifest itself. A demonstration of this section is shown in Figure 7.8.

Software Architecture Document	
Introduction:	• Describe the scope of your program and a glossary of acronyms and abbreviations to provide clarity to readers of this document.
Architecture Goals:	• Describe software technologies that will be implemented in the portal from a high-level view.
Use Case View:	• Illustrate Use-Case Models to describe system behavior of a portal.
Logical View:	• Describe a high-level conceptual view of your portal system. Elaborate the interfaces, classes, packages, and portlet subsystems.
Data Flow:	• Describe how data will flow into and out of the individual portlet subsystems and how it will be persisted on the portal back-end.
Deployment Flow:	• Describe how the portal system will be deployed.
Data Views:	• Describe the database and XML tables that will be implemented in your portal deployment.
Requirements Matrix:	• Display all of the Use Case requirements and their associations with the individual portlet subsystems in a table for easy reference.

Figure 7.7

The Architecture Goals section of the SAD outlines how the target system will be used, as well as the system's operating environment. Although this section is generally text describing your system's goals, Figure 7.8 is included to visually illuminate those objectives. The text that follows Figure 7.8 demonstrates this.

The target portal system shown in Figure 7.9 will be deployed though J2EE components — specifically, servlets and Java Server Pages (JSPs) on the Web tier that runs in the portal's portlet container. Database queries will be performed through Web Service components that will aggregate content from disparate data sources. Programmatic security will be performed on individual portlets using profile information on an LDAP Directory server so that relevant content can be targeted to specific user communities. Additionally, RSS syndication feeds, XML updates using dom4j libraries, and a JDO Abstract Layer will be implemented to feed data to individual portlet subsystems, and the portal application will reside on a target platform that runs the Linux operating system.

The Use Case View section of the SAD demonstrates the functional requirements on the system. The use-case model shown in Figure 7.10 is further refined during the construction phase to reflect architecturally significant functionality.

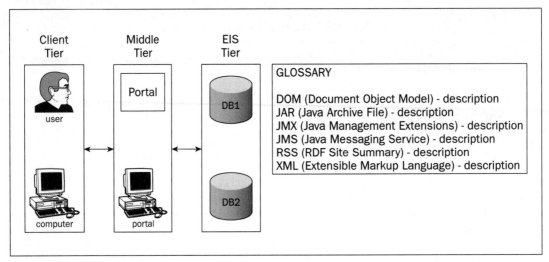

Figure 7.8

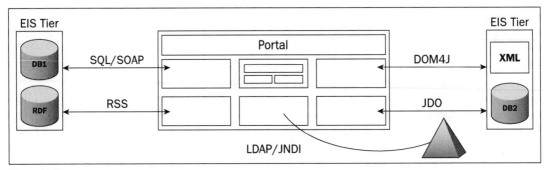

Figure 7.9

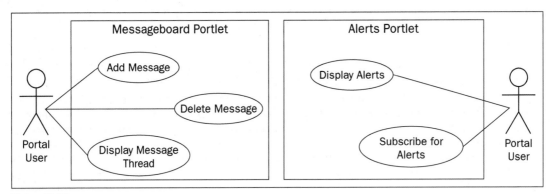

Figure 7.10

The Logical View section of the SAD with respect to portals should summarize all of the portlet subsystems from an organizational perspective that includes all of the frameworks, classes, packages, and interface layers that will be deployed on your system. It is important to remember that this section does not need to provide too much granularity, but enough to convey a coherent message about your system and how the different portlet components will work together and avoid integration collisions.

The Data Flow section of the SAD, shown in Figure 7.9, demonstrates the flow of data from external data sources into and out of the portal implementation. This section can help portlet integrators better understand port and interface requirements that will enable them to secure socket connections and facilitate profile creation to ensure that pertinent Web content is revealed to privileged users.

The Deployment Flow section of the SAD describes the topology of the deployed system. In Figure 7.11, a very simple view exhibits the tiered components that will be developed for the portal deployment.

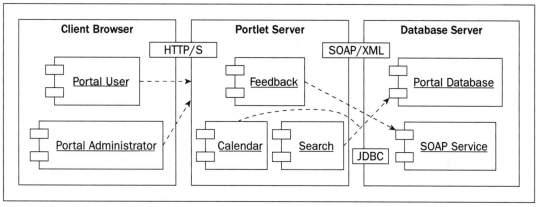

Figure 7.11

The Data Views section of the SAD elucidate the XML and database schema views of your system. These views typically represent high-level views of that data in data-flow diagrams to provide the SAD's readers with an idea of table structures for implementation and to protect individual portlet developers from encroaching on one another's data persistence structures.

The Requirements Matrix section of the SAD relates the use case artifacts to one another for easy reference. A matrix correlates requirements with technical deliverables in your system. This can be an invaluable tool for portal programs to coordinate portlet development with stakeholder expectations for deployment.

Shall Statements and User Stories

Shall statements and User Stories are lightweight requirements capturing mechanisms that can be used with any simple editor or spreadsheet application to expedite your design activities. The basic idea of these artifacts is to perform conceptual modeling and to capture high-level requirements for your system. Typically, shall statements are written in the form of "This system shall perform . . .," where the functional and nonfunctional activities are explained to the shareholders of a system. User Stories are short paragraphs that are artifacts of the XP methodology, which specify what your deployed system will deliver to satisfy stakeholder expectations.

Class-Responsibility-Collaborator Cards (CRCs)

Class-Responsibility-Collaborator cards are a great means to capture responsibilities associated with classes. Figure 7.12 demonstrates what a CRC card looks like. The idea of CRC cards as design tools is to formulate potential classes and assign responsibilities to them.

Class: Messageboard	
Responsibilities:	**Collaboration:**
Add Messages Delete Messages Show Message Threads	messageThread

Class: Calendar	
Responsibilities:	**Collaboration:**
Add Appointments Delete Appointments Show Appointments	dbPersistence Date

Figure 7.12

Of course, the use of CRC cards can appear primitive to design teams that might feel the need for more robust modeling tools to implement their design goals. But they really are powerful mechanisms that you can use to carve up the complexity of an application into manageable parts. You can also use them to clearly define the responsibilities between those parts during the early stages of design so that premature complexity is not introduced into one's modeling activities.

Storyboarding

Once all of your portal user interfaces have been identified, consideration should be given to developing storyboards based on some of your use case scenarios. A storyboard typically consists of sample HTML files or other program visualizations that outline the sequence of events that can occur during normal operations of your portal. This practice also gives your design team a better understanding of your Web application's real estate.

Storyboarding can be accomplished by printing out all of your screenshots from your template HTML files to ensure that all of the navigation flows have been completed, and then have them posted to a wall in a fashion similar to what is shown in Figure 7.13. You might try using red spools of thread attached to tacks to establish navigation flows in your portal application.

This visualization technique is a fairly inexpensive solution for your modeling team, and can be effective in understanding data flows in your application.

Another great practice to capture all of your high-level processing activity comes from the traditional structured approach to modeling called a **context diagram** (see Figure 7.14), which captures the flow of information between a system and external entities. The system scope defined in this figure delineates all of the portal system boundaries from a conceptual perspective without bogging itself down with finer details. The context diagram generally serves as a springboard for more detailed investigation during your analysis activities.

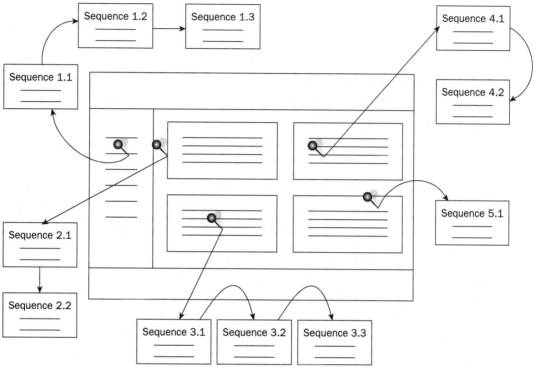

Figure 7.13

Figure 7.15 describes some of the lightweight XP life cycle processes that occur in planning and production operations, which are demonstrated at www.extremeprogramming.org. Along with those activities, open-source tools are shown to complement those tasks to satisfy design and configuration management procedures in that process. Embedded inside the figure shown are some open-source tools that could be used to facilitate those processes. With XP, the key is not to tie yourself down with time-consuming modeling tasks. The emphasis should be on the code itself—that is the end-game that will satisfy the project's stakeholders. To avoid **analysis-paralysis,** as well as tying your team in knots over capturing design models, your design planning should be done on a whiteboard so that changes can be accommodated in an easy fashion and resources are not expended on designs that can vacillate in structure and behavior during early modeling activities. Part of this modeling necessitates storyboarding to understand application flows and real-estate concerns. As far as bug tracking is concerned, open-source tools such as Scarab, BugRat, and iTracker can be used to enable developers to work without interruption from testers. Automated testing procedures could be generated using open-source tools such as ANT, JUnit, and JMeter, and scheduled to run during off-hours so they won't impede development. Lastly, ANT and CheckStyle could automate your code peer reviews and be incorporated into your acceptance testing. CheckStyle is an ANT library extension that can found at http://checkstyle.sourceforge.net/anttask.html.

Context Diagram

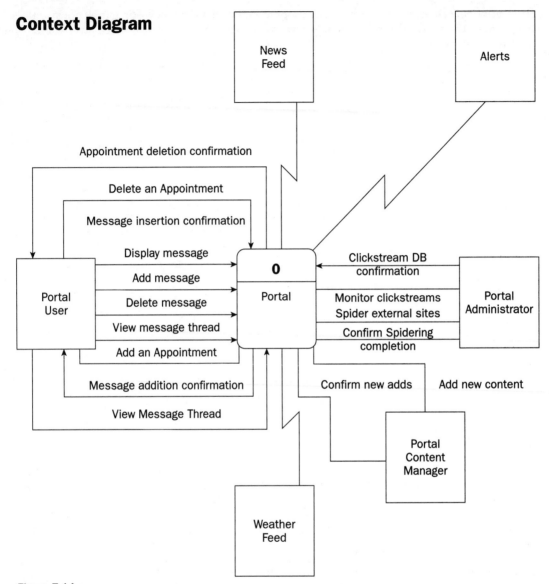

Figure 7.14

As indicated in the XP processes diagram shown in Figure 7.15, careful consideration should be given to the deployment of a collaboration server during the inception phase of your deployment so that knowledge can propagate through the disparate participating groups in your program. Product discoveries that are captured and put on these servers will increase knowledge flows and free personnel from explaining lessons learned to other participants. The idea is to keep everyone involved "clued-in" to all activities so that changes or decision-making at one end of the development spectrum do not go unnoticed by those on the other end.

Portal development efforts evolve into nasty shouting matches and finger-pointing when CM processes have not been properly deployed and adhered to. Automation of these CM activities is paramount to control the complexities that naturally arise among the different portlet developers of your portal system.

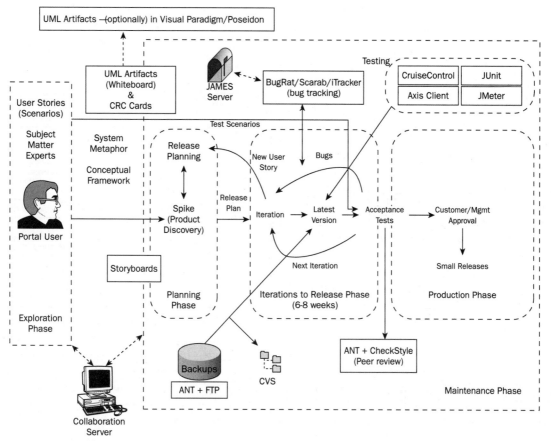

Figure 7.15

Design Models for Visualization That Are Not in UML

In Scott Ambler's book *Agile Modeling,* he provides a practical approach to modeling that enables you to deploy UML artifact-generation best practices on your system. UML does not address two very important features of enterprise modeling: **user interface design** and **data persistence design**. Scott suggests crafting storyboards to visualize your User Interface design to address real estate and navigation concerns and to craft Data Flow Diagrams to enhance data content awareness [AMBLER].

The Data Flow Diagram (DFD) in Figure 7.16 illustrates how data flows from external entities through known processes into and out of a portal application. DFDs are great visualization models that portray all of the relevant inputs/outputs, processes, and persistence mechanisms on your system.

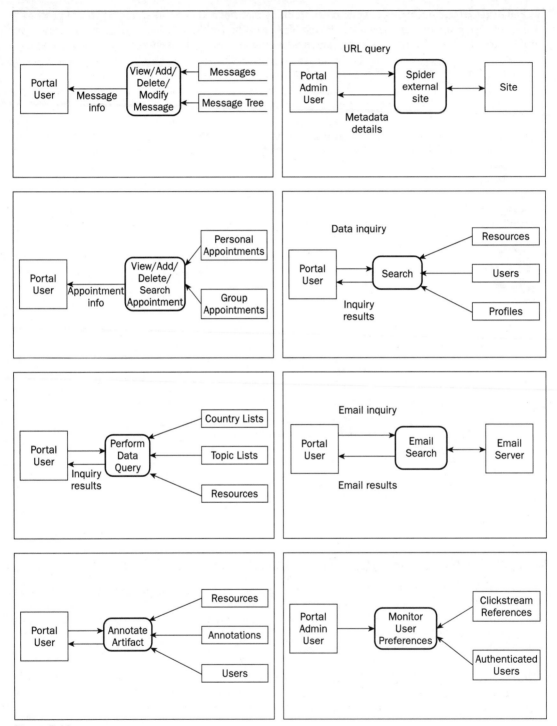

Figure 7.16

Design Decisions

A design decision is generally an architectural or implementation decision that lies outside of the requirements determined by external shareholders. From an architectural perspective, portal designers need to understand their user communities and their development resources in order to put forth a coherent implementation plan. Often, this understanding can assist portal architects in determining whether a commercial framework is needed for deployment, or a development team can roll their own. Figure 7.17 shows a few design decisions that a portal deployment might consider, along with system requirements that relate to the Requirements section previously described. Remember that the requirements listed are only a subset of possible needs that should be addressed prior to development, but they definitely are relevant and deserve consideration.

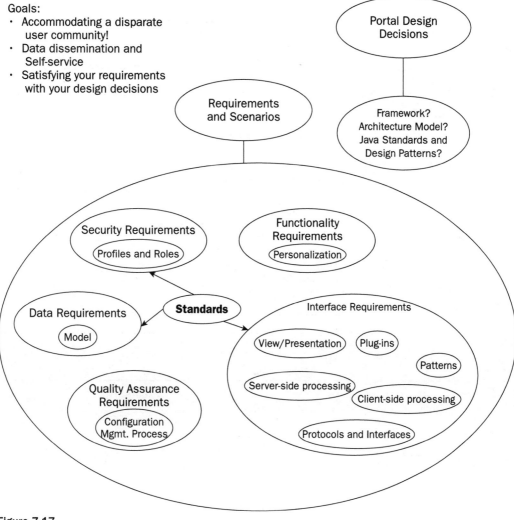

Figure 7.17

The following sections describe design decisions that relate to portal architectures. Prior to beginning an expensive portal procurement decision-making process, an understanding of the different portal architectures could be beneficial when evaluating the different portal offerings.

Model 1 Architecture

A lack of strong enterprise-level development expertise combined with tight scheduling could warrant the Model 1 design. If this is the case, and the program needs to forgo the procurement of a portal framework, using Java Server Pages and servlets with a basic Web container could satisfy your needs. Typically, the Model 1 strategy, which is considered "page-centric," can be deployed with a home page containing embedded pages. With this model, the leftNav.jsp page shown in Figure 7.18 would contain an XML-generated taxonomy that would enable users to navigate through Web content.

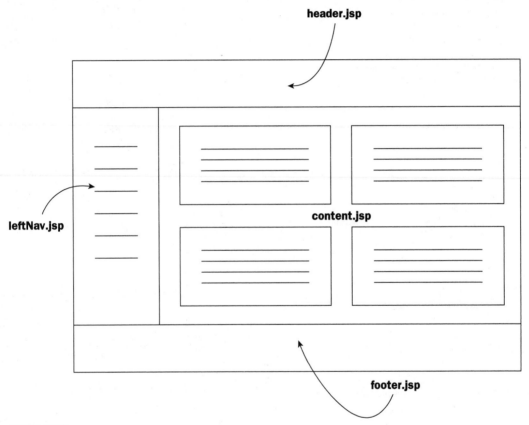

Figure 7.18

Many project designers have spent large investments in portal applications because they bought into the hype of the portal vendors, later deciding that their decision was a bad one. With the help of open-source portal frameworks such as JetSpeed (Pluto), LifeRay, eXo, and Jportal, which implement the JSR-168 specification, developers can build applications without costly expenditures. Additionally, developers can build standardized portlets that can be reused on all of these disparate portal platforms.

For enterprise portals, which service a large community of users and provide self-service capabilities along with information dissemination, an implementation should consider a framework model that can handle heavy loads of information and modifications. The procurement of non-standard portal systems should take into consideration the huge development costs that can be incurred for the services of developers who are cognizant of proprietary product extensions on these closed systems. Concern might also be given to understanding how new components can be enabled in their frameworks. The upside to acquiring a ready-made portal framework is that they come with ready-made tables for data persistence and numerous tools that enable easy portlet customization and configuration of portlet visualization preferences.

Model 2 Architecture

As previously mentioned, the Model 1 architecture is well-suited for simple applications, but most Web applications have navigation and flow control difficulties that necessitate the use of the Model 2 Architecture (M2A), shown in Figure 7.19. With the M2A, which is also referred to as the **Model-View-Controller (MVC)**, multiple views of the same data (model) can be rendered to the user community based on their navigation selections from the view. Most J2EE-compliant portal frameworks implement an MVC solution that uses a servlet controller to render appropriate JSP visualizations. M2A implementations, like Jakarta Struts, can be more cumbersome than Model 1 systems because of labyrinthine parameter-passing through an XML file (`struts-config.xml`) used by a controller servlet. This development complexity can be overcome, however, by time and experience. With M2A implementations, users can control and deploy Web components in an easier fashion than hard-coding dependencies inside the code itself, which presents maintenance problems when things change.

Model 2X Architecture

The Model 2X Architecture (M2XA), shown in Figure 7.20, demonstrates a slight difference between it and a Model 2 implementation. With M2XA, XML is generated by a servlet or JSP component and is transformed into presentation script prior to being sent to a browser for presentation. These transformations are generally performed by XSL stylesheets. The use of XSL stylesheets enables developers to render different views with the same data.

The benefits of M2XA for portal applications are twofold: a single stylesheet can be developed to present a unified view, and a portlet's look and feel can be made at runtime, just like an application that implements the Decorator pattern. A great reference for the M2XA can be found at www.orbeon.com/model2x/.

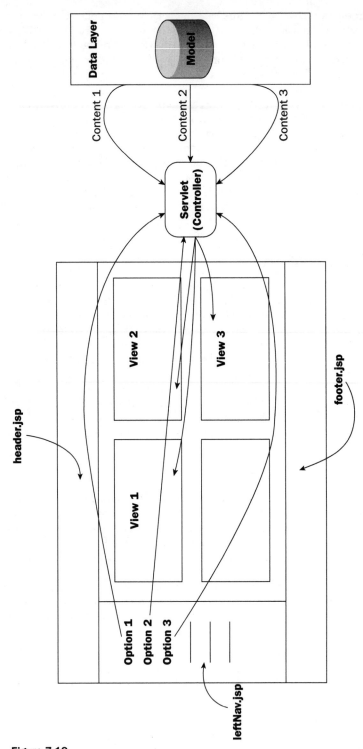

Figure 7.19

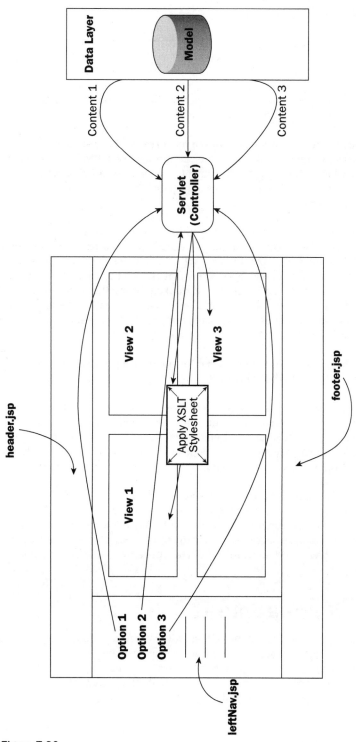

Figure 7.20

Search Utilities

Every portal deployment needs a reliable search utility to enable users to quickly find data that is reliable and suits their needs. Some common search engines include Verity, Autonomy, Inktomi, Convera, Google, and the open-source offering called Lucene. Navigating through a portal using taxonomies is fine for some, but it can become tiresome when the amount of content available is overwhelming. When the sheer size of a site's content can be too much to chew on, and you need to filter out content to get what you need, then a search utility is warranted.

Most search engines perform queries against a database, XML, or binary data set generated from an indexing mechanism. Some search engines use robots to survey the Internet so that they can aggregate more content for their databases. Web documents are retrieved and indexed. When you enter a query at a search engine Web site, your input is checked against the search engine's keyword indices. The best matches are then returned to you as hits.

Two of the more prevalent text-searching capabilities involve searches by keyword and concept. A keyword search usually searches the metadata associated with an artifact for the user-specified keyword and returns all documents that are affiliated with it. Some search engines omit text submitted with the search request so that they can search for terms that are deemed more relevant. This operation means that words such as "a" and "the" might be overlooked during the search operation. Furthermore, some engines discriminate between uppercase and lowercase characters in a search string, others do not. A problem with keyword searching is that words that are spelled the same but have different meanings result in ambiguous content returns from your query.

A concept search attempts to determine what the query string actually means and tries to obtain content that is statistically related to the string query.

In addition to these two types of searches, search engines enable users to refine their queries to target content they need. Some of that refinement includes the capability to search for two or more words and to exclude words that might confuse the engine database. Boolean operators in the form of words or symbols are part of that query refinement. Boolean operators such as AND, OR, and NOT, as well as +, -, enable the search operation to combine and subtract terms from the request.

Finally, most search engines return query results based on relevancy ratings. These relevancy ratings are generated by the number of times the keyword appears in that document; the more often it does, the more relevant the artifact is ranked. Keyword counts in documents are not an important distinguishing feature as to the importance, or relevancy, of a document. Sometimes a document may use a common word repeatedly, which could result in that document being irrelevant for your needs.

Content Management

On many portal applications, comprehensive solutions are needed to deliver content in a controlled fashion through content management applications. Data management encompasses content facilitation through workflow applications known as **content management tools** that provide management and publishing operations for Web content distribution. The implementation of content management systems typically occurs after a working system has been deployed and the portal implementers understand the content they possess.

Two open-source products, OpenCMS and Jakarta's Slide, can be used to control Web content flow in portal deployments. You should examine many of the key features of these content management systems to ensure that your system can deploy Web applications in an efficient manner with these tools. Here is a list of capabilities that you should look for in a content management application:

❑ **Content Publishing** entails the ability to draw information from a persistence store for publication. This can be a database or an XML-based storage mechanism.

❑ **Asset Management** means that all types of content, from document-based files to graphical images, can be handled in an efficient manner so that redundancies are avoided.

❑ **Workflow Management** necessitates the creation of user profiles that delineate user roles and rights to Web artifacts. Once these have been established, users can pull down a document for edit or modification, after which the document can be pushed back into a workflow so that someone else can work on it. When the end of the workflow chain has been reached, the artifact is generally marked for publication.

❑ **Versioning** enables developers to track changes through a history log. More important, it enables versions to be rolled back when problems are found with deployed distributions, and baseline releases can be constructed and fielded to targeted systems.

❑ **Scheduling** enables content managers to distribute their content during "off-hour" times so that server implementations are not overloaded and can handle the new content flows in an efficient manner.

❑ **Personalization** is a tall order for most deployments, because it requires profiles and sophisticated rules to be set up so that targeted content can be distributed to user communities in an easy manner. Personalization is generally phased into a content management process because of the complexities involved in building rules and relevant target communities.

Content management systems can be beneficial to your portal deployments, because they ensure that document standards propagate properly across your system and that portlet components can be managed efficiently in your portal operations.

Design Pattern Considerations in Your Portal

Clearly, there are many ways to implement a design that cannot be expressed adequately in this chapter alone. Hopefully, the introduction of high-level pattern constructs and brief discussion of the implementation of Java standards in this chapter can facilitate your design decisions on your portal deployments. Java language and implementation standards can also help control complexity so that consistent levels of quality can be attained in your development activities. This in turn can lead to increased partner adoption and portlet maintenance. Last, the adoption of design patterns should be applied so that best practices are propagated in your portal deployment and development operations can be hastened.

Much has been written during the last few years about **design patterns** and their use in Java development, so rather than go into great elaboration of their use, we felt that it would be more beneficial to provide high-level concepts of patterns that might be used in your portal deployments and to encourage you to explore them from the online Javaworld newsletter and from the *Core J2EE Patterns* book [ALUR].

Using Java Standards

For many mission-critical development portal efforts, decisions need to be made about expensive software procurements to satisfy your development needs. In order to protect this investment, it is wise to consider standards when you make your purchasing decision because there is nothing worse than dumping a lot of money into a particular framework only to learn after you have obtained it that it is a closed, proprietary system that does not work well with other systems. To guarantee that this does not happen to you, you should become familiar with software standards and other application frameworks' use of them. Regrettably, systems that do rely heavily on proprietary extensions often force your project to hire expensive expertise to help you deploy your program with their framework.

Figure 7.21 illustrates some of the Java standards that could be considered for portal development. It is important to remember that these need to be established prior to procuring a portal framework or integrating existing applications into a homegrown portal application. Always be cognizant of the latest versions of the standards listed in Figure 7.21, and the effects that newer versions of those standards might have on your design decisions.

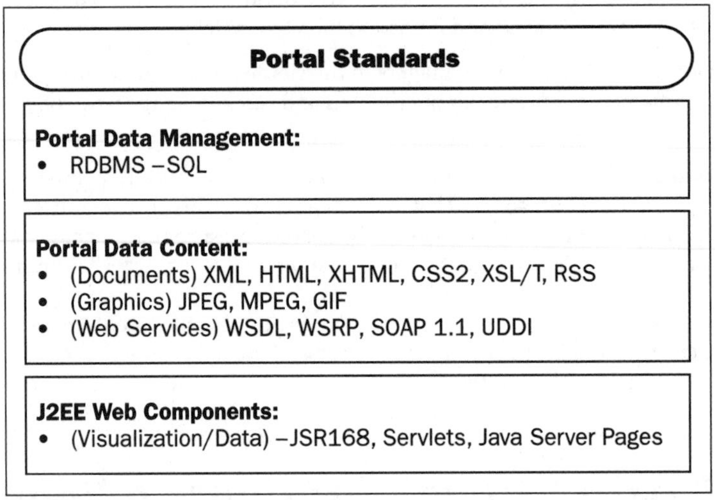

Portal Standards

Portal Data Management:
- RDBMS – SQL

Portal Data Content:
- (Documents) XML, HTML, XHTML, CSS2, XSL/T, RSS
- (Graphics) JPEG, MPEG, GIF
- (Web Services) WSDL, WSRP, SOAP 1.1, UDDI

J2EE Web Components:
- (Visualization/Data) –JSR168, Servlets, Java Server Pages

Figure 7.21

Figure 7.22 illustrates some of the portal standards that should be considered before building your portal application.

On many portal implementations, a business case for adherence to language standards that relate to individual portlets needs to be made so that proprietary extensions are not adopted by a program that disallows code reuse and promotes vendor lock-in. Being exposed to proprietary data formats, one inevitably gets increasingly locked into the solutions of a particular vendor, which in turn limits the options for application software. This ultimately enables vendors to dictate enhancement prices and introduces unnecessary risks to your system. (What if the vendor closes up shop because of low market share? Or what if the vendor adopts a technology strategy that differs from its previous software release that you implemented, which forces your development team to rewrite existing applications?)

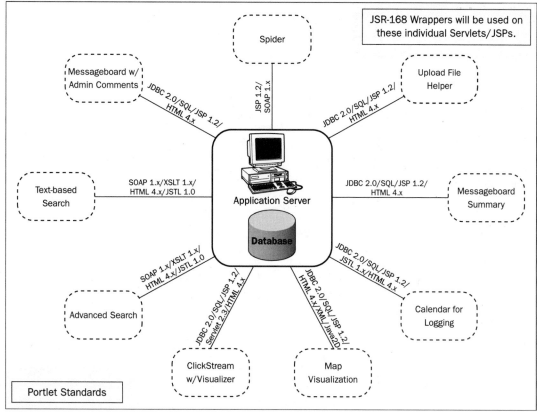

Figure 7.22

When designing your portlets from a high-level view, it is always important to give all of the portal participants an idea of what protocols and standards will be applied in their deployment. Figure 7-17 shows this, which could be an invaluable tool for discussion among different development groups. A system like this ensures that all necessary pieces of your deployment are accounted for.

Figure 7.23 depicts a portal overview from a developer's perspective, and one that can be considered in your portal development. These represent a subset of a much larger superset catalog of Gang of Four [GoF] and J2EE patterns, but the idea presents some best practices when designing your portal.

In many instances, the portal framework can handle operations in its own manner, but in case you want to roll your own, the preceding discussion can offer you some insight as to how the application of best practices in the form of design patterns can be applied.

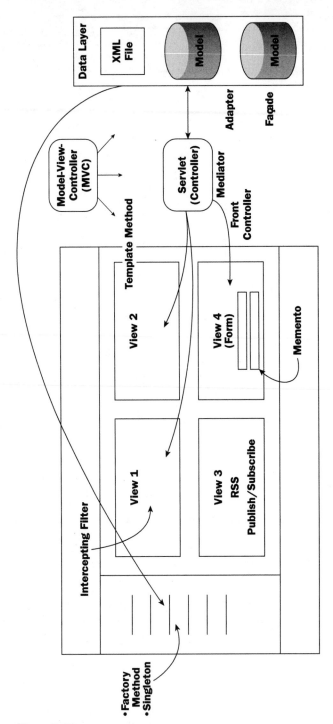

Figure 7.23

Model-View-Controller (MVC) Pattern

In the portal architecture shown in Figure 7.23, the **MVC Pattern** is where the servlet controller renders different views to the portal façade from a disparate set of data sources.

The **model** is the piece that has no specific knowledge of its controllers or its views. The portal system maintains relations between the different models and views and broadcasts content to the views when the model changes state. The **view** is typically the piece that manages the visualizations of the model data. The **controller** is the piece that manages user interaction with the model data.

The MVC Pattern is used with many frameworks because of its ability to handle content delivery complexities that are prominent in many enterprise systems. Jakarta's Struts and BEA's WebFlow are two notable implementations that use this in their frameworks.

Template Method Pattern

A good practice when developing JavaBeans in your portal applications is to use the Template Method Pattern [GoF] to enforce a common design across the portal back-end. The Template Method Pattern can be used so that modifications to your `get` and/or `set` methods will not affect your presentation view.

In the portal display in Figure 7.23, the JavaBean applications on the back-end implement the Template Method Pattern to manage the logic in the accessor (`get`/`set`) methods.

Memento Pattern

In the sample portal visualization shown in Figure 7.23, the view labeled #4 indicates that a form will be rendered to the user display. In many cases, the form will use JavaScript to perform validation testing so that activities will be performed on the client side in order to alleviate unnecessary operations on the server. This is a good practice for some Web applications, especially portals that perform heavy server operations, but sometimes incompatibilities in browsers allow inconsistent behaviors to occur.

The **Memento Pattern** [GoF] will persist the state of the form entries so that submits retain that data in the form text fields, and can perform server-side validation operations on that data.

Facade Pattern

The **Façade Pattern** [GoF] is used in the portal application shown in Figure 7-23 to facilitate tedious operations that are associated with a database connection. Some of the operations that would warrant the use of a façade include the following: database connection handling, driver setups, and SQL statement construction.

Adapter Pattern

The **Adapter Pattern** [GoF] could be applied in the aforementioned portal application as a means to rewrite legacy code implementations to share data from the back-end data stores. By wrapping existing code with an object adapter, the application can support existing interfaces by adapting the interface of the parent class.

The Adapter Pattern provides a mechanism to convert one interface into another. This is necessary when a newer interface has superceded an older one. Instead of recoding the implementation of the older interface, that implementation can be wrapped by an adapter that implements the newer interface. Calls to the new interface methods are then translated into calls to the older interface methods. This enables the legacy code to be extended to allow for more functionality, without having to rewrite existing code.

Factory Method Pattern

The **Factory Method Pattern** [GoF] can be used to instantiate objects, such as a factory, by abstracting the creation and initialization of these objects from the user. This enables the client to focus on the application without being concerned with the object creation details. In our sample portal display, it can be used to generate a `taxonomy` object (from an XML file) that will generate queries as the user traverses the navigation tree.

Singleton Pattern

The **Singleton Pattern** [GoF] ensures that only one instance of a class is created, and provides a single point of access to an object. In the portal example shown in Figure 7-23 a Singleton can be used to open a database connection or to generate a navigation tree from an XML file.

Front Controller Pattern

The **Front Controller Pattern** [ALUR] is part of the J2EE Presentation Tier Patterns library. The Front Controller Pattern is similar to the MVC Pattern, and is actually used within the context of it, but it differs in that no model, or data access component, is associated with it. Referring to our sample portal shown in Figure 7-23, a Servlet controller is used to render different JSP views to the portal display.

Note the following important features of the Front Controller Pattern: It allows for the handling of requests in a centralized location, which facilitates maintenance, and can perform authorization checks without having to spread unnecessary logic across multiple applications.

Intercepting Filter Pattern

The **Intercepting Filter Pattern** [ALUR] is another J2EE Presentation Tier Pattern that was introduced with the Servlet 2.3 specification. This Pattern allows for the pre-processing and post-processing of user requests, as well as the capability to alter response headers and data when processing requests.

In the portal display, the Intercepting Filter Pattern can be used to swap presentation views within a portlet, meaning that the data sent back from the back-end database can be processed to render data in XML format so that an XSL stylesheet can be applied to the data to present a different user view.

Client-Side Processing

Client-side processing refers to the application processing done at the browser. All browsers have been enabled to interpret scripting instructions that would usually be sent to the server. This activity reduces the load on the server's back-end.

Sadly, many challenges are present in browsers because of inconsistencies in their adherence to scripting standards. One of the most troublesome problems with browsers is inconsistencies with their implementations of the Document Object Model (DOM). The DOM standard is used to access elements and attributes of a Web document. These inconsistencies force developers to increase their development efforts to support different browser incompatibilities. To work around this issue, some portal efforts perform more server-side processing, which places a great load on the back-end. Other workaround measures involve allowing only limited amounts of client-side processing, and the application of best practices obtained through other development endeavors.

JavaScript

Different Web browsers, and different versions of the same Web browser, will often treat the similar JavaScript documents slightly differently. This browser incompatibility becomes a more salient issue the more your portal application applies it in its client-side processing. The trick to is to establish a JavaScript standard, and apply it across all of your portal applications that use JavaScript. With all portal applications that use JavaScript, make sure you're aware of your presentations when JavaScript has been disabled in your browser.

Always remember to propagate your proven scripting practices across your portal development efforts. One best practice to apply across your JavaScripting effort in your portal is to put your JavaScript source in a separate JavaScript (`.js`) file. When this is done, the JavaScript source can be referenced with the script tag in the following manner: `<script src="">`.

Server-Side Processing

According to the JSR-168 Portlet Specification, portlets share many of the same attributes as servlet components. The following table compares the two Web components to highlight their commonalities and differences.

Capabilities	Portlets	Servlets
Specialized container management	X	X
Life cycle management in container	X	X
Web interaction via request/response paradigm	X	X
Generates markup fragments	X	
Binds to a URL		X
Uses predefined modes and states to indicate application behaviors	X	
Ability to store transient state data in container sessions for both application and private scope	X	
Sets the application response character encoding set		X
Ability to set HTTP headers on a response		X
Ability to implement the `Request` interface for programmatic security activities	X	X

Figure 7.24 describes the request-handling operations that occur during portlet processing in a portal that implements the JSR-168 Portlet Specification APIs. The portlet container processes the action initiated by the portal user first, and then renders the portlet fragments in no specific order to refresh the user display.

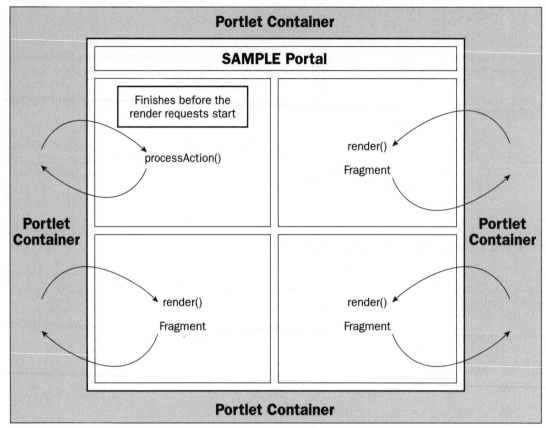

Figure 7.24

Java Plug-ins

Java Plug-ins enable Web applications to supplant a browser's default virtual machine so that more up-to-date JVMs can be applied to that application. The Java Plug-in, which requires a one-time download, enables applications to be consistent in their operations by overriding browser inconsistencies.

The first time a Web browser encounters a Web page that specifies the use of the Java Plug-in, the browser must download and install the required files for proper operation. On most portals' applications, a link should be provided to show users where a plug-in can be obtained to run their application. After the Java Plug-in has been downloaded, subsequent invocations of Web pages that are reliant on the plug-in will retrieve it from the local hard drive when an applet component is rendered.

The implementation of applets and Java Plug-ins in your portal deployments typically needs stake-holder "buy-in" prior to acceptance. This consideration needs to be addressed because of bandwidth and firewall issues that might prevent users from downloading the plug-in to access portlets that use them. To gain better clarity on the implementation of the Java Plug-in on your portal implementation with two of the most common browsers, Netscape and Internet Explorer, developers should refer to Sun's Java Plug-in reference at: http://java.sun.com/products/plugin/.

Web Services for Remote Portals (WSRP)

Web Services for Remote Portals (WSRP) is a new technology that will be an important feature of the JSR-168 Portlet Standard Specification. It enables the plug-n-play of visual UI Web services with portals or any other Web applications. WSRP services will allow content providers to expose content or applications in a non-intrusive manner that does not require application-specific adaptation by consuming applications.

The intention of WSRP is to facilitate the integration of Web applications through a standard set of Web service interfaces. A simple sequence of steps (shown in Figure 7.25) is performed when adding portlets through Web services in portals. When a user puts a portlet on one of the portal pages, the portal requests the creation of a corresponding portlet instance on the WSRP service's side, by calling the createPortletInstance operation and obtaining a portlet instance handle that it uses in subsequent requests. It can then obtain markup to embed from the WSRP service by calling the getPortletMarkup operation and displaying that markup within a portlet. If the obtained markup contains links or forms with associated actions, and the user clicks into the portlet on one of these links or forms, the portlet triggers the corresponding action in the WSRP service by calling the performAction operation. When the portal doesn't need the portlet instance anymore because the portlet is removed from a user's page, it requests to discard the portlet instance on the WSRP service's side by calling the destroyInstance operation. A good reference on WSRP implementation can be found at www-106.ibm.com/developerworks/library/ws-wsrp.

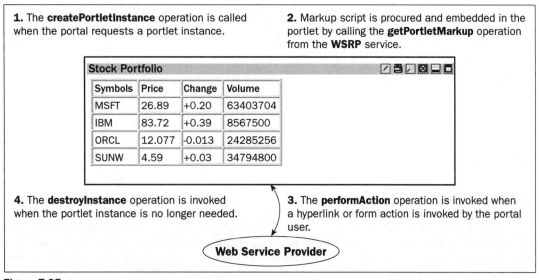

Figure 7.25

WSRPs are Web-service visualization components that accumulate content from disparate external sources for portal presentation. WSRP services can be discovered when they are published publicly or when they've been incorporated into a service directory from which they can be discovered dynamically. This is shown visually in Figure 7.26

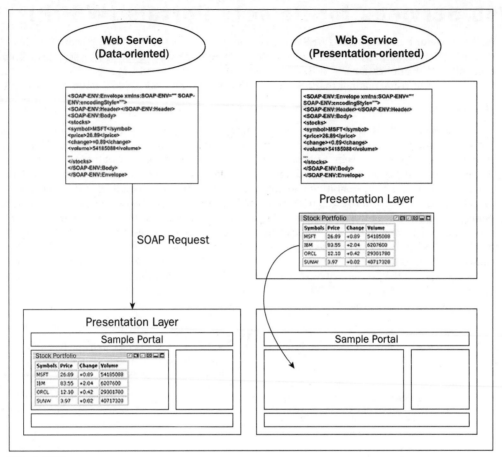

Figure 7.26

Portal Navigation

Good navigation design and consistency are essential ingredients for any successful Web site. The navigation scheme is basically the road map of your site, marking content routes and directions to further data information areas. One of the most important jobs of a portal designer is to accommodate an eclectic user base by presenting a clear vision of the navigation and search activities. Flexibility should always be designed into your navigation system to allow for easy modifications that inherently occur because of new data integrations.

Navigation types come in many flavors, but the four most common are as follows: embedded links, breadcrumb trails, top-bottom-left navigation bars, and site maps. Embedded links are commonplace in all portal applications; they are added to Web page bodies through the `<a href></a>` link construct. Breadcrumb trails enable users to backtrack through previous page links that they visited earlier. Navigation bars, located on the top/bottom/left portions of your Web page, are the most common form of navigation in portals. Navigation taxonomies are typically used on the left navigation bar to scroll down a page for content selections. On most Web sites, a site map is provided to give users a high-level view of the content available on the site. The problem for portals is that the content is so varied and complex that is difficult to categorize this in an easy-to-read fashion, and it's even harder for a developer to build this functionality in a dynamic fashion. The JetSpeed framework from Jakarta uses an XML file to track the content and portlets available to users. JetSpeed uses the Portal Structure Markup Language (PSML), which is demonstrated in Listing 7.1.

Listing 7.1: PSML File Used in JetSpeed Portal

```
<portlets user="default" xmlns="http://xml.apache.org/jetspeed/2000/psml">
  <controller
name="org.apache.jetspeed.portal.controllers.RowColumnPortletController">
    <parameter name="sizes" value="70%,30%"/>
    <parameter name="mode" value="row"/>
  </controller>
  <skin>
    <property name="selected-color" value="#990000"/>
    <property name="title-color" value="#FFCC00"/>
  </skin>
  <portlets>
    <controller
name="org.apache.jetspeed.portal.controllers.RowColumnPortletController"/>
    <entry type="ref"
parent="http://jakarta.apache.org/jetspeed/channels/jetspeed.rss">
    </entry>
    <entry type="ref" parent="http://www.xmlhack.com/rsscat.php">
    </entry>
  </portlets>
  <portlets>
    <controller
name="org.apache.jetspeed.portal.controllers.RowColumnPortletController"/>
    <entry type="ref" parent="http://www.mozilla.org/news.rdf">
      <parameter name="itemDisplayed" value="5"/>
    </entry>
    <entry type="ref" parent="http://www.apacheweek.com/issues/apacheweek-
headlines">
      <parameter name="showTitle" value="false"/>
    </entry>
    <reference id="P-ed09142736-10018" path="group/apache/page/news"/>
  </portlets>
</portlets>
```

Figure 7.27 shows most of the navigation devices that a portal should offer its users to enable them to navigate through content.

Typically, these navigation components include tree-like taxonomy structures consisting of hyperlinks; breadcrumb trails, to indicate where the user is and has been previously; and a site map, which aggregates all of the important pages that a user needs to be cognizant of from the developer's perspective. The portlet.xml file deployment descriptor, which is part of the JSR-168 specification, defines the metadata that can be used to build a site map application on portal applications.

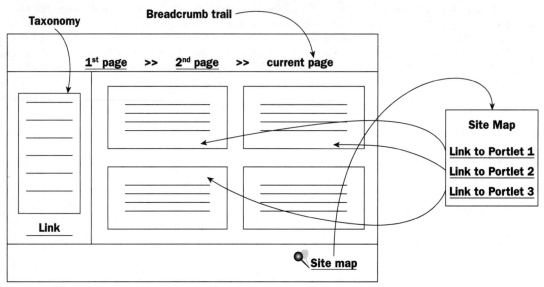

Figure 7.27

Portal Navigation Using Taxonomies

Taxonomies are important features of portal content organization. Most portals use some kind of navigation scheme to arrange their content terms into a hierarchical structure for user browsing provisioning. There are many ways to generate taxonomies. The preceding code sample demonstrates a taxonomy generator that reads an XML file displayed in Listing 7.2 and creates content links for a user to navigate through, using dom4j libraries.

This particular application uses an open-source product called dom4j to extract links from the hierarchical data in the XML file. dom4j is a great application for parsing and manipulating content that resides in XML files. As their site mentions (www.dom4j.org/), it offers full support for JAXP, SAX, DOM, and XSLT. It also has XPath support for navigating XML documents, and is based on Java interfaces for flexible implementations. For those standards-junkies, it is not considered a standard because it does not fully support the DOM standard.

Listing 7.2: TopicGenerator.java

```
001: package portals;
002: /**
003:  * @author MM
004:  *
005:  * To change this generated comment edit the template variable "typecomment":
006:  * Window>Preferences>Java>Templates.
007:  * To enable and disable the creation of type comments go to
008:  * Window>Preferences>Java>Code Generation.
009:  */
010: import java.net.*;
```

```
011: import java.util.*;
012: import javax.naming.*;
013: import org.dom4j.*;
014: import org.dom4j.io.*;
015: public class TopicGenerator {
016:    protected static String EXPANDED_SYMBOL = "- ";
017:    protected static String COLLAPSED_SYMBOL = "+ ";
018:    protected static String LEAF = "&#149; ";
019:    protected static String SPACER = " ";
020:    protected static String TOPIC_CSS_CLASS = "SelectedTopic";
021:    private Document document;
022:    public TopicGenerator() throws NamingException {
023:      Context initCtx = new InitialContext();
024:      Context ctx =  (Context) initCtx.lookup("java:comp/env");
025:      String topicsDirectory = (String) ctx.lookup("topicsDirectory");
026:      setFilename(topicsDirectory + java.io.File.separator + "Topic.xml");
027:    }
028:    public TopicGenerator(String fileName) throws Exception {
029:      parseDocument(fileName);
030:      if (this.document == null)
031:        throw new Exception("Problem initializing TopicGenerator");
032:    }
033:    public void setFilename(String fileName) {
034:      parseDocument(fileName);
035:    }
036:    private void parseDocument(String fileName) {
037:      try {
038:        SAXReader reader = new SAXReader();
039:        document = reader.read(fileName);
040:      } catch (DocumentException de) {
041:        System.out.println("Problem initializing TopicGenerator.");
042:        de.printStackTrace();
043:      } catch (MalformedURLException me) {
044:        System.out.println("Malformed URL.");
045:        me.printStackTrace();
046:      }
047:    }
```

The addElement method shown in Lines 48–79 adds hyperlinked elements to the navigation tree. The implementation of the StringBuffer class is preferred over a String class concatenation because of significant performance differences.

```
048:    private void addElement(StringBuffer sb, Set set, Element element, String topicId,
049: String topicParamName, String href, String extraParams, int level) {
050:      if (level != -1) {
051:        // write current node
052:        for (int i = 0; i < level*4; i++)
053:          sb.append(TopicGenerator.SPACER);
054:        if (element.elements().isEmpty())
055:          sb.append(TopicGenerator.LEAF);
056:        else if (set.contains(element))
```

```
057:            sb.append(TopicGenerator.EXPANDED_SYMBOL);
058:          else sb.append(TopicGenerator.COLLAPSED_SYMBOL);
059:          String thisTopicId = element.attributeValue("value");
060:          if (topicId.equals(thisTopicId))
061:            sb.append("<a class=\"" + TopicGenerator.TOPIC_CSS_CLASS + "\" ");
062:          else sb.append("<a ");
063:          sb.append("href=\"");
064:          sb.append(href);
065:          sb.append('?');
066:          sb.append(topicParamName);
067:          sb.append('=');
068:          sb.append(thisTopicId);
069:          sb.append(extraParams);
070:          sb.append("\">" + element.attributeValue("text") + "</a><br>");
071:        }
072:        if (set.contains(element) || level == -1) {
073:          Iterator it = element.elementIterator();
074:          while (it.hasNext()) {
075:            Element currElement = (Element) it.next();
076:            addElement(sb, set, currElement, topicId, topicParamName, href,
      extraParams, level + 1);
077:          }
078:        }
079:      }
```

The generateParams method receives a HashMap object from the getTopics method so that it can generate the parameters needed for navigation. Please note that it is always a good practice to check the input parameters that are passed into a method prior to performing operations on them. Lines 81–82 verify that the object value is not null and contains some items to process.

```
080:    private String generateParams(HashMap params) {
081:      if (params == null || params.isEmpty())
082:        return "";
083:      StringBuffer toReturn = new StringBuffer();
084:      Iterator keys = params.keySet().iterator();
085:      while (keys.hasNext()) {
086:        String currParam = (String) keys.next();
087:        String currParamValue = (String) params.get(currParam);
088:        if (currParamValue != null) {
089:          toReturn.append('&');
090:          toReturn.append(currParam);
091:          toReturn.append('=');
092:          toReturn.append(currParamValue);
093:        }
094:      }
095:      return toReturn.toString();
096:    }
```

The getTopics method on Line 97 establishes a tree structure based on the taxonomies residing in the Topic.xml file discovered from the code shown on Lines 23–26. The overloaded getCountriesList method shown on Line 110 receives a string country value and returns a string of country items along with the country selected by the user.

```
097:    public String getTopics(String topicId, String topicParamName, String href,
HashMap params) {
098:      if (topicId == null)
099:        topicId = "";
100:      Element taxonomy = (Element)
document.selectSingleNode("/navigation/taxonomy");
101:      List list = taxonomy.selectNodes("//topic[@value='" + topicId +
"']/ancestor-or-self::*");
102:      Set expandedNodeSet = new HashSet(list);
103:      StringBuffer toReturn = new StringBuffer();
104:      addElement(toReturn, expandedNodeSet, taxonomy, topicId, topicParamName,
href, generateParams(params), -1);
105:      return toReturn.toString();
106:    }
107:    public String getCountriesList() {
108:      return getCountriesList("");
109:    }
110:    public String getCountriesList(String cc) {
111:      StringBuffer toReturn = new StringBuffer();
112:      Element countriesRoot = (Element)
document.selectSingleNode("/navigation/countries");
113:      Iterator allCountries = countriesRoot.selectNodes("//country").iterator();
114:      while (allCountries.hasNext()) {
115:        Element currCountry = (Element) allCountries.next();
116:        String currCC = currCountry.attributeValue("value");
117:        toReturn.append("<option class=\"smalltext\" name=\"CC\" value=\"");
118:        toReturn.append(currCC);
119:        toReturn.append("\"");
120:        if (currCC.equals(cc))
121:          toReturn.append(" SELECTED");
122:        toReturn.append('>');
123:        toReturn.append(currCountry.getTextTrim());
124:        toReturn.append("</option>");
125:      }
126:      return toReturn.toString();
127:    }
128:    public String getTopics(String topicId, String topicParamName, String href)
{
129:      return getTopics(topicId, topicParamName, href, (HashMap) null);
130:    }
```

The overloaded getTopics method on Lines 131 and 137 returns the Topics values shown in using the getTopics method on Line 97. The topics that are returned become part of the taxonomy tree for user navigation.

```
131:    public String getTopics(String topicId, String topicParamName, String href,
String cc, HashMap params) {
132:      if (params == null)
133:        params = new HashMap();
134:      params.put("country", cc);
135:      return getTopics(topicId, topicParamName, href, params);
136:    }
```

```
137:    public String getTopics(String topicId, String topicParamName, String href,
String cc) {
138:       HashMap params = new HashMap();
139:       params.put("country", cc);
140:       return getTopics(topicId, topicParamName, href, params);
141:    }
```

Although the TopicGenerator method is used as a JavaBean component by our Web component in Figure 7.27, it is generally a good practice to create a test application with your bean to ensure that it works properly prior to deployment, and to demonstrate to others how the methods in it should be accessed. The main method, which starts on Line 142, uses an absolute class path to invoke the TopicGenerator method with the Topic.xml file that will be used to navigate the taxonomy tree.

```
142:    public static void main(String[] args) throws Exception {
143:       TopicGenerator tg = new
TopicGenerator("c:\\apache\\tomcat4124\\webapps\\mojo\\WEB-
INF\\classes\\Topic.xml");
144:       System.out.println(tg.getTopics("1", "mammals", "test.html"));
145:       System.out.println(tg.getCountriesList());
146:       System.out.println(tg.getTopics("1", " mammals", "", ""));
147:    }
148: }
149:
```

The data elements in the Topics.xml file in Listing 7.2 are invoked by the TopicsGenerator.java routine in Listing 7.3 to build a taxonomy tree. The two most important elements of this file are the countries and topic items. The XML file represents the topic and country data in a hierarchical manner that is easy to manipulate with the DOM4J libraries.

Listing 7.3: Topic.xml

```
<navigation>
  <countries>
    <country value="USA">United States</country>
  </countries>
  <taxonomy text="Default Taxonomy" value="test">
      <topic value="10000000" text="Mammals">
      <topic value="10000001" text="Beaver"/>
      <topic value="10000002" text="Bighorn Sheep"/>
      <topic value="10000003" text="Bison"/>
      <topic value="10000004" text="Black Bear"/>
      <topic value="10000005" text="Bobcat"/>
      <topic value="10000006" text="Cottontail Rabbit"/>
      <topic value="10000007" text="Elk"/>
      <topic value="10000008" text="Moose"/>
      <topic value="10000009" text="Raccoon"/>
      <topic value="10000010" text="Skunk"/>
      <topic value="10000011" text="Squirrel"/>
      <topic value="10000012" text="White-tailed Deer"/>
      <topic value="10000013" text="Wife"/>
```

```
        <topic value="10000014" text="Wolf"/>
        <topic value="10000015" text="Existentialists">
        <topic value="10000016" text="Camus"/>
        <topic value="10000017" text="Kafka"/>
        <topic value="10000018" text="Sartre"/>
  </taxonomy>
</navigation>
```

The source code in the TopicGenerator.java application generates the taxonomy navigation piece in the left navigation of the mocked-up portal page in Figure 7-28. An open-source library object model called dom4J (www.dom4j.org/) was used to manipulate an XML file so that taxonomy data could easily be read in and manipulated, enabling a navigation component to drill on the XML data and generate queries during the navigation process.

Figure 7.28 demonstrates how a taxonomy editor could be deployed using the source code. As a user navigates through the taxonomy, new queries are generated and the results of those queries can be rendered in the content section of a portal application, or inside of a portlet itself. The example in Figure 7.28 highlights the chosen topic "Bighorn Sheep" and generates a query, which returns a taxonomyIndex of 10000002 and a country attribute of USA. Consideration should be given to the use of XML parsers that act on XML files for navigation components because they're easy to manipulate and help avoid the hard-coding of links in your applications.

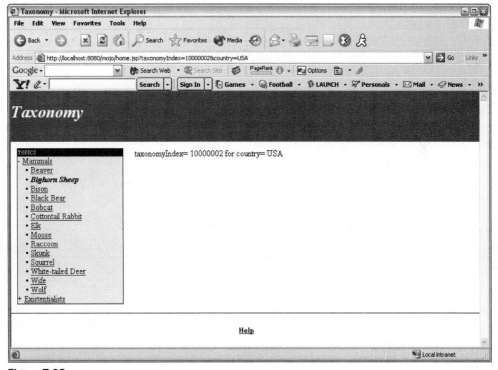

Figure 7.28

Portlet Integration Plan

Portlet Integration Plans typically outline the overall components that are needed to successfully deploy an enterprise portal. These integration pieces include hardware, software, portlet overviews, requirements, database schemas, and administrative information needed for proper implementation. Figure 7.29 exhibits a sample Portlet Integration Plan, which starts out as a portlet survey and evolves into a working document to facilitate the integration of portlets into a portal system.

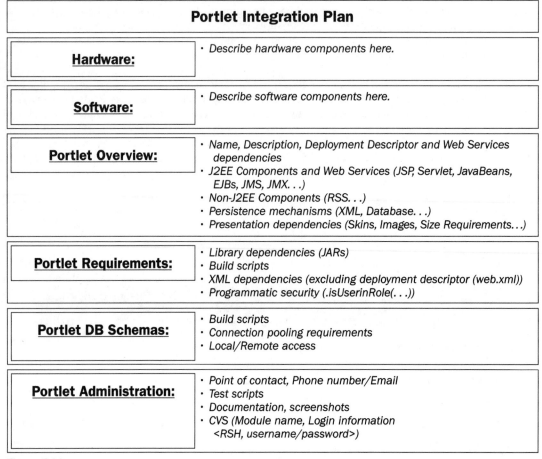

Portlet Integration Plan	
Hardware:	• Describe hardware components here.
Software:	• Describe software components here.
Portlet Overview:	• Name, Description, Deployment Descriptor and Web Services dependencies • J2EE Components and Web Services (JSP, Servlet, JavaBeans, EJBs, JMS, JMX. . .) • Non-J2EE Components (RSS. . .) • Persistence mechanisms (XML, Database. . .) • Presentation dependencies (Skins, Images, Size Requirements. . .)
Portlet Requirements:	• Library dependencies (JARs) • Build scripts • XML dependencies (excluding deployment descriptor (web.xml)) • Programmatic security (.isUserinRole(. . .))
Portlet DB Schemas:	• Build scripts • Connection pooling requirements • Local/Remote access
Portlet Administration:	• Point of contact, Phone number/Email • Test scripts • Documentation, screenshots • CVS (Module name, Login information <RSH, username/password>)

Figure 7.29

Hardware specifications describe the operating system, RAM, and disk space requirements, as well as any peripheral devices, so that portlet integrators realize where their portlet subsystems will be situated, and to let others know up front if the system being deployed has any shortcomings that might affect the fusion of their individual applications. Additionally, portal implementations generally reside on more than one box, so network dependencies and system topologies can be outlined here to elucidate how things will fit together on the enterprise system.

Software specifications outline all of the portal binary installations and the Web applications that will run in it. It is important to note what software versions will be used, especially with open-source applications, because of their easy availability and continuous release and update schedules.

Portlet overview plans describe the individual portlets and any deployment descriptor or Web services dependencies that the integrators need to understand so that disparate portlet developers will not interfere with each other's portlet subsystems. All J2EE components (JSPs, servlets, EJBs, and so on) need to be outlined, as well as non-J2EE applications. Persistence mechanisms should be publicized in small detail, such as XML or database tables, to let the integration team know which ANT/SQL or SQL scripts are needed to support the portlet applications. Lastly, presentation dependencies need to be made known so that real estate concerns and visualization needs can be addressed.

Portlet requirements illustrate library dependencies such as Java Archive (JAR) files, ANT build scripts, XML dependencies, and programmatic security concerns. XML parsers are a big part of portal implementations, considering the incursion of SOAP services and taxonomy applications, so it is paramount that portal integrators understand the XML parsers used by the different portlet development groups so that library collisions can be avoided. As far as programmatic security is concerned, it is important to understand the different methods of the Request interface. This enables you to access role information from a servlet context so that you can distinguish privileges, enabling you to make determinations about the delivery of Web content in your portlets. In Figure 7.30, programmatic security is performed to ensure that users with administrator role privileges are shown the AdminView page and all others will be shown the GuestView.

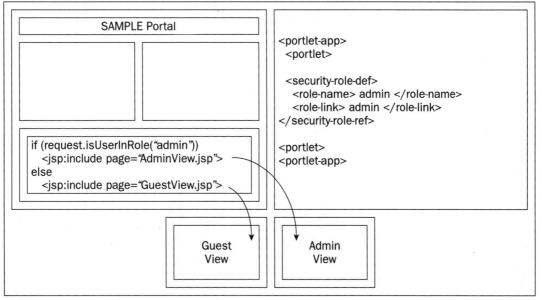

Figure 7.30

The Portlet Integration Plan is a living document that should reflect changes that are realized through discovery by both the developers and the system integrators. A "Lessons Learned" section should be appended to the document during each portal integration drop.

Summary

One conclusion that should be obvious from this chapter's discussions about requirements gathering and making portal design decisions is that portal design is difficult. However, one should realize that investment protection with standards is a good bet when evaluating portal framework products, and proper requirements and modeling processes will facilitate your operations.

The confluence of portlet subsystems into a unified portal view is a daunting modeling task to undertake, which is compounded by technical aspects of the implementation of the finalized design. Even if you feel that you've stayed up-to-date with all of the technologies needed for implementation, the task still remains formidable. Thankfully, if you plan on using Java technologies in your portal implementations, all of their technologies are related and designed to complement each other, which should help you in the long run. Some of the modeling tasks and design decisions described in this chapter could prove beneficial in your portal development programs, but one thing is for sure: There is no turnkey solution for deploying portals.

Lastly, your portal framework should be considered a "choreography piece" for all of the portlet subsystems that reside in it, and it is important to set modest goals for your first portal implementation. The greater the number of features or bells and whistles, the more likely it will be that the project becomes overly complex, the delivery date delayed, and the resulting product flawed or unreliable. Determine what key features are needed in order for the portal to succeed. Begin with a modest list of goals and fight against project creep so that early successes can flourish and significant successes can be realized in the future.

8

Effective Client-Side Development Using JavaScript

A lot of application development is focused on the middle or back-end tier where business logic and data storage are performed. These tiers comprise the vast majority of an application's guts and complexity. An equally important aspect, however, is the development of the client itself. This is the portion of the application that the customer or user interfaces with in order to accomplish a specific task.

No matter what your application architecture is comprised of, be it Java servlets, Java Server Pages (JSP), Perl Common Gateway Interface (CGI) scripts, Microsoft .Net components, and so on, your Web-based application, in the end, will consist of HyperText Markup Language (HTML) displayed in a browser. By itself, HTML is static. It can only display text or a variety of form elements for data entry. In the past, Web developers would design client interfaces to enable users to enter data into designated fields and then submit the page to a server located somewhere on the network. The server would then perform all the operations on the submitted data, from validation to applying business rules. This essentially equated to server-side data processing. When Web-based applications were in their infancy, this process was accepted as the de facto standard.

As Web-based applications evolved, they became much more complex, and better methods for handling the client needed to be worked out. Issues concerning network latency and application performance also needed to be addressed. In order to solve some of these problems, some of the data processing needed to be moved from the server to the client itself. Performing some of the workload on the client allowed for a couple of things to happen. First, certain data validations and processing could be done in the client browser, relieving the server of the burden to take the time to perform these functions. Second, it could reduce the amount of network activity needed to perform a given task.

In order to perform these types of client-side operations, many browsers have integrated the ability to run **JavaScript**. JavaScript is an interpreted, object-oriented programming language that can be added to an HTML page, which can add great flexibility to a Web page. JavaScript is not unlike other programming languages. It contains the ability to use operators, expressions, conditionals, loops, functions, etc. In addition to those basic features, however, JavaScript has built-in functions that allow direct access to a Web page's content. Adding JavaScript to a client application not only can help a developer cut down on unnecessary network traffic, it can also provide the ability to develop a more complicated and efficient client by adding power, flexibility, and even interactivity. This all can equate to a more useful and fulfilling experience for the user.

While adding JavaScript to a development architecture in order to take advantage of its features, the developer must consider a few issues. One such issue is how various browsers have integrated the use of JavaScript. The two main Web browsers, Microsoft Internet Explorer (IE) and Netscape Communicator, differ slightly in how they interpret JavaScript code. Because of this, developers of Web applications that use JavaScript have to develop and test their code in both browsers (and different versions within the same browser) to ensure that the application will run properly. The majority of JavaScript code does run in both browsers without any changes needed. The main difference is how each browser views the Web page **Document Object Model**, or **DOM**. It was mentioned earlier that JavaScript has built-in functions that can be used to gain access to a Web page's content. This process is accomplished through the interaction between the JavaScript code and the browser's DOM. Because both IE and Netscape use different DOM models, the JavaScript code necessary to access it is slightly different. The differences in JavaScript code for both IE and Netscape are highlighted in the various examples and discussions that follow in this chapter.

This chapter provides a recipe for efficiently developing Web clients for multiple browsers. The chapter starts out by describing how JavaScript is declared in the client and how it can be used to perform generic functions such as data validation. The chapter then describes increasingly more complex ways to utilize JavaScript. This includes **auto-population** and **auto-validation**, how to manage the client space through an efficient combination of JavaScript and HTML form elements, and how JavaScript can be used to dynamically change the look of the client. Throughout the examples, you will also find references to code differences that are needed so that each of these capabilities can be successfully run in different client browsers. Applying these characteristics to the client will aid the portal development process by removing unnecessary processing on the server, allowing for greater flexibility and power on the client, and enriching the user experience.

Declaring JavaScript

To create and run JavaScript, all that is needed is a Web browser and a text editor. Because JavaScript runs inside of the HTML page, the code can be generated along with the HTML tags. There are two ways, however, to include JavaScript code into an HTML page. The first method is to write the code in-line—that is, to include the code in the same file as a hard-coded HTML page or in the same script that dynamically generates an HTML page. To do this, the JavaScript is entered inside of the `<script>` tag. The `<script>` tag is usually, but not required to be, listed at the top of the HTML page inside of the `<head>` tag. The following code snippet shows how to declare the use of in-line JavaScript code:

```
<html>
  <head>
    <script language="javascript">
      // Javascript code goes here.
    </script>
  </head>
</html>
```

The other method is to create the JavaScript code in a separate file and include the file from the HTML page:

```
<html>
  <head>
    <script language="javascript" src="lib/javascript/jsfile.js">
    </script>
  </head>
</html>
```

In the preceding example, the JavaScript code is located in the file `jsfile.js`, located in the directory `lib/JavaScript`. This is a relative path from the location of the HTML file. No special tags are needed inside of the separate JavaScript file in order for the code to be loaded and executed.

Whether to include the JavaScript code in-line or in a separate file depends on the Web-based application as well as simple personal preference. Adding the code in-line is most appropriate if the JavaScript needed is specific only to that HTML page or if some of the JavaScript has to be dynamically built based on the contents of the page. For example, if the HTML page is dynamically generated and the JavaScript code must reflect certain aspects of that page, which may be different each time, it will also be necessary to dynamically generate the JavaScript code at the same time. On the other hand, some JavaScript functionality may be shared among several different Web pages. In that case, it would be more appropriate to place the JavaScript code in a file and have each Web page include the file. This reduces the amount of code written and enables the developer to adhere to the paradigm of code reuse. In many cases, however, it is necessary to use both approaches.

To have a Web page use JavaScript code written both in-line and in a separate file, simply combine the syntax for both approaches. The following code snippet shows how this is declared:

```
<html>
  <head>
    <script language="javascript" src="lib/javascript/jsfile.js">
    </script>
    <script language="javascript">
      // Javascript code goes here.
    </script>
  </head>
</html>
```

Validating Data

As described in the opening paragraphs, one advantage of using JavaScript on the client is performing client-side field validation. Using JavaScript in the client browser enables a developer to perform data validation before it is sent back to the server for further processing, and because the validation is being performed on the client instead of the server, feedback to the user concerning any data errors is obtained much quicker.

Two basic components are part of performing field validations. The first is to create a function that will perform the logic necessary for the validation, and the second is to add the process that calls the function. There are some differences between writing JavaScript functions versus writing functions in other programming languages. In JavaScript, a function is declared without a reference to whether something is returned by the function or not. It is also a loosely typed language, and arguments sent into the function are not declared to be of a certain data type. The following example shows a JavaScript function that accepts a single parameter:

```
function validateDateField(parameter1)
  // Javascript code for this function goes here.
}
```

You can use several methods to call JavaScript functions on a Web page. What you choose, of course, depends on the intended goal. If the goal is to perform validation on an entire form, the call to a function is usually accomplished from an HTML button. Following is the code necessary to call a JavaScript function from an HTML button:

```
<html>
  <head>
    <script language="javascript">
      function validateForm() {
        // Javascript code goes here.
      }
    </script>
  </head>
  <body>
    <form>
      <input type="button" value="Validate" onClick="validateForm()">
    </form>
  </body>
</html>
```

The preceding example shows the HTML <input> tag using the JavaScript onClick event handler to call the function validateForm without any arguments. A function can also be called directly from the field on which the validation is to be performed. The following code snippet lists a JavaScript function call from an HTML text field. Notice that this example has a reference to the object this being passed to the function from the HTML field:

```
<html>
  <head>
    <script language="javascript">
      function validateField(fieldObj) {
        // Javascript code goes here.
      }
    </script>
  </head>
  <body>
    <form>
      <input type="text" name="today" onChange="validateField(this)">
    </form>
  </body>
</html>
```

The preceding example shows the HTML <input> tag using the onChange event handler to call the function validateField with a single argument. In this case, the argument is the pre-defined object this, which is used by JavaScript event handlers to send a field object reference to the function. The function can then perform operations on the field by referencing the function's parameter name.

There are two other ways to call a function to perform an operation with regard to a field element on a Web page. One way would be to call the function with no reference to the field (no argument). In that case, the function itself would have to create a reference to the field. The second way is to send a reference to the field, but not using the this object. This second approach would involve getting a reference to the field from the browser's DOM itself. As mentioned earlier, IE and Netscape require that JavaScript reference the DOM in different ways. To make the same call to the function validateField with a reference to the field object via the DOM, the developer must ensure that appropriate syntax is used, based on the client browser. In order to send the reference in the Netscape browser, for example, the argument sent to the JavaScript function should look like the following:

```
<input type="text" name="today" onChange="validateField(document.forms[0].today)">
```

To send the reference in the IE browser, use the following call:

```
<input type="text" name="today" onChange="validateField(document.all.today)">
```

The same syntax (for example, document.all.today) would be used by the function to get a reference to the field from inside the function itself. Ideally, the this object would be used because in order to access the object, no code difference between Netscape and IE is needed. If either of the other two methods were used, it would most likely be necessary to create the reference to the field object inside the function rather than send it to the function. This is because the developer would have to use programming logic to first determine whether the client browser is either Netscape or IE. This can be done in a JavaScript function, but not in the HTML document where the <input> tag is listed.

Actually, IE is little more flexible when it comes to interpreting JavaScript. When accessing a document's form and form elements, IE is able to process both the statements document.forms[0].today and document.all.today. Netscape, however, can only process the statement document.forms[0].today. This flexibility in IE, however, is only valid when accessing the form object of the main document. Later in this chapter, in the section "Layering and DHTML," the concept of layering is introduced. This is done through the <span> and <div> tags. When using these tags, IE will have to access the layer's form elements through the document.all object. This will be made a bit clearer when layering is discussed. Although the initial examples in this chapter only need to access elements from the document.forms[0] object, we will use document.all to access the elements in the IE browser for consistency.

There are several ways to have JavaScript determine which browser is being used to run the application. The approach chosen depends on how much information the developer wants—for example, you may want to determine not only which browser, but also which browser versions. The code examples checking for a Netscape browser, for example, will work for Netscape 4.x browsers but not Netscape 6.0. A couple of examples of how to determine which browser is being used are outlined in the following code:

```
<html>
    <head>
<script language="javascript">
        var Netscape = false;
        // Method #1
        if (document.layers) { Netscape = true; }
        // Method #2
```

225

```
            if (navigator.appName == "Netscape") { Netscape = true; }
            function validateField() {
              var field;
              if (Netscape) {
                field = document.forms[0].today;
              }else {
                field = document.all.today;
              }
              // Rest of Javascript code.
            }
        </script>
    </head>
    <body>
    <form>
      <input type="text" name="today" onChange="validateField()">
    </form>
    </body>
</html>
```

Once the browser type is determined and the field object reference is generated according to the proper syntax, the object's properties can be obtained and modified using the same code for both browsers. At this point, the developer can proceed with the validation of the field data. In the preceding case, the validation is for a date that was entered into a text field. As is typical of most applications, the code used to accomplish a specific task can be written in different ways. The following listing shows one possible solution for performing a date validation on a text field in an HTML document:

```
function validateDateField(fld) {
    // 'fld' was sent to this function using the this object.
    // The date should be in the YYYYMMDD format.
    var dateValue = fld.value;
    // Use pattern matching to make the first check for 8 digits.
    if (!/^\d{8}$/.test(dateValue)) {
      alert("The date must be in the format YYYYMMDD.");
      return false;
    }
    var year = dateValue.substring(0,4);
    var mon = dateValue.substring(4,6);
    var day = dateValue.substring(6,8);
    if (year < 1900 || year > 2100) {
      alert("The year must be between 1900 and 2100");
      return false;
    }else if (mon < 01 || mon > 12) {
      alert("The month must be between 01 and 12");
      return false;
    }else if (day < 01 || day > 31) {
      alert("The day must be between 01 and 31");
      return false;
    }
    return true;
}
```

Ideally, the date validation routine would also check the day against the month — to ensure, for example, that a non-leap year did not list a month and day of 0229. If the date that the user entered into the text field is not in the proper format, the developer can alert the user to this fact and require that the value be changed before the form is submitted to the server. The validation in the previous example was performed on a text field.

A developer can use several other types of fields on a Web page to gather data from the user, including text areas, radio buttons, check boxes, single pick lists, and multiple-selection pick lists. Except for the text area field, the other HTML data entry types have their values obtained by JavaScript in a different manner than that of the text field. The following examples show how JavaScript can obtain the value, or values, from each of these different types of fields. Once the value or values are retrieved, the developer can then perform whatever validation needs to be done.

```
function validateField(fld) {
  // This validation is for radio button or checkbox fields.
  // The only difference between checking values from a group of
  // radio buttons or checkboxes is that more than one checkbox
  // can be 'checked'.
  var val = ""
  for (var i=0; i<fld.length; i++) {
    if (fld[i].checked) {
      val = fld[i].value;
      // Add rest of validation here.
    }
  }
}
function validateField(fld) {
  // This validation is for single or multiple select fields.
  // The only difference between checking values from a single select
  // or multiple select field is that the multiple select field can
  // have more than one option selected.
  var val = ""
  for (var i=0; i<fld.options.length; i++) {
    if (fld.options[i].selected) {
      val = fld.options[i].value;
      // Add rest of validation here.
    }
  }
}
```

With the ability for a developer to access each data entry field on a Web page, much of the data processing that previously took place on the server can now take place on the client. This not only provides immediate feedback to the user about incorrectly formatted data, it also relieves some of the processing load on the server. If the data had to be sent back to the client from the server based on an error, this client-side validation would also reduce the amount of traffic on the network compared to server-side validation.

Adding Functionality

Besides checking field values for proper formatting, JavaScript can also be used to enhance an application by adding flexibility and functionality. Developing client applications requires more than just displaying necessary data entry fields. The Graphical User Interface, or GUI, that the user interacts with must be easy to work with and must flow in a manner that promotes a natural progression. The developer must ensure that the GUI is not crowded or confusing for users, and enables them to accomplish their task. The following two sections describe a couple of these functional capabilities.

Field Auto-Population

Sometimes the developer can aid users by integrating processes that require filling out data fields based on user input. Take, for example, a banking form that deals with currency and exchange rates. It would be nice if the conversion to or from a specified currency could automatically be performed by the application itself, rather than having the user fill in the data. JavaScript can be used to perform just such a function. Listing 8.1 shows the code that is used to convert U.S. dollars to Kenyan shillings automatically. This saves users the time needed to manually make the calculation and enter the data.

Listing 8.1: Field Auto-Population

```
01: <html>
02:   <head>
03:     <script language="javascript">
04:       var Netscape = false;
05:       if (navigator.appName == "Netscape") { Netscape = true; }
06:
07:       function convertToKsh(fld) {
08:         var dollars = fld.value;
09:
10:         // Make sure that only numbers were entered.
11:         if (!/^\d$/.test(dollars)) {
12:           alert("Only numbers can be entered in the Dollar field.");
13:           return;
14:         }
15:
16:         var rate = 79;
17:         var shillingField;
18:         if (Netscape) {
19:           shillingField = document.forms[0].shillings;
20:         }else {
21:           shillingField = document.all.shillings;
22:         }
23:         shillingVal = dollars * rate;
24:         shillingField.value = shillingValue;
25:       }
26:     </script>
27:   </head>
28:   <body>
29:   <form>
30:     U.S. Dollars:
31:     <input type="text" name="dollars" onChange="convertToKsh(this)">
32:     <p>
33:     Kenyan Shillings:
34:     <input type="text" name="shillings" onFocus="javascript:onBlur()">
35:   </form>
36:   </body>
37: </html>
```

The preceding code illustrates general functionality for performing auto-population of fields. Note two additional items in the code. One, the value entered into the dollar field is checked to ensure that only numbers were used. This check is performed on line 11. Two, code was added to ensure that the user could not delete or change the value that was automatically populated into the shillings field. This is done on line 34. In this case, the JavaScript event handler onFocus is called when the user selects that field. The onFocus event handler responds by calling another JavaScript event handler, onBlur. When the event handler onBlur is called, the field is immediately de-selected and no longer maintains focus (that is, the mouse cursor is no longer on that field), so the user cannot perform any operation on it.

Field Auto-Validation

Another benefit that JavaScript can offer to enhance a client application is related to the concepts of data validation and field auto-population. The concept of **auto-validation** can be created based on a combination of user input and business rules. Take, for example, a form used to provide payment options for some kind of online business. If the user selects payment by credit card, the field into which the user would enter the credit card number now becomes a mandatory field to fill out. If the user chooses COD, however, the field for a credit card number should not be used. Instead, maybe an address field is now mandatory. Using a combination of the code examples previously used, the developer can use JavaScript to handle the various scenarios that may arise to ensure that the proper data is submitted to the server. Listing 8.2 shows how this can be accomplished.

Listing 8.2: Auto-Validation

```
01: <html>
02:   <head>
03:     <script language="javascript">
04:       var Netscape = false;
05:       if (navigator.appName == "Netscape") { Netscape = true; }
06:
07:       function checkOptions() {
08:         var payment;
09:         var creditcard;
10:         var address;
11:         var form;
12:
13:         if (Netscape) {
14:           form = document.forms[0];
15:         }else {
16:           form = document.all;
17:         }
18:
19:         payment = form.payment;
20:         creditcard = form.creditcard;
21:         address = form.address;
22:
23:         var paymentValue = "";
24:         var creditcardValue = creditcard.value;
25:         var addressValue = address.value;
26:
27:         for (var i=0; i<payment.options.length; i++) {
28:           if (payment.options[i].selected) {
29:             paymentValue = payment.options[i].value;
```

```
30:                 if (paymentValue == "COD") {
31:                     // Ensure there is an address.
32:                     if (addressValue == "") {
33:                         alert("Please enter an address.");
34:                         return false;
35:                     }else {
36:                         creditcard.value = "";   // For good measure.
37:                         // Could perform check on address format.
38:                         break;
39:                     }
40:
41:                 }else if (paymentValue == "credit") {
42:                     // Ensure there is a credit card number.
43:                     if (creditcardValue == "") {
44:                         alert("Please enter a Credit Card number.");
45:                         return false;
46:                     }else {
47:                         address.value = "";   // For good measure.
48:                         // Could perform check for card number format.
49:                         break:
50:                     }
51:                 }
52:             }
53:         }
54:
55:         if (paymentValue == "") {
56:             // Neither value was selected.
57:             alert("Please select a payment method");
58:             return false;
59:         }
```

Line 5 determines which browser is being used. Lines 13–17 then use the proper syntax based on the browser type to obtain a reference to the form. Lines 27–53 check the field values and perform the auto-validation based on certain criteria. If a payment value has not been determined, an alert (line 57) is generated and prompts the user.

```
60:
61:             form.submit();
62:         }
63:     </script>
64:   </head>
65:   <body>
66:   <form method="post" action="http://validationtest.com/test.jsp">
67:     Payment Options:
68:     <select name="payment" size="3">
69:       <option>
70:       <option value="credit">Credit Card
71:       <option value="COD">COD
72:     </select>
73:     <p>
74:     Credit Card Number:
75:     <input type="text" name="creditcard" size="20">
76:     <p>
```

```
77:     COD Address:
78:     <textarea name="address" rows="50" cols="4"></textarea>
79:     <p>
80:     <input type="button" value="Submit" onClick="checkOptions()">
81: </form>
82: </body>
83: </html>
```

Last, if all validation is successful, JavaScript is used to submit the form. This is shown on line 61. Lines 66–81 then create the HTML code necessary to generate the fields used in the form. Of the 83 lines of code listed, 59 are JavaScript-specific code.

Listing 8.2 shows several different aspects of how JavaScript can be used on the client to perform some sort of operation. As you can imagine, a larger form that contains many more field elements may also require an equally large amount of JavaScript code to perform all the functions that are necessary. It must be reiterated that all of the JavaScript code can be removed from the HTML file and stored in a separate file. Refer to the earlier example showing how an HTML page can reference a JavaScript file. Although this means that multiple files need to be maintained, it does reduce the amount of clutter in any one file and can separate presentation tags from field and form processing instructions. The requirements for performing real-world client-side form processing can be much more complex than the preceding example, but as you can see, JavaScript can add a lot of functionality to what a developer is able to do on the client before it is sent back to the server for further processing.

Space Management

When designing a Web page, the developer must determine the proper layout of field elements in the GUI (browser) to ensure that the form has a smooth flow and does not appear overly crowded. If the form seems to be too large or excessively busy-looking, the user may get confused or frustrated. The following sections describe some of these scenarios and offer possible solutions.

Multiple-Value Picklists

Handling a field that may contain numerous options to choose from is one common scenario confronting developers. Take, for example, a field that may require the user to select multiple country values.

Two HTML field elements are used to provide the user with the capability to select more than one option. The first is a group of **check boxes**. The second is a **select list** that is designated with the `multiple` attribute. A country listing can span several hundred options. If check boxes are used, several hundred check boxes need to be displayed on the form, for what amounts to a single field. The problem can be further compounded by having more than one field that requires this country list. Compared to check boxes, using the multiple select list can reduce the amount of space that is used on the form, but it also presents other challenges.

Another attribute for the `<select>` tag is `size`. The value of this attribute is used to determine how many options in the list are visible to the user. To save space on the form, the size indicated is usually not very large. If, for example, the size is designated to display ten options, there will still be several hundred country values that are not visible in the list. While users can use the vertical scroll bar to maneuver through the list, it may not be possible to visually display all of the selected values at the same time. This may make it difficult or confusing for users when they are reviewing the form. It also presents the possibility that a user may unknowingly de-select a value because not all of the active selections were visible. In addition, if more than one field needs to use the same list, each of the country values must be coded into each of the select field's `<option>` tags. This could potentially cause a lot of duplicate data being transferred over the network.

Either solution will work, but neither one is ideal for presenting the field and its values to the user in a visually acceptable manner while avoiding data duplication. One possible solution, however, can be achieved with JavaScript. Using JavaScript, the developer can create a mechanism whereby the selection of country values is made in a secondary window, and only the selected values are displayed on the main form. This would solve each of the three problems described earlier. The space needed to display the field is small, all of the selected values are visible to the user, and no duplicate data is loaded into the browser. The third point is possible because only one list of country values is needed. Any field that requires this list will simply reuse the single pick list component. Listing 8.3 shows the JavaScript and HTML code used to generate this mechanism.

Listing 8.3: Pop-Up Picklist Window

```
01:  <html>
02:   <head>
03:    <script language="javascript">
04:     var Netscape = false;
05:     if (navigator.appName == "Netscape") { Netscape = true; }
06:     var pickArr = new Array();
07:     pickArr[0] = "Algeria";
08:     pickArr[1] = "Belgium";
09:     pickArr[2] = "China";
10:     pickArr[3] = "Denmark";
11:     pickArr[4] = "England";
12:     pickArr[5] = "France";
13:     // The rest of the countries
```

Create the pick list in a JavaScript array. This has to be done only one time, no matter how many fields on the form will use the pick list:

```
14:     function picklist(fldname) {
15:      var fldObj;
16:      if (Netscape) {
17:        fldObj = document.forms[0].fldname;
18:      }else {
19:        fldObj = document.all.fldname;
20:      }
```

Generate a reference to the field that will hold the selected values from the pick list:

```
21:     var CODE = "<html">;
22:     CODE += "<script language='javascript'>";
23:     CODE += " FIELD_OBJ = null;";
24:     CODE += " function sendVal() {";
25:     if (Netscape) { CODE += " var fld = document.forms[0].pick;"; }
26:     else { CODE += " var fld = document.all.pick;"; }
```

```
27:        CODE += "   var vals = opener.getPickVals(fld);";
28:        CODE += "   FIELD_OBJ.value = vals;";
29:        CODE += "   window.close();";
30:        CODE += " }";
31:        CODE += "</scri" + "pt">";
```

Several things are taking place in the preceding code snippet. Line 21 begins the process of storing HTML code in the JavaScript variable CODE. This code will be used to generate the HTML page that will display the picklist form. Along with the HTML, JavaScript code is also being generated, which will be used to gather the selected picklist values and send them back to the main form. Line 27 creates a reference to the JavaScript object opener. This object is a reference to the browser window that opened the picklist window. It then calls the JavaScript function getPickVals, which resides in the main browser window. Lastly, Line 31 concatenates two strings that form the closing <script> tag. It is important to note that the browsers usually will not be able to process the code unless this is done. The reason is because you are essentially having JavaScript code write more JavaScript. If line 31 were written CODE += "</script>", the browser would interpret that as the end of JavaScript code for that Web page, when in fact it is only the end of the JavaScript code intended for the new window.

```
32:        CODE += "<body><form>";
33:        CODE += "<center><b>Country Picklist</b></center>";
34:        CODE += "<p>";
35:        CODE += "<center><select name="pick" size="10" multiple>";
36:        for (var i=0; i<pickArr.length; i++) {
37:           CODE += "<option>" + pickArr[i];
38:        }
39:        CODE += "</select></center>";
40:        CODE += "<p><center>";
41:        CODE += "<input type='button' value='Select' onClick='sendVal()'>";
42:        CODE += "<input type='button' value='Close' onClick='window.close()'>";
43:        CODE += "</center></form></body></html>";
```

The preceding lines of code use the JavaScript array defined earlier to create the HTML code necessary to generate the country picklist, as well as the buttons used to either save the selected values or close the window.

```
44:        PickWin = window.open("","newwindow");
45:        PickWin.document.open();
46:        PickWin.document.write(CODE);
47:        PickWin.document.close();
48:        PickWin.FIELD_OBJ = fldObj;
49:        PickWin.focus();
50:     }
```

The JavaScript function finishes by opening a new window and writing the HTML content to its document. Line 48 shows how the picklist window obtains a reference to the field on the main form that will receive a copy of the selected picklist values.

```
51:     function getPickVals(picklist) {
52:        var vals = "";
53:        for (var i=0; i<picklist.options.length; i++) {
```

```
54:           if (picklist.options[i].selected) {
55:               if (vals != "") { vals += "\n"; }
56:               vals += picklist.options[i].text;
57:           }
58:       }
59:     return vals;
60:   }
61:  </script>
62: </head>
```

The last JavaScript function is used to gather the selected picklist values, store them in a JavaScript variable, and then return the variable to the calling function. The calling function, starting on line 24, will then send the values back to the field on the main form.

```
63:  <body><form>
64:     <input type="button" onClick="picklist('storage')">
65:     <textarea name='storage' rows="5" cols="40">
66:  </form></body>
67: </html>
```

Lines 63–67 finish the Web page example by creating a button that will launch the picklist window, and the field that will receive the selected picklist values.

The preceding example shows several different JavaScript capabilities that can be used to enhance the flexibility of a Web page. Lines 6–12 show how JavaScript can use the power of arrays to store values locally and then use those values for virtually any purpose. JavaScript was also used to store HTML and JavaScript code for use in another browser window. References to form elements were not only passed to different functions, but also to different browser windows. As in some earlier examples, JavaScript was also used to retrieve data from, and add data to, HTML form elements. The code on lines 44–47 shows how JavaScript can open new windows and write content directly to the window's document. Each of these capabilities can be used individually or in combination, as shown in this example, to form a process that will aide the developer in making the client application a more robust tool for the user to accomplish the task at hand.

Repeating Values

Another issue that frequently causes problems for Web site developers is that of repeating fields. For example, an online mortgage company may have a form that requires users to enter all of their current loans. This may just be a single text field, but it is unknown at the time that the user displays the form exactly how many entries will be required. A simple solution may be to provide the user with an HTML <textarea> field to list all of their entries in the one field. This may not be appropriate either, however, because with multi-line entries, there may not be a way to tell where one piece of information ends and another begins.

To ensure that the information about different loans is not mixed, the developer may force the user to use a different text field for each individual item. This brings us back to the developer's dilemma of how to display just the right amount of text fields when it is unknown how many they will need. Different users will also require a different number of these fields.

One possible solution to this problem would be to design a way for the user to enter a number indicating how many fields they will use. The form would then be submitted back to the server, the proper number of fields would be added, and the new form would be redisplayed to the user. Again, however, we face the issue of extra submissions over the network, which could cause performance problems.

Another issue is that of the additional fields taking up more space on the form as a whole. What if the information that needed to be repeated were not just a single text field for a piece of loan information but rather a three- or four-field group that was used to gather information about a person's previous addresses. If a user wanted to add five previous addresses, the amount of extra fields on the form could get out of hand. This approach certainly would not help with the issue of space management. To further complicate matters, what if the user decided later that they needed to list seven addresses, not just five? Handling the data already listed in the five fields along with adding additional fields could cause quite a programming headache.

Another approach to solving the problem is to guess at a reasonable number of repeating values that the user is likely to need and just display all of the fields. While this may not contribute to additional performance problems due to the lack of extra submission calls, the form will most likely still be too cluttered for the user. There is also the chance that the user may need more fields than was initially anticipated. Clearly, a much better approach must be used, one that satisfies both the issue of not adding unnecessary performance roadblocks and maintaining appropriate space management.

One possible approach to finding this improved solution would be to build a repeating group mechanism that would require only one field element for each repeatable field, regardless of how many times it is needed. Buttons would be associated with each repeating group, whether it be one or multiple fields, which would allow the user to add new values and maneuver back and forth among the values. This mechanism can be accomplished by using JavaScript arrays to store the data locally for each repeating group. As the user adds or maneuvers among the existing values in the repeating group, the currently displayed values are quickly stored in the appropriate array by way of the current index. The new values to be displayed, if any, are then retrieved from the array and put into the HTML fields on the form.

To the user, this process is seamless and immediate. Not even the users need to know how many repeating values they will be using because the mechanism is built to auto-increase to virtually an unlimited number, memory not withstanding. In this case, JavaScript is used to take the storage of field data off of the form itself, to memory locations in an array. This greatly enhances the developer's capability to acquire good space management. Listing 8.4 provides an example of how a generic repeating group mechanism can be built.

Listing 8.4: Repeating Group Mechanism

```
001: <html>
002:  <head>
003:   <script language=javascript>
004:    var repfields = new Array();
005:    repfields['street'] = new Array();
006:    repfields['street'][0] = 'street';
007:    repfields['street'][1] = 'city';
008:    repfields['street'][2] = 'state';
009:
010:    var rep = new Array();
011:    rep['street']=new Array();
012:    rep['city']=new Array();
013:    rep['state']=new Array();
```

Create JavaScript arrays for the fields in the repeating group as well as for the storage of field data.

```
014:
015:    function scroll(pgrpname, direction) {
016:        // pgrpname = parent group name
017:        //    This is the name of first field in the repeating group.
018:        //    Used as basis for getting the name of the text fields
019:        //    holding the record number you are on as well as for
020:        //    obtaining references to the data storage arrays.
021:        // direction = indicates which button was clicked
022:
023:        // This example does NOT check which browser is being used.
024:
025:        var REC = eval("document.forms[0]." + pgrpname + "Recno");
026:        var OF = eval("document.forms[0]." + pgrpname + "Ofno");
027:        var Recnum = REC.value   // number of current record
028:        var Ofnum = OF.value     // number of last record
```

Obtain references for the fields that track what repeating group index the user is on. The eval function is used to create the reference based on a hard-coded string and the value of a variable. Using variables passed into the function in this manner enables the developer to create a more flexible script.

```
029:        var newRec, newOf;
030:        var moveAhead = 0;
031:        var moveToLast = 0;
032:
033:        if (direction == "prev") {
034:            if (Recnum == 1) {
035:                alert("You are on the first record");
036:                return;
037:            }
038:            newRec = eval(Math.abs(Recnum)-1);
039:            newOf = Ofnum;
040:            moveAhead = 1;
041:
042:        }else if(direction == "first") {
043:            if (Recnum == 1) {
044:                alert("You are on the first record");
045:                return;
046:            }
047:            newRec = 1;
048:            newOf = Ofnum;
049:            moveAhead = 1;
050:
051:        }else if(direction == "next") {
052:            if (Recnum == Ofnum) {
053:                alert("You are on the last record");
054:                return;
055:            }
056:            newRec = eval(Math.abs(Recnum)+1);
057:            newOf = Ofnum;
058:            moveAhead = 1;
059:
```

```
060:        }else if(direction == "last") {
061:            if (Recnum == Ofnum) {
062:                alert("You are on the last record");
063:                return
064:            }
065:            newRec = Ofnum;
066:            newOf = Ofnum;
067:            moveAhead = 1;
068:
069:        }else if(direction == "new") {
070:            newOf = eval(Math.abs(Ofnum)+1);
071:            newRec = newOf;
072:        }
```

Use conditional statements to determine which button was selected and then determine the new repeating group index numbers. Notice here how the Math.abs function is used inside of the eval function. The Math.abs function is used to convert a numeric string into a number that can be used in a mathematical operation. This conversion itself must be wrapped in the eval function so that the mathematical expression can be performed correctly.

```
073:        var flds = eval("repfields['" + pgrpname + "']");
074:        var currfld, ele, eleName, eleVal;
```

Line 73 obtains a reference to the JavaScript array that holds the name of each field that is part of the repeating group. This example had only one repeating group, so some of the code could have been hard-coded, rather than dynamically creating object references. Except for additional JavaScript array declarations (see lines 5-8), the code in this listing, however, is written in a manner that will support the use of multiple repeating groups with no additional code changes.

```
075:        for (var i=0; i<flds.length; i++) {
076:            currfld = flds[i];
077:            ele = eval("document.forms[0]." + currfld);
078:            eleName = ele.name;
079:            eleVal = ele.value;
080:            if (!eleVal) { eleVal = " "; }
081:
082:            if (direction == "prev" || direction == "next") {
083:                rep[eleName][Recnum] = eleVal;    //store current value
084:                ele.value = rep[eleName][newRec]; //get old value
085:
086:            }else if(direction == "first") {
087:                rep[eleName][Recnum] = eleVal;
088:                ele.value = rep[eleName][1];
089:
090:            }else if(direction == "last") {
091:                rep[eleName][Recnum] = eleVal;
092:                ele.value = rep[eleName][Ofnum];
093:
094:            }else if(direction == "new") {
095:                rep[eleName][Recnum] = eleVal;
096:                if (Recnum == Ofnum) {
097:                    // The user hit the 'new' button while on the last
```

```
098:                      // element. Let's make sure that we only advance the
099:                      // numbers if there is a value in one of the fields.
100:                      if (eleVal && !hasBlanks(eleVal)) { moveAhead = 1; }
101:
102:                  }else {
103:                      // The user hit the new button but not on the last
104:                      // element. Let's look ahead to see what values are
105:                      // stored for the last elements. If both are empty,
106:                      // only advance the current record number to match
107:                      // the 'of' number.
108:                      lastVal = rep[eleName][Ofnum];
109:                      if (lastVal && !hasBlanks(lastVal)) { moveAhead = 1; }
110:                      else { moveToLast = 1; }
111:                  }
112:                  ele.value = "";
113:              }
114:          }
```

Get a handle to the actual field element. Once the reference is created, store the current value in the storage array and obtain the new value, if any, to display in the field. This example only uses text fields. If other types of fields are used (such as radio buttons or picklists), you will have to add the JavaScript syntax necessary to process those types.

```
115:          if (moveAhead) {
116:              REC.value = newRec;
117:              OF.value = newOf;
118:
119:          }else if(moveToLast) {
120:              REC.value = Ofnum;
121:          }
```

Last, change the repeating group counters to display the appropriate index number.

```
122:      }
123:
124:      function hasBlanks(str) {
125:          var len = str.length;
126:          var spot = "";
127:          var sym = 0;
128:
129:          for (var i=0; i<len; i++) {
130:              spot = str.substring(i, i+1);
131:              if (spot != " ") {
132:                  sym = 1;
133:                  break;
134:              }
135:          }
136:          if (sym) { return false; }
137:          else { return true; }
138:      }
```

The function hasBlanks is used to ensure that a field does not contain only spaces. This is necessary because a space is a valid character as far as JavaScript is concerned. When the user selects the New button in the repeating group, a check is performed to ensure that at least one of the fields has a value. If not, the counters are not moved. Using `hasBlanks` ensures that a field with only spaces is not mistakenly identified as a field with a true value.

```
139:   </script>
140:  </head>
141:  <body bgcolor="cadetblue">
142:   <form name="myform">
143:    <center>
144:     <table border=2>
145:      <tr><td>
146:       Street: <input name='street' type='text' size='50'>
147:      </td></tr>
148:      <tr><td>
149:       City: <input name='city' type='text' size='30'>
150:      </td></tr>
151:      <tr><td>
152:       State: <input name='state' type='text' size='3'>
153:      </td></tr>
154:
155:      <tr><td>
156:       <input type=button value='<<' onClick='scroll("street","first")'>
157:       <input type=button value='Prev' onClick='scroll("street","prev")'>
158:       <input type=button value='Next' onClick='scroll("street","next")'>
159:       <input type=button value='>' onClick='scroll("street","last")'>
160:          
161:       <input type=button value='New' onClick='scroll("street","new")'>
162:          
163:       Record: <input type='text' value='1' name='streetRecno' size='2'>
164:       Of <input type='text' value='1' name='streetOfno' size='2'>
165:      </td></tr>
166:     </table>
167:    </center>
168:   </form>
169:  </body>
170: </html>
```

Figure 8.1 shows a screen capture of what the repeating group mechanism looks like to the user.

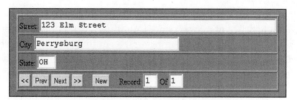

Figure 8.1

The preceding repeating group example gives the user the capability to create new repeating group records, as well as to move back and forth among the existing values. This mechanism could be expanded to include such things as searching and deleting within the repeating group as well. In order to add these, or any other, capabilities, simply add an HTML button with the appropriate arguments to the `scroll` function and then modify the function to incorporate the new logic. While the repeating group mechanism offers the developer several advantages, some side effects are inherent to the mechanism model. These may or may not become issues for the developer or the user. The first issue is that only one value for each of the repeating group fields is visible to the user at any one time. The rest of the values are hidden in the JavaScript data storage array. Adding a search capability could help alleviate this problem by making it easy to quickly find other values.

The other issue is that of submitting the form data to the server for processing. Because the value for each field in the repeating group is stored in a JavaScript array, the form cannot be submitted as usual. If it were, only the current value for each field would be transmitted to the server and the rest of the data would be lost. If this type of repeating group mechanism is used, the developer must create a new strategy for getting all of the repeating group values in the JavaScript array back to the server for processing.

When a Web page is submitted, the HTML fields and their values are sent over the network as a sort of hashtable to be accessed by the server program. Given this, the values in the JavaScript array must be put in an HTML field first, and then the form can be submitted as usual. It is up to the developer to determine the best solution for this process. If the values are simply added to a <textarea> field, for example, they must be added in such a manner that they are easily extracted as individual values when the code is interpreted by the server-side program.

One possible solution is to store the values in an XML format and then add it to a field. Taken a step further, the entire document could have all of its values stored in an XML format. This could be accomplished by having JavaScript gather all of the values and create the XML document. The XML could then be put in one or more <textarea> fields and submitted to the server. When building a client Web page, the developer will have to weigh the advantages and drawbacks of certain design strategies. In the case of the repeating group mechanism, the advantages of space management and virtually unlimited repeating group entries will most likely outweigh the drawbacks that result from the design.

Dynamic Actions

Up to this point, we have used JavaScript to perform some general, but still powerful, capabilities. Validating data, transferring field values, forcing mandatory data entry, and space management are but a few of these capabilities. They provide the basis for transforming a static Web page into a functional application that can include built-in business rules.

Sometimes, however, this is not enough. There may be times when a truly more dynamic approach is needed for certain characteristics of a Web page. Previously, our code example showed one possible solution for how an application can use a component — in this case, a picklist — more efficiently. The component, however, always remained the same. The values of the picklist never changed. In most cases, this would be the normal characteristic for such a component. Suppose, however, the values of a picklist needed to change dynamically based on some action by the user.

Take, for example, a Web page for a travel agency. The page may have a picklist from which the user can select the country to which they would like to travel. Instead of having one large country picklist, however, the page may have one picklist that lists the continents and another for the countries on the continent. When the user selects one of the continent values, the other picklist will display the countries for that particular continent. As the user selects different continent values, the country picklist must dynamically change its values. One way to solve this problem is to submit the form back to the server and have the server rebuild the Web page with the appropriate set of picklist values. This could be very time-consuming, however, especially if the user wants to change the picklist several times.

This is another good example of how JavaScript can help the developer build a dynamic client without having to submit the form to the server. With JavaScript, a picklist's values can change dynamically in response to some user action. Listing 8.5 shows how this dynamic action can take place.

Listing 8.5: Dynamically Changing a Picklist

```
01: <html>
02:  <head>
03:   <script language="javascript">
04:    var Netscape = false;
05:    if (navigator.appName == "Netscape") { Netscape = true; }
06:
07:    var africaArr = new Array();
08:    africaArr[0] = "Algeria";
09:    africaArr[1] = "Kenya";
10:    africaArr[2] = "South Africa";
11:
12:    var europeArr = new Array();
13:    europeArr[0] = "Belgium";
14:    europeArr[1] = "Germany";
15:    europeArr[2] = "Italy";
16:    europeArr[3] = "Switzerland";
17:
18:    // The rest of the country arrays.
```

Create the picklists using JavaScript arrays. These will be used by JavaScript to switch the values of the single `<select>` object picklist.

```
19:    function picklist(pickObj) {
20:     var ctryPick;
21:     var continent;
22:     for (var i=0; i<pickObj.options.length; i++) {
23:      if (pickObj.options[i].selected) {
24:        continent = pickObj.options[i].value;
25:      }
26:     }
27:     if (Netscape) {
28:      ctryPick = document.forms[0].countries;
29:     }else {
30:      ctryPick = document.all.countries;
31:     }
```

Lines 22–26 determine which continent value the user selected. The code then proceeds to create a reference to the `picklist` object that holds the country values.

```
32:     while (ctryPick.options.length > 0) {
33:      ctryPick.options[0] = null;
34:     }
```

Remove any values from the country picklist in preparation for adding a new list of values. It is important to remove the old values first, rather than just overwrite them with the new values, because the old list may be longer than the new list.

```
35:     var new_opt;
36:     if (continent == "africa" ) {
37:        for (var i=0; i<africaArr.length; i++) {
38:           new_opt = new Option(africaArr[i],"");
39:           ctryPick.options[i] = new_opt;
40:        }
41:
42:     }else if (continent == "europe") {
43:        for (var i=0; i<europeArr.length; i++) {
44:           new_opt = new Option(europeArr[i],"");
45:           ctryPick.options[i] = new_opt;
46:        }
47:
48:     }else if(continent == "na") {
49:     // Continue with the rest of the conditional statements.
50:     . . . . . . .
51:     }
```

Lines 35–51 determine which continent was selected and then use the appropriate country array to populate the country picklist by creating new options and adding them in order to the `picklist` object. Keep in mind that there are several different ways to perform this last portion of logic. A separate JavaScript array was created for each of the continent countries. The preceding example used a separate `for` loop for each of the country arrays, depending on which continent was selected. This code could be reduced by creating a single reference to the appropriate array so that only one `for` loop is needed. This can be accomplished through the built-in JavaScript function `eval`. The following lines of code could replace lines 35–51 with this new approach:

```
35:     var new_opt;
36:     var pickArr = eval(continent + "Arr");
37:     for (var i=0; i<pickArr.length; i++) {
38:        new_opt = new Option(pickArr[i], "");
39:        ctryPick.options[i] = new_opt;
40:     }
```

As you can see, the number of lines of code needed to perform the action was reduced from 17 lines to just 6. Line 36 is the key to this code reduction. The `eval` function will convert a string value to its equivalent object value. In this case, the string was the value of the variable continent (e.g., europe) and the string `Arr` to form the new string `europeArr`. If you remember from earlier in the example, there is a JavaScript array object with the same name. With this change, there is no longer any need for conditional statements to determine which continent was selected. It also reduces code maintenance because the hard-coded continent values in the conditionals are, again, no longer needed.

```
47:     if (Netscape) {
48:        history.go(0);
49:     }
50:     }
51:  </script>
```

The JavaScript function is finally ended with another check to determine whether Netscape is the client browser. If it is, a call to another built-in JavaScript function, `history.go`, is made. JavaScript has access to many of the browser's objects. One of these is the `history` object, which keeps track of where the user has been. The `go` function is used to navigate the browser to some previous URL that the user has visited. If, for example, line 48 used the code `history.go(-2)`, the browser would be directed to load the URL that the user visited two pages ago. In this case, however, the argument used was 0. The number 0 represents the current URL in the `history` object. This essentially refreshes the current page. If Netscape is being used as the client browser, this refresh action is essential in order to get the full impact of the dynamic picklist change. When new values are added to the country picklist, some of the new values may be longer than any of the previous values that were displayed in the picklist. In IE, the new picklist `<select>` object is automatically resized when the new values are added. This is not the case with Netscape.

In effect, this means that if the longest value in the old picklist was ten characters long, only the first ten characters for each of the new picklist values will be displayed. Any new value that has more than ten characters will still have its full value available for selection, but the whole value will not be seen by the user. If, however, the page is refreshed, Netscape will then be able to perform the proper resizing of the `<select>` object so that each value can be seen in its entirety.

```
52:   <head>
53:   <body>
54:    <form>
55:      Select a continent to display the countries available:
56:      <select name="continents" onChange="picklist(this)">
57:       <option value="africa">Africa
58:       <option value="europe">Europe
59:       <option value="na">North America
60:       // Add the other continent values
61:      </select>
62:      <p>
63:      Destination countries:
64:      <select name="countries" size="5">
65:      </select>
66:    </form>
67:   </body>
68: </html>
```

The example code finishes by generating the HTML code for the two picklist objects. Notice on line 56 that the JavaScript event handler `onChange` is used to call the main JavaScript function picklist with the `this` object argument.

As you can see from the various examples in this chapter, JavaScript can be used with increasing complexity to produce functionality that is hidden from the user but, at the same time, can produce a GUI that enables the user to complete as much work as possible on the client. As mentioned earlier, a developer designing a client application must take into consideration more than the requirement of gathering certain data.

Certain visual aspects of the GUI will, if done properly, assist the user in completing the intended goal. The easier it is for a user to complete the intended task, the greater the likelihood that it will actually be done. If the developer is designing a GUI for a company's internal use, such as a payroll form, there is little likelihood that a poorly designed data entry form would keep the user from completing the task of using the form, as that is part of the user's job. Conversely, if the Web page's purpose is to get a potential customer to purchase something that the company is selling, a poorly designed page may result in reduced sales if the user gets frustrated or loses interest before completing the process. It is up to the developer to find unique or innovative ways to build a robust client framework that will help in solving the many issues of performance, visual aesthetics, and space management. In the preceding code samples, performance was enhanced by moving a portion of the GUI off of the main form and creating dynamically changing picklists, a solution that helped with space management.

Layering and DHTML

Several of the previous examples have dealt with, in one way or another, the issue of managing the space used on a form so that the GUI is not overly crowded or confusing for the user. Another seemingly common issue that developers face is the problem of having an overly large amount of fields that need to fit on a Web page form. This section focuses on how JavaScript can be used to display multiple forms in the same space, and how it can be used in a creative manner to dynamically move objects on an HTML page.

Forms and Layers

Trying to place all of the fields in a way that will maintain the intended workflow usually results in an overly crowded number of fields placed horizontally or a form that is so long vertically that the user feels overwhelmed. Unfortunately, the amount of fields that have to be used may be out of the control of the developer.

What the developer does have control over is how to design the GUI to best accommodate the large number of fields. This scenario, however, doesn't offer the developer a lot of options. Two general options are to split the work among several server calls or have the client handle multiple views. The first option would require the fields to be arranged into key sections, with one section displayed at a time. Once the user submits the current section back to the server for processing, the next section is displayed. This continues until all sections are completed.

There are many potential problems with this approach. In addition to the possibility of slow response times, there is also the problem of handling cases in which the user does not complete all of the sections. Keeping track of what the user has and has not done can be quite a challenge for the developer.

This leaves the second option, which is similar to the first, except everything is handled on the client side. The goal would be, again, to divide the field elements into logical groupings and display only one group at a time to the user. This could possibly be accomplished with pop-up windows, but a more elegant solution would be to employ the use of layers. Layering involves adding field elements to the `form` object of a layer. Each layer is placed in the same position as the other layers, but only one layer is visible at any one time. Moving from one form to another simply involves hiding the current layer and displaying the new layer. The term "layer" in this context is somewhat of a misnomer and should not be taken literally. Netscape utilizes the `<layer>` tag to create a `layer` object. This tag is properly interpreted only by the Netscape browser. IE does not recognize such a tag. In order to get the effect of layering in IE, the `<span>` or `<div>` tags must be used. Fortunately, Netscape also can use the `<span>` and `<div>` tags to achieve layering as well.

Each layer is part of the browser's `document` object. The layer itself also contains a `document` object, and is where the `form` object that contains the layer's field elements resides. It was stated earlier that both IE and Netscape access the browser's DOM in slightly different ways. In all of the previous examples, the field elements were associated with the window's `document.form` object. Thus, JavaScript access to these elements was performed through a `document.forms[0].`*elementname* call. Both IE and Netscape were able to access the fields through this manner. It was also stated that IE could access the field elements through a `document.all.`*elementname* call, and the preceding examples had IE access the elements through this manner. This was done to keep the code examples consistent for when we addressed the issue of layers.

Netscape's DOM includes a set of arrays for the various children of the `document` object. Layer objects in Netscape are accessed through the document's array of layers—`document.layers[`*layername*`]`. IE uses `document.all` to gain access to all objects on a form, be it an image, link, or layer. Therefore, in the case of JavaScript in IE, access to a `layer` object can only be done by using `document.all(`*layername*`)`. Listing 8.6 shows a Web page consisting of three different sections, each associated with a different layer.

Listing 8.6: Layering Example

```
001:  <html>
002:  <head>
003:   <style type="text/css">
004:    #maindiv{position:absolute; left:10; top:10}
005:    #sub1div{position:absolute; left:10; top:10; visibility:hidden}
006:    #sub2div{position:absolute; left:10; top:10; visibility:hidden}
007:   </style>
```

The layer's characteristics are defined within the `<style>` tag. Here is where you define such things as the layer's location on the Web page, along with its visibility status. Note that the layer #maindiv does not contain a visibility attribute. By default, a layer is visible unless otherwise stated.

```
008:
009:   <script language="javascript">
010:    Netscape = false;
011:
012:    if (navigator.appName == "Netscape") { Netscape = true; }
013:
014:    CurrentLayer = "maindiv";
015:    CurrentForm = "mainform";
016:
017:    //
018:    // switchForm - hides one layer (form) and displays another.
019:    //
020:    function switchForm(from, to) {
021:        if (Netscape) {
022:            document.layers[from].visibility = "hidden";
023:            document.layers[to].visibility = "visible";
024:
025:        }else {
026:            document.all(from).style.visibility = "hidden";
027:            document.all(to).style.visibility = "visible";
028:        }
029:
030:        CurrentLayer = to;
031:        CurrentForm = to.replace(/div$/,"form");
032:    }
```

The JavaScript function switchForm is key to the layering functionality. This is where the layer views are switched. The currently visible layer, identified by the from variable, is hidden, whereas the selected layer, identified by the to variable, becomes visible.

```
033:    </script>
034:    </head>
035:    <body bgcolor="cadetblue">
036:
037:    <!-- MAIN FORM -->
038:    <div id="maindiv">
```

The layer's content is now defined within the <div> tag. The id attribute value must match a valid name listed within the <style> tag at the beginning of the script. This tag will contain its own <form> tag in which the field elements of the layer are defined.

```
039:    <form name="mainform">
040:     <center>
041:     <font size='+2'>Individual Biography</font><p>
042:     <table>
043:      <tr>
044:       <td align="right">Name:</td>
045:       <td><input name="name" type="text" size="50"></td>
046:      </tr>
047:      <tr>
048:       <td align="right">SSN:</td>
049:       <td><input name="ssn" type="text" size="12"></td>
050:      </tr>
051:      <tr>
052:       <td align="right">Marital Status:</td>
053:       <td>
054:        <input name="marital" type="radio" value="s">Single
055:        <input name="marital" type="radio" value="m">Married
056:        <input name="marital" type="radio" value="d">Divorced
057:        <input name="marital" type="radio" value="w">Widowed
058:       </td>
059:      </tr>
060:      <tr>
061:       <td align="right">Date of Birth:</td>
062:       <td><input name="dob" type="text" size="10"></td>
063:      </tr>
064:      <tr>
065:       <td align="right">Place of Birth:</td>
066:       <td><input name="pob" type="text" size="40"></td>
067:      </tr>
068:      <tr>
069:       <td valign="top" align="right">Address:</td>
070:       <td>
071:        <textarea name="address" rows="5" cols="60"></textarea>
072:       </td>
073:      </tr>
074:     </table>
075:     </center>
076:     <p>
```

```
077:      <center>
078:      <a href="javascript:void(0)" onClick='switchForm("maindiv", "sub1div")'>
079:         Physical Characterisitcs</a>
080:      <br>
081:      <a href="javascript:void(0)" onClick='switchForm("maindiv", "sub2div")'>
082:         Occupation</a>
083:      </center>
```

Lines 78 and 81 list the code used to link the main form to the other layers. The anchor uses the JavaScript event handler onClick to call the function switchForm. The arguments to the function represent the layer to hide and the layer to make visible.

```
084:      <p>
085:      <center>
086:       <input type="button" value="Save Record">
087:      </center>
088:     </form>
089:   </div>
090:
091:
092:   <!-  SUB FORM 1  ->
093:   <div id="sub1div">
094:    <form name="sub1form">
095:     <center>
096:     <font size='+2'>Physical Characteristics</font><p>
097:     <table>
098:      <tr>
099:       <td align="right">Height (in.):</td>
100:       <td><input name="height" type="text" size="10"></td>
101:      </tr>
102:      <tr>
103:       <td align="right">Weight (lbs.):</td>
104:       <td><input name="weight" type="text" size="10"></td>
105:      </tr>
106:      <tr>
107:       <td align="right">Eye Color:</td>
108:       <td><input name="eyes" type="text" size="30"></td>
109:      </tr>
110:      <tr>
111:       <td align="right">Hair Color:</td>
112:       <td><input name="hair" type="text" size="30"></td>
113:      </tr>
114:      <tr>
115:       <td align="right">Glasses/Contacts:</td>
116:       <td>
117:        <input name="glasses" type="radio" value="yes">Yes
118:        <input name="glasses" type="radio" value="no">No
119:        <input name="glasses" type="radio" value="unk">Unknown
120:       </td>
121:      </tr>
122:      <tr>
123:       <td valign="top" align="right">Distinguishing Marks:</td>
124:       <td><textarea name="marks" rows="5" cols="60"></textarea></td>
```

```
125:      </tr>
126:      </table>
127:      </center>
128:      <p>
129:      <center>
130:        <input type="button" value="Save" onClick='switchForm("sub1div",
"maindiv")'>
131:      </center>
132:      </form>
133:    </div>
```

Line 91 starts the code for the first subform. As mentioned in line 5, the subform is not initially displayed to the user. Line 130 again uses a reference to the JavaScript function switchForm, which is used to display the subform. Line 136 begins the code for the second subform. Its characteristics are similar to the first subform.

```
134:
135:    <!-- SUB FORM 2 -->
136:    <div id="sub2div">
137:     <form name="sub2form">
138:      <center>
139:      <font size='+2'>Occupation</font><p>
140:      <table>
141:       <tr>
142:         <td align="right">Name of Employer:</td>
143:         <td><input name="employer" type="text" size="50"></td>
144:       </tr>
145:       <tr>
146:         <td align="right">Job Title:</td>
147:         <td><input name="jobtitle" type="text" size="40"></td>
148:       </tr>
149:       <tr>
150:         <td align="right">Job Start Date:</td>
151:         <td><input name="jobstartdate" type="text" size="10"></td>
152:       </tr>
153:       <tr>
154:         <td align="right">Salary:</td>
155:         <td><input name="salary" type="text" size="10"></td>
156:       </tr>
157:      </table>
158:      </center>
159:      <p>
160:      <center>
161:        <input type="button" value="Save" onClick='switchForm("sub2div",
"maindiv")'>
162:      </center>
163:      </form>
164:    </div>
165:   </body>
166: </html>
```

This layering example shows a very generic view of how individual field groupings can be separated from the rest of the Web page field elements. Switching among the layers is a seamless process and enables the user to concentrate on only a small portion of the total fields at any one time. This helps keep the GUI from appearing too cluttered or confusing.

The fields in the preceding example were set up as simple text or radio button fields for simplicity. The forms could be made much more complex and flexible by integrating the characteristics of some of the previous examples, such as repeating groups, multiple-option picklist pop-up windows, or dynamically changing picklists. As with some of the other examples, the advantages also come with some drawbacks. The drawbacks for the layering capability are similar to those of the repeating group in that not all of the field values are visible to the user at the same time, and the Web page cannot be submitted in the typical manner. This second point is true for layering because each layer has its own <form> and only one form can be submitted at a time. A possible solution to this is the same as the solution for the repeating group, which is to have JavaScript gather all of the field values, create an XML document, store the XML document in one or more <textarea> fields, and submit the form with the field, or fields, to the server for processing.

Figures 8.2 and 8.3 show screen captures for the initial layer as well as the **Physical Characteristics** layer.

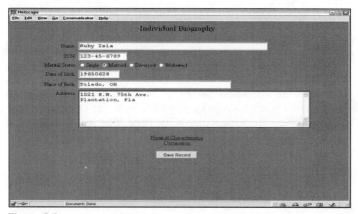

Figure 8.2

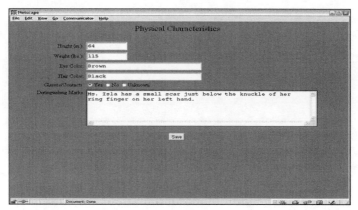

Figure 8.3

Movable Layers

Using layers to hide and display form elements begins the process of transforming a static general-purpose Web page into a dynamic, user-friendly user interface. This additional creativity and functionality is known as **DHTML**, or **Dynamic HTML**. DHTML introduces a new type of user interaction to the Web page, and JavaScript is the key to making this happen. The new and exciting ways in which JavaScript is being used to help create DHTML Web pages are rapidly growing. Items such as menu bars, toolbars, various types of charts, games, animations, and so on are bringing Web pages to new heights and making the user experience much more rewarding. One of the more interesting items is the capability to track mouse events. With the capability to track the user's mouse movements in conjunction with the use of layers, a developer can create an application in which the user is able to move objects around the Web page. This type of capability could be used to create a JavaScript game or the dynamic placement of form elements. Listing 8.7 shows how to create a Web page that enables the user to click and drag two images around the browser window.

Listing 8.7: Moving Layers with Mouse Movements

```
001: <html>
002:  <head>
003:   <style type="text/css">
004:       #img1 {position:absolute; left:50; top:100; width:244; z-index:0}
005:       #img2 {position:absolute; left:110; top:145; width:144; z-index:0}
006:   </style>
```

Lines 4 and 5 create the layers that will be used. Notice that they each list the property z-index. This property is used to place the layers in a stacking order. A value of 0 means that the layer is on the bottom of the stack. If two layers share the same space on the page, the layer with the highest z-index will be visible.

```
007:   <script language="javascript">
008:    var Netscape = false;
009:    if (navigator.appName == "Netscape") { Netscape = true; }
010:
011:    // Set zIndex property.
012:    function setZIndex(obj, zOrder) { obj.zIndex = zOrder; }
013:
014:    // Position an object at a specific pixel coordinate.
015:    function shiftTo(obj, x, y) {
016:      if (Netscape) {
017:        obj.moveTo(x,y);
018:      } else {
019:        obj.pixelLeft = x;
020:        obj.pixelTop = y;
021:      }
022:    }
023:
024:    // Holds reference to selected element.
025:    var selectedObj;
026:
027:    // Holds location of mouse click relative to element.
028:    var offsetX, offsetY
029:
030:    // Find out which element has been clicked on.
031:    function setSelectedElem(evt) {
```

```
032:        if (Netscape) {
033:            // Declare local var for use in upcoming loop
034:            var testObj;
035:
036:            // Make copies of event coords for use in upcoming loop.
037:            var clickX = evt.pageX;
038:            var clickY = evt.pageY;
039:
040:            // Loop through all layers (starting with frontmost layer)
041:            // to find if the event coordinates are in the layer.
042:            for (var i = document.layers.length - 1; i >= 0; i-) {
043:                testObj = document.layers[i];
044:                if ((clickX > testObj.left) &&
045:                    (clickX < testObj.left + testObj.clip.width) &&
046:                    (clickY > testObj.top) &&
047:                    (clickY < testObj.top + testObj.clip.height)) {
048:
049:                    // Set the global var to the layer and bring it forward.
050:                    selectedObj = testObj;
051:                    setZIndex(selectedObj, 100);
052:                    return;
053:                }
054:            }
055:
056:        }else {
057:            // Use the IE event model to get the targeted element.
058:            var imgObj = window.event.srcElement;
059:
060:            // Make sure it's one of image layers.
061:            if (imgObj.parentElement.id.indexOf("img") != -1) {
062:                // Now set the var to the style property of the element
063:                // bring it forward.
064:                selectedObj = imgObj.parentElement.style;
065:                setZIndex(selectedObj,100);
066:                return;
067:            }
068:        }
```

The call to the function setZIndex on lines 51 and 65 causes the selected layer to always appear to float on top of any other layer as they pass over one another.

```
069:
070:        // If we are here, the user probably clicked on the background.
071:        selectedObj = null;
072:    }
```

The function setSelectedElem, which starts on line 31, is used to determine which, if any, layer was selected by the user. If one is within the right coordinates of the mouse click, some global variables are set and will be used by other functions.

```
073:
074:    // Drag an element.
075:    function dragIt(evt) {
```

```
076:        // operate only if a fish is selected
077:        if (selectedObj) {
078:          if (Netscape) {
079:            shiftTo(selectedObj, (evt.pageX - offsetX),
080:                                 (evt.pageY - offsetY));
081:          }else {
082:            shiftTo(selectedObj, (window.event.clientX - offsetX),
083:                        (window.event.clientY - offsetY));
084:            // Prevent further system response to dragging in IE.
085:            return false;
086:          }
087:        }
088:      }
```

Moving the layer on the page is done through the function dragIt, which is listed on line 75. As the user drags the mouse over the browser window, this function is continuously called to provide updates about where to move the selected layer. It is called so often and quickly that the movement of the layer seems to be extremely fluid.

```
089:
090:    function engage(evt) {
091:      setSelectedElem(evt);
092:
093:      if (selectedObj) {
094:        // Set vars that remember where the click is in relation
095:        // to the top left corner of the element so we can keep
096:        // the element-to-cursor relationship constant throughout
097:        // the drag.
098:        if (Netscape) {
099:          offsetX = evt.pageX - selectedObj.left;
100:          offsetY = evt.pageY - selectedObj.top;
101:
102:        }else {
103:          offsetX = window.event.offsetX;
104:          offsetY = window.event.offsetY;
105:        }
106:      }
107:      return false;
108:    }
```

Line 91 makes a call to the method setSelectedElem, which will determine if the user clicked the mouse on a layer object. Line 93 determines whether an object, or valid layer, was selected. This is important to ensure that the variables listed later in the function are not changed when the user doesn't click on a layer.

```
109:
110:    // Restore elements and global vars to initial values.
111:    function release(evt) {
112:      if (selectedObj) {
113:        setZIndex(selectedObj, 0);
114:        selectedObj = null;
115:      }
116:    }
```

```
117:
118:    // Turn on event capture for Netscape.
119:    function setNavEventCapture() {
120:       if (Netscape) {
121:          document.captureEvents(
122:                  Event.MOUSEDOWN | Event.MOUSEMOVE | Event.MOUSEUP);
123:       }
124:    }
125:
126:    // Assign event handlers used by both Netscape and IE.
127:    function init() {
128:       if (Netscape) { setNavEventCapture(); }
129:
130:       // Assign functions to each of the events.
131:       // This is used for both Netscape and IE.
132:       document.onmousedown = engage;
133:       document.onmousemove = dragIt;
134:       document.onmouseup = release;
135:    }
```

The function init on line 127 is used to set up the event handling of the mouse actions. Each user-defined method (engage, dragIt, release) assigned to handle the events will receive an event object as a parameter even though it is not listed as such. Netscape requires an additional step to set up the event handlers, which is listed in the function setNavEventCapture on line 119.

```
136:    </script>
137:    </head>
138:    <body onLoad="init()">
139:      <span id="img1">
140:        <img name="i1" src="earth.gif" border=0>
141:      </span>
142:      <span id="img2">
143:        <img name="i2" src="castle.gif" border=0>
144:      </span>
145:    </body>
146: </html>
```

Lines 139–144 finish the code example by creating the contents of the two layers. In this case, the contents include only images.

Summary

In designing a portal, the client is but a portion of the entire architecture. Just as a portal can be designed using different tools and be comprised of varying components, the client itself can also be designed using different user interfaces. This chapter dealt solely with the browser-based client. Using JavaScript on the client can add great flexibility to a developer's schema for designing an application.

As shown in several examples, JavaScript can be used for simple field validations or more complex, dynamic interaction with the browser window. This gives the developer a wider range of options when delegating the workload between the various portal components. Although this chapter demonstrated several key aspects of how to utilize JavaScript in a client browser to help solve a variety of problem-solving scenarios, it is by no means an exhaustive list.

The developer will face plenty of additional common and unique circumstances in designing the application's client component. While JavaScript can offer the developer a large number of options to choose from, it is imperative, as mentioned earlier in the chapter, to understand how JavaScript can be deployed successfully in a multi-browser environment. There are not only differences in how JavaScript is used within different browsers, but also within different versions of the same browser. Any application that employs JavaScript must be thoroughly tested in a variety of browsers and browser versions to ensure the greatest possibility of success.

Developing Applications and Workflow for Your Portal

This chapter focuses on the development of JSR 168 portlet applications for portal servers that are compliant with the JSR 168 standard. It provides a general overview of the necessary portlet concepts, portlet architecture, and the development process, including compilation and deployment. You will also build a portlet that explores each of these areas.

The enterprise portal that we will use to build our portlet applications is the eXo portal platform, which supports JSR 168 and is an open-source solution. You will learn about the eXo portal platform's architecture and create a sample portlet that touches on the Model-View-Controller paradigm, which eXo also supports for portlet development.

The Portlet Architecture

Before creating our portlet, you should understand why we even need a portlet specification in the first place. What are the benefits for a developer, an IT manager, and a vendor? For developers, the portlet specification provides a standard way to develop portlets, and thus makes portlet code reusability a reality. Imagine being able to maintain only one set of portlet code that will work on any JSR 168–compliant portal server with minimal if any alterations to the configurations. For IT managers, the major benefit is that now their department's portlets support any portal vendors that are JSR 168 compliant. This allows for greater flexibility with little engineering involvement when providing their portlets to the market place. For vendors, the specification creates the capability to provide all sorts of tools — from IDEs to application servers — and it increases the market size for these tools.

A portal contains the user's individual portlets, which can be added, removed, and customized by the user. Portlets are what make up a portal's presentation layer. They are user interface components that are customizable by users, and they can be added to and removed from the portal dynamically. They also process user requests and generate content on demand through the portlet container.

The Portlet Container

A portlet container is used to manage portlets throughout their life. The container enables developers to call specific methods during the lifetime of the portlet. It is up to the developer to decide which methods to implement. As a general rule, developers should always extend the `GenericPortlet` class when creating their portlets. The `GenericPortlet` class calls specific `render` methods based on the current mode of the portlet. These methods are described in the following table.

Method	Description
doEdit	This is called by the `render` method when the portlet is going into `EDIT` mode. `EDIT` mode should be used for the specific purpose of editing the portlet. For example, if we had a stock portfolio portlet and it contained a list of stocks, when we click edit we should be able to edit the list of stocks in our portfolio.
doView	This is called by the `render` method when the portlet is going into `VIEW` mode. `VIEW` mode is the main mode that the portlet will be in. The main content of your portlet should be displayed during this mode. For example, if we had a football standings portlet, the standings should be displayed when in `VIEW` mode.
doHelp	This is called by the `render` method when the portlet is going into `HELP` mode. `HELP` mode should be used to display specific help on the usage of the portlet. Taking the stock portfolio example from `doEdit`, `HELP` mode might describe the appropriate way to edit and enter the stocks and their symbols into the portlet.

Other methods can be accessed with or without extending from the `GenericPortlet` class. These methods enable the developer to handle different functionality that is not necessarily based on the current mode of the portlet. These additional methods are shown in the following table.

Method	Description
init	The `init` method is called by the container when the portlet is created and is used to initialize the portlet and prepare it for use. For example, if your portlet needed to load specific configurations from a database or external data sources, this would be a great time to do it.
destroy	The `destroy` method is called by the container when the container destroys the portlet, enabling you to clean up anything that may require special attention. For instance, if a database connection were open, this would give you a chance to close the open connections and clean up neatly when the portlet is destroyed.
processAction	The `processAction` method is called by the container when a user submits changes to the portlet. This is an essential method that enables you to process data submitted by the user from the portlet. For example, you could have a form that requests the user's birth date. When the user submits the form, `processAction` is called, enabling you to process the information and decide what to display to the user, as well as change the mode of the portlet if you desire.
render	The `render` method is called whenever the portlet needs to be redrawn. In most cases, you will not need to handle this method because `doView`, `doEdit`, and `doHelp` exist in the `GenericPortlet` class and are automatically called by the `render` method.

The four methods that you will interact with most when developing a portlet are the doView, doEdit, doHelp, and processAction methods. These methods appear similar to servlets because they are passed request and response objects. Depending on the methods used with them, these objects can be used to do the following:

❑ Gain access to the portlet's preferences objects in order to maintain state.

❑ Get parameters submitted by users through forms.

❑ Obtain session information.

❑ Gather security information about the user, such as user-role information.

❑ Change different aspects of the portlet and how it is rendered. For example, the title can be changed through the response object.

There are many more interaction and runtime specifics dealing with the portlet and users of the portlet.

Figure 9.1 shows what a basic portlet in VIEW mode looks like and provides a brief description of the different components of the portlet container window, as well as what methods each component invokes when clicked.

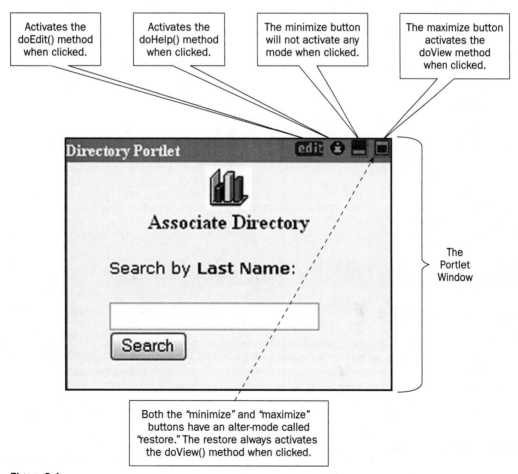

Figure 9.1

The portlet container handles user interaction with the visual components of a portlet and also enables the developer to change specific attributes about the portlet. We have not yet talked about how to maintain state and special configurations with portlets. The next section describes the maintenance of user state through the portlet preferences.

Portlet Preferences

The JSR 168 specification provides a way for developers to maintain user information about a portlet, including state information. This is done through the use of the `PortletPreference` object. We will use this object in-depth when we create our example portlet later in this chapter. This object will aid us in storing different information about the portal and enable us to retrieve preference information when necessary. For a more detailed look at portlet preferences, please see Chapter 1.

Using the `setValues` and `getValues` methods, we can retrieve the necessary preferences for our portlet. The `store` method is used to save changes to the `PortletPreference` object; however, changes can only be made inside the `processAction` method and toward the end of execution. The `PortletPreference` object also has a way to validate that the data we are about to save using the `store` method is correct. This is done by implementing the `PreferenceValidator` class. If this class is implemented, any calls to `store` will trigger the `validate` method of the `PreferenceValidator` class before the changes to the `PortletPreference` object are saved.

The initial preferences are stored in the `portlet.xml` file along with the `PreferenceValidator` class for the specified portlet. This is the key area to save initial preference information you want to load at runtime. You will see a working example of this later, in "The Directory Portlet" section of this chapter.

JSP Tag Library

The portlet specification also provides a JSP tag library, which makes it easier for you to develop JSP pages and process portlet information. This tag library is setup in the `web.xml` file for the portlet. Following is an example of the `<taglib>` entry:

```
<taglib>
    <taglib-uri>http://java.sun.com/portlet</taglib-uri>
    <taglib-location>/WEB-INF/taglib.tld</taglib-location>
</taglib>
```

JSP tag libraries have been created for Web applications as well. *Do not confuse the two.* The portlet tag library is specifically used for accessing the portlet API and portlet information.

Packaging a Portlet

Portlets are packaged very similarly to Web applications (in `.war` files). As a matter of fact, they are even created with the extension `.war`. Everything is contained in the `.war` file, just as it would be in a normal `.war` file, with the addition of a `portlet.xml` file (which is a deployment descriptor describing the portlet in detail and storing preference information). The `portlet.xml` also aids in security configurations for the portlet. It can restrict the portlet from being run on any protocol other than HTTPS. This should definitely be helpful if you have to develop an online banking portal or an e-commerce billing system.

The eXo Portal Platform

The eXo portal platform is a JSR 168-compliant, open-source portal that supports portlets developed according to the JSR 168 specification. It supports two methods of portlet development. One is the standard development architecture using the guidelines in the JSR 168 specification, and the other enhances the development of portlets by using a Model-View-Controller architecture. You will look at one example of each development approach in this chapter. The Directory portlet example was developed using the standard method, and the Loan Calculator portlet example was developed using the MVC approach.

The following sections describe several of the features and tools that the eXo platform provides in order to make the development process and usage of JSR 168-compliant portlets simple and robust.

The eXo Portal

The eXo portal is built around the Java Server Faces (JSR 127) specification, which is a Web framework paradigm based on the Model-View-Controller (MVC) method of development, which enables developers to interact with the Web layer's components and events in a fashion that is similar to Swing. This enables the easy retrieval of a portlet's content and user preferences. The eXo portal is completely compliant with the JSR 168 specification, which enables you to create portlets based on the specification and run them on the eXo portal.

Hot Deployment

The Hot Deployment feature is comprised of two technologies that together provide a lightweight and fast solution for hot deployment. The technologies are **JbossMX** and **Pico Container**. Pico Container handles the resolving of dependencies, while JbossMX's main focus is hot deployment of the Web archive. This means that you can deploy the portlets you create while the server is running. This is a great feature, because it can be quite a nuisance during development, or even while doing production upgrades, to have to stop the server in order to install new portlets. This will save you a significant amount of time during the development process.

Customization Tool

The eXo platform also provides a customization tool that provides administrators with the capability to configure the portlet with minimal effort and almost no programming knowledge. The customization tool is a "what you see is what you get" (WYSIWYG) complete portal and portlet editor. The customization tool is shown in Figure 9.2.

The customization tool enables you to decide which portlets are in your portal, what their titles are, and how they are laid out. It also enables you to add and edit tabs, as well as adjust and edit columns. It's a very flexible and easy-to-use tool, especially during the testing process when you need to test more than one portlet at a time.

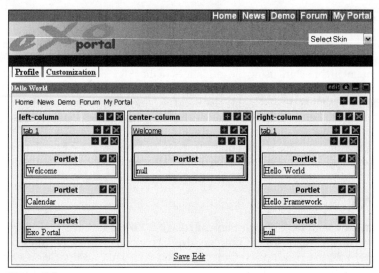

Figure 9.2

Setup and Installation of eXo

There are two main distributions of eXo, as is the case with most open-source products: the source distribution and the binary distribution. If you download the binary distribution, all you have to do is extract the platform and run it. The latest Java Virtual Machine is required to be present on your machine in order for it to function correctly. The following steps enable you to run the eXo binary distribution:

1. If you are familiar with Jboss, the eXo platform directory structure will look familiar to you. eXo uses a consolidated version of the Jboss server. Change directory to `install_directory/exo-portal/exo-jboss/bin`.

2. On a Unix system, run the shell script `exo.sh`. On a Windows system, run the batch file `exo.bat`. This will execute the server and integrate the eXo portal with Jboss.

3. The final step of the installation process is to simply go to the following URL, where you should see the eXo portal running:

`http://localhost:8080/exo/faces/layout/blue-lagoon/portal.jsp`

The source distribution is provided for developers who want to compile the source code themselves and execute the platform. Build procedures change daily, as does the code, so it is important to keep up with the latest changes on the eXo Web site (www.exoportal.org), especially the Forums section.

Understanding the eXo Directory Structure

The eXo directory structure has numerous similarities with the Jboss directory structure. This is because it is tightly bundled with Jboss and Tomcat. Just in case you have never used Jboss before, this section explains each directory and what it is used for in relation to the eXo platform. Figure 9.3 illustrates the components of the eXo directory structure.

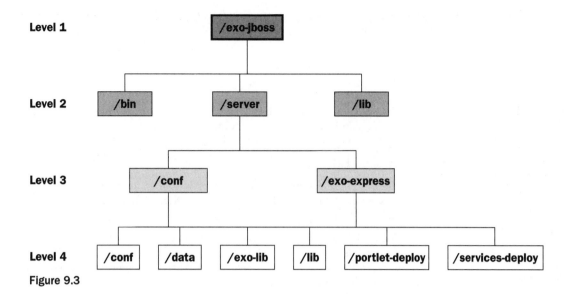

Figure 9.3

Referring to Figure 9.3, at **level 1** we have the directory /exo-jboss. This is the top-level directory and doesn't contain any files. At **level 2,** we have three new directories, which are described in the following table.

Directory	Description
/bin	The /bin directory contains all the scripts necessary for starting and shutting down the portal server. It contains the exo.sh and exo.bat files previously explained in the section "Setup and Installation of eXo."
/server	The /server directory simply contains the level 3 directories shown in Figure 9.3.
/lib	The /lib directory contains all the libraries necessary to run JBoss. Libraries contained here have a global effect across the server. In other words, a library file in this directory does not need to be included in the portlet's WEB-INF/lib directory.

The **level 3** directories contain default configuration information and are described in the following table.

Directory	Description
/conf	The /conf directory enables you to define a default web.xml file that will be used by all Web applications and portlet applications.
/exo-express	The /exo-express directory is the start of the simplest form of the eXo portal server.

The **level 4** directories contain several key directories that are used for the following: configurations of portlets, hot deployment, libraries the portlets use, and eXo services. These directories are described in the following table.

Directory	Description
/conf	The /conf directory enables you to configure security features, logging features, and deployment configurations.
/data	The /data directory contains information related to the hypersonic database that comes with eXo.
/exo-lib	The /exo-lib contains libraries explicit to eXo. If any of these libraries are contained in the level 2 /lib directory, they do not need to be included here.
/lib	The /lib directory enables the deployment of libraries that will affect all the portlets and Web applications on this server. Again, if any of these libraries are contained in the level 2 /lib directory, they do not need to be included here.
/portlet-deploy	The /portlet-deploy directory is the directory in which you would put your portlet WAR files. This is the hot deployment directory and the main directory you will be dealing with when developing portlets.
/services-deploy	The /services-deploy directory is made specifically to contain eXo service (.es) files.

The preceding tables describe the key directories in the eXo platform and their uses. This should provide you with a good understanding of how the eXo portal platform is structured.

The Directory Portlet

In this section, you will learn how to design, develop, and configure the Directory portlet example. This example portlet focuses on all the main aspects of portlet development and shows you how to handle each facet of the development process. Deployment of the Directory portlet will take place on the eXo portal platform, which was discussed in the previous section.

The **Directory portlet** is a portlet that enables the user to find a fellow employee in their company directory. The user can search for the associate by last name, first name, or e-mail address. If the user were to search for a last name for which multiple entries existed, the portlet displays each entry on a separate line. The company directory information is stored in a MySQL database and is accessed via JDBC. Figure 9.4 shows what the portlet looks like in the portlet VIEW mode.

In the portlet VIEW mode, the Directory portlet is available for someone to enter a search. It is currently set up to search by last name. That can be changed in EDIT mode. If we search for an associate with the last name of Smith, the portlet will submit the form and call the processAction method, which will then search for the associate, display the results, and return the portlet to VIEW mode. Figure 9.5 displays the results of the search.

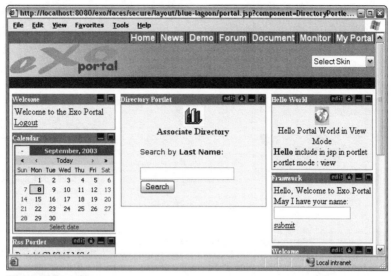

Figure 9.4

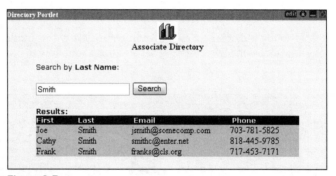

Figure 9.5

You can see in Figure 9.5 that the results showed up in VIEW mode even though they were submitted from VIEW mode. This is an interesting concept and is not as complex as it may seem. Basically, when the form is submitted, it posts the information to the processAction method and returns to the same view it was in before submission unless explicitly changed during the processAction method. When it returns from the process action, the doView method is executed again, enabling us to display the results of the search.

The edit screen shown in Figure 9.6 enables the user to decide which method to search by. The user can select either last_name, first_name, or email as a search criteria. When the Apply button is pressed, the processAction method is triggered. The processAction method sets a preference indicating what the user selected and returns the user to VIEW mode, which in turn uses the preference as the new search criteria.

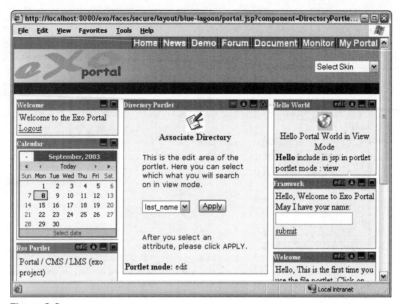

Figure 9.6

Finally, the portlet HELP mode is displayed, as shown in Figure 9.7. In this mode, we can offer the user specific details about how to use the Directory portlet and tips about how to search the associate directory if need be.

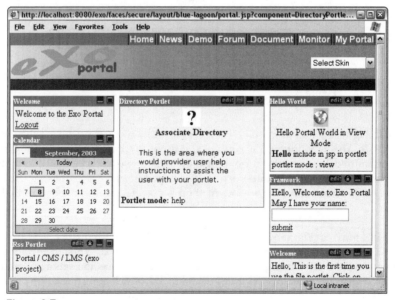

Figure 9.7

You may have noticed throughout these screenshots that the icons have changed for each mode. This is completely configurable and is simple HTML code. You can always determine programmatically what mode you are in or about to be in throughout the life cycle of the portlet. This enables ultimate customization of what we allow the user to view, depending on the mode of the portlet. All these techniques are demonstrated when you view the source code for each component of the directory portlet.

Developing the Directory Portlet

In the previous section, you saw what the directory portlet looks like in HELP, VIEW, and EDIT portlet modes. Now we will concentrate heavily on the construction of the portlet, examining all the source code in great detail. Do not be overwhelmed by the code, for the general concepts that make up the portlet are fairly painless to grasp, especially if you have done any kind of Web application development in the past.

Before examining the source code, you need to take a look at the various files that make up the Directory portlet. The files are described in the following table.

File	Description
DirectoryPortlet.java	This is the main portlet source file that subclasses the GenericPortlet class; it contains methods for handling the different modes and events that are triggered during the life cycle of a portlet. The methods it contains are as follows:
	init — handles portlet initialization.
	processAction — handles action events created by the user.
	doView — handles VIEW mode render requests.
	doEdit — handles EDIT mode render requests.
	doHelp — handles HELP mode render requests.
	destroy — this method is not defined in our sample, but could be added to it if we needed any clean-up code.
DirectoryValidator.java	This file contains the DirectoryValidator class, which implements the interface PreferencesValidator and includes a validate method. The validate method is executed from a processAction call when a PortletPreferences.store method is executed. Its main purpose is to ensure that the preferences data about to be stored to the preferences is correct. If it isn't correct, you can throw a ValidatorException from the validate method, thus aborting the PortletPreferences.store procedure.
DirectoryView.jsp	This JSP file is included in when the doView method is executed from the DirectoryPortlet class. It contains the search form that the user can use to search for an employee in the associate directory. It also contains the logic for connecting to the MySQL database and issuing a SQL statement to query the appropriate information from the database. Once it obtains information from the database, it displays it to the user from within itself and does not use another JSP to display the information.

Table continued on following page

File	Description
`DirectoryEdit.jsp`	This JSP file is included when the `doEdit` method is executed from the `DirectoryPortlet` class. It contains a form that enables the user to select the search criteria (last name, first name, e-mail) to search by. When the user clicks Submit, the form data is processed by `processAction` and the portlet's mode is changed to `VIEW`.
`DirectoryHelp.jsp`	This JSP file is included when the `doHelp` method is executed from the `DirectoryPortlet` class. It contains help information that aids the user in the use of the portlet.
`DirectoryResources.` `properties`	This file simply contains one property that allows you to set the default title for the portlet. The line looks like this: `javax.portlet.title=` `Directory Portlet`.
`portlet.xml`	This is the deployment descriptor file for the portlet. It contains all kinds of configuration data that pertains to the directory portlet. Examples of such data include security constraints, initial preferences, user attributes, and so on.
`web.xml`	This is the Web archive deployment descriptor; it contains servlet mappings, tag libraries, display name, and so on.
`taglib.tld`	This file is the template for the JSP tag library.

The MySQL Database

The MySQL database, `dbdirectory`, used in the directory portlet example has a very simplistic design. It contains one table called `tblCoworkers` with four columns: `first_name`, `last_name`, `email`, and `phone`. The database is used by `DirectoryView.jsp` to accomplish the user search request. The following code demonstrates a SQL script that could be created to configure the database in MySQL:

```
// Create the Database
CREATE DATABASE IF NOT EXISTS dbdirectory;

// Create the table
CREATE TABLE IF NOT EXISTS TBLCOWORKERS
(
    FIRST_NAME VARCHAR(100),
    LAST_NAME VARCHAR(100),
    EMAIL VARCHAR(100),
    PHONE VARCHAR(100)
);

// Here is the syntax for inserting a record
INSERT INTO TBLCOWORKERS (FIRST_NAME, LAST_NAME, EMAIL, PHONE)
VALUES ('Joe', 'Smith','jsmith@somecomp.com', '703-781-5825');
```

Now that we have examined the files, directory structures, and databases that make up the directory portlet example, let's take a look at the source code. We will analyze each source code example, providing you with a detailed informational breakdown of what is taking place within each major section.

The DirectoryPortlet Class

This class is the main portlet class that extends the `GenericPortlet` class. It implements the following methods: init, doView, doEdit, doHelp and processAction. The following code shows the initial creation of the `DirectoryPortlet` class and the init method:

```
/**
 * Created: 2003
 */

import javax.portlet.*;

/**
 * Class  : DirectoryPortlet extends GenericPortlet
 * Desc   : Use to process portlet events
 */
public class DirectoryPortlet extends GenericPortlet
{
    private static final String TEMPLATE = "/WEB-INF/templates/html/";

    /**
     * Method : init
     * Desc   : Handles the initialization of the portlet
     */
    public void init(PortletConfig config) throws PortletException {
        super.init(config);
    }
}
```

In the preceding code, we needed to import the package `javax.portlet.*` to gain access to the Portlet API. After the import, we defined the `DirectoryPortlet` class and extended the `GenericPortlet` class. The `GenericPortlet` class contains all the necessary portlet methods that we can define to control our portlet. The init method is now defined and does nothing more than call its superclass.

The doView method handles the doView calls from the render method, enabling you to determine what to do in VIEW mode. It also includes the `DirectoryView.jsp`, which enables you to process user search requests.

```
public void doView(RenderRequest request, RenderResponse response)
                        throws PortletException, IOException
{
    // Get a preferences object for this portlet
    PortletPreferences prefs = request.getPreferences();

    // Obtain a windows state object that can be used to determine
    // the state of the portlet
    WindowState state = request.getWindowState();
```

The first thing we want to do is determine the state of the portlet. If it is in NORMAL or MAXIMIZED mode, we will handle the request:

```
    // If we are in the NORMAL or MAXIMIZED state execute this block of
    // code
    if (state == state.NORMAL || state == state.MAXIMIZED) {
        Writer writer = response.getWriter();
```

Next, we display the icon we want to be viewed on the portlet for this mode:

```
    writer.write("<center><img src='/DirectoryPortlet/images/directory.jpg'/></center>");
    writer.write("<center><b>Associate Directory</b></center><br>");
```

Finally, we obtain the portlet context and a dispatcher, and then include the `DirectoryView.jsp`, passing it the `request` and `response` objects before it is included. This gives `DirectoryView.jsp` the chance to decide what it will display:

```
        PortletContext context = getPortletContext();
        PortletRequestDispatcher rd = context.getRequestDispatcher(TEMPLATE +
            "DirectoryView.jsp");
        rd.include(request, response);
    }
  }
```

The `doEdit` method enables you to process edit requests from the user. The `EDIT` mode in this portlet is for tracking what criteria the user wants to search by:

```
/**
  * Method : doEdit
  * Desc   : Handles portlet edit events
  */
public void doEdit(RenderRequest request, RenderResponse response)
                          throws PortletException, IOException
{
    // Get a preferences object for this portlet
    PortletPreferences prefs = request.getPreferences();

    // Obtain a windows state object that can be used to determine the state
    // of the portlet
WindowState state = request.getWindowState();
```

The following code determines the current state of the portlet. As long as it is in NORMAL or MAXIMIZED, we will proceed accordingly:

```
    // If we are in the NORMAL or MAXIMIZED state execute this block of code
    if (state == state.NORMAL || state == state.MAXIMIZED) {
        Writer writer = response.getWriter();

        writer.write("<center><img src='/DirectoryPortlet/images/edit.jpg'/></center>");

        writer.write("<center><b>Associate Directory</b></center><br>");
```

At this point, we include the `DirectoryEdit.jsp` and pass it `request` and `response` objects, respectively.

```
        PortletContext context = getPortletContext();
        PortletRequestDispatcher rd = context.getRequestDispatcher(TEMPLATE +
            "DirectoryEdit.jsp");

        rd.include(request, response);
    }
}
```

The following code shows the `doHelp()` method. The directory portlet example doesn't provide much help to the user because of its simplicity. We could expand this method if we had a much more complex portlet that was going to be commercially used. At the end of this method, we include `Directory Help.jsp` to aid in help processing:

```
/**
  * Method : doHelp
  * Desc   : Handles portlet help events
  */
public void doHelp(RenderRequest request, RenderResponse response)
                            throws PortletException, IOException
{
    // Get a preferences object for this portlet
    PortletPreferences prefs = request.getPreferences();

    // Obtain a windows state object that can be used to determine the state
       of the portlet
    WindowState state = request.getWindowState();

    // If we are in the NORMAL or MAXIMIZED state execute this block of code
    if (state == state.NORMAL || state == state.MAXIMIZED) {
        Writer writer = response.getWriter();

        writer.write("<center>
           <img src='/DirectoryPortlet/images/help.jpg'/></center>");

        writer.write("<center><b>Associate Directory</b></center><br>");

        PortletContext context = getPortletContext();

        PortletRequestDispatcher rd = context.getRequestDispatcher(TEMPLATE +
            "DirectoryHelp.jsp");

        rd.include(request, response);
    }
}
```

The `processAction` method is the final method in the `DirectoryPortlet` class. It provides you with the capability to process action events as they are occurring. For instance, if a user submits data from a form in EDIT mode, a `processAction()` call will be made, enabling you to handle the form submission and then take appropriate action. Now to step through the code for a better understanding of this key method:

```
/**
 * Method : processAction
 * Desc   : Handles portlet Action events
 */
public void processAction(ActionRequest aReq, ActionResponse aRes) throws
                                  PortletException, IOException
{
```

It is important to grab a `preferences` object in case we need to store information submitted by the user. We will determine this based on the current mode of the portlet.

```
// Get preferences object
PortletPreferences prefs = aReq.getPreferences();

// Get the search string the user sent
String searchString = aReq.getParameter("searchString");
```

If we are in VIEW mode, then we want to retrieve the current search string that the user submitted and use `setRenderParameter` to save it as a parameter that can be used by `DirectoryView.jsp` to search the associate directory:

```
// Check to see what mode we are in and process action accordingly
if (aReq.getPortletMode().equals(PortletMode.VIEW)) {
    if (searchString == null) {
        searchString = prefs.getValue("searchString","not_supplied");
    }

    aRes.setRenderParameter("searchString", searchString);

} else if (aReq.getPortletMode().equals(PortletMode.EDIT)) {
    boolean editOK = false;
    String errorMsg = null;
```

If we are in EDIT mode, we know that the form submission is coming from `DirectoryEdit.jsp`. This means that we need to obtain the search type that the user selected from the combo box and store it as a preference for later use:

```
    try {
        // Get selection string from combo box
        String selected = aReq.getParameter("cmbSearchType");

        // Make sure the preference we want to modify is modifiable
        if (prefs.isModifiable("userSelection")) {
            prefs.setValue("userSelection", selected);

            // Store preferences
            prefs.store();
            editOK = true;
        } else {
            System.out.println("Error:processAction(): PortletPreferences
                    not modifiable, check deployment descriptor");
            editOK = false;
```

```
        }
    } catch (ValidatorException ex) {
        System.out.println("Error:processAction():Validation Exception - "
            + ex);
        editOK = false;
        errorMsg = ex.getMessage();
    } catch (Exception e) {
        System.out.println("Error:processAction():Exception - " + e);
        e.printStackTrace(System.out);
    }
```

The setPortletMode method is one of the really neat features of the Portlet API. We can use the set PortletMode method to literally change the mode we want the portlet to be in once processAction is complete. In the following code snippet, we are setting it to VIEW mode even though we were originally in EDIT mode. This will execute the doView method when processAction has finished processing:

```
try {
    // Redirect to view mode
    if (editOK) {
        aRes.setPortletMode(PortletMode.VIEW);
    } else {
        aRes.setRenderParameter("error", errorMsg);
    }
} catch (Exception e) {
    System.out.println("Error:processAction():Exception:Redirect - " +
        e);
    e.printStackTrace(System.out);
}
}
```

The DirectoryValidator Class

In the processAction() method described in the previous section, we executed a store method to save information related to the search criteria supplied by the user. In the method, we executed a prefs.store call. This method does not require a validator class, but we highly recommend that you use one. For one thing, it will save you a lot of time debugging if something goes wrong with the store method. In addition, it provides you with a means to prevent errors from occurring in the store method, and a tactic to clean up gracefully.

The PreferencesValidator that is used for your portlet is defined in the portlet.xml file. In this example, the DirectoryValidator class is created and contains a method called validate(), which makes sure that the user supplied a selection before pressing the Submit button from EDIT mode. If the selection is empty, a ValidatorException is thrown, halting the store() operation. The following example shows the code used in the directory portlet:

```
public class DirectoryValidator implements PreferencesValidator {
/**
    * Method : validate
    * Desc   : This method is called with the preference store() method
    *          is invoked.
    */
```

```
public void validate(PortletPreferences prefs) throws ValidatorException {
    String sSelection = prefs.getValue("userSelection","");

    // Check to make sure that there is a userSelection preference
    if (sSelection.equalsIgnoreCase("")) {
        throw new ValidatorException("Invalid userSelection Preference!!",null);
    }
}
```

The DirectoryView JSP File

The DirectoryView.jsp file is displayed in VIEW mode and is included when doView is called in the DirectoryPortlet class. This file contains the logic that is needed to perform the search of the associate directory. It creates a JDBC connection to a MySQL data source, which stores the associate directory information. When a search is submitted by the user, a processAction method is called and returns the search string the user submitted to this JSP. When the search string is received, DirectoryView.jsp searches the associate directory for matches and displays them on the portlet. Let's examine the source code of DirectoryView.jsp more closely:

```
<%@ page import="javax.portlet.*" %>
<%@ page import="java.sql.*" %>
<%
// Get the request and response objects to be used in this jsp
RenderRequest renderRequest = (RenderRequest)
            request.getAttribute("javax.portlet.request");

RenderResponse renderResponse = (RenderResponse)
            request.getAttribute("javax.portlet.response");

// Obtain a preferences object
PortletPreferences prefs = renderRequest.getPreferences();

// Get the current user selection
String sSelection = prefs.getValue("userSelection", "last_name");

// If something went wrong set it to 'last_name'
if (sSelection == null) {
    sSelection = "last_name";
}
%>
```

The user form is created with the method set to post and the action set to something you have probably never seen before. We use renderResponse.createActionURL to create an action URL. This will post the user form information to the processAction method of the DirectoryPortlet class:

```
<form method="post"
      action="<%=renderResponse.createActionURL().toString()%>">
    <input type="text" name="searchString" size="25">
    <input type="submit" value="Search" name="btnSearch">
</form>
```

At this point, we want to get the search string that the user submitted and then create our connection to the MySQL database so that we can find the appropriate associates:

```
<%
// Get the search string
String sSearchStr = request.getParameter("searchString");

if (sSearchStr != null && !sSearchStr.equals("")) {
    // Setup a connection to a MySQL database
    String sDriverName = "jdbc:mysql://LT-JVitale.mcdonaldbradley.local/dbDirectory";

    String sClassName = "com.mysql.jdbc.Driver";

    Class.forName(sClassName);

    // Create connection
    Connection connection = DriverManager.getConnection(sDriverName);

    connection.setAutoCommit(false);

    Statement statement = connection.createStatement();

    String sSQLCommand = null;
```

The following code segment determines which criteria to search by. Remember that the user can change this in EDIT mode, so we have to handle all three cases:

```
    // Decide what to search by
    if (sSelection.equalsIgnoreCase("last_name")) {
        sSQLCommand = "SELECT * FROM tblcoworkers WHERE last_name = '" +
                sSearchStr + "'";
      } else if (sSelection.equalsIgnoreCase("first_name")) {
        sSQLCommand = "SELECT * FROM tblcoworkers WHERE first_name = '" +
                    sSearchStr + "'";
    } else {
        sSQLCommand = "SELECT * FROM tblcoworkers WHERE email = '" +
                    sSearchStr + "'";
    }

    // Execute SQL statement
    ResultSet resultset = statement.executeQuery(sSQLCommand);

    // Return the results below in a table formatted fashion
%>
```

We broke up this code to save space. Basically, what you would do in order to retrieve the results is spin through the ResultSet and obtain the column values for each record. Then, you would display them in an HTML-formatted table:

```
<%
   // Display next result if there is any
   while(resultset.next()) {
       resultset.getString("first_name");
       resultset.getString("last_name");
       resultset.getString("email");
       resultset.getString("phone")
   }

   // Clean up connection
   statement.close();
   connection.close();
%>
```

The DirectoryEdit JSP File

The `DirectoryEdit.jsp` file is accessed when the user selects `EDIT` mode on the portlet. This JSP file enables the user to edit the search type that `VIEW` mode uses for searching the associate directory. When the form is submitted, the contents are sent to the `processAction` method of the `DirectoryPortlet` class. If successful, the portlet is set to `VIEW` mode and will show the reflected changes. Now, let's inspect the important parts of the `DirectoryEdit.jsp` code:

```
<%@ page import="javax.portlet.*"%>
<%
// Get the request and response objects to be used in this jsp
RenderRequest renderRequest = (RenderRequest)
         request.getAttribute("javax.portlet.request");

RenderResponse renderResponse = (RenderResponse)
           request.getAttribute("javax.portlet.response");
%>
```

The following JSP snippet is the form that posts information to the `processAction` method of the `DirectoryPortlet` class:

```
<form method="post"
       action="<%=renderResponse.createActionURL().toString()%>"
   <select size="1" name="cmbSearchType">
       <option selected value="last_name">last_name</option>
       <option value="first_name">first_name</option>
       <option value="email">email</option>
   </select>
   <input type="submit" value="Apply" name="btnApply">
</form>
```

This following simple code shows how to access the portlet mode using the Portlet API:

```
<b>Portlet mode:</b>
<font color="#0000FF"><%= renderRequest.getPortletMode().toString() %></font>
```

The web.xml File

The web.xml files for portlets have the same general structure that Web application web.xml files have. They contain configurations specific to the Web application portion of the portlet. The XML fragments that follow highlight the important parts of the web.xml file:

```
<web-app>
    <display-name>DirectoryPortlet</display-name>
    <description>
        This application is a portlet. It can not be used outside a portal.
        This web.xml file is mandatory in each .par archive file.
    </description>
```

Notice that the <servlet> and <servlet-mapping> tags all point to the portlet:

```
<servlet>
    <servlet-name>DirectoryPortlet</servlet-name>
    <servlet-class>DirectoryPortlet</servlet-class>
</servlet>
<servlet-mapping>
    <servlet-name>DirectoryPortlet</servlet-name>
    <url-pattern>/DirectoryPortlet</url-pattern>
</servlet-mapping>
```

The next section defines the JSP tag library to use for this portlet:

```
<taglib>
    <taglib-uri>http://java.sun.com/portlet</taglib-uri>
    <taglib-location>/WEB-INF/taglib.tld</taglib-location>
</taglib>
</web-app>
```

The portlet.xml File

The portlet.xml file is the deployment descriptor for the portlet and contains configuration, security, cache, and initial preference information. The following code shows the core elements for the directory portlet example:

```
<portlet-app>
  <portlet>
    <description lang="EN">Directory Portlet</description>
    <portlet-name>DirectoryPortlet</portlet-name>
    <display-name lang="EN">Directory Portlet</display-name>
    <portlet-class>DirectoryPortlet</portlet-class>
    <expiration-cache>-1</expiration-cache>
    <supports>
      <mime-type>text/html</mime-type>
      <portlet-mode>edit</portlet-mode>
      <portlet-mode>help</portlet-mode>
    </supports>
    <supported-locale>en</supported-locale>
```

```
    <resource-bundle>DirectoryResources</resource-bundle>
    <portlet-info>
      <title>Directory Portlet</title>
      <short-title>DirectoryPortlet</short-title>
      <keywords>Directory</keywords>
    </portlet-info>
```

The `<portlet-preferences>` tag is a key tag for you to take note of. Here is where you define the initial preferences that you want to load into memory when the portlet is initialized:

```
    <portlet-preferences>
      <preference>
        <name>userSelection</name>
        <value>last_name</value>
      </preference>
      <preferences-validator>DirectoryValidator</preferences-validator>
    </portlet-preferences>
    <security-role-ref>
      <role-name>trustedUser</role-name>
      <role-link>auth-user</role-link>
    </security-role-ref>
  </portlet>
  <user-attribute>
    <description lang="EN">
      Pre-defined attribute for the telephone number of the user at work.
    </description>
    <name>workInfo/telephone</name>
  </user-attribute>
  <security-constraint>
    <portlet-collection>
      <portlet-name>TimeZoneClock</portlet-name>
    </portlet-collection>
    <user-data-constraint>
      <transport-guarantee>CONFIDENTIAL</transport-guarantee>
    </user-data-constraint>
  </security-constraint>
</portlet-app>
```

Deploying the Directory Portlet in eXo

The steps to deploy a portlet on the eXo portal platform are fairly straightforward. The key is to make sure that you package the Web archive (.war) file correctly, with all the files in the appropriate directory structure. Figure 9.8 illustrates the correct directory structure and the files in those directories prior to archiving.

To package the portlet into a Web archive (.war) file, we would use the JAR tool that is provided with the Java SDK. Once our DirectortyPortlet.war file is created, all we have to do is drop it into the hot deployment directory of eXo called portlet-deploy and the portlet will be automatically deployed by JBoss. Then, we simply bring up the eXo portal in a Web browser, log in, go to the customization page, and add the portlet to the portal. The Directory portlet will now be viewable and useable.

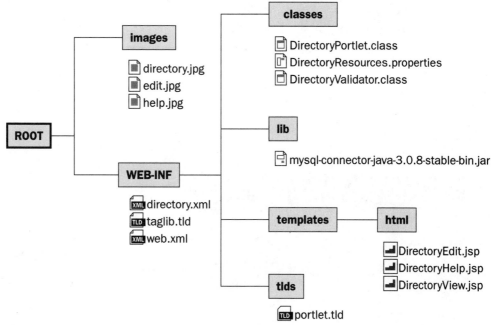

Figure 9.8

Portlet Creation the Model-View-Controller (MVC) Way

The eXo portal platform provides a means for you to develop your portlets according to the MVC paradigm. The MVC paradigm was orignally created by SmallTalk developers and has since been adopted for programming GUI-driven applications. The MVC paradigm divides an application into three componets: the model, the view, and the controller. The controller has access to both the model and the view and is the basis for the paradigm. The model talks to the view and can notify it of any changes to the model, but it does not have any references to the controller. The view has a reference to the model in order to communicate with the model and retrieve data from it. The view can also communicate with the controller, but its main purpose for communication with the controller is to notify it when updates to the view are successful.

In the portal world, the portlet acts as the controller, which creates the model object that can be used to access any enterprise or back-end data sources. The portlet or the controller will send the data out to the appropriate views. In the portal case, the data is dispatched to the JSPs that process the data. The JSPs aid in changing the view and rendering a visual display of the data that has been processed, all the while communicating with the controller. Figure 9.9 depicts the MVC paradigm as it applies to portlets.

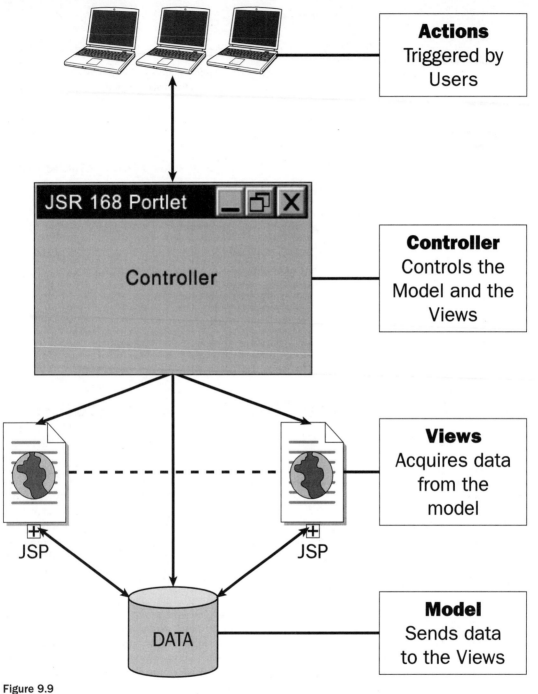

Figure 9.9

The MVC Loan Calculator Portlet

We have created a Loan Calculator portlet that makes use of the MVC paradigm using the eXo portal platform. The official name of this portlet in code is the MVCPortlet and we refer to it by this name throughout this section. The MVCPortlet portlet and controller configurations are defined in the portlet.xml file located in the MVCPortlet\WEB-INF directory. Specific controller information is defined in a separate XML file called controllers.xml, which is pointed to from the portlet.xml file. The following XML snippets are taken from the portlet.xml file and illustrate how the framework is set up and how a controller is configured:

```
<portlet>
```

Here, the basic portlet name and class are defined for the portlet:

```
<description lang="EN">MVC Portlet Test</description>
<portlet-name>MVCPortlet</portlet-name>
<display-name lang="EN">MVCPortlet</display-name>
<portlet-class>exo.portal.portlet.ExoPortletFramework</portlet-class>
```

Within the <init-param> tags, the portlet controller file is defined:

```
<init-param>
   <description>Portlet Controller</description>
   <name>controller-url</name>
   <value>controllers.xml</value>
</init-param>
</portlet>
```

The controllers.xml file displayed in the following code handles the different modes that can occur during a portlet's life cycle. This differs from the Directory portlet example in which we had to handle each mode in code by extending from the GenericPortlet class. The controllers handle the VIEW, EDIT, and HELP modes when they are encountered, and forward the requests to the XML specified classes and JSPs:

```
<controllers>
   <name>MVC Portlet Test</name>
   <identifier>Hello MVC Portlet Test</identifier>
```

The view controller results in two possible actions that can occur. One is the default action, ShowMVCPortletAction, which is called when no action parameters have been supplied. The other is the MVCPortletAction, which is called when action parameters are supplied:

```
<view-controller>
   <default-action>ShowMVCPortletAction</default-action>
   <action name="ShowMVCPortletAction" class="mvctest.MVCPortletAction">
      <forward name="success" page="MVCPortlet.jsp"/>
      <forward name="error" page="MVCPortlet.jsp"/>
   </action>
```

```
        <action name="MVCPortletAction" class="mvctest.MVCPortletAction">
            <forward name="success" page="MVCPortlet.jsp"/>
            <forward name="error" page="MVCPortlet.jsp"/>
        </action>
    </view-controller>
```

The help controller is executed when the portlet is in HELP mode:

```
    <help-controller>
        <default-action>MVCPortletHelpMode</default-action>
        <action name="MVCPortletHelpMode" class="mvctest.MVCPortletHelpMode">
            <forward name="success" page="MVCPortletHelp.jsp"/>
            <forward name="error" page="MVCPortletHelp.jsp"/>
        </action>
    </help-controller>
```

The edit controller is executed when the portlet is in EDIT mode:

```
    <edit-controller>
        <default-action>MVCPortletEditMode</default-action>
        <action name="MVCPortletEditMode" class="mvctest.MVCPortletEditMode">
            <forward name="success" page="MVCPortletEdit.jsp"/>
            <forward name="error" page="MVCPortletEdit.jsp"/>
        </action>
        <action name="MVCPortletAction" class="mvctest.MVCPortletAction">
            <forward name="success" page="MVCPortlet.jsp"/>
            <forward name="error" page="MVCPortlet.jsp"/>
        </action>
    </edit-controller>
```

The appropriate action classes are called when processing of the action message is needed. In order to process an action, you must extend the ActionHandler interface. You must then override two execute methods to handle two different types of action events: the RenderRequest event and the ActionRequest event. RenderRequest events are executed when the portlet is asked to be visible on-screen. ActionRequests are executed when an action has occurred within the portlet, as shown in the following code:

```
public class MVCPortletAction extends  ActionHandler {
  public void init() throws Exception {
  }
  public void execute(PortletContext context, ActionRequest request)
      throws Exception
  {
    // Add ActionRequest handling code here
  }
  public void execute(PortletContext context, RenderRequest request)
      throws Exception
  {
    // Add RenderRequest handling code here
  }
}
```

Figure 9.10 illustrates the GUI interface of the Loan Calculator portlet in action. In EDIT mode, the Loan Calculator portlet enables you to edit the loan amount; the term, in months; and the interest rate. When a user clicks Calculate, VIEW mode is displayed, showing the values entered in EDIT mode, plus the newly calculated monthly payment.

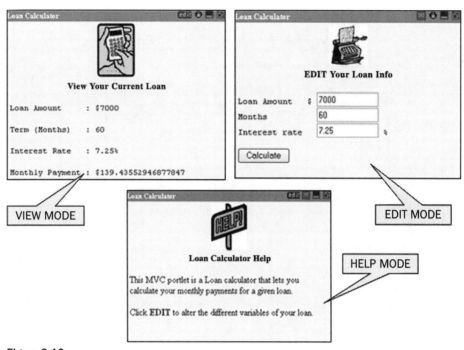

Figure 9.10

Most of the structure for the Java classes and JSP code is the same as the Directory portlet example, with the exception of the previously explained MVC additions. Therefore, there is no need to show the entire source code here. You can, however, download it from the book's Web site at www.wrox.com. Two source examples are worth noting. One is the MVCPortletAction class used for handling user submissions of forms, and the other is an example from the MVCPortletEdit.jsp, which shows you how to switch portlet modes from within a JSP. The following example shows the code for the MVCPortletAction class:

```
package mvctest;
import javax.portlet.*;
import exo.portal.portlet.actions.ActionHandler;
public class MVCPortletAction extends  ActionHandler {
  public void init() throws Exception {
  }
  public void execute(PortletContext context, RenderRequest request)
          throws Exception {

    System.out.println("MVCPortlet inside RenderRequest execute() method.");

  }
```

```
    public void execute(PortletContext context, ActionRequest aReq)
           throws Exception {

    // Get preferences object
    PortletPreferences prefs = aReq.getPreferences();

    if (prefs != null) {
        String  sLoanAmount = aReq.getParameter("loanAmount");
        String  sLoanTerm =   aReq.getParameter("loanTerm");
        String  sLoanRate =   aReq.getParameter("loanRate");

        double dLoanAmount  = Double.parseDouble(sLoanAmount);
        double dLoanTerm    = Double.parseDouble(sLoanTerm);
        double dLoanRate    = Double.parseDouble(sLoanRate);

        double dLoanPayment = 0.0d;
        double dRate        = 0.0d;
        dRate = dLoanRate / 1200;

        // Loan Calculation Algorithm
        dLoanPayment = dLoanAmount * dRate /
                    (1.0d - (Math.pow(1.0d/(1.0d + dRate), dLoanTerm)));

        String sLoanPayment = String.valueOf(dLoanPayment);

        try {
            prefs.setValue("loanAmount", sLoanAmount);
            prefs.setValue("loanTerm", sLoanTerm);
            prefs.setValue("loanRate", sLoanRate);
            prefs.setValue("loanPayment", sLoanPayment);

            // Store preferences
            prefs.store();
        } catch (ValidatorException ex) {
            // Handle Exception
        } catch (Exception e) {
            // Handle Exception
        }
    }
  }
}
```

The final code excerpt is taken from MVCPortletEdit.jsp and illustrates how to change the mode of a portlet from a JSP:

```
RenderResponse pRes =
      (RenderResponse) request.getAttribute("javax.portlet.response");

// Create a Portlet URL
PortletURL pURL = pRes.createActionURL();

// Set the portlet mode to VIEW
pURL.setPortletMode(PortletMode.VIEW);
```

The eXo portal platform is very flexible and it enables you to take different approaches to developing portlets. The portlet examples presented here demonstrated how to develop JSR 168 portlets in standard fashion and also how to take advantage of the MVC development structure that eXo supports.

Web Applications versus Portlet Applications

You now know that the structure of a portlet is very similar to that of a Web application, which suggests the obvious question: Should you convert your Web applications into portlet applications? This raises some important points, so we will now discuss some distinctions between the two.

It should be readily obvious to you by now that Portlet applications and Web applications are similar but not the same. If Portlet applications were merely a newer version of Web applications, then they would have replaced Web applications, instead of building upon them.

Fundamentally, though, Portlet applications and Web applications have a major distinction in their designs. Web applications control the interaction with the client tier — the Web browser. This means that they provide all content in the page, as well as control layout and application flow control. Portlet applications have fundamentally different design assumptions. They have two types of logic: **action logic** and **render logic**. Portlet applications also do not control where they appear on the page. Portlets have specific modes that should be taken into account (VIEW, EDIT, and HELP). These modes are the basis for portlet design. Therefore, you have to figure out if it makes more sense to create a portlet or a Web application for the data you want to present.

One other key point to keep in mind when comparing Portlet applications and Web applications is that portlets are generally thought of as individual applications contained in a portal, which can be added, removed, and customized by the user. Remember that the architecture for portlets in general usually does not rely on other portlets in the user's portal in order to function. This could be a significant factor in your decision as to whether you want to create a Web application or a portal application.

We think you will find that even though portlets are built on the Web application architecture, this does not automatically make the use of Web applications obsolete. Rather, it just provides you with more options for development, and it is up to you to decide which is right for the task at hand. Therefore, whether you should convert your Web applications into portlet applications must be determined on a case-by-case basis.

Summary

This chapter focused on development of JSR 168 portlet applications for portal servers that are compliant with the JSR 168 standard. In it, you were exposed to a general overview of portlet concepts, including portlet architecture and the development process, which explained the compilation and deployment of portlets.

You created your own portlet, the Directory portlet, as a solid JSR 168–compliant portlet example. In doing so, you were able to cover all the core components of portlet development and examine portlet concepts in depth. You used the open-source eXo portal platform to build and deploy your portlet applications, and looked at the Model-View-Controller paradigm that eXo supports for portlet development.

The final part of the chapter discussed Web applications versus portlet applications. In the next chapter, you will explore the concepts of building Web services for your portal.

10

Portlet Integration with Web Services

Throughout this book, we have discussed portal development as it relates to the user interface. This chapter, however, focuses on the information transmission between your portal and your enterprise information stores with Web services. Portlets are a great way to provide a front-end-user interface to back-end data sources, and Web services provide a standard interface for the transmission of that information. Traditional Web services are data-oriented and presentation-neutral, and must be aggregated and styled in order to provide presentation. On the other hand, the OASIS WSRP (Web Services for Remote Portlets) specification introduces a presentation-oriented Web service interface façade for remote portlets that mixes application and presentation logic. WSRP defines how a portlet can be invoked remotely by another portal, and is a mechanism for simpler integration between portals and Web services.

In this chapter, we describe the basic concepts of Web services and portal integration; build examples of portlets interacting with traditional Web services; and provide an overview of the WSRP specification. All source code for the examples in this chapter, including the code referred to but not listed, is on the book's Web site, at www.wrox.com.

Basic Concepts

Unless you have been in a cave for the last few years, you know that Web services are software applications that can be discovered, described, and accessed based on XML and standard Web protocols over computer networks. The messaging foundation of Web services is SOAP (Simple Object Access Protocol). WSDL (Web Service Definition Language) is used for describing the interfaces of SOAP Web services, and UDDI (Universal Description, Discovery, and Integration) registries are used for discovering and finding such Web services. Because there is community acceptance and standards agreement on these specifications to promote interoperability between applications, any portal developer should understand these basic concepts and know how to integrate with Web services. As this book is geared toward portal developers and is not a Web services tutorial, we do not explain every detail of the SOAP, WSDL, and UDDI specifications. We do, however, briefly discuss the SOAP message syntax, show you SOAP messaging and WSDL examples, discuss Web services as they relate to portlet development, and show you examples of portlets integrating with sample Web services using Apache Axis.

If you are entirely new to Web services, we recommend that you spend some time looking at the Web Services Primer at http://webservices.xml.com/, as well as the Sun Java documentation at http://java.sun.com/webservices. The examples in this chapter use the Apache Axis framework to deploy our Web services, and in one case, use Axis-generated objects to communicate with them. For more information about Apache Axis, please visit their Web site (http://xml.apache.org/axis).

One of the first things that you should understand is the format of the SOAP message syntax. An entire Web service message is encapsulated by a SOAP **envelope**, optional header information (mostly security-related information) is contained in the SOAP **header**, and the body of your Web service messages is contained in the SOAP **body**.

The following code shows a sample SOAP request asking for the last stock trade price for a ticker symbol, taken from the first example in the SOAP 1.1 specification. [SOAP] The SOAP body contains the main request, and the SOAP envelope wraps the entire message. On lines 4–7 is the SOAP body of the message, which wraps the application-specific information (the call to `GetLastTradePrice` in the SOAP body). A Web service receives this information, processes the request in the SOAP body, and returns a SOAP response. In this example, there was no SOAP header, but if there were such a header, it would precede the SOAP body as another child of the SOAP envelope:

```
01: <SOAP-ENV:Envelope
02:   xmlns:SOAP-ENV="http://schemas.xmlsoap.org/soap/envelope/"
03:   SOAP-ENV:encodingStyle="http://schemas.xmlsoap.org/soap/encoding/">
04:   <SOAP-ENV:Body>
05:       <m:GetLastTradePrice xmlns:m="Some-URI">
06:           <symbol>DIS</symbol>
07:       </m:GetLastTradePrice>
08:   </SOAP-ENV:Body>
09: </SOAP-ENV:Envelope>
```

The WSDL for this Web service would list the SOAP message format for the requests and responses. The SOAP response in the following code, much like the request in the preceding code, contains the "guts" of the application's message in the SOAP body. No presentation is included in the SOAP response; therefore, any portal calling this Web service will have to add presentation to the results:

```
<SOAP-ENV:Envelope
    xmlns:SOAP-ENV="http://schemas.xmlsoap.org/soap/envelope/"
    SOAP-ENV:encodingStyle="http://schemas.xmlsoap.org/soap/encoding/"/>
    <SOAP-ENV:Body>
        <m:GetLastTradePriceResponse xmlns:m="Some-URI">
            <Price>34.5</Price>
        </m:GetLastTradePriceResponse>
    </SOAP-ENV:Body>
</SOAP-ENV:Envelope>
```

If you developed a portlet to call the `GetLastTradePrice` Web service with a request shown in the first nine lines of code, you would have to do a little bit of extra work to add presentation to the response shown in the second group. The service itself provides no graphics, and simply sends an XML message response. Because SOAP messages are presentation-neutral, they must be styled (usually with stylesheets) to produce content. A simple scenario of the interaction between a portal and a Web service is shown in Figure 10.1. This figure shows three important concepts:

❑   The use of a Web service as a façade to the data source

❑   The interaction between a portlet in a portal and a Web service

❑   Taking the contents of the SOAP response and applying presentation

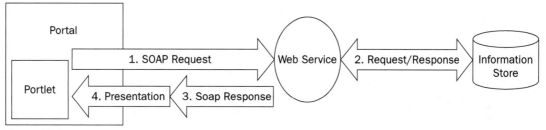

Figure 10.1

In Figure 10.1, a portlet sends a SOAP request to a Web service, which in turn makes a request to an information store. When the Web service is able to respond, it sends a SOAP response back to the portal. At this point, however, another process must take place in order to style the response content. Often, the presentation process could use XSL (the eXtensible Stylesheet Language) with a stylesheet in order to style the content for display in the portlet. Of course, this example could become more complicated if the portlet speaks to several Web services and needs to aggregate content before styling the information. As a result, your design needs to accommodate such complexity. As we discussed in the last chapter, such a design can be accomplished by using the Model-View-Controller (MVC) paradigm. Portlet development with Web services using MVC can take a very similar approach, with the Web services representing the model. In a portlet architecture with Web services, your Portlet developed with the Java Portlet API may act as the *controller,* and delegate presentation to other components, including JSPs. In the next section, you will see several examples of building portlets that integrate with traditional, data-centric Web services, following the MVC paradigm.

Integrating with Traditional Web Services

Portlets may be used as controllers to connect to your Web services, and dispatch presentation to other components, such as JSPs. Figure 10.2 shows a typical example of how you can develop your portlets to the MVC paradigm. In Figure 10.2, the portlet gets initialization information from the portlet descriptor as well as the names of the JSPs for `VIEW` mode, `EDIT` mode, and `HELP` mode. The portlet, using the `doView()`, `doEdit()`, and `doHelp()` methods inherited from the class `javax.portlet.GenericPortlet`, is able to dispatch to the proper presentation defined by the mappings in the portlet deployment descriptor. Depending on your Web services, your portlet itself may initiate the call to the Web service, or your JSPs may invoke a class or a bean to call the Web service.

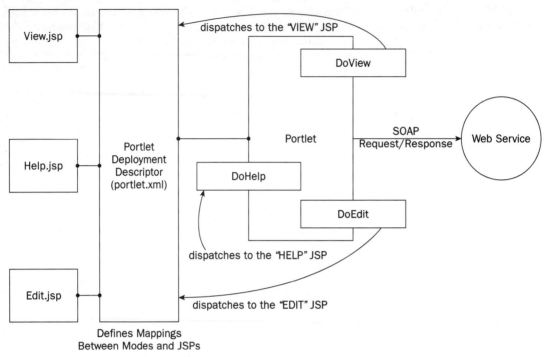

Figure 10.2

Figure 10.2 provides a good overview of how your portlets can be designed, whereby your portlets act as controllers to JSPs based on the VIEW/EDIT/HELP modes of your portlet. This takes advantage of the MVC paradigm, and can help you when you develop your portlets — regardless of whether you will be interacting with Web services.

Sun Microsystems developed some excellent sample portlets that follow this model, and these JSPs are used in several open-source portlet containers, which are available at http://developers.sun.com/prodtech/portalserver/reference/techart/jsr168/index.html. In their design, they have created a JSPPortlet class that extends the javax.portlet.GenericPortlet class that performs the redirection to the appropriate VIEW, EDIT, and HELP pages. This class is extended by their sample portlets, and a UML class diagram for their design is shown in Figure 10.3.

Figure 10.3 shows the design of Sun's example JSP portlets, where JSPPortlet is a superclass for dispatching the presentation of the portlet, based on the contentPage, editPage, and helpPage parameters in a portlet descriptor. The demonstration portlets that extend JSPPortlet are WeatherPortlet, NotepadPortlet, and BookmarkPortlet, all of which are good examples that you can use to understand portlet development. A partial listing of the code for JSPPortlet is shown in the following code. Because this code was developed by Sun Microsystems, we are listing the copyright:

```
/*
 * Copyright 2003 Sun Microsystems, Inc. All rights reserved.
 *
 * Redistribution and use in source and binary forms, with or without
 * modification, are permitted provided that the following conditions
 * are met:
```

```
 *
 * - Redistributions of source code must retain the above copyright
 *   notice, this list of conditions and the following disclaimer.
 *
 * - Redistribution in binary form must reproduce the above copyright
 *   notice, this list of conditions and the following disclaimer in
 *   the documentation and/or other materials provided with the
 *   distribution.
 *
 * Neither the name of Sun Microsystems, Inc. or the names of
 * contributors may be used to endorse or promote products derived
 * from this software without specific prior written permission.
 *
 * This software is provided "AS IS," without a warranty of any
 * kind. ALL EXPRESS OR IMPLIED CONDITIONS, REPRESENTATIONS AND
 * WARRANTIES, INCLUDING ANY IMPLIED WARRANTY OF MERCHANTABILITY,
 * FITNESS FOR A PARTICULAR PURPOSE OR NON-INFRINGEMENT, ARE HEREBY
 * EXCLUDED. SUN AND ITS LICENSORS SHALL NOT BE LIABLE FOR ANY DAMAGES
 * SUFFERED BY LICENSEE AS A RESULT OF USING, MODIFYING OR
 * DISTRIBUTING THE SOFTWARE OR ITS DERIVATIVES. IN NO EVENT WILL SUN
 * OR ITS LICENSORS BE LIABLE FOR ANY LOST REVENUE, PROFIT OR DATA, OR
 * FOR DIRECT, INDIRECT, SPECIAL, CONSEQUENTIAL, INCIDENTAL OR
 * PUNITIVE DAMAGES, HOWEVER CAUSED AND REGARDLESS OF THE THEORY OF
 * LIABILITY, ARISING OUT OF THE USE OF OR INABILITY TO USE SOFTWARE,
 * EVEN IF SUN HAS BEEN ADVISED OF THE POSSIBILITY OF SUCH DAMAGES.
 *
 * You acknowledge that Software is not designed, licensed or intended
 * for use in the design, construction, operation or maintenance of
 * any nuclear facility.
 */
package com.sun.portal.portlet.samples.jspportlet;
import javax.portlet.*;
import java.io.*;
import java.util.*;
public class JSPPortlet extends GenericPortlet {
  private PortletContext pContext;
  public void init(PortletConfig config) throws PortletException {
    super.init(config);
    pContext = config.getPortletContext();
  }
  public void doView(RenderRequest request,RenderResponse response)
    throws PortletException,IOException {
    String contentPage = getContentJSP(request);
    response.setContentType(request.getResponseContentType());
    if (contentPage != null && contentPage.length() != 0) {
      try {
        System.out.println("Dispatching to content page: " +
            contentPage);
        PortletRequestDispatcher dispatcher =
            pContext.getRequestDispatcher(contentPage);
        dispatcher.include(request, response);
      } catch (IOException e) {
        throw new PortletException("JSPPortlet.doView exception",
        e);
      }
    }
  }
}
```

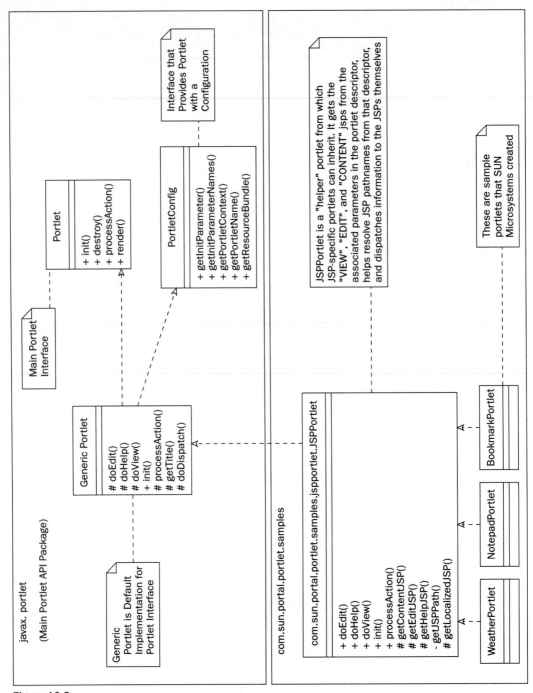

Figure 10.3

In the preceding listing, you saw that the doView() method uses the PortletRequestDispatcher object to dispatch the listing to the content page, specified in the portlet descriptor. In the same way, the doEdit() and doHelp() methods that were deleted from this listing delegate the view to the appropriate JSPs. In the following code, additional methods from JSPPortlet continue such delegation. The getContentJSP() page returns the localized JSP for the VIEW mode of the portlet. In the same manner, getEditJSP(), and getHelpJSP() in the file return the localized JSPs for the EDIT and HELP JSP pages, respectively. In the following code, the class resolves the localized path in the getLocalizedJSP() and getJSPPath() methods:

```
    protected String getContentJSP(RenderRequest request)
  throws PortletException {
    PortletPreferences pref = request.getPreferences();
    String contentPage = pref.getValue("contentPage","");
    return getLocalizedJSP(request.getLocale(), contentPage);
  }
  /* NOTE:
    getEditJSP() and getHelpJSP() were removed from this listing
    for space-saving purposes. They are very similar to getContentJSP().
  */
  protected String getLocalizedJSP(Locale locale, String jspPath) {
    String realJspPath = jspPath;
    if (locale != null) {
      int separator = jspPath.lastIndexOf("/");
      String jspBaseDir = jspPath.substring(0, separator);
      String jspFileName = jspPath.substring(separator+1);
      PortletContext pContext = getPortletContext();
      String searchPath = getJSPPath(jspBaseDir,
                                     locale.toString(),
                                     jspFileName);
      if (pContext.getResourceAsStream(searchPath) != null) {
        realJspPath = searchPath;
      } else {
        if (!locale.getCountry().equals("")) {
          searchPath = getJSPPath(jspBaseDir,
                                  locale.getLanguage(),
                                  jspFileName);
          if (pContext.getResourceAsStream(searchPath) != null) {
            realJspPath = searchPath;
          }
        }
      }
    }
    return realJspPath;
  }
  private String getJSPPath(String jspBaseDir,
                            String localeStr, String jspFileName) {
    StringBuffer sb = new StringBuffer();
    sb.append(jspBaseDir)
      .append("_")
      .append(localeStr)
      .append("/")
      .append(jspFileName);
    return sb.toString();
  }
}
```

The preceding code samples show some of the major methods of `JSPPortlet.java`. Its `doView()`, `doEdit()`, and `doHelp()` methods get the appropriate JSPs from the portlet's descriptor. They dispatch to the appropriate pages, calling the `getContentJSP()`, `getEditJSP()`, and `doHelpJSP()` methods, depending on the mode of the portlet. As you can see, the Java class can be a very helpful class for JSP redirection. We will extend this class in our example portlets in this chapter.

The next section provides an example of two different designs for integrating with Web services using such an architecture, explaining the pros and cons of each. In one example, the portlet delegates complete responsibility to its corresponding JSP pages for its respective modes; in the other, the Web service is called from the portlet and sends data information to the corresponding JSPs.

A Simple Example

For this example, we will develop a very simple portlet connecting to a simple Web service. Because we often see a lot of "stock quote" examples for Web services, which get boring after a while, we've created an example that is a little different. For this example, we will build a simple Llama portlet that shows inventory for a llama farm, based on results returned from a Llama Inventory Web service. The results from the Web service are based on a common XML Llama schema. This portlet acts only in VIEW and HELP modes.

We will show two approaches for invoking the Llama Web service: one showing and using SOAP and WSDL messaging, and one using objects generated with Web service tools. The first approach will show the "gory details" of SOAP and WSDL because it is sometimes helpful to see this in order to understand how SOAP and WSDL work. (It is also very helpful when you are debugging!) In the first approach, we'll provide an example of delegating responsibility to a JSP that calls the Web service and styles the SOAP message. In the second approach, we'll show you an example of using Axis-generated objects for communicating with your Web service. Both approaches focus on the Llama Inventory Web service.

First Approach: SOAP and WSDL Messaging

Our first approach has been created more for instructional (tutorial) use than for production. This will help you understand SOAP "on the wire," and some of the nitty-gritty details of WSDL. At the end of this section, you should have an appreciation for what "automatic" Web service integration tools do for you.

The WSDL that our Web service uses for this example is based on a "common llama schema" shared by many llama farms. The WSDL for this example, for `"Bonnie's Llama Farm"`, is shown in the following code sections. As you can see by looking at the `LlamaResults` element in the WSDL, inventories consist of a list of llamas, including each llama's international identifier, its age, a description, a name, the type of llama it is (usually a stud, weanling, cria, or female), and a URL for its image on the Web. The types section is shown here, which indicates the schema that we are using:

```xml
<?xml version="1.0" encoding="UTF-8" ?>
<definitions targetNamespace="http://trumantruck.com/bonniellama"
        xmlns="http://schemas.xmlsoap.org/wsdl/"
        xmlns:apachesoap="http://xml.apache.org/xml-soap"
        xmlns:impl="http://trumantruck.com/bonniellama"
        xmlns:soapenc="http://schemas.xmlsoap.org/soap/encoding/"
        xmlns:soap="http://schemas.xmlsoap.org/wsdl/soap/"
        xmlns:xsd="http://www.w3.org/2001/XMLSchema">

<!- types section ->
 <types>
```

```
  <schema xmlns="http://www.w3.org/2001/XMLSchema">
   <simpleType name="LlamaTypes">
    <restriction base="string">
     <enumeration value="STUD"/>
     <enumeration value="INTACT WEANLING MALE"/>
     <enumeration value="ADULT FEMALE"/>
     <enumeration value="FEMALE CRIA"/>
     <enumeration value="WEANLING FEMALE"/>
     <enumeration value="WEANLING MALE (NON-INTACT)"/>
    </restriction>
   </simpleType>
   <element name="LlamaResults">
    <complexType>
     <sequence>
      <element name="Llama" minOccurs="0">
       <complexType>
        <sequence>
         <element name="identifier" type="string"/>
         <element name="age" type="string" minOccurs="0"/>
         <element name="description" type="string" minOccurs="0"/>
         <element name="name" type="string"/>
         <element name="type" type="impl:LlamaTypes"/>
         <element name="imgurl" type="string" minOccurs="0"/>
        </sequence>
       </complexType>
      </element>
     </sequence>
    </complexType>
   </element>
   <element name="getLlamasInput" type="xsd:anyType"/>
  </schema>
 </types>
```

Next, we must define our message declarations, our port type declarations, and our bindings. These parts of the WSDL are shown in the following code:

```
 <!- message declarations ->
 <message name="getLlamasRequest">
  <part element="impl:getLlamasInput" name="part"/>
 </message>
 <message name="getLlamasResponse">
  <part element="impl:LlamaResults" name="getLlamasReturn"/>
 </message>

 <!- port type declarations ->
 <portType name="BonniesLlamaFarmInfoService">
  <operation name="getLlamas">
   <input message="impl:getLlamasRequest"/>
   <output message="impl:getLlamasResponse"/>
  </operation>
 </portType>
 <!- bindings ->
 <binding name="BonniesLlamasSoapBinding"
          type="impl:BonniesLlamaFarmInfoService">
```

```
    <soap:binding style="document"
                  transport="http://schemas.xmlsoap.org/soap/http"/>
   <operation name="getLlamas">
    <soap:operation soapAction=""/>
    <input name="getLlamasRequest">
     <soap:body namespace="http://trumantruck.com/bonniellama"
          use="literal"/>
    </input>
    <output name="getLlamasResponse">
     <soap:body namespace="http://trumantruck.com/bonniellama"
          use="literal"/>
    </output>
   </operation>
  </binding>
  <service name="BonniesLlamaFarmInfoServiceService">
   <port name="GetLlamas" binding="impl:BonniesLlamasSoapBinding">
    <soap:address
          location="http://localhost:80/axis/services/BonniesLlamas"/>
   </port>
  </service>
</definitions>
```

As you can see by looking at the WSDL in the preceding code, the `getLlamas()` operation returns an XML schema-defined list of llamas for an inventory. We know this by looking at the port type declaration section of the WSDL, which indicates that the output message is `impl:getLlamasResponse`, which is defined in the message declarations as type `LlamaResults`, which was defined in our types section at the beginning of the WSDL.

If you don't get overly excited by inspecting WSDL and looking at the details of SOAP messages, don't worry. We are showing you this because it is helpful for an understanding of these concepts. In the second approach, which follows, we'll show you how your developer tools do the WSDL-to-Java conversion so that you don't have to manipulate the wire format. For debugging purposes, it is helpful to understand SOAP interactions, just as it is helpful to understand WSDL.

An example SOAP message that is returned from the `getLlamas()` operation is shown in the following code:

```
<soapenv:Envelope
    xmlns:soapenv="http://schemas.xmlsoap.org/soap/envelope/"
    xmlns:xsd="http://www.w3.org/2001/XMLSchema"
    xmlns:xsi="http://www.w3.org/2001/XMLSchema-instance">
 <soapenv:Body>
  <LlamaResults>
   <Llama>
       <identifier>289892</identifier>
       <age>6</age>
       <description>Black and White Tuxedo Llama</description>
       <name>Sergio</name>
       <type>STUD</type>
   </Llama>
   <Llama>
       <identifier>32983</identifier>
```

```
        <age>2</age>
        <description>Champagne and White-Colored Female</description>
        <name>Victoria</name>
        <type>ADULT FEMALE</type>
        <imgurl>http://www.trumantruck.com/Llama32983.JPG</imgurl>
    </Llama>
  </LlamaResults>
</soapenv:Body>
</soapenv:Envelope>
```

The preceding code shows the example results for querying this Llama Inventory service. If we understand the format of the messages by looking at the WSDL (or by looking at the SOAP messages), we can certainly style the output with XSLT. Because this example will not utilize EDIT mode, our portlet descriptor provides pages only for VIEW and HELP mode, as shown in the following code:

```
<portlet>
   <portlet-name>Llama Portlet</portlet-name>
   <portlet-class>
         LlamaPortlet
   </portlet-class>
   <init-param>
    <name>llama.url</name>
    <value>http://localhost:80/axis/services/BonniesLlamas</value>
   </init-param>
   <expiration-cache>3600</expiration-cache>
   <supports>
    <mime-type>text/html</mime-type>
    <!-- We are not supporting EDIT mode in this portlet -->
    <!-- <portlet-mode>EDIT</portlet-mode>   -->
    <portlet-mode>HELP</portlet-mode>
   </supports>
   <portlet-info>
    <title>Bonnie's Llamas</title>
   </portlet-info>
   <portlet-preferences>
    <preference>
      <name>contentPage</name>
      <value>/llama/llamaView.jsp</value>
    </preference>
    <preference>
      <name>helpPage</name>
      <value>/llama/llamaHelp.jsp</value>
    </preference>
   </portlet-preferences>
</portlet>
```

As previously mentioned, we will extend Sun's JSPPortlet class for this example, which will redirect our portlets to the proper JSP pages, based on the portlet descriptor shown in preceding code. In the following code, we create our Llama portlet, which delegates everything to the VIEW JSP in the doView() method. Because this is a simple portlet that only displays information that is not changeable, we don't utilize the doEdit() method. We don't override the doHelp() method from JSPPortlet, because we are not sending any parameters to our HELP page, and the inherited method already does the dispatching for us:

```
import javax.portlet.*;
import java.io.*;
import com.sun.portal.portlet.samples.jspportlet.JSPPortlet;
public class LlamaPortlet extends JSPPortlet
{
  private String m_llamaURLString;
  public void init(PortletConfig config)
  throws PortletException, UnavailableException
  {
    String llamaURLString;
    super.init(config);
    m_llamaURLString = config.getInitParameter("llama.url");
  }
  public void doView(RenderRequest request,RenderResponse response)
  throws PortletException, IOException {
    try
    {
      request.setAttribute("llamaURL", m_llamaURLString);
      super.doView(request, response);
    }
    catch ( Exception ex )
    {
      ex.printStackTrace() ;
      response.setProperty("expiration-cache","0");
      PortletRequestDispatcher rd =
              getPortletContext().getRequestDispatcher(
          "/llama/llamaServiceUnavailable.html");
      rd.include(request,response);
    }
  }
}
```

As you can see in the preceding code, the portlet gets the llama.url parameter from the portlet deployment descriptor in the portlet's init() method, and sets it as an attribute in the RenderRequest object for the JSP to receive. The following code shows the SP that styles the SOAP message. This JSP uses the XTAGS tag library, the IO tag library, and the PORTLET tag library to present information in the portlet's VIEW mode. The IO tag library and the XTAGS library come from Jakarta Taglibs, an open-source repository for custom tag libraries that provides convenient tags for JSP processing. The PORTLET tag library is used for passing portlet parameters to JSPs:

```
<%@ taglib uri="http://jakarta.apache.org/taglibs/xtags" prefix="xtags" %>
<%@taglib uri="http://jakarta.apache.org/taglibs/io" prefix="io" %>
<%@ taglib uri="http://java.sun.com/portlet" prefix="portlet" %>
<portlet:defineObjects/>

<%
  String llamaURL= (String)renderRequest.getAttribute("llamaURL") ;
%>

<xtags:style xsl="http://localhost/webproject/llama2view.xsl">
<io:soap url="<%=llamaURL%>" SOAPAction="">
  <io:body>
      <SOAP-ENV:Envelope
```

```
            xmlns:SOAP-ENV="http://schemas.xmlsoap.org/soap/envelope/"
          SOAP-ENV:encodingStyle="http://schemas.xmlsoap.org/soap/encoding/">
            <SOAP-ENV:Header/>
            <SOAP-ENV:Body>
                <ns1:getLlamas
              xmlns:ns1="http://localhost:8080/axis/services/BonniesLlamas">
                </ns1:getLlamas>
            </SOAP-ENV:Body>
        </SOAP-ENV:Envelope>
    </io:body>
</io:soap>
</xtags:style>
```

As you can see, the JSP in the preceding code first uses the IO tag library to send the SOAP message to our getLlamas() Web service call, and then styles the result with the XTAGS library and a stylesheet. The stylesheet is shown in the following code:

```
<xsl:stylesheet version="1.0"
    xmlns:xsl="http://www.w3.org/1999/XSL/Transform">
  <xsl:output method="xml" indent="yes" encoding="utf-8"/>
  <xsl:template match="LlamaResults">
   <center><IMG SRC="http://localhost/webproject/bonniesllamas.jpg"/><br/>
   <hr/>
   <b>Inventory for Bonnie's Llama Farm</b></center>
   <TABLE BORDER="1">
    <tr><TD><B>Name</B></TD><TD><B>Type</B></TD><TD><B>Description</B></TD>
        <TD><B>ID</B></TD><TD><B>Image</B></TD>
    </tr>
    <xsl:for-each select="Llama">
      <tr><td><xsl:value-of select="name"/></td>
          <td><xsl:value-of select="type"/></td>
          <td><xsl:value-of select="description"/></td>
          <td><xsl:value-of select="identifier"/></td>
          <xsl:if test="imgurl">
            <td>
              <IMG width="100" height="100">
              <xsl:attribute name="src">
                <xsl:value-of select="imgurl"/>
              </xsl:attribute>
              </IMG>
            </td>
          </xsl:if>
      </tr>
    </xsl:for-each>
   </TABLE>
  </xsl:template>
</xsl:stylesheet>
```

The stylesheet in the preceding code styles the SOAP response, which looks like the code shown earlier in the example SOAP message. As you can see, the stylesheet creates a table of llamas, showing the name, type, description, and identifier. If the <imgurl> element exists, it creates an image in the table. The results are shown in Figure 10.4, in which you can see the inventory of llamas at Bonnie's Llamas.

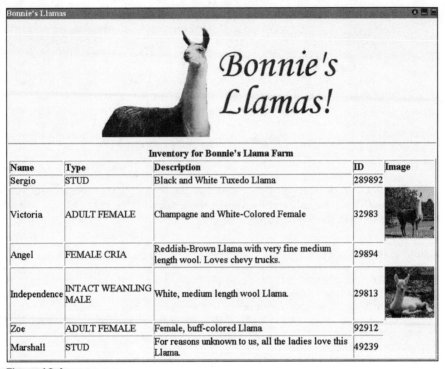

Inventory for Bonnie's Llama Farm

Name	Type	Description	ID	Image
Sergio	STUD	Black and White Tuxedo Llama	289892	
Victoria	ADULT FEMALE	Champagne and White-Colored Female	32983	
Angel	FEMALE CRIA	Reddish-Brown Llama with very fine medium length wool. Loves chevy trucks.	29894	
Independence	INTACT WEANLING MALE	White, medium length wool Llama.	29813	
Zoe	ADULT FEMALE	Female, buff-colored Llama	92912	
Marshall	STUD	For reasons unknown to us, all the ladies love this Llama.	49239	

Figure 10.4

As you can see by looking at the results in Figure 10.4, our portlet works! Having examined this part of the example, you should have an understanding of what WSDL is, what SOAP messaging looks like, and how portals can interact with JSP pages.

Although this code was created as an exercise to help you learn how to interact with portlets, the authors have in practice learned difficult lessons in utilizing the Java IO tag libraries and XTAGS in building portlet views:

❏ They are often hard to maintain, depending on the versions of certain libraries and parsers that are deployed with them.

❏ In the preceding example, the JSP page makes the call to the Web service. A better use of the MVC paradigm is to enable your portlet to call your Web service, passing the information to the JSPs.

In addition, the authors have seen that it is sometimes a pain to deal with WSDL and SOAP messages directly. Instead, you can delegate this responsibility to your favorite Web services toolkit (such as Apache Axis). Our next approach takes a different design approach, and uses Java objects that were created by the Axis toolkit.

Second Approach: Working with Generated Objects

This section takes a different (and better) approach to building the portlet that talks to Bonnie's Llama service. We will change the portlet code and the JSP code, but everything else will stay the same.

If you don't enjoy parsing SOAP messages yourself (a likelihood that probably represents a good 99 percent of the world) and would like your Web services toolkit to do it for you, read on! Most toolkits enable you to do a WSDL-to-Java conversion, and vice-versa, when you are creating clients to talk to Web services, or when you are building new Web services. The toolkit performs the marshalling (converting XML to objects) and unmarshalling (converting objects to XML) for you, so that you don't have to. With Axis, it is easy. You may use the `Axis-wsdl2java` Apache Ant task that is included with the latest version of Axis, or you may call the Axis converter directly with the Apache Axis `WSDL2Java` class by typing the following, assuming that the Axis libraries are in your classpath:

```
% java org.apache.axis.wsdl.WSDL2Java BonniesLlamas.wsdl
```

Based on the WSDL listed earlier, the tool automatically generates Java code and classes, placing it in the package dictated by the target namespace. Because the target namespace of the WSDL was `http://trumantruck.com/bonniellama/`, the tool places the generated Java source and classes in the directory `com/trumantruck/bonniellama`, representing the new package that was created by the following code generation:

```
BonniesLlamaFarmInfoService.class
BonniesLlamaFarmInfoService.java
BonniesLlamaFarmInfoServiceService.class
BonniesLlamaFarmInfoServiceService.java
BonniesLlamaFarmInfoServiceServiceLocator.class
BonniesLlamaFarmInfoServiceServiceLocator.java
BonniesLlamasSoapBindingStub.class
BonniesLlamasSoapBindingStub.java
LlamaTypes.class
LlamaTypes.java
_LlamaResults.class
_LlamaResults.java
_LlamaResults_Llama.class
_LlamaResults_Llama.java
```

The object most meaningful to our application is the `LlamaResults_Llama` class. This class represents the characteristics of each llama from the schema. Of course, the names of the classes Axis generates are not always pretty, but given well-formed and valid WSDL, Apache Axis should be able to create classes that you can easily use to interact with Web services. Because Axis generates the code for you, you can certainly change the names of the classes and recompile for better-looking class names. In this case, we will simply use the classes that Axis generated for us. The code for our second portlet shows the llama inventory:

```
//import the Axis-generated classes
import com.trumantruck.bonniellama.*;
import javax.portlet.*;
import java.io.*;
import java.net.*;
//import the Sun JSP portlet that we will extend
import com.sun.portal.portlet.samples.jspportlet.JSPPortlet;
public class LlamaPortlet2 extends JSPPortlet
{
  private String m_llamaURLString;
  public void init(PortletConfig config)
  throws PortletException, UnavailableException
```

```
{
  String llamaURLString;
  super.init(config);
  m_llamaURLString = config.getInitParameter("llama.url");
}
public void doView(RenderRequest request,RenderResponse response)
throws PortletException, IOException
{
  //Get the list of Llamas from the web service & send it on to the JSP!
  try
  {
    _LlamaResults_Llama[] llamas = getLlamas();
    request.setAttribute("llamas", llamas);
    super.doView(request, response);
  }
  catch ( Exception ex )
  {
    ex.printStackTrace() ;
    response.setProperty("expiration-cache","0");
    PortletRequestDispatcher rd =
        getPortletContext().getRequestDispatcher(
            "/llama/llamaServiceUnavailable.html");
    rd.include(request,response);
  }
}
```

In the preceding code, we extend Sun's JSPPortlet class, and because we are only concerned about the functionality in VIEW mode for this example, we only override the doView() method to call the Web service before the superclass. In this portlet, we created a getLlamas() method that used our Axis-generated classes to call our Web service. This method — the final part of our portlet — is listed in the following code:

```
/*
 * This method uses the generated stuff from Axis' WSDL2Java
 */
private _LlamaResults_Llama[] getLlamas() throws Exception
{
  BonniesLlamaFarmInfoServiceService bonnie = new
            BonniesLlamaFarmInfoServiceServiceLocator();
  URL serviceURL = new URL(m_llamaURLString);
  //Get the getLlamas() service
  BonniesLlamaFarmInfoService service = bonnie.getGetLlamas(serviceURL);
  //Get the LlamaResults()
  _LlamaResults lr = (_LlamaResults)service.getLlamas(null);
  //Finally, get the list of Llamas!
  _LlamaResults_Llama[] llamas = lr.getLlama();
  return (llamas);
}
}
```

In the preceding code, we use the classes generated by Apache Axis in the getLlamas() method. In that method, we use the generated classes to talk to our Web service, and get a marshaled object version of the list of llamas returned in the SOAP response. In the doView() method, we call getLlamas() to get the list of the llama inventory, and we use that list of llamas as an attribute in the `RenderRequest` object before calling the superclass that will dispatch us to the JSP page. The following code shows the JSP page that adds presentation to the list of llamas:

```
<%@ taglib uri="http://java.sun.com/portlet" prefix="portlet" %>
<portlet:defineObjects/>
<%
   com.trumantruck.bonniellama._LlamaResults_Llama[] llamas =
       (com.trumantruck.bonniellama._LlamaResults_Llama[])
                       renderRequest.getAttribute("llamas");
%>
<center><IMG SRC="http://localhost/webproject/bonniesllamas.jpg"/><br/>
 <hr/><b>Inventory for Bonnie's Llama Farm</b></center>
 <TABLE BORDER="1">
  <tr><TD BGCOLOR='yellow'><B>Name</B></TD>
      <TD BGCOLOR='yellow'><B>Type</B></TD>
      <TD BGCOLOR='yellow'><B>Description</B></TD>
      <TD BGCOLOR='yellow'><B>ID</B></TD>
      <TD BGCOLOR='yellow'><B>Image</B></TD>
  </tr>
<%
  for (int i = 0; i < llamas.length; i++)
  {
      String url = llamas[i].getImgurl();
%>
 <tr><td><%=llamas[i].getName()%></TD><TD><%=llamas[i].getType()%></TD>
     <TD><%=llamas[i].getDescription()%></TD>
     <TD><%=llamas[i].getIdentifier()%></TD>
 <%
   if (url != null)
   {
 %>
     <TD><IMG width=100 HEIGHT=100 SRC='<%=url%>'></TD>
  <%
   }
   %>
</TR>
 <%
  }
  %>
</TABLE>
```

In the preceding code, we get the list of llamas as an array by obtaining that attribute from the `renderRequest` object that was set in our portlet. We create a table identical to the HTML table that we generated in the earlier approach with a stylesheet, looping the length of array, and getting the required information from each llama returned from our Web service. The result is the same portlet that was shown in Figure 10.4.

As you can see, this approach is a little easier than dealing directly with the SOAP messaging. It is also a better way to enable your portlet to call your Web service; the only responsibility your JSP has is to present the data that your portlet passes. Using the unmarshalling and marshalling features that Apache Axis provides for you, you can handle the business logic of your application without having to delve in the guts of SOAP messaging and WSDL parsing.

In this section, you have examined a few examples of building portlets that communicate with Web services. As a result, you should be able to use the concepts presented in other chapters of this book to build complex portlets that communicate with any Web service. In this section, we used Apache Axis, but any Web services toolkit should be able to provide the same functionality. Another good example of portlet integration with Web services is Sun's Weather Portlet, distributed with many open-source portlet containers, such as Exo Portal on SourceForge (http://sourceforge.net/projects/exo).

Web Services for Remote Portlets (WSRP)

As you have seen, traditional Web services are presentation-neutral, and as a result, we portlet developers need to provide presentation logic for the Web services we invoke. In addition, we sometimes need to aggregate content from multiple Web services to provide a combined view. Over the past few years, many vendors and technologists have discussed creating presentation-oriented Web service interfaces for portlets so that they can be called remotely. However, without a standard interface definition for all portlets, developers would have a frustrating time creating plug-and-play portlets from different Web services. The OASIS Web Services for Remote Portlets (WSRP) specification aims to simplify the integration through standard Web service interfaces for presentation-oriented interactive Web services. WSRP defines how a portlet can be invoked remotely, through a Web service, by a portal. This section provides the "big picture" of WSRP: how it works, and how you can build portlets that will work well remotely.

Web Services for Remote Portlets are user-facing, interactive Web services that include presentation. [SCHAECK] These presentation-oriented Web services enable remote portlets to be displayed in local portals. Using WSRP services, your portal can quickly bring remote portlet content and display it locally. Your portal can also expose local portlets remotely for other portals to use. Luckily for the portlet developer, no special portlet code is needed! The WSRP specification (as well as the Java Portlet specification) provides important guidelines for standard user-interface markup, a topic that is covered in the section "WSRP Guidelines for Portlet Developers," later in this chapter. Other than that, the portlet container does all the hard work for you. Making your portal consume remote portlets or produce local portlets remotely should be a simple configuration step.

To begin understanding WSRP, you should understand a few terms:

- ❑ WSRP Producers—Producers are presentation-oriented Web services that host portlets that are able to render markup fragments and process user interaction requests. Producers provide Web service interfaces for self-description (metadata), markup, registration between producers and consumers, and portlet management.

- ❑ WSRP Consumers—Consumers are portals or applications that communicate with presentation-oriented Web services (remote portlets). They gather the markup delivered by the portlets and present the aggregation to the end-user.

- ❑ Remote Portlets—Remote portlets are those portlets that are hosted and disseminated by a WSRP producer through a Web services interface. These portlets can be developed with the Java Portlet API, much like the examples in this book—and they use standard WSRP markup.

You can see all of these WSRP players in action in Figure 10.5. In this figure, both WSRP consumers and producers are portals, and the consumer speaks SOAP to the producer to indicate a portlet that resides on a remote server. Unlike traditional Web services, the SOAP bodies of WSRP messages contain presentation information, including portlet markup.

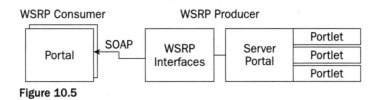

Figure 10.5

In Figure 10.5, note that a standard Web service interface (the block that says WSRP Interfaces) enables the consumer portal to include remote portlets from the producer. This is what WSRP is all about! When a portal uses a remote portlet, it typically uses a generic portlet proxy to invoke the Web service, and it invokes it much like it would invoke a local portlet. Because all remote portlets have the same interface definition, the same proxy can be used for all remote portlets. A diagram of this interaction is shown in Figure 10.6. As you can see, the process of the portal calling the proxy is very similar to calling a portal using a local interface.

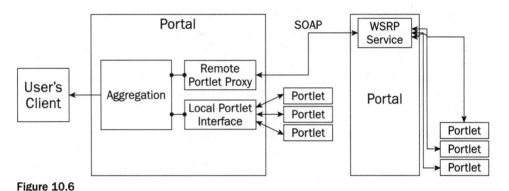

Figure 10.6

As simple as Figure 10.6 looks, a few complexities of producer-consumer interaction can result. A typical process flow, based on the Web Services for Remote Portlets Specification 1.0, is shown here [WSRP]:

1. The consumer discovers the producer via a UDDI server or other type of registry. In this step, the consumer may receive registration requirements for consumer-producer relationships, metadata about the producer describing the requirements for consumer-producer interactions, as well as the types of portlets that are available for consumption.

2. The consumer and the producer establish a relationship, exchanging capability information. This may include security and business requirements, and this relationship ultimately results in the consumer learning the full capabilities (all available remote portlets) of the producer. Many times, this involves a **registration** step.

3. The consumer and the end-user establish a relationship, which may require authentication, based on the producer's security requirements. This step may also consist of enabling the user to customize content sent by the producer.

4. The consumer sends a request for a markup from a remote portlet to the producer, receives the page, and presents this content to the end-user.

5.   Portlet interactions take place, based on user input events; and based on the event that is triggered, the consumer may send this action event for processing, leading to step 4.

6.   Eventually, the producer and consumer end their relationship, and resources are cleaned up.

The next section discusses some of the WSRP services that are involved in this process.

Types of WSRP Services

To enable a flexible infrastructure for remote portlets, WSRP services range from very simple to complex. Many portlets are very simple (such as our llama example, which used only VIEW and HELP modes), but some portlets require complex user interaction and operate based on transient and persistent state. As you can imagine, this requires a little bit of work underneath the covers when complex portlets become remote portlets. In fact, WSRP has defined Web service operations to handle all these scenarios. This section describes each of the services that are available with WSRP standard portals.

Discovery, Registration, and Deregistration Services

WSRP providers can publish their remote portlets in a registry (such as a UDDI server) so that WSRP consumers can discover information about the portlets. These registries provide the portlet name, an overall description, supported markup types, and the WSRP interface description in WSDL. Although registries support most capabilities for discovery, calling the WSRP getServiceDescription() operation on the Web service returns the full capabilities of the service. This also returns what is required for a consumer to communicate with the producer (if registration is required).

If there is a requirement for registration, WSRP provides these services. To register, the consumer calls the register() operation, passing in registration data. This registration data includes information about the consumer, the protocol extension it supports, and portlet states and modes it is willing to manage. A unique registrationHandle is returned from the registration operation to refer to this registration process. To later deregister, the consumer calls the deregister() operation, supplying the initial registrationHandle so that the producer may release resources related to that consumer.

Simple WSRP Services — Stateless "View Only" Modes

The simplest WSRP service would be one that provides "view only" access to a portlet without tracking state changes, much like in our llama example in the last section. In our llama example, we simply provided a page for VIEW mode, which invoked a Web service; and a HELP page, which provided documentation about the portlet. For such an example, if our portlet container were a WSRP producer and wanted to expose our llama portlet as a remote portlet, it would need to register a WSRP service that provides a getMarkup() operation, which returns a WSRP markup fragment listing the llama inventory.

More Complex Services — Interactive WSRP Services

As remote portlets require more end-user interaction, it is usually necessary to pass state information between the producer and the consumer based on that end-user interaction. Many times, this state information is session-based, meaning that the relationship between the end-user and the portlet ends after the session ends. Often, persistent state information between end-users and remote portlets also needs to be saved and passed. As a result, WSRP provides services for performing these interactions. The method performBlockingInteraction() provides action handling for each user interaction, and it passes state information, as well as other parameters, before the consumer calls getMarkup() to see the resulting WSRP content. Based on the parameters passed in the performBlockingInteraction() operation, both the consumer and producer can communicate changes in state, regardless of whether they are persistent or session-based. The `initCookie()` operation is used for passing cookie information, and `releaseSessions()` is called by the consumer in order to inform the producer that it will no longer be using a set of sessions.

Portlet Management Services

A producer can expose a portlet management interface and enable a consumer to clone and customize the portlets that the producer offers, enabling **consumer-configured portlets**. Using WSRP portlet-management services, an administrator on the consumer portal can configure properties about the producer's remote portlet for use by the consumer. Operations in the Portlet Management Interface are as follows:

- ❑ `getPortletDescription()` provides information about the portlets it offers.

- ❑ `clonePortlet()` enables the consumer to request the creation of a new portlet from an existing portlet.

- ❑ `getPortletPropertyDescription()` enables the consumer to discover the type and description of the properties of a portlet, which could be useful in generating a user interface for configuring the portlet.

- ❑ `getPortletProperties()` enables the consumer to fetch the current values of the portlet's properties.

- ❑ `setPortletProperties()` enables the consumer to set the current values of the portlet's properties.

- ❑ `destroyPortlets()` is used to inform the producer that the consumer-configured portlet will no longer be used.

WSRP Markup Guidelines for Portlet Developers

Although we have listed some of the major WSRP Web services, you won't have to call those WSRP services (unless you are developing a portlet container!). Because your portlet container will do most of the hard work as a consumer or producer of remote portlets, all you have to do is develop your portlets with your Java Portlet API, using *standard markup* required by the WSRP and Java Portlet specification. For the most part, portals utilize HTML and XHTML, and WSRP lists guidelines for what is allowed and not allowed. This section provides an explanation of these guidelines.

Disallowed XHTML and HTML Tags

When building HTML- or XHTML-based portlets, you must not use the following tags: `<body>`, `<frame>`, `<frameset>`, `<head>`, `<html>`, and `<title>`. Using those tags will make the producer a non-interoperable producer; and although many consumers may allow it, it may cause erratic behavior in some consumer environments.

Cascading Style Sheets (CSS) Style Definitions

The WSRP specification defines a set of CSS definitions in order to provide a common look and feel — regardless of whether the portlet is displayed locally or remotely. These styles affect the decorations around the portlets, but not the content of the portlets themselves. This section defines the styles that are listed in the WSRP specification. The behavior of the elements that use these CSS classes is dependent on the portlet container, so you may want to experiment with the open-source portal of your choice that uses these styles.

Font Style Classes

The WSRP specification provides style classes that are related to font attributes. If the developer wants a certain font type to be larger or smaller, he or she should use the `font-size` style, setting it to a relative size. The following table shows the font style classes from the WSRP specification.

Style	Description
portlet-font	This style is for font attributes of "normal" fonts, and it is used for the display of non-accentuated information.
portlet-font-dim	This style is for font attributes similar to the portlet-font style, but displayed in a lighter "dimmed" color.

The following code shows a WSRP-compliant fragment of markup for the font style CSS classes:

```
<!- Portion of a Portlet Fragment->
<p class="portlet-font">This is a test of normal font</p>
<p class="portlet-font" style="font-size:larger">
  This should be bigger
</p>
<p class="portlet-font-dim">This should be dimmed a little bit.</p>
```

Message Style Classes

Message style definitions affect the rendering of a paragraph and may affect the attributes of text, depending on the portal customization settings. For example, depending on the customization parameters, portals may display error messages in red, success messages in green, and so on. The following table describes the message style class definitions dictated by the WSRP specification.

Style	Description
portlet-msg-status	Used for displaying the status of the current operation
portlet-msg-info	Used for displaying help messages or additional information
portlet-msg-error	Used for displaying error messages
portlet-msg-alert	Used for displaying warning messages
portlet-msg-success	Used for displaying verification of the successful completion of a task

The following code shows an example of compliant error message and information message:

```
<!- code ->
<p class="portlet-msg-error">
    An error occurred as a result of this operation!
</p>
<p class="portlet-msg-info">The error that was returned was: 'Insufficient Memory
to Perform Operation'. Stack trace follows:
</p>
```

Section Style Classes

The WSRP specification provides section style definitions that affect the rendering of markup sections, such as alignment, borders, and background color. The following table lists the classes and their descriptions.

Style	Description
portlet-section-header	This style is used to show a section header.
portlet-section-body	This style is used to show normal text in a section.
portlet-section-alternate	This implies text in every other row in the section.
portlet-section-selected	This implies text in a selected range.
portlet-section-subheader	This style is used to show a subheader.
portlet-section-footer	This style is used to show a section footer.
portlet-section-text	This style is used for text that belongs to the section but does not fall in one of the other categories.

The following compliant fragment uses the section style classes:

```
<p class="portlet-section-header">
   More Java Pitfalls
</p>
<p class="portlet-section-subheader">
   50 New Time-Saving Solutions and Workarounds
</p>
<p class="portlet-section-text">
   This is a great book! Five Stars.
</p>
```

Table Style Definitions

The following table shows style sheet classes related to HTML and XHTML tables. Use these styles when styling table content.

Style	Description
portlet-table-header	This style is used for table headers (such as "Style" and "Description" in this table). Sometimes, the consumer portal will make the font of this bold, and give it a background color, making it stand out.
portlet-table-body	This style is used for normal text in a table cell.
portlet-table-alternate	This style highlights text in every other row in the table.
portlet-table-selected	This style applies to text in a selected cell range.
portlet-table-subheader	This style is for text of a subheading.
portlet-table-footer	This style is for a table footer.
portlet-table-text	This style is for text that belongs to the table but does not fall in one of the other categories.

The following code fragment shows an HTML table with compliant style tags (from our earlier llama example):

```
<!- code showing a few table styles ->
<table>
   <tr class='portlet-table-header'>
        <td>Name</td><td>Type</td>
        <td>Description</td><td>ID</td>
        <td>Image</td>
   </tr>
   <tr class='portlet-table-body'>
        <td>Marshall</td><td>STUD</td>
        <td>For some reason, all the ladies love this Llama</td>
        <td>21979</td>
        <td>http://www.trumantruck.com/marshallthepimp.jpg</td>
   </tr>
</table>
```

Form Style Definitions

Form styles define the look-and-feel of the elements in an HTML form. The following table describes the available styles.

Style	Description
portlet-form-label	This style defines text used for the descriptive label of the whole form.
portlet-form-input-field	This style is used for text of the user-input in an input field.
portlet-form-button	This style applies to text on a button.
portlet-icon-label	This style is used for text that appears beside a context-dependent action icon.
portlet-dlg-icon-label	This style defines text that appears beside a "standard" icon (for example, OK or Cancel).
portlet-form-field-label	This style applies to text for a separator of fields (for example, checkboxes, and so on).
portlet-form-field	This style is used for text for a field (input field, check boxes, and so on).

The following code fragment shows compliant portlet markup using the form style definitions:

```
<form>
   <p align="center" class="portlet-section-header">
       Llama Registration Form
   </p>
   <center>
      <table>
         <tr><td class="portlet-form-label" colspan="2">
              Please Enter The Llama Registration ID of the Llama
              You would Like to Register
```

```
                    </td>
                </tr>
                <tr><td class="portlet-form-field-label">Identification #</td>
                    <td><input name="llama_identifier" type="text"
                             class="portlet-form-input-field">
                    </td>
                </tr>
                <tr><td class="portlet-form-label" colspan="2" align="center">
                    <input name="submit" type="button"
                             class="portlet-form-button"
                             value="Register!"/>
                    </td>
                </tr>
            </table>
        </center>
</form>
```

Revising the Llama Portlet to Make It WSRP-Compliant

Finally, in order to make our llama portlet's JSP a WSRP-compliant portlet, we need to change a few things. Because we created a table in our portlet, we need to use the table style definitions shown in the table of the same name. The following code shows the change to our earlier llama example to make it compliant:

```
<%@ taglib uri="http://java.sun.com/portlet" prefix="portlet" %>
<portlet:defineObjects/>
<%
  com.trumantruck.bonniellama._LlamaResults_Llama[] llamas =
      (com.trumantruck.bonniellama._LlamaResults_Llama[])
             renderRequest.getAttribute("llamas");
%>
<p class='portlet-section-header'>Inventory for Bonnie's Llama Farm</p>
  <p class='portlet-section-body'>
    <IMG SRC="http://localhost/webproject/bonniesllamas.jpg"/>
  </p>
  <TABLE BORDER="1">
    <tr class='portlet-table-header'><TD>Name</TD><TD>Type</TD>
        <TD>Description</TD><TD>ID</TD><TD>Image</TD>
    </tr>
<%
  for (int i = 0; i < llamas.length; i++)
  {
    String url = llamas[i].getImgurl();
%>
  <tr class='portlet-table-body'>
    <TD><%=llamas[i].getName()%></TD><TD><%=llamas[i].getType()%></TD>
    <TD><%=llamas[i].getDescription()%></TD>
    <TD><%=llamas[i].getIdentifier()%></TD>

<%
  if (url != null)
  {
%>
```

```
        <TD><IMG width=100 HEIGHT=100 SRC='<%=url%>'></TD>
    <%
      }
      %>
    </tr>
  <%
    }
    %>
  </TABLE>
```

User Information

The WSRP specification, along with the Java Portlet Specification, provides a mechanism for portlets to use standardized user information in order to personalize behavior for the current user. A standard set of user attributes has been derived from the W3C P3P (Platform for Privacy Preferences) specification. Because of space limitations, we do not list them all here, but refer you to Section 11 (User Information) of the WSRP specification, available at www.oasis-open.org/committees/tc_home.php?wg_abbrev=wsrp/. This user information can be used when passing information between a producer and a consumer. These user attributes can also be used in portlet descriptors, as the Java Portlet specification suggests.

Summary

This chapter covered a lot of ground. We have provided an overview of how portals and portlets can interact with Web services. We provided a brief overview of Web services standards; discussed design strategies for building portlets that communicate with Web services; and showed you how by providing examples of portlet code interacting with services. We also discussed the Web Services for Remote Portlets (WSRP) specification, and provided guidelines for writing WSRP-compliant markup in your portlets.

11

Performance Testing, Administering, and Monitoring Your Portal

Portals have become an important tool for organizations to improve their knowledge transfer through dynamic content delivery and self-service activities for large audiences of people who rely on that information to be effective in their positions. Many institutions have already made significant investments in portals and will continue to rely on portal development activities to reign in maintenance costs that result from the proliferation of unstructured Web sites and to avoid the misplacement of information that could result in the obsolescence of critical information.

More often than not, successful portal implementations were crafted by diverse development and Web content teams that managed to operate in a consistent manner amidst the chaos that inevitably consumes these programs. This chapter discusses how development and deployment consistencies can be attained by creating and applying reliable and repeatable process methodologies using open-source tools during a program's life cycle.

Portal process coordination starts with a pragmatic understanding of what you have, what you need, and how are you going to get where you want to be. Some portal projects are lucky enough to have previously developed source code or some open-source libraries that they can easily reuse and deploy with portlet wrappers, but others might need to develop new programs that have to integrate with previously developed code. The trick is to "sync-up" all of these applications through configuration management, testing, and network management procedures.

It is paramount that all software programs implement a **configuration management** (CM) scheme to manage development operations so that development efforts can be controlled, and deployment risks and errors can be avoided.

This chapter focuses on a few open-source technologies that should help assist you in your program management activities. These tools include CVS, ANT, JUnit, JMeter, Anthill, and Scarab, which are primarily used during portal development iterations. Additionally, some elaboration is provided for network management pieces that use Java Management Extensions (JMX), which are generally used during deployment and maintenance to observe, monitor, and alter your applications through controlled interfaces to ensure that they're working properly. Some portlet examples will exhibit the use of JMX MBeans to perform system administration operations. The final section of this chapter demonstrates the implementation of an open-source collaboration server called **JSPWiki,** which might be used for a portal implementation to share knowledge among the stakeholders of a portal system, to propagate best practices and lessons learned, and to share documents and exchange ideas. The point here is to provide a general overview of how open-source applications can be implemented to capture and maintain your processes properly so that your portal development and maintenance activities don't overwhelm your program. Prior to discussing some of these important tools, a brief description of an important development methodology called **continuous integration** will be touched on to emphasize the importance of testing your applications to facilitate integration activities in the latter stages of your program.

Continuous Integration

Continuous integration is an eXtreme Programming (XP) practice that obliges developers on a software program to submit tests along with their code so that automated procedures can be put in place to test in an automated fashion that code and any modifications that are made to it. Open-source tools such as CruiseControl, BusyB, and AntHill have been developed to assist in this process and have made continuous integration a practical consideration for many integration activities. The idea behind continuous integration is to facilitate integration testing up front and manage risk so that interface issues don't bog down deployment operations in the final stages of deployment.

Continuous integration encompasses the execution of automated builds from a centralized code repository from which developers check in and check out source code during their development activities. A system build is typically generated daily from this repository so that tests can be run against new code submissions to ensure that all new modifications to that code have not corrupted previously working code. More often than not, these tests are run during off-hours so as not to interfere with normal operations.

Two approaches for performing continuous integration operations with Open-source tools and a centralized code repository warrant the implementation of CVS and the newer Subversion applications., The following sections discuss these technologies to help you gain a better appreciation of these capabilities and how they can be implemented to help you manage your development challenges.

CVS

Concurrent Versioning System (CVS) is used on many development programs to manage source code artifacts and their modifications. The CVS application acts as a coordination tool to control code development and facilitate the merging of changes by different developers. This harmonization enables programs to remain in sync programmatically and ensures that developers work off a common source code set. Additionally, CVS repositories allow common releases to be tagged so that ongoing operations can check out working copies of files and roll back code to procure targeted builds for release.

In Figure 11.1 is a brief overview of CVS, and some its operations are demonstrated to provide you with a better appreciation of its use. Developer 1 is shown checking out the portal module and all of the code and libraries associated with the portal module. This action is generally taken when a programmer is starting out and needs to access the baseline code for a program. Developer 2 is adding an archived file called `messageboard.jar` to the CVS repository. Notice the -kb flag appended to the add statement. This is used to ensure that the file being archived is marked as binary.

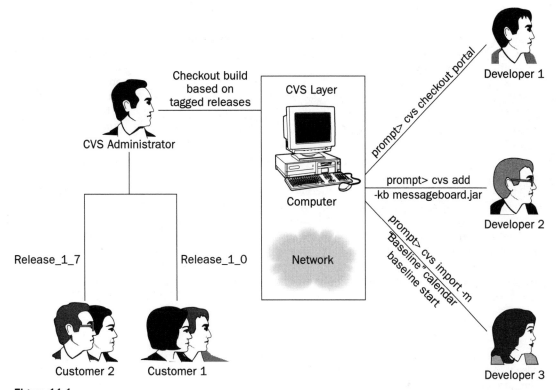

Figure 11.1

Most problems on application deployments that use CVS are the result of developers checking in code improperly, which often means checking in or adding binary libraries without the -kb option. The absence of this flag during CVS add operations will cause problems on your system and can be hard to track down during your development activities, so consideration might be given to using the cvswrappers file to ensure that files that end in jar are included in add and import operations as binary files. Developer 3 is performing an import operation of an entire module under the name "portal" to the CVS repository. The same consideration needs to be given to binary files during this operation also.

A system administrator who is responsible for maintenance of a CVS repository generally tags builds for deployment to customer sites. This person will check out code submitted by the program's developers according to the tag associated with the code marked during the life cycle of the project.

A great resource that should help you get a better handle on CVS and its utilization can be found at www.cvshome.org/docs/manual/. Because CVS is such an important tool used in many of the CM processes described later in this chapter, additional command-line operations are provided in this section to enhance your learning.

The CVS tool requires the implementation of a server application to process user requests for source code from the repository. Accounts must be established on the server to allow access to the code, along with CVS group privileges. To access that server, a client application must implement a communication protocol to gain access to the repository. The following paragraphs discuss two means of accessing data from the CVS library: through a password server and with an `ssh` script.

For a client to access a CVS repository that uses a password server, the CVSROOT environment variable must be established to expedite the checking in/out of source code. The CVSROOT environment variable takes the following form:

```
:pserver:<username>@<hostname>:<cvs-repository-path>
```

If this is not performed by the client, then the user is forced to type the following at the command line, or in their CVS IDE tool dialog window: **-d :pserver:\<username\>@\<hostname\>:\<cvs-repository-path\>** for every CVS operation, which can be quite painful if you need to perform many CVS operations.

Ssh (Secure shell) client access is a safer alternative to using a password server for CVS operations. Ssh is a program that enables users to log into remote computers, execute commands, and transfer files from one machine to another. Ssh provides strong authentication and secure communications over unsecured channels. Ssh would be used to protect against sinister snoopers who might log all of the incoming/outgoing traffic on your system, especially passwords or any other information that is passed in the clear. Additionally, Ssh can prevent IP spoofing — whereby unknown remote hosts pretend to be trusted hosts — because it never trusts the network. To use Ssh in your CVS activities, you must set the environment variable CVS_RSH equal to ssh, and then use the following code to perform your CVS operation:

```
cvs -d :ext:<username>@<hostname>:<cvs-repository-path> command
```

CVS updates to your working directory are performed by using the `update` command to capture new files that might have been checked in by other users. An example for an update to your files would be `cvs update <module-name>`.

To add files that you have worked on, you must use the `commit` operation. CVS examines each directory and subdirectory below the current working directory. Any files that CVS knows about will be checked for changes. When changes are committed to the CVS repository, CVS opens your default editor and asks that you comment on the changes to the file(s) being checked in. A window similar to the following will be shown:

```
CVS:----------------------------------
CVS: Enter Log.  Lines beginning with 'CVS:' are removed automatically
CVS:
CVS: Committing in .
CVS:
CVS: Modified Files:
CVS:  example/portal/sample.tld example/portal/sample.jar
CVS:----------------------------------
```

The removal of files from CVS repositories often is a tricky proposition for developers, unless they've performed this action a few times before. A file is marked for removal by using the *remove* statement in the following manner: `cvs remove` *\<filename\>*. After that is done, the file needs to be deleted from your working directory. The CVS application puts this file in a subdirectory called `Attic`, which makes that file transparent to future operations on it.

To compare files in your working repository with a centralized CVS repository, the `diff` command can be used. To understand the history of a file, a user can type **cvs history –c** *<filename>* to display when a particular file has been checked in. Additionally, file information can be displayed with the `log` command.

One salient shortcoming of the CVS application is that it does not lock files to prevent two or more users from making modifications on the same file, necessitating the need to merge those files upon commitment to the CVS repository. This merging can be quite messy, especially if a large number of changes are made by a different set of users to a particular file. A new open-source application called Subversion (http:// subversion.tigris.org) addresses the nonlocking aspect of CVS and has been developed to supercede CVS, which promises to make it a more robust tool for code management.

Subversion

Subversion is an alternative open-source revision control system to CVS that was developed by the Tigris.org group (http://subversion.tigris.org) for software configuration and management. With Subversion, software developers can monitor modifications in their code and work independently of other developers with confidence that complicated merge operations are not needed. The Subversion file system tracks changes to it by storing files in a tree structure. Recall that a big problem with CVS is that two or more users can modify the same file at the same time, which can cause files to become out-of-sync. To get back into sync, those files have to be manually merged to accommodate changes made by multiple users.

Figure 11.2 demonstrates how complicated merges required with the use of CVS are avoided with Subversion.

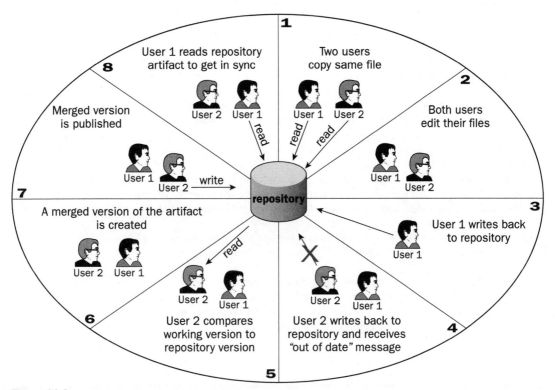

Figure 11.2

Subversion's strengths, which make it an attractive alternative to the CVS source control management tool, are as follows:

❏ It shares many CVS features, with the exception of the annotation task, which has been put off until after the 1.0 release.

❏ File contents are versioned.

❏ Commit operations are atomic, meaning that until an entire commit has been successful, updates to that repository are considered incomplete.

❏ The open-source Apache Web server acts as a network server to enable WebDAV protocol operations to act upon the code repository.

❏ It uses a binary "diff"-ing mechanism to store successive revisions of a file.

Although CVS is a great tool that has been implemented on many software development programs, consideration should be given to Subversion and its wider range of capabilities to facilitate your configuration management activities.

JUnit

Unit testing is typically performed to verify that subsystem components function properly with different types of user input. With unit testing, a predetermined set of tests are run against static data from a controlled environment. On many portal implementations, these tests act on back-end JavaBean components and their methods.

Countless numbers of CVS and ANT script integrations have been published to describe how developers and testers can use these technologies to perform continuous integration activities. Rather than repeat some of these implementations, this section explores a slightly different perspective that might be considered to accommodate your testing activities.

Test teams generally like unit tests because testers consider code to be correct by examining input/output conditions of the code during their testing. This view can sometimes appear myopic to stakeholders, who consider the entire code set and how it works from an operations perspective. Therefore, overall testing procedures should aggregate both views to determine whether a program is working properly.

JUnit is an open-source test framework found at www.junit.org that enables developers to easily automate unit testing of their source code creations from source code repository builds. The example shown in the following code demonstrates how JUnit and CVS can be used to satisfy your test objectives.

The dialog box shown in Figure 11.3 illustrates the use of an open-source ANT library found at www.kasisoft.de/build/ant/interactive/ called **Interactive ANT**.

With Interactive ANT, users can create drop-down lists and text fields for dynamic user inputs. The `build-portal-tests.xml` file enables users to browse the local directory file system for the directory in which tests will be run, select pre-determined tests for execution, select the JUnit run mode, and query the user as to whether the code being tested should be checked out of CVS prior to running unit tests.

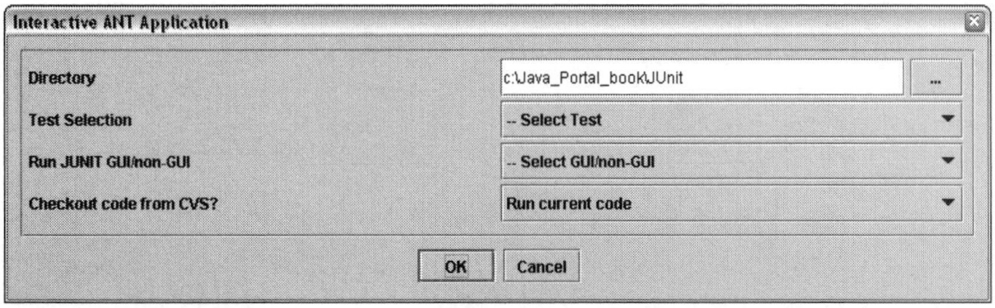

Figure 11.3

The following code shows the ANT script that actually executes the JUnit tests based on the user inputs from the interactive dialog application. The first section of the script initializes property values concerning file paths and CVS dependencies. Naturally, these could also be sent through the command line or from an external properties file. The file classpaths are defined for the JAR files that are needed to run the interactive display:

```
001: <?xml version="1.0"?>
002: <project name="junitTest" default="help">
003:
004:    <property environment="env"/>
005:    <property file="build.properties"/>
006:    <property name="deploy.dir" value="./deploy" />
007:    <property name="app.name" value="PORTAL"/>
008:    <property name="lib.path" value="."/>
009:
010:    <!- CVS ->
011:    <property name="cvs.username" value="emilyStephenA" />
012:    <property name="cvs.hostname" value="localhost" />
013:    <property name="cvs.dir" value="c:\cvsrep" />
014:    <property name="cvs.module" value="CVSTests" />
015:
016:    <!- Setup the system classpath ->
017:    <path id="system.classpath">
018:      <pathelement path="${lib.path}/AntelopeTasks.jar"/>
019:      <pathelement path="${lib.path}/portal_interactive.jar"/>
020:      <pathelement path="${env.ANT_HOME}"/>
021:    </path>
022:
023:    <!- task definitions ->
024:    <taskdef name="if" classname="ise.antelope.tasks.IfTask"
classpathref="system.classpath" />
025:    <taskdef name="interactive" classname="portal.Interactive"
classpathref="system.classpath" />
026:
```

The `run_interactive_display_test` target that starts on line 27 uses the Interactive ANT libraries to render the user GUI shown in Figure 11.3 so that users can dynamically declare directory, test selection, GUI, and CVS flag information that will be used to run the JUnit tests. The if-then-else logic operations are enabled by the `Antelope` libraries to trigger proper target execution for testing:

```
027:    <target name="run_interactive_display_test">
028:      <interactive verbose="off">
029:        <input property="dir" text="Directory" type="dir"
value="c:\Java_Portal_book\JUnit" />
030:        <input property="test" text="Test Selection" type="test" />
031:        <input property="junit" text="Run JUNIT GUI/non-GUI" type="junit" />
032:        <input property="cvs" text="Checkout code from CVS?" type="cvs" />
033:      </interactive>
034:      <echo> Directory : ${dir} </echo>
035:      <echo> Test selection : ${test} </echo>
036:      <echo> JUnit run selection : ${junit} </echo>
037:      <echo> Checkout code from CVS? : ${cvs} </echo>
038:
039:      <if name="cvs" value="Checkout code from CVS">
040:        <antcall target="cvs_code_checkout"/>
041:      </if>
042:
043:      <if name="test" value="- Select Test">
044:        <echo> No test selected. Please select a test. </echo>
045:        <else>
046:          <if name="junit" value="- Select GUI/non-GUI">
047:            <echo> No JUnit option selected. Please select a JUnit option.
</echo>
048:            <else>
049:              <if name="test" value="Test1">
050:                <echo> Test1 selected </echo>
051:                <if name="junit" value="Run w/ GUI">
052:                  <antcall target="portal_test1_gui"/>
053:                <else>
054:                  <antcall target="portal_test1_nongui"/>
055:                </else>
056:                </if>
057:              <else>
058:                <if name="test" value="Test2">
059:                  <echo> Test2 selected </echo>
060:                  <if name="junit" value="Run w/ GUI">
061:                    <antcall target="portal_test2_gui"/>
062:                  <else>
063:                    <antcall target="portal_test2_nongui"/>
064:                  </else>
065:                  </if>
066:                <else>
067:                  <echo> All tests [Test1/Test2] selected </echo>
068:                  <if name="junit" value="Run w/ GUI">
069:                    <antcall target="portal_test1_gui"/>
070:                    <antcall target="portal_test2_gui"/>
071:                  <else>
072:                    <antcall target="portal_test1_nongui"/>
073:                    <antcall target="portal_test2_nongui"/>
074:                  </else>
075:                  </if>
076:                  </else>
077:                </if>
078:              </else>
079:              </if>
080:            </else>
```

```
081:           </if>
082:         </else>
083: </if>
084:    </target>
085:
```

The `run_commandline_test` target that starts on line 86 determines which test to select for operation. If the test name selected is `Test1`, then a text string will be echoed to the console with the value `Test1`. Otherwise, the target `portal tests`, not shown in this script, will be called:

```
086:    <target name="run_commmandline_test">
087:      <!-- read from properties files -->
088:      <echo>Directory        : ${dir} </echo>
089:      <echo>Test selection   : ${test} </echo>
090:
091:      <if name="test" value="- Select a test">
092:         <echo> No test selected </echo>
093:         <else>
094:            <if name="test" value="Test1">
095:               <echo> Test1 </echo>
096:            <else>
097:               <antcall target="portal_tests"/>
098:            </else>
099:            </if>
100:         </else>
101:      </if>
102:    </target>
103:
```

The `portal_test1_gui` and `portal_test2_gui` targets that start on lines 104 and 115 run JUnit tests in a GUI display so that users can visually determine if their tests have passed or failed in their operations:

```
104:    <target name="portal_test1_gui">
105:      <java fork="yes" classname="junit.awtui.TestRunner"
106:            taskname="junit" failonerror="true">
107:      <arg value="validateFormTestCase1"/>
108:      <classpath>
109:        <pathelement path="${lib.path}" />
110:        <pathelement path="${java.class.path}" />
111:      </classpath>
112:    </java>
113:    </target>
114:
115:    <target name="portal_test2_gui">
116:      <java fork="yes" classname="junit.awtui.TestRunner"
117:            taskname="junit" failonerror="true">
118:      <arg value="validateFormTestCase2"/>
119:      <classpath>
120:        <pathelement path="${lib.path}" />
121:        <pathelement path="${java.class.path}" />
122:      </classpath>
123:    </java>
124:    </target>
125:
```

The `portal_test1_nongui` and `portal_test2_nongui` targets that start on lines 126 and 143 run JUnit tests from the command line. The `JUnitReport` test descriptors will output their test results in an XML file for observation and analysis:

```
126:    <target name="portal_test1_nongui">
127:       <echo message="Running JUnit tests." />
128:       <junit printsummary="true">
129:         <formatter type="xml" />
130:         <test name="validateFormTestCase1" />
131:         <classpath>
132:           <pathelement location="." />
133:         </classpath>
134:       </junit>
135:       <junitreport todir=".">
136:         <fileset dir=".">
137:           <include name="TEST-*.xml" />
138:         </fileset>
139:         <report format="frames" todir="." />
140:       </junitreport>
141:    </target>
142:
143:    <target name="portal_test2_nongui">
144:       <echo message="Running JUnit tests." />
145:       <junit printsummary="true">
146:         <formatter type="xml" />
147:         <test name="validateFormTestCase2" />
148:         <classpath>
149:           <pathelement location="." />
150:         </classpath>
151:       </junit>
152:       <junitreport todir=".">
153:         <fileset dir=".">
154:           <include name="TEST-*.xml" />
155:         </fileset>
156:         <report format="frames" todir="." />
157:       </junitreport>
158:    </target>
159:
```

The `cvs_code_checkout` target that starts on line 160 performs checkout operations on the CVS repository, as well as move and delete activities on the file system. After files have been checked out from CVS, the code is compiled from the `compile_portal_tests` target:

```
160:    <target name="cvs_code_checkout">
161:       <echo message="Checking out test code from CVS." />
162:       <cvs cvsRoot=":pserver:${cvs.username}@${cvs.hostname}:${cvs.dir}"
163:           command="co ${cvs.module}"
164:           dest="${lib.path}" />
165:       <!- move files for easy access ->
166:       <move todir="${lib.path}">
167:         <fileset dir="${lib.path}\CVSTests"/>
168:       </move>
169:       <delete dir="${lib.path}\CVSTests"/>
```

```
170:        <!– compile code –>
171:        <antcall target="compile_portal_tests"/>
172:    </target>
173:
```

The `compile_portal_tests` target on line 174 compiles the baseline code checked out from CVS repository. The `help` target that start on line 181 could be used to add help text to facilitate operations for new users:

```
174:    <target name="compile_portal_tests">
175:      <echo message="Compiling Portal test code." />
176:      <javac srcdir="${lib.path}"
177:             destdir="${lib.path}"
178:             classpathref="system.classpath" />
179:    </target>
180:
181:    <target name="help" description="Help">
182:      <echo message="JUnit application"/>
183:      <echo message=""/>
184:      <echo message="Place help instructions here. "/>
185:      <echo message=""/>
186: </target>
187:
188: </project>
```

The `taskdef` definitions on lines 24–25 associate task names with their library class names. Task definitions require two attributes: the name that identifies the unique task, and the full name of the class that implements this task. Our Interactive ANT example uses two open-source libraries that can be downloaded from the Internet: Antelope (http://sourceforge.net/projects/antelope) and Interactive ANT, which can be procured from (www.kasisoft.de/build/ant/interactive/). The Antelope libraries enable users to implement Java-like `if`/`else` constructs in your ANT scripts. The Interactive ANT libraries allow users to easily create interactive displays to add script behavior on the fly.

As previously mentioned, vast amounts of JUnit test materials and references can be found online, as well as in journals and books, but a simple primer should suffice to refresh your memory in case you might have forgotten some of the steps needed to successfully deploy JUnit tests. Feel free to skip ahead if this material is not for you.

The `validateFormTestCase2` program in the following code runs three tests on the methods of the `validateForm` application in the code that follows it. Notice the `assert` operations that are performed on the returned values from the accessor methods of the JavaBean. These operations are considered **back-box** testing because our only concern is that if we add a value in the test sent to an application, that same value is returned when we try to invoke it later:

```
import junit.framework.TestCase;
public class validateFormTestCase2 extends TestCase {
    public void testCase2() {
      validateForm vForm = new validateForm();
          assertTrue(vForm != null);
        vForm.setTelephoneNumber("703-555-1212");
        assertTrue("703-555-1212" == vForm.getTelephoneNumber());
  }
```

```
   public void testCase3() {
    validateForm vForm = new validateForm();
    assertTrue(vForm != null);
    vForm.setBirthDate("04-12-1963");
    assertTrue("04-12-1963" == vForm.getBirthDate());
  }
 public void testCase5() {
    validateForm vForm = new validateForm();
        assertTrue(vForm != null);
      vForm.setSsn("123-45-6789");
     assertTrue("123-45-6789" == vForm.getSsn());
 }
 }
```

The `validateForm` application in the following code is a simple JavaBean application that runs on the server back-end and is used by a Web component that runs in an application server's Web container. The JUnit test in the preceding code will invoke the `get` and `set` operations in this class to determine whether the internal methods behave properly when user inputs are run against them. The `validate` method uses regular expressions to determine whether user inputs are correct. If no errors have been found, the JSP that uses this validation form can be assured that all data input by the user is proper and well-formed:

```
import java.util.*;
import java.text.*;
import java.util.regex.*;
public class validateForm {
     private String telephoneNumber;
     private String birthDate;
     private String ssn;
  private Hashtable errors;
    public boolean validate() {
    boolean errorsFound=false;
          if (telephoneNumber.equals("")) {
       errors.put("telephoneNumber","Please enter a valid telephone #");
              errorsFound=true;
          } else {
             if (!(telephoneNumber.matches("\\+?([0-9]+-)+([0-9]+-)+[0-9]+"))) {
                 errors.put("telephoneNumber","Please enter a valid telephone
format ### - ### - ####");
       errorsFound=true;
             }
         }
        if (ssn.equals("")) {
             errors.put("ssn","Please enter a valid Social Security #");
     errorsFound=true;
         }
        else {
    if (!(ssn.matches("(\\d{3}\\-?)+(\\d{2}\\-?)+\\d{4}+"))) {
                 errors.put("ssn","Please enter a valid SSN: ### - ## - ####");
                 errorsFound=true;
           }
       }
        if (birthDate.equals("")) {
```

```
                    errors.put("birthDate","Please enter a valid date");
            errorsFound=true;
              } else {
                  if (!(birthDate.matches("(\\d{4}\\-?)+(\\d{2}\\-?)+\\d{2}+"))) {
                      errors.put("birthDate","Please enter a valid date format: (yyyy-
mm-dd)");
            errorsFound=true;
                  }
              }
              return errorsFound;
      }
      public String getErrorMsg(String s) {
        String errorMsg =(String)errors.get(s.trim());
        return (errorMsg == null) ? "":errorMsg;
      }
      public validateForm() {
        telephoneNumber="";
        birthDate="";
        ssn="";
        errors = new Hashtable();
      }
```

The following code performs get and set operations for the validateForm bean that is used by a JSP for validation activities:

```
    // getters
    public String getTelephoneNumber() {
      return telephoneNumber;
    }
    public String getBirthDate() {
      return birthDate;
    }
    public String getSsn() {
      return ssn;
    }
    // setters
    public void setTelephoneNumber(String tn) {
          telephoneNumber=tn;
      }
      public void setBirthDate(String bd) {
          birthDate=bd;
      }
      public void setSsn(String s) {
          ssn=s;
      }
    }
    }
```

In summary, during portal development, it is very easy for a program's complexity to grow exponentially because of design and technology miscalculations. To staunch this occurrence, attention should be given to developing unit tests for your applications throughout your programming activities to mitigate deployment risks on your portal program. Once these tests have been crafted, you should archive them in your code repositories for future retrieval and implementation.

AntHill

Earlier in this chapter, we discussed the use of CVS, ANT, and JUnit applications for continuous integration operations. Typically, the implementation of these technologies for testing necessitates the manual setting up of scripts to run those applications. The ANT script shown in the preceding section, named `junitTest`, checks out the latest baseline code from the CVS repository; compiles those files; deploys those files as libraries in Java Archive (JAR) format; runs unit tests with JUnit on all of the individual components; and verifies that bugs were not introduced into the working baseline.

Rather than manually integrate those parts into a single ANT script and develop a separate script for scheduling test execution, consider using a really nifty open-source application called Anthill to perform those same activities. Anthill was developed by Urbancode and can be found at www.urbancode.com/ projects/anthill/default.jsp. Anthill uses Jakarta Apache's ANT tool to automate build processes so that multiple users can build code together from a consistent baseline that resides in a centralized source code repository. AntHill requires the following open-source applications for deployment:

❑ Tomcat v4.1.24 or higher — Anthill deploys as a Web application, so the `anthill.war` file that is included with the Anthill distribution should be installed in the `/webapps` directory of the Tomcat server.

❑ Any e-mail server application — Our example uses the open-source application called JAMES v2.1. JAMES can be downloaded from the Internet at http://james.apache.org/. Once installed, a user account needs to be established so that build notifications can be broadcast. Generally, this involves installing and running the JAMES server with the `run` script, telnet-ing to the default port number 4555, and adding a user account. A default user login is **root/root;** from there you can type **help** to get more information on operations that can be performed by the user. These activities include the following: user account actions, user account information displays, and forwarding tasks. See Chapter 3 for more information on JAMES.

❑ ANT — The ANT utility can be found at http://ant.apache.org. It is a Java-based build tool that uses XML scripts to target build operations.

❑ CVS — CVS can be procured from www.cvshome.org. Once it has been properly installed on your system, a file named `project.version` needs to be added to the CVS module directory being tested. The number placed in that file is incremented by one for each consecutive build performed by AntHill on that module.

The Projects section of Figure 11.4 indicates that a project named Portal Test was run at a designated build interval indicated by a timestamp. A successful run renders a green background indication around the build time. An unsuccessful run displays a red background, indicating that unit tests have discovered an error, which could warrant further investigation.

The Build link associated with the individual projects enables users to create non-scheduled builds on the fly. When clicked, a Web page is rendered to the user display that shows the current version number of that task. Along with that is a checkbox, indicating that a new build will be executed; and a text field, which must have a new build version input associated with it.

The Anthill application enables users to modify test properties through a Web browser. The `anthill. build.script` property can be designated so that the testing framework can execute JUnit test scripts on demand or at desired time intervals. All scheduled test scripts should reside in a folder that is relative to the project root directory.

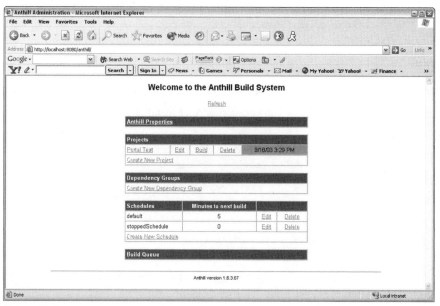

Figure 11.4

Figure 11.5 shows a Web-based administrative display that enables users to designate test properties for test operations. Some of the important configuration considerations include e-mail setup values, Anthill home path information, and the URL that will be accessed from Anthill.

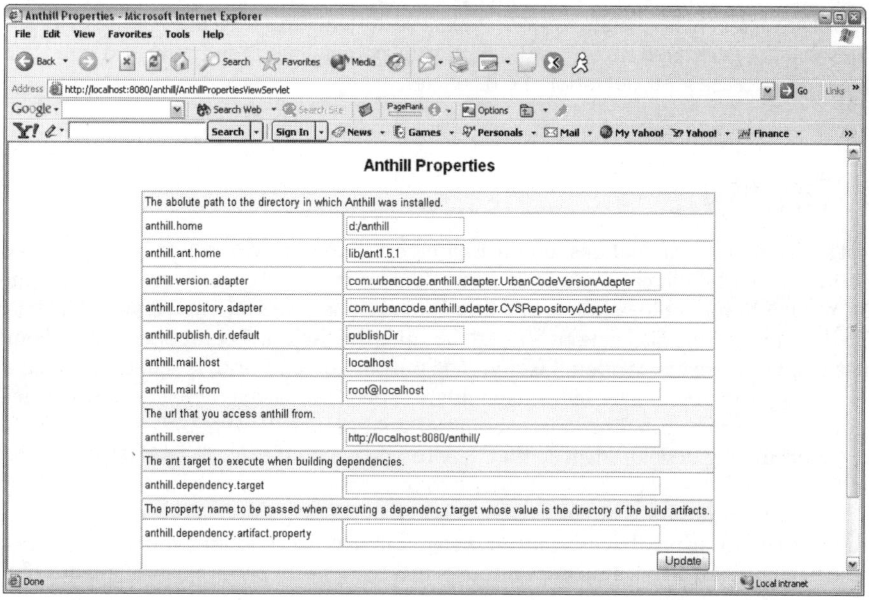

Figure 11.5

AntHill implements a property file called `anthill.properties` to save system configuration values that are modified by the user. This file maintains the attributes shown in the following table.

Property	Description
`anthill.home`	Location of Anthill installation (for example, `d:/anthill`)
`anthill.ant.home`	Location of ANT installation (for example, `lib/ant1.5.1`)
`anthill.version.adapter`	Controls the format of the version number Anthill uses during scheduled builds (for example, `com.urbancode.anthill.adapter.UrbanCodeVersionAdapter`)
`anthill.repository.adapter`	Component responsible for interaction with the source control repository (for example, `com.urbancode.anthill.adapter.CVSRepositoryAdapter`)
`Anthill.publish.dir.default`	Location to place artifacts after a build is completed (for example, `publishDir`)
`Anthill.mail.host`	Mail server IP address or DNS name (for example, `localhost`)
`Anthill.mail.from`	Address that will show up on notification alerts (for example, root@localhost)
`Anthill.server`	Address where URL address will be accessed on the server (for example, `http://localhost:8080/anthill/`)

As with all testing tools, configuring them is the most difficult part of their implementation. Once they have been properly set up, your automated builds will enhance your program's testing and integration processes. The idea here is to build your unit tests with JUnit and then use Anthill to apply those tests to build files that are generated from your CVS repository using the scheduling and build activities of the Anthill tool to increase your operational efficiencies.

Load Testing

For most software implementations, unit tests are performed in a controlled fashion. This differs from **load testing,** which evaluates dynamic user and content transactions on a system in a semi-controlled manner. You might intend to simulate 50+ user transactions on a system, but you can't be absolutely sure which simulated user is being processed, because the threaded components you would use for those users can operate in a random fashion. The purpose of load testing is to ensure that a system delivers the functionality that system stakeholders expect, rather than what testers and developers want their unit tests to accomplish. Load tests are important because they enable testers to discover system software faults during development so that they can be rectified prior to final deployment. Load tests come in many forms, but you might consider two in your testing operations: **stress** and **configuration**.

Stress tests are run to ensure that a deployed system can handle a specified number of users, and to gain a better understanding of how a system performs when those users perform simultaneous transactions on it. Stress tests are generally run to take measurements on a system that has a significant amount of users performing simultaneous transactions. Configuration tests are executed to evaluate the software/hardware configurations on a system to ensure that a system is deployed satisfactorily and meets all of the system requirements established by the stakeholders of a program.

Tests that simulate stress loads are critical to all Web-based deployments, but they're especially pertinent for portal deployments because portals are built to service large user communities through portlets, which, taken as a whole, perform many independent back-end operations simultaneously. Load test implementations monitor and report on the performance and scalability of a system to ensure that high performance is attained. Performance and scalability are two primary concerns for most portal deployments because of their dependence on back-end data sources for dynamic content and their need to handle transactional operations as user loads are increased on a system. Traditionally, portlet usage projections are generated during the requirements phase of a portal project but are not realized until the portal application is deployed and is accessible to the user community. The open-source application **JMeter** can be used to test those projections and your Web site's behavior under measured stress levels during development so that bottlenecks in your applications can be corrected and re-engineered prior to deployment.

JMeter

JMeter is a Jakarta Apache offering (http://jakarta.apache.org/jmeter/) that runs as a Java Swing application to measure and test nonfunctional behavior of Java applications, databases, LDAP directory server lookups, and Web components. JMeter simulates user loads through threaded applications that are set up through its console application. JMeter also renders graphical analyses of scheduled tests on designated applications and enables users to archive test data results for future observation and interpretation.

It would be hard to argue that many portal development efforts have not benefited from the implementation of open-source products in their deployments. Compressed development cycles have led to widespread implementation of open-source libraries to accommodate tight delivery timelines. As a result of this, developers often deploy libraries that have been developed independently from their teams. This reliance on free open-source libraries has gained prominence in development circles and poses a difficult dilemma for teams that are challenged to deploy reliable enterprise systems with no in-depth knowledge of these libraries in their systems. This occurrence has warranted the implementation of unit and load tests to monitor software integrations and to correct performance obstacles early in their development timetables so that unexpected issues do not arise in the latter stages of a program because of these library components.

Tools such as JMeter are especially helpful in ensuring early in your development that latency issues don't wreak havoc on your production systems. JMeter enables both developers and testers to optimize their systems for speed and scalability because throwing more hardware at a latency problem is not always the best solution to overcoming inefficient code. There are no hard-and-fast rules for this, but most portal deployments should gear themselves towards realistic goals and strive for them.

JMeter enables development teams to be more conscientious about an application's latency issues throughout the development process. Performance management of enterprise Web applications is challenging, so planning performance goals should be part of your design and development activities. That includes forecasting the number of concurrent users and the response times you expect to deliver on your production system.

Before delving into the use of the JMeter console, let's examine the use of a JMeter ANT task developed by ProgrammerPlanet (www.programmerplanet.org/ant-jmeter/) to perform Web-based testing. The task shown in the following code enables developers to run their JMeter test plans from the command line and output run logs to a flat file that can be rendered to HTML format using an XSLT stylesheet:

```xml
<?xml version="1.0"?>
<project name="test" default="jmeter-ant">

    <property name="basedir" value="d:\JMeter_1.8"/>
    <taskdef name="jmeter"
classname="org.programmerplanet.ant.taskdefs.jmeter.JMeterTask"/>
    <target name="jmeter-ant">
        <echo> basedir= ${basedir} </echo>

        <jmeter jmeterhome="d:/JMeter_1.8"
                testplan="d:/JMeter_1.8/portal_tests/TestPlan_1.jmx"
                resultlog="d:/JMeter_1.8/portal_tests/TestPlan_1.jtl"/>
        <xslt in="d:/JMeter_1.8/portal_tests/TestPlan_1.jtl"
              out="d:/JMeter_1.8/portal_tests/TestPlan_1.html"
              style="d:/JMeter_1.8/portal_tests/jmeter-results-report.xsl"/>

    </target>
</project>
```

The XSLT provided with the download renders test metrics to an HTML file for examination in a Web browser. Additional views can be provided by modifying the custom ANT tasks file and outputting the data to a different file and stylesheet that accommodate the data view you want to render.

The JMeter console is a Java Swing application that enables simple dialog boxes to set up load tests to stress your system and monitor the results. Figure 11.6 shows this console. From it, testers and developers can create threaded sessions to emulate specified numbers of concurrent users for load testing. User dialog boxes enable users to set up different forms of user requests. The screen shown in Figure 11.6 indicates that requests can for created the following operations: FTP, HTTP/S, SOAP/XML RPC, LDAP lookups, Java applications, and JDBC calls. Graphic visualizations can be added to those requests, including Spline displays, as well as Aggregate and Tree reports.

The screenshot in Figure 11.7 shows how a user can test a JDBC connection. In this example, a SELECT statement is performed on a table called report. This test can also be configured to perform twenty simultaneous requests using the same query operation, to see how the database handles multiple requests on the same table. Most data-intensive Web applications that depend on back-end database queries to generate dynamic content should incorporate tests like these to ensure that their connection pooling operations are working properly, and that their JDBC connection drivers can handle known amounts of requests. JMeter enables testers to discover database invocation shortcomings through JDBC calls so that corrective actions can be made to assuage these problems throughout a portal application's life cycle. Rather than have some tester "fat-finger" database requests, users can pull up archived tests, run them with JMeter, and determine whether their system is running properly or needs corrective measures.

As you explore the JMeter application, you will discover the great potential it possesses to satisfy your load testing needs for your portal application. The JMeter site includes a rich set of resources that users can sift through to better understand the load testing tool's capabilities. The basic idea here is to manage project risk by using tools such as JMeter early in your development schedules to understand how your system components work as a whole under varied user scenarios and stress levels. This inevitably will improve your application quality and accelerate your delivery timelines.

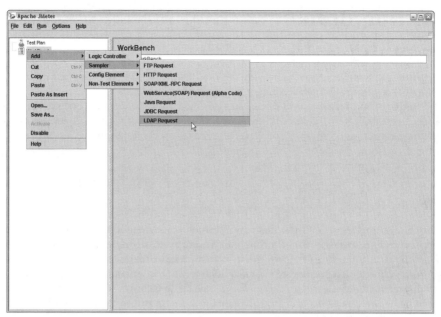

Figure 11.6

Figure 11.7

Portal Requirements/Bug Management and Traceability with Scarab

Requirements and bug-tracking activities are important software management tasks during portal development that necessitate the consolidation of requirement deliverables in a centralized repository and a monitoring tool to audit the status of those tasks during a project's life cycle. Several high-quality open-source tools such as Scarab, Bugzilla, BugRat, and iTracker are readily available for download on the Internet to perform these operations for you. This chapter concentrates on the Scarab application (www.tigris.org/) and its use of Web components to provide robust requirements and bug-tracking coverage for your portal initiatives.

Scarab

Software change tracking is an important configuration management activity that is needed to manage software and design artifact changes throughout the life cycle of your program. Software and design modifications are a continuous concern throughout a project's lifetime — either the developers want to change their technical perspectives or the stakeholders want to amend their original requirements. To address this recurring challenge, tracking software needs to be implemented to maintain the flow of a project, to maintain high levels of software quality assurance, and to remind all party members about a program's requirements and their adherence to them. Uncontrolled requirements tracking and change modifications could lead to pandemonium on a program.

With Scarab, users can view a program's requirements, customer feature requests, as well as bug discoveries and fix details through easy-to-use navigation windows and keyword queries from a browser display.

A bug-tracking system is essentially a centralized data repository for problem reports. Those reports can be software bugs, hardware defects, stakeholder feedback, or any other incidents and issues. Two important benefits of a bug-tracking and requirements-tracking system are its collaborative nature and its tracking management capabilities.

Two essential considerations with an open-source bug-tracking system include the following: Java implementation for cross-platform compatibility and database independence. When procuring such a system for your program, forethought also must also be given to users and their ability to do the following:

- ❑ Create/edit/close issues
- ❑ Obtain attachment support so that issue clarity can be provided
- ❑ View logging operations
- ❑ Broadcast e-mail notifications about project status
- ❑ Perform searches on issues
- ❑ Generate reports and import/export issue data

Administrative operations should allow users with admin privileges to perform project and user locking activities, as well as have the capability to determine user-level permissions. Fortunately, Scarab meets all of these requirements.

As with all requirements and bug-tracking tool implementations, problem discovery and explanation clarity are paramount in resolving problems. When such a tool has been put in place, users should be strongly encouraged to do the following:

- ❑ Put in as much relevant detail as they can. Duh!

- ❑ Keep issues distinct and separate from one another.

- ❑ Use their e-mail addresses so that problem ambiguities can be resolved faster.

- ❑ Broadcast alerts or e-mails to developers who have bugs assigned to them.

- ❑ Include URLs that indicate where the bug is located.

Additional open-source applications that are needed for Scarab deployments include the following:

- ❑ Tomcat v4.1.24 or later — Scarab deploys as a Web application that can be built using ANT scripts included in their distribution. After a successful build, a Web Archive (WAR) is created, which can be dropped into the `/webapps` directory of the Tomcat server.

- ❑ An e-mail server — JAMES v2.1 (http://james.apache.org/). See Chapter 3 for more information on JAMES. All new accounts will be sent a confirmation code to ensure that users properly register with the Scarab system. If you intend to run Scarab locally on your PC without a mail server running on your box, it is possible to trick the system by updating the user account you have created in the `turbine_user` table by manually setting the `CONFIRM_VALUE` to `CONFIRMED`. The `CONFIRM_VALUE` is normally established when a user receives an e-mail from the Scarab tool after registering and returning a confirmation e-mail.

- ❑ A database — Our implementation uses the open-source database MySQL, which can be found at www.mysql.com/. User table scripts are provided with the Scarab distribution and can be applied using the ANT build script with the `create-db-schema` target name.

Scarab Tasks

The Scarab tasks page contains many important tabbed features that enable users to monitor issues. Figure 11.8 illustrates the tabbed sections, which indicate what relevant data is available to users and what fields need to be filled out and submitted so that they will be persisted in the back-end repository. The following table describes the tabbed sections available from the tasks page.

Tab Name	Description
Attributes	Contains static issue information, including when an issue was committed and last modified.
	A text area is provided so that users can enter comments regarding their reasons for a change.
	Alternatively, users can move and copy issues from this section.
Personnel	Displays the user personnel name of the person who created the task.
Comments	A text area that enables users to add comments that will be associated with the task being viewed.

Table continued on following page

Tab Name	Description
Attachments/ Dependencies/URLs	Renders a Browse button that enables users to attach files with the task issue along with comments in a text area. This attachment function requires that the user indicate the mime-type of the file being attached to the task.
	Text and drop-down components are rendered so users can specify dependencies as Issue IDs, Types, and Reasons.
	Related links can be input as URL and text descriptions.
History	Provides timestamps of critical events associated with task issues. All newly created issues reveal the date they were created, who created them, and why they were created.

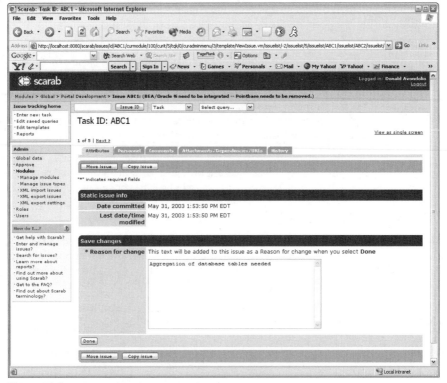

Figure 11.8

Scarab employs a very vigorous issue management strategy when committing, tracking, and modifying issues. Relationships are tracked between issues, so it is possible to track an issue through specific query operations, or when reviewing other issues. All software changes are tracked along with information about who made changes and when source code modifications were committed.

With Scarab, issue types are created so that a unique set of attributes and options can be used to describe issues in a purposeful manner. Attributes within an issue type are defined by the project administrator and affect issues only within that issue type. Each project has a unique set of issue types.

Issue attributes are used to categorize issues for tracking and analysis. Each issue type has a unique set of attributes, such as Summary, Description, Priority, Milestone, Status, Resolution, and Severity. The Scarab system deploys with a default set of values for attributes, but it can be easily customized by your project administrator. The User Search page shown in Figure 11.9 enables users to perform keyword searches on user-specified criteria. Search results can be refined by specifying filters as well as desired amounts of data to be rendered on the user display. When user names are returned from a user query, Scarab users with proper privileges have the option of modifying these roles or deleting them entirely from the user repository.

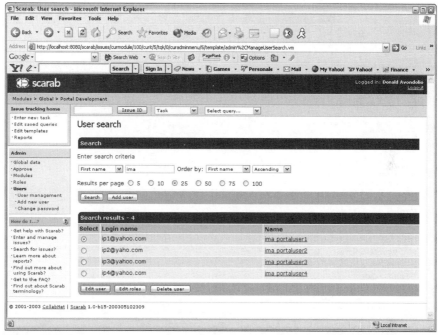

Figure 11.9

In the Scarab Role Administration screen displayed in Figure 11.10, users can edit, delete, and add new roles for the project modules. When a user opts to edit a user role, this is achieved by selecting the radio button associated with the role to be edited, and clicking the Edit button on the Role List display. From there, the user can enable or disable roles permissions that relate to the following: Domains, Issues, Items, Modules, Users, and Votes. Generally, these permissions relate to the following functions: Edit, Attach, Add, Configure, Assign, Enter, Search, Approve, Delete, and Manage.

The screenshot in Figure 11.11 demonstrates how query results are rendered when issue queries are performed. After a result set has been returned from a user query, the user has the option of selecting individual query items so that they can be saved for future interpretation. These same queries can be saved to an Excel spreadsheet or a tab-separated display in a browser window that can be printed for future reading. This query capability is important for aggregating common problems so that they can be recognized and rectified in a timely fashion.

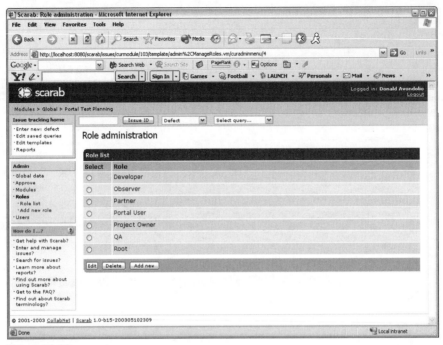

Figure 11.10

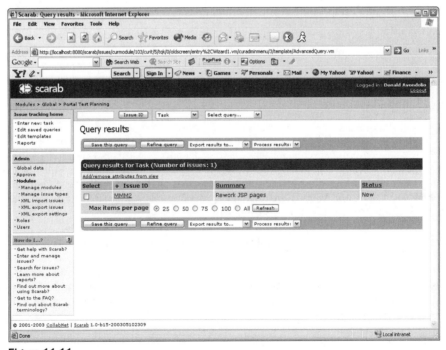

Figure 11.11

Another important feature of the Scarab application is the capability for users to import issues into the system to be tracked during a program's life cycle. An export function also enables users to save issue libraries so that they can be archived and transported to other Scarab implementations.

In summary, the Scarab tool can be a valuable asset in your portal development because it enables all program stakeholders to monitor and assess the health of their project from a user-friendly browser application. The database back-end provides great flexibility in capturing issues and their states throughout the life cycle of a program. Tracking tools such as Scarab can facilitate your requirements for monitoring and reporting needs, as well as bug tracking activities, so that your project can achieve success with its deployment and maintenance operations.

Portal Administration with JMX

In the past, many portal applications managed their disparate subsystems through applications and Web-based console applications using proprietary APIs to control data and operations on that information. These operations were often costly in terms of toolset training, and challenging in regard to its usefulness to implementers when monitoring data. In addition to that, system configurations were often saved and modified manually to flat files that became susceptible to corruption through user mismanagement and mishandling, resulting in unreliable operations.

The introduction of Java Management eXtensions (JMX) APIs and libraries now enables developers to create applications that perform system management operations of deployed systems through standards-based interfaces using the Java programming language. These interfaces were developed so that role, security realm, and database components could be easily administered by managed resources known as **agents,** thus avoiding the introduction of errors by manual operations.

JMX was rolled out with the Tomcat 4.1 distribution in a Struts-enabled administrative console. In Tomcat's 5.x distribution, JMX MBeans were captured in the `catalina-admin.jar` file. This admin console offers a graphical administration tool that authorizes developers to expose application-specific information about J2EE and Java-based applications and the resources they act upon.

To really appreciate the power of JMX, it is important to understand its benefits. According to the JMX specification, JMX provides the following:

❑ A management agent that provides a standard manner to manage Java applications, devices, and services

❑ The integration of autonomous modules with the management agent, which produces a scalable management architecture

❑ The capability to leverage standard Java technologies such as JNDI, JDBC, and JTS

❑ JMX smart agents that can be managed through HTML browsers or by SNMP protocols

Figure 11.12 illustrates part of the JMX specification. It offers a high-level view of how JMX can be used on your system to control the applications and Web components that operate on your system.

The following code listings are sample JSR 168 portlet implementations that emulate functions that reside in the Tomcat 5.x administration console application. The purpose of this code is to demonstrate how to use **Dynamic** MBeans in your portlet applications using simple J2EE Web components.

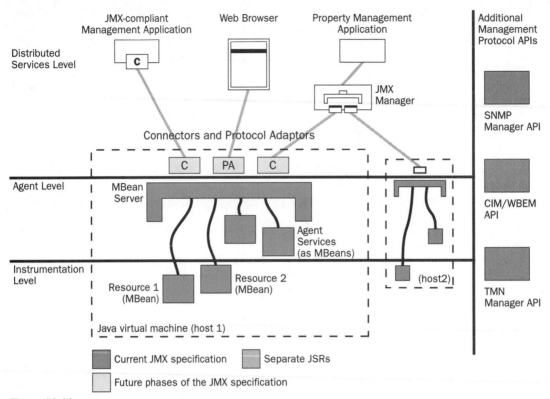

Figure 11.12

The JMX Instrumentation Level provides an interface to resources so that they can be managed. This interface is known as a **managed resource** and is called an **MBean**. The Instrumentation Level supports four flavors of MBeans: **Standard** MBeans, **Dynamic** MBeans, **Open** MBeans, and **Model** MBeans. Proper MBean implementations can be made by gaining a better understanding the four different MBean types.

Standard MBeans explicitly define their management interfaces so that get and set operations can be performed on them fairly easily. The JMX agent uses **introspection** to discover the state and behavior of classes and their superclasses through Standard MBeans. According to the JMX specification, the name of an MBean's Java interface must be formed by adding the MBean suffix to the MBean's fully qualified Java class name. Therefore, if an MBean class you have created is named Test, then the Java interface that you need to implement with that class should be named TestMBean.

Dynamic MBeans implement the DynamicMBean interface to enable runtime modification of system attributes and events. Dynamic MBeans expose attributes and methods without introspection but through a JMX agent. The DynamicMBean interface is displayed in Figure 11.13. When a DynamicMBean is registered in a JMX agent, an application can make calls through the accessor methods (getters/setters) and the invoke method to obtain the names of a component's attributes and operations.

«Interface» Dynamic MBean

getMBeanInfo(): MBeanInfo
getAttribute(attribute:String): Object
getAttributes(attributes:String[]): AttributeList
setAttribute(attribute:Attribute): void
setAttributes(attributes:AttributesList): AttributeList
invoke(actionName:String,
       params:Object[],
       signature:String[]): Object

Figure 11.13

Open MBeans were developed as a mechanism to discover new managed objects at runtime. Open MBeans are capable of managing data and operations during runtime without requiring the recompilation of management applications. Open MBeans are particularly useful when a management application does not necessarily have access to the Java classes of an agent. Model MBeans use a set of interfaces to provide both static and dynamic behavior. Descriptors are used with Model MBeans to serve as metadata stores.

A great reference that you should consider looking at to better appreciate JMX and its management and instrumentation capabilities is Mike Janowski's *JMX Programming* (Wiley, 2002).

Now that you have a basic understanding of some high-level concepts concerning MBean implementation, the question becomes, How do you actually write code to implement them? You must first procure an application server that runs an MBean server. Jakarta's Tomcat server starts an MBean server when the application server is started. If you don't believe it, look at the Java console on which you ran startup for Tomcat. Next, you should delve through the source code of the `catalina-admin.jar` file in the Tomcat distribution that stores the Struts-enabled files to see how MBeans are used in the admin console. To run the console, start Tomcat and type this URL: http://<Tomcat hostname>:<Tomcat port number>/admin. Prior to performing this activity, however, you should modify the `tomcat-users.xml` file in Tomcat's /conf directory to include the `admin` keyword to the `role` attribute. This will enable you to log in to the admin console as tomcat/tomcat.

If you don't want to dawdle through the console code, you might consider the following code. This JSR 168 portlet cuts through the complexity that the Struts console admin tool possesses. This simple example instantiates an `MBeanServer` object so that users and roles can be displayed and a new user can be added:

```
001: import java.io.IOException;
002: import java.io.Writer;
003: import java.net.*;
004: import javax.portlet.*;
005: import javax.management.*;
006: import javax.servlet.*;
007: import org.apache.commons.modeler.Registry;
008:
009: public class JMXPortlet1 extends GenericPortlet {
010:
011:     public JMXPortlet1() {}
012:
013:     public void init(PortletConfig config)
014:         throws PortletException {
015:         super.init(config);
016:     }
017:
```

The `doView` method on line 18 is used to render the content of the `JMXPortlet1` portlet application. Our example code determines whether the Tomcat MBean server is running; if so, then the application will add the user Jack Stern to the system using a JMX interface and the `invoke` method of the `MBean` object on line 52:

```
018:     public void doView(RenderRequest request, RenderResponse response)
019:         throws PortletException, IOException, UnavailableException {
020:
021:         String groups[] = null;
022:         ObjectName oname = null;
023:         String objectName = null;
024:
025:         WindowState state = request.getWindowState();
026:         WindowState _tmp = state;
027:         if(state == WindowState.NORMAL) {
028:
029:             Writer writer = response.getWriter();
030:
031:             MBeanServer mserver = Registry.getRegistry().getMBeanServer();
032:             if(mserver == null) {
033:                 throw new UnavailableException("MBeanServer is not available");
034:             } else {
035:
036:                 String db="Users:type=UserDatabase,database=UserDatabase"; //
037:                 String databaseName =URLDecoder.decode(db);
038:
039:                 // add user
040:             String signature[] = { "java.lang.String", "java.lang.String",
"java.lang.String" };
041:                 Object params[] = { "jack", "jack", "Jack Stern" };
042:
043:         try {
044:                     oname = new ObjectName(databaseName);
```

```
045:                    objectName = (String)mserver.invoke(oname, "createUser",
params, signature);
046:                } catch(Exception e) {
047:                    System.out.println("Exception: " + e.toString());
048:                }
049:
050:                try {
051:                    oname = new ObjectName(objectName);
052:                    mserver.invoke(oname, "removeGroups", new Object[0], new
String[0]);
053:
054:                    if(groups == null)
055:                        groups = new String[0];
056:                    String addsig[] = new String[1];
057:                    addsig[0] = "java.lang.String";
058:                    Object addpar[] = new Object[1];
059:                    for(int i = 0; i < groups.length; i++) {
060:                        addpar[0] = (new
ObjectName(groups[i])).getKeyProperty("groupname");
061:                        mserver.invoke(oname, "addGroup", addpar, addsig);
062:                    }
063:                } catch(Exception e) {
064:                    System.out.println("Exception: " + e.toString());
065:                }
066:                writer.write("Added user: Jack Stern<br>");
```

Lines 67–107 render user, role, and group information visually inside the JMXPortlet1 portlet component. On line 70, the getAttribute method is sent the users text value to indicate that the MBean component should return all of the user names of the system and store them in string array visual output. The same getAttribute method is used on lines 84 and 98 so that role and group information can be rendered along with user name data:

```
067:                // show users
068:                try {
069:                    ObjectName dname = new ObjectName(databaseName);
070:                    String results[] = (String[])mserver.getAttribute(dname,
"users");
071:                    if(results == null)
072:                        results = new String[0];
073:                    else {
074:                        for (int i=0; i < results.length; i++)
075:                        writer.write("user[" + i + "]= " + results[i] + "<br>");
076:                    }
077:                } catch(Exception e) {
078:                    System.out.println("Exception: " + e.toString());
079:                }
080:
081:                // show roles
082:                try {
083:                    ObjectName dname = new ObjectName(databaseName);
084:                    String results[] = (String[])mserver.getAttribute(dname,
"roles");
```

```
085:                  if(results == null)
086:                      results = new String[0];
087:                  else {
088:                      for (int i=0; i < results.length; i++)
089:                          writer.write("role[" + i + "]= " + results[i] +
"<br>");
090:                  }
091:              } catch(Exception e) {
092:                  System.out.println("Exception: " + e.toString());
093:              }
094:
095:              // show groups
096:              try {
097:                  ObjectName dname = new ObjectName(databaseName);
098:                  groups = (String[])mserver.getAttribute(dname, "groups");
099:                  if(groups == null)
100:                      groups = new String[0];
101:                  else {
102:                      for (int i=0; i < groups.length; i++)
103:                          writer.write("groups[" + i + "]= " + results[i] +
"<br>");
104:                  }
105:              } catch(Exception e) {
106:                  System.out.println("Exception: " + e.toString());
107:              }
108:
```

Lines 109–111 demonstrate how the `PortletRequestDispatcher` interface is used to delegate Web content to the components that handle and render it. The path defined as a string on line 110 must be relative to the context root to propagate properly:

```
109:                  PortletContext context = getPortletContext();
110:                  PortletRequestDispatcher rd =
context.getRequestDispatcher("/WEB-INF/templates/html/JMXExample.jsp");
111:                  rd.include(request, response);
112:          }
113:      }
114:
115:      public void doEdit(RenderRequest request, RenderResponse response)
116:          throws PortletException, IOException {}
117:
118:      public void doHelp(RenderRequest request, RenderResponse response)
119:          throws PortletException, IOException {}
120:
121: }
122:
```

This program performs the same functionality as the Struts admin console shown in Figure 11.14, where user name, password, and full name inputs are submitted by the console user to add users to the back-end database. Once a unique user name has been submitted in the Tomcat admin console, the Web page will render that data back to the display so that users will know that a successful submission has been made.

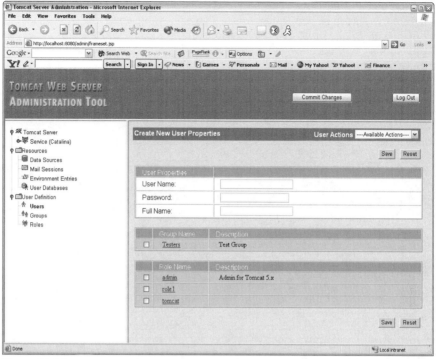

Figure 11.14

To set up new data sources using JMX MBeans, you can implement the JMX portlet shown in the following example. This portlet implements JSR 168 libraries for portlet visualization:

```
01: import java.io.IOException;
02: import java.io.Writer;
03: import java.net.*;
04: import javax.portlet.*;
05: import javax.management.*;
06: import javax.servlet.*;
07: import org.apache.commons.modeler.Registry;
08:
09: public class JMXPortlet2 extends GenericPortlet {
10:
11:     public JMXPortlet2() {}
12:
13:     public void init(PortletConfig config)
14:         throws PortletException {
15:         super.init(config);
16:     }
17:
```

Prior to adding a new data source to the back-end persistence mechanism, an `MBeanServer` instance must be created, as shown on line 31. Once the action of creating a new data source has been executed properly in lines 46–86, the newly created data source can be exercised by other portlet users to perform database operations. Improper entries will trigger error messages to alert the portal user that improper parameter values were submitted in the portlet application:

```
18:     public void doView(RenderRequest request, RenderResponse response)
19:         throws PortletException, IOException, UnavailableException {
20:
21:         String groups[] = null;
22:         ObjectName oname = null;
23:         String objectName = null;
24:
25:         WindowState state = request.getWindowState();
26:         WindowState _tmp = state;
27:         if(state == WindowState.NORMAL) {
28:
29:             Writer writer = response.getWriter();
30:
31:             MBeanServer mserver = Registry.getRegistry().getMBeanServer();
32:             if(mserver == null) {
33:                 throw new UnavailableException("MBeanServer is not available");
34:             } else {
35:
36:                 String objectName = "";
37:                 String signature[] = { "java.lang.String", "java.lang.String" };
38:                 Object params[] = { "testMySQL", "javax.sql.DataSource" };
39:
40:                 String resourcetype = "Global";
41:                 String path = "";
42:                 String host = "";
43:                 String domain = "Catalina";
44:                 ObjectName oname = null;
45:
46:                 try {
47:                     oname = new ObjectName(domain +
48:                                     ":type=Resource" +
49:                                     ",resourcetype=Global" +
50:                                     ",class=" +
51:                                     params[1] +
52:                                     ",name=" + params[0]);
53:
54:                     if(mserver.isRegistered(oname)) {
55:                         System.out.println("Invalid name...");
56:                     }
57:                     oname = ResourceUtils.getNamingResourceObjectName(domain,
resourcetype, path, host);
58:                     objectName = (String)mserver.invoke(oname, "addResource",
params, signature);
59:                 } catch(Exception e) {
60:                     System.out.println("Exception: " + e);
61:                 }
62:
```

```
63:                    // set up attributes
64:                    String attribute = null;
65:                    try {
66:                        oname = new ObjectName(objectName);
67:                        attribute="url";
68:                        mserver.setAttribute(oname, new
Attribute(attribute,"jdbc:mysql://localhost/mysqlDB"));
69:                        attribute="driverClassName";
70:                        mserver.setAttribute(oname, new
Attribute(attribute,"org.gjt.mm.mysql.Driver"));
71:                        attribute="username";
72:                        mserver.setAttribute(oname, new
Attribute(attribute,"dbUser"));
73:                        attribute="password";
74:                        mserver.setAttribute(oname, new
Attribute(attribute,"dbUser"));
75:                        attribute="maxActive";
76:                        mserver.setAttribute(oname, new Attribute(attribute,"4"));
77:                        attribute="maxIdle";
78:                        mserver.setAttribute(oname, new Attribute(attribute,"2"));
79:                        attribute="maxWait";
80:                        mserver.setAttribute(oname, new Attribute(attribute,"5000")); /
81:
82:                    } catch(Exception e) {
83:                        System.out.println("Exception: " + e);
84:                    }
85:
86:                    writer.write("Added datasource: mysqlDB<br>");
```

Lines 87–89 demonstrate how the `PortletRequestDispatcher` interface is used to delegate Web content to the components that handle and render it. The path defined as a string on line 88 must be relative to the context root to propagate properly:

```
87:                    PortletContext context = getPortletContext();
88:                    PortletRequestDispatcher rd = context.getRequestDispatcher("/WEB-
INF/templates/html/JMXExample.jsp");
89:                    rd.include(request, response);
90:        }
91:    }
92:
93:    public void doEdit(RenderRequest request, RenderResponse response)
94:        throws PortletException, IOException {}
95:
96:    public void doHelp(RenderRequest request, RenderResponse response)
97:        throws PortletException, IOException {}
98:
99: }
100:
```

The console shown in Figure 11.15 displays the results of running the code in the preceding listing. All of the properties that were initialized in this code are shown in the data source display so that they can be configured dynamically by the user.

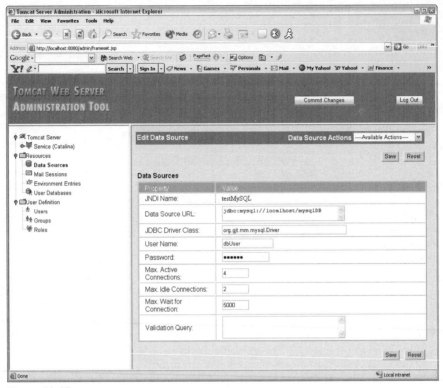

Figure 11.15

Prior to the introduction of JMX libraries in application servers, many of these applications provided proprietary interfaces for adding and modifying components on them. The problem with these products was that their implementations tied you to their system. Your individual applications, which acted inside their frameworks, often became coupled with their server components, which made modifications expensive and difficult to rectify. Thankfully, the industry trend for these application servers was the migration to JMX components to manage your resources with standards-based tools and the Java programming language. Development and implementation of MBeans on your portal systems greatly enhances your system's portability so that your components can easily plug into any JMX-compliant server.

Portal Collaboration with JSPWiki

Up till now, this chapter has focused on open-source tools that you might consider to perform testing and monitoring activities on your portal implementation. Portal process methodologies and tools, however, warrant further discussion about how all of these technologies can be brought together in a collaborative fashion to ensure the success of your project. Therefore, this chapter finishes with a brief overview of an open-source tool called JSPWiki (www.jspwiki.org/Wiki.jsp).

On most portal initiatives, cross-project communication needs to be managed to capture and promote requirements adherence as well as development knowledge among the disparate portlet development teams. Often, this development knowledge includes how and where things were installed, what applications and libraries are being implemented, and what pitfalls were discovered and should be avoided by the development teams. This knowledge can also be used by the testing team personnel to craft and target suitable test plans. To perform these operations, a collaboration server needs to be integrated into your development plans. This chapter briefly discusses a new open-source tool call JSPWiki that was derived from the more mature PERL-based Wiki tool to perform these actions for you.

Ideally, you want a collaboration server to provide a comprehensive solution for document and task management, and a calendar to create events and member tasking. JSPWiki can't currently provide you with all of these capabilities, because of its relative newness, but it will enable you to capture and openly exchange knowledge on your portal program in an unfettered fashion.

JSPWiki is written with Java Server Pages (JSPs), runs in a Web container, and implements a simple text syntax to craft Web pages and cross links between pages. Plug-ins can be implemented to enhance its functionality. Additionally, links can be included to add behavior and enhance the user experience.

Figure 11.16 shows a JSPWiki display that has implemented a template plug-in to override the default presentation. Several different template facades can be added to the /templates directory of your JSPWiki installation. To enable these templates, the **template** key in the **jspwiki.properties** file must be modified from the **default** value to the template façade that is desired. In Figure 11.16, the **mrg** template is used. The JSPWiki page in Figure 11.16 might be used to encourage its viewers to freely contribute suggestions and comments on the technologies that are described on the web page. Additionally, documents can be uploaded for knowledge transfer and a simple search query can be invoked to track down artifacts.

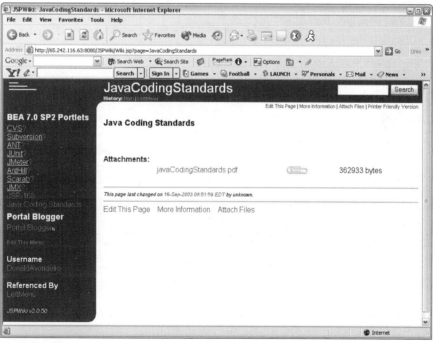

Figure 11.16

In the display, all of the technologies that are demonstrated in this chapter are hyperlinked so that users can freely add or read text annotations about them. The question mark (?) next to some of the links indicates that the topic is new and has not had any user input added to it. The Portal Blogger link enables users to navigate to an external blogger application.

Summary

Phew! That was a lot of material to cover in one chapter. Please remember that this chapter addressed only a few applications that can be used to test, administer, and monitor your portal development operations. Numerous open-source tools are available to perform these same tasks, so it is important to acquaint yourself with these tools in the open-source community and their applicability to your testing, monitoring, and administration needs. Feedback systems are paramount when implementing a portal application — to ensure that good communication channels allow the flow of ideas and development best practices to propagate through a program so that successful implementations can be realized.

To optimize complex systems like portals, consideration should always be given to relevant system processes that automate user code distribution and management, testing, bug-tracking and network component management. The tools we have examined in this chapter illustrate an assortment of approaches that can be used to implement practical testing and oversight processes so that your portal implementation can be successful. Getting things right in your portal system through the enactment of these tools is a prudent thing to do and will improve your operations in the long run.

12

Unifying the Enterprise Application Space Through Web Start

Web browsers have become the standard interface for displaying and using data on the Internet. Its inherent functional limitations, however, may not make it fully suitable for certain applications. With rapid developments in technology, increasingly complex applications will be in demand. While popular portal applications may best be displayed in a browser, some general and niche portals may require a richer client interface — one that will serve in a manner that Web browsers cannot. Just as the current portal framework was a generational leap from the older, individual static Web page, a newer generation of portal applications is being built using *rich clients*, which function in a way that the standard Web browser simply cannot. These rich clients may offer asynchronous processing, complex event handling, or more stylistic Graphical User Interface (GUI) components. They are able to offer the user more functionality and a flexible application that is tailored to their needs.

Users typically are able to find these features in their favorite desktop word processing, graphics, or presentation applications. They like the rich behavior and the fact that it resides on their own computer, so they can work offline, anywhere and anytime. There are some problems with these rich, "thick" clients, however, insofar as they are used as part of an enterprise application solution. Issues may arise when it comes to installing the application on hundreds, maybe thousands, of computers. It may be even more difficult to obtain new versions of the application or simple updates for a bug fix.

One innovative product that is trying to bridge the gap between the benefits of a rich client and the disadvantages of its pitfalls is Sun's **Java Web Start**. Java Web Start is based on the **Java Network Launch Protocol (JNLP)** and the Java 2 platform. JNLP is tabbed as a deployment solution that provides Java developers with the capability to deploy and maintain rich, thick Java clients that can be stored and executed locally on a user's desktop. It has even become a standard component of the Java 2 Standard Edition (J2SE) platform (as of Java version 1.4). The prospects of what Java Web Start can offer are very enticing for both Java developers and portal application builders alike.

This chapter discusses various aspects of Java Web Start, including its installation, configuration, packaging, and invocation. It also describes JNLP and how Java Web Start utilizes it, as well as the security aspects of building a Java application that is distributed through Java Web Start. The chapter concludes with a sample application that shows how to put all of the pieces together. This chapter does not, however, provide in-depth details about writing Java applications, as the focus is on how Java Web Start can be used to deploy virtually any type of Java application as part of an enterprise solution. The challenge of building the appropriate client application for a given scenario is left up to you, the Java Web Start application developer.

Rich Clients

Users are enthralled with what the Web technology wave has brought them. Using a Web browser to surf the net in order to find virtually any piece of information on any topic is very appealing. However, users are not likely to forego their favorite desktop applications, such as Microsoft Word, Microsoft PowerPoint, or Adobe Acrobat, for some webified version that tries to serve the same purpose. The reason is that a browser-based application has limits as to how functional, interactive, or complex it can be. Typical desktop applications written in languages such a C, C++, Java, and Visual Basic are greatly superior in what they can offer to the user experience. These types of applications can be very complex as far as capabilities are concerned, while at the same time be very easy to use for the typical person. Using these richer types of clients in an enterprise application can offer both the user and the developer many opportunities for accomplishing the task at hand.

As mentioned earlier, one of the problems with the use of these rich clients is that they can sometimes be complicated to install, and possibly even harder to upgrade. Moreover, a company may have hundreds or even thousands of desktop computers on which these clients are intended to be run. It may be very difficult to ensure that each computer is able to obtain the current version of your application. This is typically a logistics issue, as the target computers may be spread throughout a country or even over multiple continents. The personnel performing installations may be overwhelmed. The task of application distribution, installation, and maintenance can be a daunting one. Not everyone may get the bug fix or upgraded version in a timely fashion. These types of problems have led many companies to view the Web-based application boom as a panacea because of its simplicity and cost-effective deployment and maintenance. It is very easy to deploy a Web server and develop a Web-based application for use in a Web browser. A company's employees or customers could all come to the same place to obtain the application as well as receive upgrades or enhancements dynamically. The problem again, however, is that by going to these **thin** clients, users relinquish some functionality for ease of development, distribution, and maintenance. Traditionally, the richer, thick clients were more functional, but harder to deploy and maintain.

What was needed was something to bridge the gap between the ease of Web-based deployment and the functionality of a rich client. Delivering an interface that was richer than simple HTML but still inside the Web application framework became an attractive goal to pursue for both developers and implementers. Building a Java-based client application in such an architecture was an effort that had its problems. Early attempts at accomplishing this task led to the introduction of the **applet**. A Java applet, as you probably know, was an attempt to run a Java application from the user's Web browser. For a while, this approach was fairly popular because it delivered a rich Java application front-end to the user via a Web browser.

It soon became apparent, however, that running an applet introduced its own set of problems. Differences in various browsers' Java Runtime Environment (JRE), as well as long download times, proved to be problematic for developers. Although the Java language was quickly making advances and

Java Swing was becoming popular for use in Java GUIs, the Web browsers were not as fast at incorporating these enhancements into their JREs. Greater strides had been achieved in the Java platform for developing richer application interfaces, but the problem of effectively deploying and maintaining a rich application on the client remained. A promising solution to this problem has started to unfold in the form of the JNLP technology and Java Web Start.

Java Web Start

Java Web Start is Sun's Reference Implementation (RI) of JNLP and is essentially a wrapper for easily deploying a Java application and its rich GUI. Virtually any Java application can be used in this framework. Because the Java application will ultimately reside on the client machine, its speed and response time are not necessarily dependent on the network. This enables a user to employ it in an offline mode, which is something that a browser-based application typically cannot do. This may not always be the case, however, if the application is used as part of an enterprise portal solution that requires access to remote data sources. In any case, a Java application can take advantage of the many aspects of the Java 2 platform, which offers far greater capabilities than a standard browser-based application. The promise of JNLP and Java Web Start is to combine the flexibility, functionality, and power of rich Java application clients with the ease of deploying and maintaining the Web-based architecture.

Once a client machine has Java Web Start installed (described shortly in the section "Downloading and Installing Java Web Start"), it is ready to download and deploy a Java application, which sits inside a Web server's Web space and has been added to a JNLP framework. In its simplest form, the client clicks an HTML link that references a JNLP file. The JNLP would then upload the Java application to the client machine. Once the application resides on the client machine, it can be launched from either the computer's Start Menu (under Windows), a desktop icon, or via the browser link again. Although a Web browser is required to obtain the initial installation of the application, a browser is not needed for the application's continued use. This can be an appealing feature, as the Java application can be associated with the user's desktop just like any other application. The initial download of the application can be time-consuming because the entire application code must be uploaded to the client, but subsequent application invocations will be very quick because the application is running locally on the client. This initial time lag to launch the application may be unappealing to browser users, but the benefits that the user will obtain from subsequent application startups will far outweigh that initial delay. Each time the application is launched on the client, a check determines whether the local version is the most current. If a newer version is detected on the server, the new update is automatically uploaded to the client. This capability enables users to maintain the most recent version of an application or receive bug fixes without having to do anything but launch the application. This auto-check is done whether the user starts the application from the browser or a desktop icon. Figure 12.1 shows a graphical representation of the Java Web Start workflow. This graphic was taken from the Java Web Start architecture document, which can be found at http://java.sun.com/products/javawebstart/architecture.html.

Although the Java application is initially launched, and subsequently downloaded, from a Web browser, it will run in the client's installed Java 2 JRE, rather than the Web browser's JRE. This means that the application will run in a dedicated Java environment and not be dependent on the browser to provide the necessary framework. This alleviates the aforementioned problem of browser incompatibilities when running Java applets. Because applets seemingly no longer play as large a role in deploying client Java applications as was once envisioned, the JNLP framework, along with Java Web Start, is ready to take over the role of distributing these rich clients as single applications or full-fledged intranet enterprise application solutions.

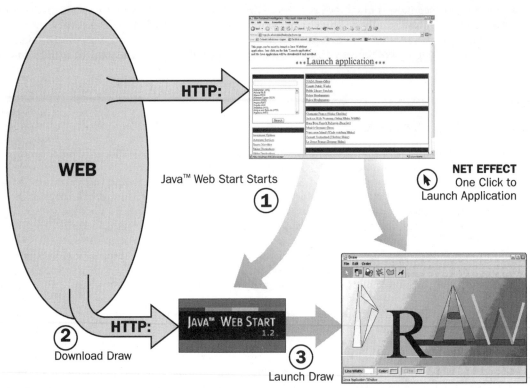

Figure 12.1

Java Web Start offers many capabilities that were previously lacking in other attempts to distribute rich Java applications. Automatic downloads and updates along with quick application startup (after the initial loading) are appealing features for both developers and users. As mentioned earlier, a Java application loaded on the client machine via Java Web Start also has the look and feel of other desktop applications because it can be started from the Start Menu or a desktop icon. This is an appealing feature for users who like standard desktop application loading. The locally stored applications are also very secure. Although they are stored on the client's machine, the application still adheres to the same applet-like security sandbox architecture. Security restrictions forbid an application from performing such functions as accessing the local hard drive or obtaining resources from other hosts, and the application has limited access to the client's system properties. Just like applets, however, a Java application loaded from Java Web Start can be signed, and the user can grant certain privileges that will allow it to go outside the security sandbox. Signing application code to perform such operations is discussed in the section "Code Signing," later in this chapter.

As you can imagine, the possibilities for creating and running complex, innovative, and user-friendly Java applications on a client machine with JNLP and Java Web Start are virtually limitless. It can be as simple as a single application or as complex as an entire enterprise application portal. The direction and vision are up to the developer. As far as deploying portal solutions goes, there are a couple of different scenarios in which a developer can use Java Web Start as a deployment mechanism. As mentioned earlier, the vast majority of portals used today are Web-based portals that use HTML clients. The complexities and logic of running these portals is concentrated on the server, where, for example, Java applications are being employed. The client is still a thin application of very little functionality (in and of itself). The addition of

JavaScript code can make an HTML Web page more interactive and flexible, but there are still limits as to what can be done. With Java Web Start, an entire Java application with great flexibility can now be run locally. This application itself could represent the entire application portal. When a user performs some action on the Java application interface, the entire GUI does not have to be redrawn, as in the case of a Web-based portal. The Java 2 platform offers great functionality in dynamically updating only specific components of the user interface, without affecting other components. Essentially, an enterprise application portal built on top of the Java 2 platform can be the launching point for many other subapplications (also known as **portlets**). The developer can achieve a similar framework while still maintaining a typical Web-based HTML portal architecture. In this case, the portal may contain several portlets that, when activated, use JNLP and Java Web Start to launch Java applications stored locally on the client machine. This enables a generic portal framework to contain complex portlet applications. Having Java applications on the client enables the continued progression of portal framework architectures.

Getting Started

Setting up and using Java Web Start to launch a Java application is a relatively simple process. Several steps need to be taken in order to accomplish this, but you should not run into any problems. The following subsections provide the details for building and deploying Java applications through JNLP using Java Web Start from a developer's perspective. These topics include downloading and installing Java Web Start, how JNLP is used, what is needed to package an application, how to sign application code, and how to link an HTML page to the JNLP file.

Downloading and Installing Java Web Start

It was mentioned in the introduction that Java Web Start is now integrated in the J2SE platform. Once the J2SE is installed on the computer, no other action is needed in order to make Java Web Start available for use. If a previously installed JRE did not include Java Web Start, a small update package can be downloaded. If no JRE has previously been installed on the client machine, another, albeit much larger, download file can be obtained. In either case, an executable file will be downloaded. After the download is complete, simply double-click on the file and follow the installation wizard. Once the installation is complete, you are ready to begin the process of deploying a Java application using Java Web Start. All of the downloads, from the J2SE to the individual Java Web Start packages, can be downloaded by going to Sun's Java Web Start Web site, which is located at http://java.sun.com/products/javawebstart/download.html.

Configuring the Web Server

Java Web Start utilizes the existing Web technology architecture in order to deploy applications and perform auto-update functions. It uses the Hypertext Transfer Protocol (HTTP) and Web servers to accomplish this. In order for Java Web Start to behave properly, however, the JNLP that is used to actually launch the application must be registered in the Web server as a new Multipurpose Internet Mail Extension (MIME) type. The MIME type lets the Web server know what application to launch when it receives a request for such a file type. This action is similar to how other desktop applications are launched — for example, when a file with the extension .doc is requested and Microsoft Word is automatically launched. The new MIME type that must be configured is `application/x-java-jnlp-file`.

Different Web servers have different methods for configuring their MIME types. Simply check the documentation for the Web server to see which file and format you must use. Some Web servers may already have the MIME type configured in their default settings. If you are using Apache Tomcat 4.0.x or later, for example, simply check the `web.xml` file located in the `conf` directory. It should already be configured to handle the JNLP extension. How the JNLP is used and configured is discussed in the next section.

Under the various MIME type mappings, the following entry should be listed:

```
<mime-mapping>
    <extension>jnlp</extension>
    <mime-type>application/x-java-jnlp-file</mime-type>
</mime-mapping>
```

Once the Web server is configured to handle the JNLP extension, simply restart the server. Any request that wants to access a file with the extension .jnlp will now be properly handled.

Creating the JNLP File

Now that the Web server is configured to handle requests for JNLP files, it is time to create one. The JNLP file is a descriptor file for specifying what the application is composed of, where to find the necessary files, what icon to associate with the application, and so on. The format of the file is the Extensible Markup Language (XML). The contents of the file are described in the Java Network Launching Protocol and API specification, which can be found at http://java.sun.com/products/javawebstart/download-spec.html. JNLP is also described in the Java Web Start Developer's Guide. Probably the easiest way to create a JNLP file, however, is to obtain an existing one and simply modify it to suit your needs. Listing 12.1 shows an example of what a JNLP file might look like.

Listing 12.1: Sample JNLP File

```
01: <?xml version"1.0" encoding="UTF-8"?>
02: <jnlp
03:     spec="1.0+"
04:     codebase="http://server:port/web_server_location"
05:     href="myFile.jnlp">
06:   <information>
07:     <title>The title of the application</title>
08:     <vendor>Company name</vendor>
09:     <homepage href="homepage.html"/>
10:     <description>A full description of the application</description>
11:     <icon href="images/myicon.gif"/>
12:     <offline-allowed/>
13:   </information>
14:   <security>
15:     <all-permissions/>
16:   </security>
17:   <resources>
18:     <j2se version="1.3"/>
19:     <jar href="myjar.jar"/>
20:     <jar href="classes12_01.jar"/>
21:   </resources>
22:   <application-desc main-class="myPackage.MyClass"/>
23: </jnlp>
```

Several other tags and attributes can be used for other specialized needs. For example, Java Web Start can be used to launch Java applets by using the `applet-desc` element in the JNLP file. Consult the Java Web Start Developer's Guide for a full description of the available tags.

The first line in the preceding code simply states the XML version and encoding. This tag is optional but is almost always included in the file. The main tag in a JNLP file is the `<jnlp>` tag. This tag includes four main subelements: `<information>`, `<security>`, `<resources>`, and `<application-desc>`. It also contains several attributes. These attributes and subelements are described in greater detail in the following sections.

`<jnlp>` Attributes

Lines 3–5 list the attributes of the `<jnlp>` tag. The first one, `spec`, is used to denote the JNLP specification version. This attribute is optional and defaults to the value `1.0+`. The next attribute is `codebase`, which is used as the base location for locating a resource on the Web server listed in any `href` attribute. The last attribute listed, `href`, is used to denote the name of the JNLP file itself.

`<information>` Subelement

The `<information>` subelement listed in lines 6–13 is used to provide some general information about the application. The `<title>` tag is simply used to name the application. This title will appear on various Java Web Start interfaces to distinguish this application from other Java Web Start applications. The `<vendor>` tag is normally used to denote the vendor, or organization, that built the application. The third tag in the listing is the `<homepage>` tag, which contains only the single attribute `href`. The value of the attribute is a Uniform Resource Locator (URL) that points to a Web page which Java Web Start uses when the user wants to obtain more information about the application. As mentioned previously, the value of an `href` attribute is a relative location based on the value of the `codebase` attribute. The next tag, `<description>`, is used to apply a general statement about the application. The `<icon>` tag also takes a single `href` attribute and points to a GIF or JPEG image with which you want Java Web Start to identify the application. This icon is used for display on the client desktop as well as other Java Web Start modules. The last tag listed, `<offline-allowed>`, is used by Java Web Start to determine whether the application can be launched when the client machine is not connected to a network. The tag is also used to determine how Java Web Start will apply its auto-update functionality. By default, if this tag is not listed, the application is determined to be in an **online** mode. This means that the application cannot be launched if the client machine is not connected to a network.

`<security>` Subelement

As mentioned in the "Java Web Start" section, applications that are launched by Java Web Start adhere to the applet-like sandbox security architecture, which restricts the operations that an application can perform when it comes to such things as client system resources and hardware. The `<security>` tag can be used in the JNLP file to request permission to perform operations outside this sandbox. The `<all-permissions>` element tag is used when you want to gain full access to the client machine. When this is requested, the application code must be signed and the user will be asked if he or she wants to accept the signing certificate.

`<resources>` Subelement

The `<resources>` tag is used to specify the various resources that the application needs in order to run. This information is listed in lines 17–21. The first tag listed, `<j2se>`, is used to denote which version of the Java 2 platform the application will run in. The next two lines both list the `<jar>` tag. This tag, which takes the familiar `href` attribute, is used to tell Java Web Start where to find the Java class files that the application will use. In the preceding example, line 19 lists a JAR file that holds application code created by the developer, while line 20 lists the Oracle Java DataBase Connectivity (JDBC) driver classes. As you can see, multiple `<jar>` tags can be used inside of the `<resources>` tag. The preceding listing used only the `<j2se>` and `<jar>` tags, but other tags are available for use, including `nativelib`, `property`, `package`, and `extension`.

<application-desc> Subelement

The last subelement used in the `<jnlp>` tag is an element that lets Java Web Start know that it is launching a Java application, rather than a Java applet. The attribute `main-class` is used to denote the application class that contains the `main` method; it is used to start the application. If this class file is listed in the manifest file of the first JAR file listed, then this subelement does not have to be listed in the JNLP file.

As a side note, JNLP separately bundles an additional Application Programming Interface (API) in the `jnlp.jar` or `javaws.jar` file. This API provides additional application functionality that is not part of the J2SE API. This API describes services that enable the developer to further enhance the capabilities of a Java Web Start application. The services that are available through this API include `BasicService`, `ClipboardService`, `DownloadService`, `FileOpenService`, `FileSaveService`, `PrintService`, and `PersistenceService`. More information on how to use this API can be found in the Java Web Start Developer's Guide. In order to use this API, the appropriate JAR file must be added to your classpath for compiling purposes. Typically, the `javaws.jar` file can be found in the directory in which Java Web Start was installed.

Application Packaging

Although we have talked a lot about JNLP and how Java Web Start utilizes this protocol to deploy and maintain applications, the main part of a Java Web Start application is the application itself. In the section "Introductory Application," later in this chapter, you will examine some sample code for a small Java application as an introduction to using Java Web Start. For now, we will just assume that you have already developed a Java application that we can package accordingly.

Once the application code has been created and, we hope, tested, all that is left to do is to gather the code and package it in a JAR file, or files. The application JAR file(s), other application resource files, images, HTML files, and any other files that may be associated with the Java Web Start application must be installed under the Web server's Web space so that it is accessible to anyone with access to the network through a Web browser. The location of the files under the Web space must also be listed properly in the JNLP file so that a client that wants to access the Java Web Start application will not run into any deployment problems. Once the application has been packaged properly, it is ready to be accessed from another client machine.

Client Invocation

Now that the Java Web Start application is sitting on the server under the Web space waiting to be accessed by a client, you need to generate the client code that is needed to access the Java Web Start application. Earlier, we described how to configure the Web server such that if a request came in asking for access to a file with the extension of .jnlp, the Java Network Launch Protocol would be automatically activated. The JNLP file is then used to gather the application's resources and send them to the requesting client. In order for the client to trigger this sequence of events, a simple HTML link is the only thing needed. The syntax for this is as follows:

```
<a href="myFile.jnlp">Launch a Java Web Start Application</a>
```

The myFile.jnlp file should be found under the Web server's root document directory. This filename is the same file listed on line 5 in the first code listing presented earlier. When customers or users visit your Web page, they should be able to just click on the link to launch your Java Web Start application. However, what if the client machine that accesses your Web page does not have Java Web Start installed? If that is the case, they will not be able to launch the application. It would be nice if you could first detect whether Java Web Start were installed on the machine. That way, you could either present them with the appropriate link to your application (if it is installed) or point the user to a site where they can first download and install Java Web Start. Luckily, this is possible with a little client-side scripting. Both Netscape and Internet Explorer (IE) have scripting languages that can be used in the browser to enable you to determine whether such a product is installed. Listing 12.2 shows an example of how this can be accomplished.

Listing 12.2: Java Web Start Client Detection

```
01: <html>
02:  <head>
03:   <script language="javascript">
04:    isIE = "true";
05:    installed = "false";
06:
07:    if (navigator.appName == "Netscape") { isIE = "false"; }
08:
09:    if (isIE == "false") {
10:      mime = navigator.mimeTypes['application/x-java-jnlp-file'];
11:      if (mime) { installed = true; }
12:    }
13:   </script>
14:   <script language="VBScript">
15:    If isIE = "true" Then
16:      If Not (IsObject(CreateObject("JavaWebStart.IsInstalled"))) Then
17:        installed = false
18:      Else
19:        installed = true
20:      End If
21:    End If
22:   </script>
23:   <script language="javascript">
24:    if (installed) {
25:      document.open();
26:      document.write("<a href='myFile.jnlp'>Launch Web Start App</a>");
27:      document.close();
28:    }else {
29:      document.open();
30:      document.write("Please Download Java Web Start From " +
31:        "<a href='http://java.sun.com/products/javawebstart/" +
32:        "download.html'>Here</a>.");
33:      document.close();
34:    }
35:   </script>
36:  </head>
37: </html>
```

The first `<script>` tag, listed in lines 3–13, uses JavaScript as the scripting language. This is primarily for the Netscape browsers. Typically, client-side scripting using JavaScript is fine in both Netscape and IE, but in this case we must use different scripting code for the IE browser. Inside the tag, notice that a couple of global variables are being instantiated. These are used to keep track of which browser the client is using and whether Java Web Start is installed on the machine. The script then continues to determine if the JNLP mime type is part of Netscape's array or mime types. Line 7 is where the script determines whether the client browser is Netscape. This is just one way of determining browser type. There are other ways to determine which browser version is being used. The preceding code was tested using Netscape 4.7.7 and IE 6.0. It is possible that other browser versions may not work with the code listed. For a production application, more testing would have to be completed to ensure that the code used would work with at least the most common browsers and browser versions.

The second `<script>` tag group, listed from lines 14–22, uses Microsoft's VBScript as the scripting language. This will be used by IE browsers and ignored by Netscape browsers. The VBScript makes a similar check to determine whether Java Web Start is installed. Notice that the variables `isIE` and `installed` were instantiated within the first block of code but used here, in the second block of code. This works fine, as the scope of the variables is available within in the wrapper `<script>` tag.

The last `<script>` group is used to bring everything together. The first two areas are used to determine the variables' values based on which browser is being used. Now that those have been determined, you can use JavaScript to make a conditional statement based on whether Java Web Start is installed on the client machine. If it is, then you can simply display the link to your application's JNLP file. If Java Web Start is not installed, then you can display a message indicating that, with a link that enables the user to download Java Web Start. This will help prevent users from trying to launch a Java Web Start application when they do not have the proper component installed on their machine. Regardless of whether Java Web Start was installed, the code only displays a link on the resulting Web page. Typically, the resulting page would include more than just the link. For the sake of brevity, however, only the appropriate link is displayed.

Code Signing

It was mentioned earlier that Java Web Start applications, although running on the client machine, adhere to a restricted security sandbox architecture. This protects users from applications that can perform operations that may be harmful to the user's system. A developer, however, may need to gain access to certain resources, or perform operations that are outside the sandbox in order for the application to execute as intended. In order to accomplish this, the developer must perform a couple of operations. The first is to provide the appropriate tags in the application's JNLP file. To request full access to a client's machine, the JNLP file must contain the following code:

```
<security>
  <all-permissions/>
</security>
```

This was also listed on lines 14–16 of the first code listing, which described the contents of the JNLP file. The second step is to sign the application code. Code signing is an important security feature for both the user and the vendor of the application. For users, it means that they can first see who has signed the application, in order to determine if it is a trusted source. If a user does not know the signer, he or she can simply elect not to launch the application. For the vendor, it ensures that a third party has not tampered with the application code. If Java Web Start determines that the signed code has been altered in any way, it will not launch the application. Java Web Start applications can be signed in the same fashion as Java applets. This is done through the J2SE's **keytool** and **jarsigner**. Several steps are involved when signing your application code. These steps are outlined as follows:

1.   Create a JAR file for the application code. This can be done with the following statement:

```
jar cf myApplication.jar myApplication.class
```

2.   Create a new key in the keystore. When you run this procedure, you will be prompted for a password as well as some identification information, such as name, organization, and location. To create a new key, you run the following statement:

```
keytool -genkey -keystore testKeystore -alias testAlias
```

3.   Create a self-signed certificate. In order to sign the application code, it is necessary to have a certificate that is used to identify a trusted authority. The J2SE keytool provides a mechanism for creating a self-signed certificate, but this typically is used only for test purposes, as it does not guarantee anything about the identity of the signer. Generally, when an application that requires signed code goes into production, a trusted certificate from a **certificate authority** is used. An example of a popular certificate authority is Verisign. The following statement can be used to create a self-signed certificate that will be used when signing the application JAR file:

```
keytool -selfcert -alias testAlias -keystore testKeystore
```

4.   Ensure that everything went okay up to this point by listing the contents of the keystore. This can be accomplished with the following statement:

```
keytool -list -keystore testKeystore
```

After providing a password, the contents of the keystore will be displayed. If all went well, the contents should look something like the following:

```
Keystore type: jks
Keystore provider: SUN
Your keystore contains 1 entry:
testalias, Mar 12, 2003, keyEntry,
Certificate fingerprint (MD5):
E2:AB:2A:0C:DB:51:B3:8A:32:40:53:A6:1D:A2:B7:31
```

5.   Sign the application's JAR file by running the following command:

```
jarsigner -keystore testKeystore myApplication.jar testAlias
```

If more than one JAR file is used by the application, you must repeat the last step for each additional file. Note a couple of important points to understand about certificates and signing application code. First, the certificates usually are valid only for a given period of time. This means that when a certificate expires, another one must be generated in order to maintain a properly signed application. Second, remember that after any application modifications, the application code must be re-compiled, re-jarred, and re-signed. Otherwise, the changes made to the application will not be updated on the client machines. When a user launches the application on the client machine, Java Web Start performs its auto-update procedures by checking whether the application's JAR file(s) have changed. If the code (that is, the Java class files) has changed but has not been re-jarred, Java Web Start will not recognize that an update to the application has been made.

Introductory Application

Now that we have discussed the procedures for setting up the framework for creating and deploying a Java application using Java Web Start, let's create a small application and use the procedural steps to deploy it. This will give you the opportunity to see what exactly Java Web Start does, and displays, when a user wants to launch a Java application. Our little example application simply asks the user to try to guess a number between 1 and 100. If the user makes the correct guess, a congratulatory message is provided. If the guess is incorrect, a message will appear, indicating that the guess was either too high or too low. For our example, we will assume two things have already taken place. One, we will assume that Java Web Start has been downloaded and installed on the development machine; and two, we will assume that the Web server has already been configured for the JNLP mime type. The first thing we will do is create the Java application code for our little application game. The following code provides the source code for this application:

```java
import java.util.*;
import java.io.*;
import java.awt.*;
import java.awt.event.*;
public class GuessGame extends Frame implements ActionListener {
    Button    btn_restart;
    Button    btn_guess;
    Button    btn_close;
    TextField tf_guess;
    Label     lbl_result;
    int       the_number;
    public static void main(String args[]) {
        new GuessGame("Guess Game");
    }
    public GuessGame(String s) {
        super(s);
        btn_restart = new Button("Restart");
        btn_guess = new Button("Guess");
        btn_close = new Button("Quit");
        btn_restart.addActionListener(this);
        btn_guess.addActionListener(this);
        btn_close.addActionListener(this);
        lbl_result = new Label("Enter a number from 1 - 100");
        tf_guess = new TextField(3);
        Panel main = new Panel();
        main.setLayout(new GridLayout(3,1));
        Panel p1 = new Panel();
        Panel p2 = new Panel();
        Panel p3 = new Panel();
        main.add(p1);
        main.add(p2);
        main.add(p3);
        add(main);
        p1.add(lbl_result);
        p2.add(tf_guess);
        p3.add(btn_guess);
        p3.add(btn_restart);
        p3.add(btn_close);
        chooseNewNumber();
```

```
        setSize(400,200);
        show();
}
```

The first part of the class defines Java AWT objects that will be used as part of the GUI. The GuessGame method is then used to instantiate the GUI objects, create the layout, and display the GUI to the user:

```
public void chooseNewNumber() {
    the_number = (int)(Math.random() * 100);
    if (the_number == 0) { chooseNewNumber(); }
}
public void actionPerformed(ActionEvent e) {
    if (e.getActionCommand().equals("Quit")) {
        System.exit(0);
    }else if (e.getActionCommand().equals("Restart")) {
        chooseNewNumber();
        lbl_result.setText("Enter a number from 1 - 100");
        tf_guess.setText("");
        tf_guess.requestFocus();
    }else if (e.getActionCommand().equals("Guess")) {
        int response = Integer.parseInt(tf_guess.getText());
        if (response == the_number) {
            lbl_result.setText("Congratulations! You're Right.");
        }else if (response < the_number) {
            lbl_result.setText("Your guess was too low.");
        }else {
            lbl_result.setText("Your guess was too high.");
        }
    }
}
}
```

Now that we have created our application code, compiled it, and tested it, we are ready to move on to the next process, which is to create the JNLP file that will be used by Java Web Start. The first code listing showed what a sample JNLP file might look like, and described each component. The JNLP file that we will create for our test application is slightly different, as it does not require all the items depicted in the first code listing. The following code shows what the JNLP file for our Guess Game application looks like:

```
<?xml version"1.0" encoding="UTF-8"?>
<jnlp
    spec="1.0+"
    codebase="http://localhost:8090/javawsGame"
    href="guessGame.jnlp">
    <information>
        <title>Guess Game 1.0</title>
        <vendor>Acme Game Builders</vendor>
        <homepage href="help.html"/>
        <description>A guessing game of random numbers.</description>
        <icon href="game.gif"/>
        <offline-allowed/>
    </information>
    <resources>
```

```
        <j2se version="1.4"/>
        <jar href="game.jar"/>
    </resources>
    <application-desc main-class="GuessGame"/>
</jnlp>
```

Notice that one key item has been left out of our JNLP file: the `<security>` section is not listed. This is because our application does not require any special privileges that are outside the security sandbox. In addition, only a single JAR file is listed in the `<resources>` section because our application does not require any other resources to run. The `game.jar` file simply contains our one class, `GuessGame.class`. Everything is set. Now all we need is an interested user who would like to launch our little game application. Assuming that the client machine has Java Web Start installed, when the user visits our Web page and clicks the link that points to the application's JNLP file, Java Web Start should activate and download the application to the client. Figure 12.2 shows what the user would see.

Figure 12.2

Figure 12.3 shows what our `Guess Game` application looks like on the client machine.

Figure 12.3

That is all there is to it. Our Java Web Start application now resides on another machine. When the user wants to play the game at some other time, he or she has two options for launching it again. Users can revisit the Web page that contained the link to the JNLP file and launch it via the URL link, or they can double-click on the Java Web Start icon that is located on their desktop. In either case, if the application code has not been changed, Java Web Start will not download the application again but simply launch the locally stored copy. If users decide to launch the application from the desktop icon, they will be presented with the Java Web Start Application Manager, shown in Figure 12.4.

Figure 12.4

As you can see, the Application Manager console displays some of the information listed in the JNLP file. That is why it is important to be as descriptive and unambiguous as possible when generating your application's JNLP file. You should also notice the image icon displayed along with the application's title in the upper-left corner. This is the `game.gif` image, which we declared in the JNLP file. Under the View menu option of the Application Manager are three application groupings: **Remote Applications**, **Downloaded Applications**, and **Favorite Applications**. When Java Web Start downloads an application, it adds it to its Downloaded Applications grouping. It was mentioned earlier that it would be possible for a user to launch a Java Web Start application from several areas. Two of those mentioned were the Start Menu and from a desktop icon. After an application is initially downloaded, it can only be launched via the browser or from the Java Web Start Application Manager. Once a user has launched the application a second time, Java Web Start displays a message, asking such users whether they want to create shortcuts for those areas. Figure 12.5 displays this message.

Figure 12.5

Our little application could be downloaded and run on the client machine without having the code signed because no special access privileges were requested. In order to see the effect of how Java Web Start handles applications that have been signed, we will pretend that our application requires special privileges for accessing the client machine. This requires that the application code be signed with **jarsigner**. Earlier, you learned the procedures for generating a new self-signed certificate and how to use that certificate to sign your application JAR file. If we simply took our existing JAR file and followed the procedures for signing the code in the JAR file, however, Java Web Start would not recognize that anything had changed with our application. In order to make this happen, we must also make a change to our JNLP file. It was mentioned earlier that we did not include the `<security>` tag in our application's JNLP file. We must now add this in order to make our change complete. Lines 14–16 of the first code listing in the chapter show what the `<security>` tag should contain. Once we make that additional change, Java Web Start will detect a change in our application the next time the client tries to launch it. When the user does decide to re-launch our application, Java Web Start will display the screen shown in Figure 12.6.

Figure 12.6

The user can determine a few things from this screen. The first line indicates that the application is requesting full system access. It also lists the name of the signer. The name was entered when the key for the keystore was generated. Lastly, there is a warning to the user that Java Web Start was not able to verify the authenticity of the certificate used to sign the application code and, because of that, does not recommend that the user run the application. The last point is the reason why it is recommended that a self-signed certificate be used only for testing, and that a certificate from a trusted certificate authority be used when the application is put into production mode. Note also the Details button on the screen. If users would like more information about the certificate, they can click the Details button, and the screen in Figure 12.7 will be displayed.

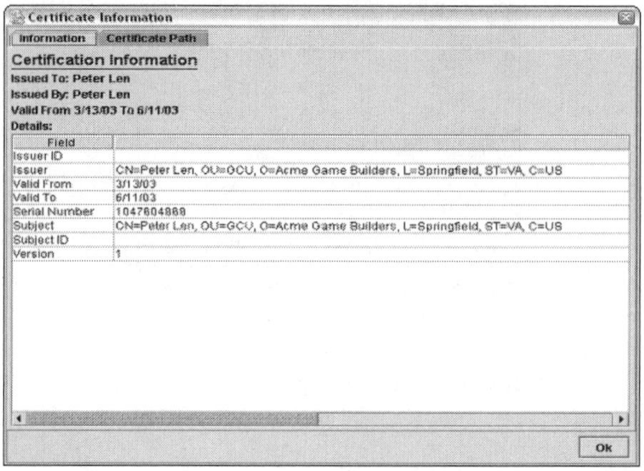

Figure 12.7

A few more details about the certificate can be obtained from this detail screen. Users can gain a little more information about the issuer as well as the dates for which the certificate is valid. After reviewing this information, users will be a little more informed before deciding whether they want to trust the signer enough to run the application. In our case, we know that our application code is not going to do anything malicious to the client machine. Java Web Start, however, does not know that. One of the strengths of using Java Web Start is its security mechanism. If someone creates an application requesting special privileges outside the security sandbox, for example, and adds the <security> tag but does not sign the application code, Java Web Start will not want to launch the application, and will display the screen shown in Figure 12.8 to the user.

Figure 12.8

Using Java Web Start can enable you to deliver a very rich client application written with the Java 2 framework to virtually any client machine that is connected to the Internet in a very efficient and secure manner. As you can see from the previous examples, it does not take much effort to install Java Web Start, develop a Java application, and make it accessible through a Web server. This capability greatly increases the options for the developer when putting together an architecture for a distributed enterprise application, especially when it comes to the new generation of portal applications. Our little Guess Game application is a simple stand-alone application, but it would be just as easy to produce a more sophisticated application that is either a portion (i.e., a portlet) of a Web-based portal or serves as a basis for an entire enterprise portal application itself. Now that you know how to use Java Web Start to deliver your Java 2 application, we will look at how this capability can be used in the larger context of portal development.

Using JWS in Portal Implementations

We have talked a lot about Java Web Start, but JWS is only the delivery mechanism for the real client in which we are interested. It is the Java 2 client application that Java Web Start downloads and updates that is the real key to how and why Java Web Start can be used as a new means for delivering an enterprise portal solution. It was mentioned earlier that Web-based portals cannot always fulfill the requirements of a client application. While Java may be used on the server via JSPs, JavaBeans, and servlets, the result is an HTML client application. There are limitations as to what can be done with an HTML page, even if it is dynamically generated. There may be circumstances in which only a portion of the page needs to be updated and a full form submission is unnecessary, or in which the layout and functionality of the client GUI is too complicated to be represented in an HTML page. The solution to these more sophisticated problems is a client that utilizes the Java 2 framework. Java offers more robust, functional, and rich client interfaces, and Java Web Start is the wrapper that can deliver them.

Current Web-based portals typically center on several key items, such as general search capabilities, news feeds, shopping, e-mail, and so on. Depending on how these various components are implemented, their levels of sophistication can vary. You may need, for example, to build a very sophisticated news channel that requires capabilities that an HTML page cannot deliver. Other times, it may be necessary to have a portlet (or portion thereof) that resides in a larger portal perform automatic checks on the server for an update without impacting anything else in the portal. The possibilities for an interface that requires a richer Java client are endless.

Two types of scenarios in which Java can be used in a portal framework are to use it as a portion of a standard Web-based portal or to use it for the entire portal itself. In the former case, it may have been necessary to use a Java application for its capability to meet a more complex requirement that was not needed for the other components of the portal. In this case, Java Web Start would be utilized to deliver the one component of the portal. As demonstrated earlier, this would require only that an HTML link to the application's JNLP file be listed in the portal. We will take a look at examples for both of these scenarios to give you a better idea of how each can be used.

Use in a Web-based Portal

Consider, for example, a portal that should implement a chat capability. Although the rest of the portal's components may work well using the Web-based HTTP architecture, the functionality needed for the chat mechanism requires a more sophisticated framework and interface. Figure 12.9 depicts a fictitious Web-based portal that has a Java-based chat component as part of one of the portal's portlets.

Figure 12.9

The content and role of the portal is not significant for our purposes. What is important is the one item in the portal that is used to launch our Java 2 chat application. Notice the link labeled Online Chat that is part of the Communication portlet located on the left side of the portal. When the mouse hovers over this link, the URL associated with it, http://localhost:8090/iportal/communication/chat/chat.jnlp, is displayed in the browser's status bar, which is located in the lower left-hand corner. This URL should now be familiar to you. When a user clicks this link, Java Web Start will launch and download a Java application to the client machine. If the user has already downloaded the application, clicking the link will simply launch the locally stored version. In this case, the portal needed a component that would enable a certain type of chat session(s) to be used. The interface needed to accomplish this is a bit more sophisticated than the HTML-rendered page can perform, so a Java application is used to build the user interface, and is integrated into the portal via a link to the application's JNLP file. Following is the code that accomplishes this:

```
. . . . . . .
<img src="write2.gif"> <br>
 <img src="<%=LINK1%>">
<a href="home.jsp?commo=written&link=1" style="text-decoration=none">
    Web Email
</a> <br>
 <img src="<%=LINK2%>">
<a href="http://localhost:8090/portal/communication/chat/chat.jnlp"
                                style="text-decoration=none">
Online Chat</a> <br>
. . . . . . .
```

The other link in this portion of the portlet, as well as all the other portal links, uses a call to a JSP page in order to accomplish its particular task. The link to the chat application, however, makes a call to a JNLP file. You have already seen the contents of a JNLP file, so we won't repeat that here. Refer to the first code listing of the chapter if you need to review the sample JNLP file presented earlier. When a user visits the portal and decides to take part in a chat session, the chat application will be launched by Java Web Start. Figure 12.10 displays what the user would then see.

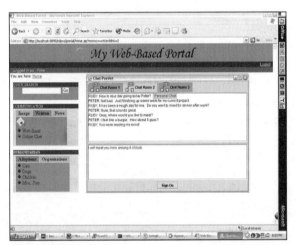

Figure 12.10

The chat application contains separate areas to maintain three different chat sessions at once. Each one could be independent of the other. As you can imagine, this functionality would be extremely difficult to produce in an HTML-based environment. A more logical choice for implementing this type of functional requirement is through a Java application, and Java Web Start is the ideal means to deliver it. While Figure 12.10 displays the application in the **content** pane of the portal, it really is a separate application running on the desktop and is not embedded in the portal itself. This enables users to continue using the portal's other components while maintaining their chat sessions. The code used to create the sample chat session is as follows:

```
import javax.swing.*;
import java.awt.*;
import java.awt.event.*;
public class ChatClient extends JPanel {
    public ChatClient() {
        ImageIcon icon = new ImageIcon("talk2.gif");
        JTabbedPane tabbedPane = new JTabbedPane();
        Component panel1 = makeSplitPane();
:        tabbedPane.addTab("Chat Room 1", icon, panel1, "Business Chat");
        tabbedPane.setSelectedIndex(0);
        Component panel2 = makeSplitPane();
        tabbedPane.addTab("Chat Room 2", icon, panel2, "Personal Chat");
        Component panel3 = makeSplitPane();
        tabbedPane.addTab("Chat Room 3", icon, panel3, "Hobbies Chat");
        //Add the tabbed pane to this panel.
        setLayout(new GridLayout(1, 1));
        add(tabbedPane);
    }
    protected Component makeSplitPane() {
        JTextArea    receive = new JTextArea("", 10, 30);
        JTextArea    send = new JTextArea("", 3, 30);
        JScrollPane  topScrollPane = new JScrollPane(receive);
        JScrollPane  bottomScrollPane = new JScrollPane(send);
        JSplitPane   splitPane = new JSplitPane(
                                 JSplitPane.VERTICAL_SPLIT,
                                 topScrollPane, bottomScrollPane);
        JButton btn = new JButton("Sign On");
        JPanel  btnPanel = new JPanel();
        btnPanel.add(btn);
        JPanel panel = new JPanel(new BorderLayout());
        panel.add("Center", splitPane);
        panel.add("South", btnPanel);
        return panel;
    }
    public static void main(String[] args) {
        JFrame frame = new JFrame("Chat Portlet");
        frame.addWindowListener(new WindowAdapter() {
            public void windowClosing(WindowEvent e) {System.exit(0);}
        });
        frame.getContentPane().add(new ChatClient(),
                                 BorderLayout.CENTER);
        frame.setSize(600, 400);
        frame.setVisible(true);
    }
}
```

As you can readily see from the preceding code, the "guts" for a real chat client are not listed. That would involve multiple Java files and more text than we have space for in this chapter. It does, however, show the basis for building a Java client that could house a chat mechanism. It also provides a sample scenario of what type of client component may require a Java interface and how it can be integrated into a general Web-based portal architecture. Another thing to keep in mind concerning the implementation of a Java application launched by Java Web Start as part of a Web-based portal is that it is generally launched via the link listed in the portlet. It was mentioned earlier that one of the benefits to running a Java application through Java Web Start is that it can be launched via other mechanisms, such as the Start Menu or a desktop icon. While this chat application can be launched through these other mechanisms as a stand-alone application, in order for it to be part of, and integrated within, the portal, it must be launched via the hyperlink in the portlet. This is neither a positive nor a negative aspect of the application or portal, but rather a consequence of being part of the portal as a whole.

Developing a Java client application can be more time-intensive and require a greater skill set than producing similar functionality through dynamically generated HTML pages. This may be necessary, though, to produce the functionality you need. Our example only required one portion of the portal to be run as a Java client application. What if several other components of the portal also required similarly sophisticated clients? At some point it may be better, or even necessary, to develop the entire portal itself as a Java application. Aside from having a richer portal client, having a Java-based portal also introduces the possibility of having individual portal components communicate with each other in a seamless manner that is not possible in an HTML-based portal. This type of functionality can provide the developer with many more options concerning the portal architecture.

Use in a Java Portal

Building a Java-based portal enables the developer to have complete control over how the portal acts and reacts to user interactions. Various types of functionality, such as drag and drop, just cannot be accomplished in Web-based portals. Using a Java client application as the portal interface allows for a much richer user experience and a more functional application. In general, a Java-based portal is simply a Java application. In order to make it accessible on the Internet, the application need only be Java Web Start–enabled, which means that it is packaged in the JNLP framework. Portals are all about obtaining, sharing, and transferring data from various data sources. The rich functionality of the Java language enables these types of processes to occur in a much smoother manner than in a typical Web-based portal. One of the big enhancements to the Java 2 environment was the introduction of Java Swing.

Java Swing

Swing was introduced as part of the Java Foundation Classes (JFC) and is a new GUI component kit that aids in the development of an application's visual components. These include such things as dialogs, window panes, menu bars, and so on. Besides Swing, the JFC also includes the Java 2D, drag and drop, and other Accessibility APIs. Swing and the JFC are an add-on to the standard Java Abstract Windowing Toolkit (AWT) packages. Swing is now a core part of the JDK 1.2 and sits atop and expands the AWT. There are many crossover classes between AWT and Swing components, such as the AWT `Frame` class and the Swing `JFrame` class, but the Swing components offer a much more powerful and elegant solution than their AWT counterpart. One of the key capabilities of the Swing toolkit is the Pluggable Look and Feel (PL&F). This feature enables developers to modify the appearance and behavior, or look and feel, of the windowing components they are developing. A second important feature of Swing is its Accessibility classes. This API introduces an important compatibility with software and hardware that is designed for people with special needs, such as those who have a sight impairment or cannot operate a mouse. The benefits that the Accessibility classes offer don't only benefit the disabled, however. Creating things such as touch-screen components are beneficial to everyone, and gives the developer additional options in developing an application. Figure 12.11 depicts where the Swing API fits into the JFC framework. This graphic is part of the document "Getting Started with Swing," which can be found at http://java.sun.com/products/jfc/tsc/articles/getting_started/index.html.

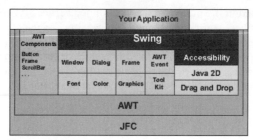

Figure 12.11

As you can imagine, using Swing components as part of a Java-based portal solution can add great flexibility and functionality not only to the portal framework itself but also to how individual components within the portal work, both as individual components and interconnected modules. There is no generic definition of how a portal is supposed to function or what types of capabilities it must have, so how a portal's user and functional requirements are converted into a Java 2 application (using the AWT or Swing) is up to the imagination and creative capabilities of the developer. Because of this, there is no way to describe or show how to build a Java-based portal, but only to show some examples of how components can be used within a portal framework or how other developers have used Java to build an existing portal or portal-like application. A couple of these examples are listed in the following section.

Java-based Portal Examples

A portal can look like many different things, depending on the goal and purpose of the portal. The main thing to determine is whether the functionality needed for the portal is better served by using a Web-based or Java-based front-end interface. We will assume here that a Java-based portal is needed due to the complexities that the interface must deliver. It was mentioned earlier that Java Swing offers a solid platform for building rich interfaces. Figure 12.12 depicts a Java-based portal that employs several different Java Swing components.

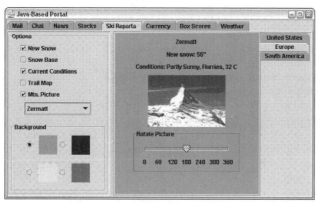

Figure 12.12

The example shows a number of features that Java Swing can offer, including a JTabbedPane, JSplitPane, JPanel, JSlider, JCheckbox, JComboBox, and JRadioButton. Notice that the tabs on the top of the application span the myriad of typical portal-type components. Unlike a Web-based portal, however, these different components could possibly be updated as the user is accessing a different part of the portal. It depends on how the application is developed, but Java offers this type of flexibility. The following example shows the code necessary to build this interface:

```java
import javax.swing.*;
import javax.swing.border.*;
import java.awt.*;
import java.awt.event.*;
public class JavaPortal extends JPanel {
    /*
     * Class constructor
     */
    public JavaPortal() {
        JTabbedPane tabbedPane = new JTabbedPane();
        tabbedPane.addTab("Mail", new JPanel());
        tabbedPane.addTab("Chat", new JPanel());
        tabbedPane.addTab("News", new JPanel());
        tabbedPane.addTab("Stocks", new JPanel());
        tabbedPane.addTab("Ski Reports", makeSkiPanel());
        tabbedPane.addTab("Currency", new JPanel());
        tabbedPane.addTab("Box Scores", new JPanel());
        tabbedPane.addTab("Weather", new JPanel());
        //Add the tabbed pane to this panel.
        setLayout(new GridLayout(1, 1));
        add(tabbedPane);
    }
```

The `JavaPortal` constructor is used to create the `Swing` objects that are added to the GUI layout. In this case, a variety of `Swing` panels are added as tabs to the `JTabbedPane`:

```java
    /*
     * makeSkiPanel - Creates the entire panel for a given tab.
     */
    protected Component makeSkiPanel() {
        JTabbedPane tabbedPane = new JTabbedPane();
        tabbedPane.addTab("United States", makeSkiDetail());
        tabbedPane.addTab("Europe", makeSkiDetail());
        tabbedPane.addTab("South America", makeSkiDetail());
        tabbedPane.setTabPlacement(JTabbedPane.RIGHT);
        JSplitPane    splitPane = new JSplitPane(JSplitPane.HORIZONTAL_SPLIT,
                                    makeSkiProps(), tabbedPane);
        return splitPane;
    }
    /*
     * makeSkiDetail - Creates the panel data for the right-side tabs.
     */
    protected JPanel makeSkiDetail() {
        JPanel skiDetail = new JPanel();
        skiDetail.setBackground(Color.green);
        JPanel inner = new JPanel();
        inner.setLayout(new BoxLayout(inner, BoxLayout.Y_AXIS));
        JLabel lbl1 = new JLabel("Zermatt");
```

```
    JPanel p1 = new JPanel();
    p1.add(lbl1);
    p1.setBackground(Color.green);
    inner.add(p1);
    lbl1 = new JLabel("New snow: 56\"");
    p1 = new JPanel();
    p1.add(lbl1);
    p1.setBackground(Color.green);
    inner.add(p1);
    lbl1 = new JLabel("Conditions: Partly Sunny, Flurries, 32 C");
    p1 = new JPanel();
    p1.add(lbl1);
    p1.setBackground(Color.green);
    inner.add(p1);
    lbl1 = new JLabel(new ImageIcon("ZERMATT.gif"));
    p1 = new JPanel();
    p1.add(lbl1);
    p1.setBackground(Color.green);
    inner.add(p1);
    JPanel p2 = new JPanel();
    p2.setBackground(Color.green);
    p2.setBorder(new TitledBorder(new EtchedBorder(), "Rotate Picture"));
    JSlider slide = new JSlider(JSlider.HORIZONTAL, 0, 360, 180);
    slide.setMajorTickSpacing(60);
    slide.setMinorTickSpacing(30);
    slide.setPaintTicks(true);
    slide.setPaintLabels(true);
    p1 = new JPanel();
    p1.add(slide);
    slide.setBackground(Color.green);
    p1.setBackground(Color.green);
    p2.add(p1);
    inner.add(p2);
    skiDetail.add(inner);
    inner.setBackground(Color.orange);
    return skiDetail;
}
/*
 * makeSkiProps - Creates the left portion of the JSPlitPane.
 */
protected Component makeSkiProps() {
  JPanel skiPanel = new JPanel();
  skiPanel.setLayout(new BoxLayout(skiPanel, BoxLayout.Y_AXIS));
  skiPanel.setBorder(new TitledBorder(new EtchedBorder(), "Options"));
  JPanel top = new JPanel();
  top.setLayout(new BoxLayout(top, BoxLayout.Y_AXIS));
  JPanel choices = new JPanel();
  choices.setLayout(new BoxLayout(choices, BoxLayout.Y_AXIS));
  choices.add(new JCheckBox("New Snow"));
  choices.add(new JCheckBox("Snow Base"));
  choices.add(new JCheckBox("Current Conditions"));
  choices.add(new JCheckBox("Trail Map"));
  choices.add(new JCheckBox("Mtn. Picture"));
  top.add(choices);
  String[]    data = {"Jackson Hole", "Whistler/Blackcomb", "Zermatt"};
```

```
JComboBox    resorts = new JComboBox(data);
JScrollPane resortPane = new JScrollPane(resorts);
JPanel       listPanel = new JPanel();
listPanel.add(resortPane);
top.add(listPanel);
skiPanel.add(top);
JPanel       bg = new JPanel();
bg.setLayout(new BoxLayout(bg, BoxLayout.Y_AXIS));
bg.setBorder(new TitledBorder(new EtchedBorder(), "Background"));
JPanel j1 = new JPanel();
j1.add(new JRadioButton());
j1.add(new JLabel(new ImageIcon("green.gif")));
j1.add(new JRadioButton());
j1.add(new JLabel(new ImageIcon("blue.gif")));
JPanel j2 = new JPanel();
j2.add(new JRadioButton());
j2.add(new JLabel(new ImageIcon("yellow.gif")));
j2.add(new JRadioButton());
j2.add(new JLabel(new ImageIcon("magenta.gif")));
bg.add(j1);
bg.add(j2);
skiPanel.add(bg);
return skiPanel;
}
```

The two `Swing` panels that are generated from the methods `makeSkiDetail` and `makeSkiProps` are created with content that will be displayed in the left and right sides of the GUI's split pane:

```
/*
 * main
 */
public static void main(String[] args) {
  JFrame frame = new JFrame("Java-Based Portal");
  frame.addWindowListener(new WindowAdapter() {
    public void windowClosing(WindowEvent e) {System.exit(0);}
  });
  frame.getContentPane().add(new JavaPortal(),
                             BorderLayout.CENTER);
  frame.setSize(600, 400);
  frame.setVisible(true);
}
}
```

As you can see, the preceding code is not enough to produce a fully functioning portal application as depicted in Figure 12.10. It merely represents a shell for how a Java-based portal application can be built, and demonstrates several options that Java Swing can offer the developer in building a portal interface.

Another example of a Java-based application is **BrowserG**. BrowserG is a freeware Java-based desktop application developed by Jeet Shahani that is based on the WebClient Java API. Documentation and download information can be found at http://browserg.mozdev.org. Figure 12.13 shows one facet of this product's functionality.

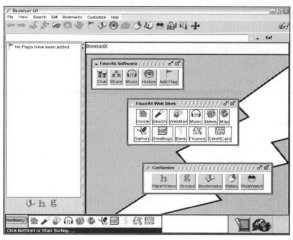

Figure 12.13

You will notice that this application utilizes moveable menu bars. These can add great flexibility, as it essentially allows for a *layering* of application interfaces. These examples show only a small part of what a Java-based application can look like or what its perceived functionality can entail. They should provide you with a good idea of how much more flexible a Java-based application (for example, a portal) can be versus an HTML Web-based portal.

Summary

Enterprise portals continue to evolve, and with it so should the technologies behind them. As portals become more sophisticated, the framework that supports them needs to be flexible enough to satisfy all of their requirements. A move to using a richer client interface in the form of a Java application is not new, but how the application can be installed and maintained on a client machine has been greatly improved with the introduction of Java Web Start. As a developer, taking advantage of the Java Web Start framework is very simple. The following list shows the relatively few steps that need to be taken to make any Java application "webified" for use by Java Web Start:

1. Download and install Java Web Start.
2. Configure the Web server to recognize `.jnlp` file requests.
3. Create a Java application.
4. Create a JNLP file for the application.
5. Package the application in a JAR(s) file and put it in the necessary location on the Web server.
6. Sign the application code if necessary.
7. Create an HTML Web page that has a link to the JNLP file.

Ultimately, using Java Web Start is beneficial for both the user and the developer. The user of a Java application delivered by Java Web Start will embrace its richness and functionality, while the developer will appreciate it for its flexibility, security, and robustness.

References

[ALUR] Alur, Deepak, John Crupi, and Dan Malks. *Core J2EE Patterns: Best Practices and Design Strategies*. Upper Saddle River, NJ: Prentice-Hall, 2001.

[AMBLER] Ambler, Scott M. *Agile Modeling: Effective Practices for Extreme Programming and the Unified Process*. Indianapolis, IN: John Wiley & Sons, 2002.

[BECKFOWLER] Beck, Kent and Martin Fowler. *Planning Extreme Programming*. Boston, MA: Addison Wesley, 2000.

[GoF] Gamma, Erich, Richard Helm, Ralph Johnson, and John Vlissides. *Design Patterns: Elements of Reusable Object-Oriented Software*. Reading, MA: Addison-Wesley, 1996.

[HOWTO] See http://jakarta.apache.org/tomcat/tomcat-5.0-doc/realm-howto.html.

[JCP] *JSR-000003 Java Management Extensions (JMX) Maintenance Release 2*, September 2, 2002.

[JSR168] *The Java Portlet Specification 1.0*, October 27, 2003.

[NIST] Computer Security Resource Center. "An Introduction to Role-Based Access Control," in *ITL Computer Security Bulletin*. National Institute of Standards and Technology, December 1995. See also http://csrc.nist.gov/publications/nistbul/csl95-12.txt.

[REALMHOWTO] The Tomcat 5 Servlet JSP Container — Realm Configuration HOWTO, http://jakarta.apache.org/tomcat/tomcat-5.0-doc/realm-howto.html.

[SCHAECK] Schaeck, Thomas. "Web Services for Remote Portals (WSRP) Whitepaper," in *OASIS Web Services for Remote Portlets TC*, 2002.

References

[SMITHK] Smith, Kevin. "Solutions for Web Services Security — Lessons Learned in a Department of Defense Program," in *Object Management Group's 2nd Workshop on Web Services Modeling, Architectures, Infrastructures and Standards. Philadelphia, PA* , April 2003.

[SOAP] *Simple Object Access Protocol 1.1, W3C Note,* May 8, 2000. See www.w3.org/TR/SOAP/.

[WSRP] *Committee Specification 1.0: OASIS Web Services for Remote Portlets,* Committee Specification 1.0, July 14, 2003.

Index

Symbols

G

H

M

Apache Software License

Version 1.1

Redistribution and use in source and binary forms, with or without modification, are permitted provided that the following conditions are met:

1. Redistributions of source code must retain the above copyright notice, this list of conditions and the following disclaimer.

2. Redistributions in binary form must reproduce the above copyright notice, this list of conditions and the following disclaimer in the documentation and/or other materials provided with the distribution.

3. The end-user documentation included with the redistribution, if any, must include the following acknowledgment:

   "This product includes software developed by the Apache Software Foundation (www.apache.org/)."

   Alternately, this acknowledgment may appear in the software itself, if and wherever such third-party acknowledgments normally appear.

4. The names "Apache" and "Apache Software Foundation" must not be used to endorse or promote products derived from this software without prior written permission. For written permission, please contact apache@apache.org.

5. Products derived from this software may not be called "Apache," nor may "Apache" appear in their name, without prior written permission of the Apache Software Foundation.

GNU Lesser General Public License

Version 2.1, February 1999

Preamble

The licenses for most software are designed to take away your freedom to share and change it. By contrast, the GNU General Public Licenses are intended to guarantee your freedom to share and change free software — to make sure the software is free for all its users.

This license, the Lesser General Public License, applies to some specially designated software packages— typically libraries — of the Free Software Foundation and other authors who decide to use it. You can use it too, but we suggest you first think carefully about whether this license or the ordinary General Public License is the better strategy to use in any particular case, based on the explanations below.

When we speak of free software, we are referring to freedom of use, not price. Our General Public Licenses are designed to make sure that you have the freedom to distribute copies of free software (and charge for this service if you wish); that you receive source code or can get it if you want it; that you can change the software and use pieces of it in new free programs; and that you are informed that you can do these things.

To protect your rights, we need to make restrictions that forbid distributors to deny you these rights or to ask you to surrender these rights. These restrictions translate to certain responsibilities for you if you distribute copies of the library or if you modify it.

For example, if you distribute copies of the library, whether gratis or for a fee, you must give the recipients all the rights that we gave you. You must make sure that they, too, receive or can get the source code. If you link other code with the library, you must provide complete object files to the recipients, so that they can relink them with the library after making changes to the library and recompiling it. And you must show them these terms so they know their rights. We protect your rights with a two-step method: (1) we copyright the library, and (2) we offer you this license, which gives you legal permission to copy, distribute and/or modify the library.

To protect each distributor, we want to make it very clear that there is no warranty for the free library. Also, if the library is modified by someone else and passed on, the recipients should know that what they have is not the original version, so that the original author's reputation will not be affected by problems that might be introduced by others.

Finally, software patents pose a constant threat to the existence of any free program. We wish to make sure that a company cannot effectively restrict the users of a free program by obtaining a restrictive license from a patent holder. Therefore, we insist that any patent license obtained for a version of the library must be consistent with the full freedom of use specified in this license.

Most GNU software, including some libraries, is covered by the ordinary GNU General Public License. This license, the GNU Lesser General Public License, applies to certain designated libraries, and is quite different from the ordinary General Public License. We use this license for certain libraries in order to permit linking those libraries into non-free programs.

When a program is linked with a library, whether statically or using a shared library, the combination of the two is legally speaking a combined work, a derivative of the original library. The ordinary General Public License therefore permits such linking only if the entire combination fits its criteria of freedom. The Lesser General Public License permits more lax criteria for linking other code with the library.

We call this license the "Lesser" General Public License because it does Less to protect the user's freedom than the ordinary General Public License. It also provides other free software developers Less of an advantage over competing non-free programs. These disadvantages are the reason we use the ordinary General Public License for many libraries. However, the Lesser license provides advantages in certain special circumstances.

For example, on rare occasions, there may be a special need to encourage the widest possible use of a certain library, so that it becomes a de-facto standard. To achieve this, non-free programs must be allowed to use the library. A more frequent case is that a free library does the same job as widely used non-free libraries. In this case, there is little to gain by limiting the free library to free software only, so we use the Lesser General Public License.

In other cases, permission to use a particular library in non-free programs enables a greater number of people to use a large body of free software. For example, permission to use the GNU C Library in non-free programs enables many more people to use the whole GNU operating system, as well as its variant, the GNU/Linux operating system.

Although the Lesser General Public License is Less protective of the users' freedom, it does ensure that the user of a program that is linked with the Library has the freedom and the wherewithal to run that program using a modified version of the Library.

The precise terms and conditions for copying, distribution and modification follow. Pay close attention to the difference between a "work based on the library" and a "work that uses the library." The former contains code derived from the library, whereas the latter must be combined with the library in order to run.

GNU Lesser General Public License Terms and Conditions for Copying, Distribution and Modification

0.   This License Agreement applies to any software library or other program which contains a notice placed by the copyright holder or other authorized party saying it may be distributed under the terms of this Lesser General Public License (also called "this License"). Each licensee is addressed as "you."

A "library" means a collection of software functions and/or data prepared so as to be conveniently linked with application programs (which use some of those functions and data) to form executables.

The "Library," below, refers to any such software library or work which has been distributed under these terms. A "work based on the Library" means either the Library or any derivative work under copyright law: that is to say, a work containing the Library or a portion of it, either verbatim or with modifications and/or translated straightforwardly into another language. (Hereinafter, translation is included without limitation in the term "modification.")

"Source code" for a work means the preferred form of the work for making modifications to it. For a library, complete source code means all the source code for all modules it contains, plus any associated interface definition files, plus the scripts used to control compilation and installation of the library.

Activities other than copying, distribution and modification are not covered by this License; they are outside its scope. The act of running a program using the Library is not restricted, and output from such a program is covered only if its contents constitute a work based on the Library (independent of the use of the Library in a tool for writing it). Whether that is true depends on what the Library does and what the program that uses the Library does.

1. You may copy and distribute verbatim copies of the Library's complete source code as you receive it, in any medium, provided that you conspicuously and appropriately publish on each copy an appropriate copyright notice and disclaimer of warranty; keep intact all the notices that refer to this License and to the absence of any warranty; and distribute a copy of this License along with the Library.

   You may charge a fee for the physical act of transferring a copy, and you may at your option offer warranty protection in exchange for a fee.

2. You may modify your copy or copies of the Library or any portion of it, thus forming a work based on the Library, and copy and distribute such modifications or work under the terms of Section 1 above, provided that you also meet all of these conditions:

   a) The modified work must itself be a software library.

   b) You must cause the files modified to carry prominent notices stating that you changed the files and the date of any change.

   c) You must cause the whole of the work to be licensed at no charge to all third parties under the terms of this License.

   d) If a facility in the modified Library refers to a function or a table of data to be supplied by an application program that uses the facility, other than as an argument passed when the facility is invoked, then you must make a good faith effort to ensure that, in the event an application does not supply such function or table, the facility still operates, and performs whatever part of its purpose remains meaningful. (For example, a function in a library to compute square roots has a purpose that is entirely well-defined independent of the application. Therefore, Subsection 2d requires that any application-supplied function or table used by this function must be optional: if the application does not supply it, the square root function must still compute square roots.)

   These requirements apply to the modified work as a whole. If identifiable sections of that work are not derived from the Library, and can be reasonably considered independent and separate works in themselves, then this License, and its terms, do not apply to those sections when you distribute them as separate works. But when you distribute the same sections as part of a whole which is a work based on the Library, the distribution of the whole must be on the terms of this License, whose permissions for other licensees extend to the entire whole, and thus to each and every part regardless of who wrote it.

Thus, it is not the intent of this section to claim rights or contest your rights to work written entirely by you; rather, the intent is to exercise the right to control the distribution of derivative or collective works based on the Library.

In addition, mere aggregation of another work not based on the Library with the Library (or with a work based on the Library) on a volume of a storage or distribution medium does not bring the other work under the scope of this License.

3. You may opt to apply the terms of the ordinary GNU General Public License instead of this License to a given copy of the Library. To do this, you must alter all the notices that refer to this License, so that they refer to the ordinary GNU General Public License, version 2, instead of to this License. (If a newer version than version 2 of the ordinary GNU General Public License has appeared, then you can specify that version instead if you wish.) Do not make any other change in these notices.

    Once this change is made in a given copy, it is irreversible for that copy, so the ordinary GNU General Public License applies to all subsequent copies and derivative works made from that copy.

    This option is useful when you wish to copy part of the code of the Library into a program that is not a library.

4. You may copy and distribute the Library (or a portion or derivative of it, under Section 2) in object code or executable form under the terms of Sections 1 and 2 above provided that you accompany it with the complete corresponding machine-readable source code, which must be distributed under the terms of Sections 1 and 2 above on a medium customarily used for software interchange.

    If distribution of object code is made by offering access to copy from a designated place, then offering equivalent access to copy the source code from the same place satisfies the requirement to distribute the source code, even though third parties are not compelled to copy the source along with the object code.

5. A program that contains no derivative of any portion of the Library, but is designed to work with the Library by being compiled or linked with it, is called a "work that uses the Library." Such a work, in isolation, is not a derivative work of the Library, and therefore falls outside the scope of this License.

    However, linking a "work that uses the Library" with the Library creates an executable that is a derivative of the Library (because it contains portions of the Library), rather than a "work that uses the library." The executable is therefore covered by this License. Section 6 states terms for distribution of such executables.

    When a "work that uses the Library" uses material from a header file that is part of the Library, the object code for the work may be a derivative work of the Library even though the source code is not. Whether this is true is especially significant if the work can be linked without the Library, or if the work is itself a library. The threshold for this to be true is not precisely defined by law.

    If such an object file uses only numerical parameters, data structure layouts and accessors, and small macros and small inline functions (ten lines or less in length), then the use of the object file is unrestricted, regardless of whether it is legally a derivative work. (Executables containing this object code plus portions of the Library will still fall under Section 6.)

Otherwise, if the work is a derivative of the Library, you may distribute the object code for the work under the terms of Section 6. Any executables containing that work also fall under Section 6, whether or not they are linked directly with the Library itself.

6. As an exception to the Sections above, you may also combine or link a "work that uses the Library" with the Library to produce a work containing portions of the Library, and distribute that work under terms of your choice, provided that the terms permit modification of the work for the customer's own use and reverse engineering for debugging such modifications.

You must give prominent notice with each copy of the work that the Library is used in it and that the Library and its use are covered by this License. You must supply a copy of this License. If the work during execution displays copyright notices, you must include the copyright notice for the Library among them, as well as a reference directing the user to the copy of this License. Also, you must do one of these things:

a) Accompany the work with the complete corresponding machine-readable source code for the Library including whatever changes were used in the work (which must be distributed under Sections 1 and 2 above); and, if the work is an executable linked with the Library, with the complete machine-readable "work that uses the Library," as object code and/or source code, so that the user can modify the Library and then relink to produce a modified executable containing the modified Library. (It is understood that the user who changes the contents of definitions files in the Library will not necessarily be able to recompile the application to use the modified definitions.)

b) Use a suitable shared library mechanism for linking with the Library. A suitable mechanism is one that (1) uses at run time a copy of the library already present on the user's computer system, rather than copying library functions into the executable, and (2) will operate properly with a modified version of the library, if the user installs one, as long as the modified version is interface-compatible with the version that the work was made with.

c) Accompany the work with a written offer, valid for at least three years, to give the same user the materials specified in Subsection 6a, above, for a charge no more than the cost of performing this distribution.

d) If distribution of the work is made by offering access to copy from a designated place, offer equivalent access to copy the above specified materials from the same place.

e) Verify that the user has already received a copy of these materials or that you have already sent this user a copy.

For an executable, the required form of the "work that uses the Library" must include any data and utility programs needed for reproducing the executable from it. However, as a special exception, the materials to be distributed need not include anything that is normally distributed (in either source or binary form) with the major components (compiler, kernel, and so on) of the operating system on which the executable runs, unless that component itself accompanies the executable.

It may happen that this requirement contradicts the license restrictions of other proprietary libraries that do not normally accompany the operating system. Such a contradiction means you cannot use both them and the Library together in an executable that you distribute.

7. You may place library facilities that are a work based on the Library side-by-side in a single library together with other library facilities not covered by this License, and distribute such a combined library, provided that the separate distribution of the work based on the Library and of the other library facilities is otherwise permitted, and provided that you do these two things:

a) Accompany the combined library with a copy of the same work based on the Library, uncombined with any other library facilities. This must be distributed under the terms of the Sections above.

b) Give prominent notice with the combined library of the fact that part of it is a work based on the Library, and explaining where to find the accompanying uncombined form of the same work.

8. You may not copy, modify, sublicense, link with, or distribute the Library except as expressly provided under this License. Any attempt otherwise to copy, modify, sublicense, link with, or distribute the Library is void, and will automatically terminate your rights under this License. However, parties who have received copies, or rights, from you under this License will not have their licenses terminated so long as such parties remain in full compliance.

9. You are not required to accept this License, since you have not signed it. However, nothing else grants you permission to modify or distribute the Library or its derivative works. These actions are prohibited by law if you do not accept this License. Therefore, by modifying or distributing the Library (or any work based on the Library), you indicate your acceptance of this License to do so, and all its terms and conditions for copying, distributing or modifying the Library or works based on it.

10. Each time you redistribute the Library (or any work based on the Library), the recipient automatically receives a license from the original licensor to copy, distribute, link with or modify the Library subject to these terms and conditions. You may not impose any further restrictions on the recipients' exercise of the rights granted herein. You are not responsible for enforcing compliance by third parties with this License.

11. If, as a consequence of a court judgment or allegation of patent infringement or for any other reason (not limited to patent issues), conditions are imposed on you (whether by court order, agreement or otherwise) that contradict the conditions of this License, they do not excuse you from the conditions of this License. If you cannot distribute so as to satisfy simultaneously your obligations under this License and any other pertinent obligations, then as a consequence you may not distribute the Library at all. For example, if a patent license would not permit royalty-free redistribution of the Library by all those who receive copies directly or indirectly through you, then the only way you could satisfy both it and this License would be to refrain entirely from distribution of the Library.

If any portion of this section is held invalid or unenforceable under any particular circumstance, the balance of the section is intended to apply, and the section as a whole is intended to apply in other circumstances.

It is not the purpose of this section to induce you to infringe any patents or other property right claims or to contest validity of any such claims; this section has the sole purpose of protecting the integrity of the free software distribution system which is implemented by public license practices. Many people have made generous contributions to the wide range of software distributed through that system in reliance on consistent application of that system; it is up to the author/donor to decide if he or she is willing to distribute software through any other system and a licensee cannot impose that choice.

This section is intended to make thoroughly clear what is believed to be a consequence of the rest of this License.

12. If the distribution and/or use of the Library is restricted in certain countries either by patents or by copyrighted interfaces, the original copyright holder who places the Library under this License may add an explicit geographical distribution limitation excluding those countries, so that distribution is permitted only in or among countries not thus excluded. In such case, this License incorporates the limitation as if written in the body of this License.

13. The Free Software Foundation may publish revised and/or new versions of the Lesser General Public License from time to time. Such new versions will be similar in spirit to the present version, but may differ in detail to address new problems or concerns. Each version is given a distinguishing version number. If the Library specifies a version number of this License which applies to it and "any later version," you have the option of following the terms and conditions either of that version or of any later version published by the Free Software Foundation. If the Library does not specify a license version number, you may choose any version ever published by the Free Software Foundation.

14. If you wish to incorporate parts of the Library into other free programs whose distribution conditions are incompatible with these, write to the author to ask for permission. For software which is copyrighted by the Free Software Foundation, write to the Free Software Foundation; we sometimes make exceptions for this. Our decision will be guided by the two goals of preserving the free status of all derivatives of our free software and of promoting the sharing and reuse of software generally.

NO WARRANTY

15. BECAUSE THE LIBRARY IS LICENSED FREE OF CHARGE, THERE IS NO WARRANTY FOR THE LIBRARY, TO THE EXTENT PERMITTED BY APPLICABLE LAW. EXCEPT WHEN OTHERWISE STATED IN WRITING THE COPYRIGHT HOLDERS AND/OR OTHER PARTIES PROVIDE THE LIBRARY "AS IS" WITHOUT WARRANTY OF ANY KIND, EITHER EXPRESSED OR IMPLIED, INCLUDING, BUT NOT LIMITED TO, THE IMPLIED WARRANTIES OF MERCHANTABILITY AND FITNESS FOR A PARTICULAR PURPOSE. THE ENTIRE RISK AS TO THE QUALITY AND PERFORMANCE OF THE LIBRARY IS WITH YOU. SHOULD THE LIBRARY PROVE DEFECTIVE, YOU ASSUME THE COST OF ALL NECESSARY SERVICING, REPAIR OR CORRECTION.

16. IN NO EVENT UNLESS REQUIRED BY APPLICABLE LAW OR AGREED TO IN WRITING WILL ANY COPYRIGHT HOLDER, OR ANY OTHER PARTY WHO MAY MODIFY AND/OR REDISTRIBUTE THE LIBRARY AS PERMITTED ABOVE, BE LIABLE TO YOU FOR DAMAGES, INCLUDING ANY GENERAL, SPECIAL, INCIDENTAL OR CONSEQUENTIAL DAMAGES ARISING OUT OF THE USE OR INABILITY TO USE THE LIBRARY (INCLUDING BUT NOT LIMITED TO LOSS OF DATA OR DATA BEING RENDERED INACCURATE OR LOSSES SUSTAINED BY YOU OR THIRD PARTIES OR A FAILURE OF THE LIBRARY TO OPERATE WITH ANY OTHER SOFTWARE), EVEN IF SUCH HOLDER OR OTHER PARTY HAS BEEN ADVISED OF THE POSSIBILITY OF SUCH DAMAGES.

END OF TERMS AND CONDITIONS

How to Apply These Terms to Your New Libraries

If you develop a new library, and you want it to be of the greatest possible use to the public, we recommend making it free software that everyone can redistribute and change. You can do so by permitting redistribution under these terms (or, alternatively, under the terms of the ordinary General Public License).

To apply these terms, attach the following notices to the library. It is safest to attach them to the start of each source file to most effectively convey the exclusion of warranty; and each file should have at least the "copyright" line and a pointer to where the full notice is found.

<one line to give the library's name and a brief idea of what it does.>

Copyright © *<year> <name of author>*

This library is free software; you can redistribute it and/or modify it under the terms of the GNU Lesser General Public License as published by the Free Software Foundation; either version 2.1 of the License, or (at your option) any later version.

This library is distributed in the hope that it will be useful, but WITHOUT ANY WARRANTY; without even the implied warranty of MERCHANTABILITY or FITNESS FOR A PARTICULAR PURPOSE. See the GNU Lesser General Public License for more details. You should have received a copy of the GNU Lesser General Public License along with this library; if not, write to the Free Software Foundation, Inc., 59 Temple Place, Suite 330, Boston, MA 02111-1307 USA.

Also add information on how to contact you by electronic and paper mail. You should also get your employer (if you work as a programmer) or your school, if any, to sign a "copyright disclaimer" for the library, if necessary. Here is a sample; alter the names:

Yoyodyne, Inc., hereby disclaims all copyright interest in the library 'Frob' (a library for tweaking knobs) written by James Random Hacker.

<signature of Ty Coon>, 1 April 1990

Ty Coon, President of Vice

That's all there is to it!

GNU General Public License

Version 2, June 1991

Copyright © 1989, 1991 Free Software Foundation, Inc., 59 Temple Place, Suite 330, Boston, MA 02111-1307 USA.

Everyone is permitted to copy and distribute verbatim copies of this license document, but changing it is not allowed.

Preamble

The licenses for most software are designed to take away your freedom to share and change it. By contrast, the GNU General Public License is intended to guarantee your freedom to share and change free software—to make sure the software is free for all its users. This General Public License applies to most of the Free Software Foundation's software and to any other program whose authors commit to using it. (Some other Free Software Foundation software is covered by the GNU Library General Public License instead.) You can apply it to your programs, too.

When we speak of free software, we are referring to freedom, not price. Our General Public Licenses are designed to make sure that you have the freedom to distribute copies of free software (and charge for this service if you wish), that you receive source code or can get it if you want it, that you can change the software or use pieces of it in new free programs; and that you know you can do these things.

To protect your rights, we need to make restrictions that forbid anyone to deny you these rights or to ask you to surrender the rights. These restrictions translate to certain responsibilities for you if you distribute copies of the software, or if you modify it.

For example, if you distribute copies of such a program, whether gratis or for a fee, you must give the recipients all the rights that you have. You must make sure that they, too, receive or can get the source code. And you must show them these terms so they know their rights.

We protect your rights with two steps: (1) copyright the software, and (2) offer you this license which gives you legal permission to copy, distribute and/or modify the software.

Also, for each author's protection and ours, we want to make certain that everyone understands that there is no warranty for this free software. If the software is modified by someone else and passed on, we want its recipients to know that what they have is not the original, so that any problems introduced by others will not reflect on the original authors' reputations.

Finally, any free program is threatened constantly by software patents. We wish to avoid the danger that redistributors of a free program will individually obtain patent licenses, in effect making the program proprietary. To prevent this, we have made it clear that any patent must be licensed for everyone's free use or not licensed at all.

The precise terms and conditions for copying, distribution and modification follow.

Terms and Conditions for Copying, Distribution and Modification

0. This License applies to any program or other work which contains a notice placed by the copyright holder saying it may be distributed under the terms of this General Public License. The "Program," below, refers to any such program or work, and a "work based on the Program" means either the Program or any derivative work under copyright law: that is to say, a work containing the Program or a portion of it, either verbatim or with modifications and/or translated into another language. (Hereinafter, translation is included without limitation in the term "modification.") Each licensee is addressed as "you."

    Activities other than copying, distribution and modification are not covered by this License; they are outside its scope. The act of running the Program is not restricted, and the output from the Program is covered only if its contents constitute a work based on the Program (independent of having been made by running the Program).

    Whether that is true depends on what the Program does.

1. You may copy and distribute verbatim copies of the Program's source code as you receive it, in any medium, provided that you conspicuously and appropriately publish on each copy an appropriate copyright notice and disclaimer of warranty; keep intact all the notices that refer to this License and to the absence of any warranty; and give any other recipients of the Program a copy of this License along with the Program.

    You may charge a fee for the physical act of transferring a copy, and you may at your option offer warranty protection in exchange for a fee.

2. You may modify your copy or copies of the Program or any portion of it, thus forming a work based on the Program, and copy and distribute such modifications or work under the terms of Section 1 above, provided that you also meet all of these conditions:

    a) You must cause the modified files to carry prominent notices stating that you changed the files and the date of any change.

    b) You must cause any work that you distribute or publish, that in whole or in part contains or is derived from the Program or any part thereof, to be licensed as a whole at no charge to all third parties under the terms of this License.

    c) If the modified program normally reads commands interactively when run, you must cause it, when started running for such interactive use in the most ordinary way, to print or display an announcement including an appropriate copyright notice and a notice that there is no warranty (or else, saying that you provide a warranty) and that users may redistribute the program under these conditions, and telling the user how to view a copy of this License. (Exception: if the Program itself is interactive but does not normally print such an announcement, your work based on the Program is not required to print an announcement.)

    These requirements apply to the modified work as a whole. If identifiable sections of that work are not derived from the Program, and can be reasonably considered independent and separate works in themselves, then this License, and its terms, do not apply to those sections when you distribute them as separate works. But when you distribute the same sections as part of a whole which is a work based on the Program, the distribution of the whole must be on the terms of this License, whose permissions for other licensees extend to the entire whole, and thus to each and every part regardless of who wrote it. Thus, it is not the intent of this section to claim rights or contest your rights to work written entirely by you; rather, the intent is to exercise the right to control the distribution of derivative or collective works based on the Program.

In addition, mere aggregation of another work not based on the Program with the Program (or with a work based on the Program) on a volume of a storage or distribution medium does not bring the other work under the scope of this License.

3. You may copy and distribute the Program (or a work based on it, under Section 2) in object code or executable form under the terms of Sections 1 and 2 above provided that you also do one of the following:

    a) Accompany it with the complete corresponding machine-readable source code, which must be distributed under the terms of Sections 1 and 2 above on a medium customarily used for software interchange; or,

    b) Accompany it with a written offer, valid for at least three years, to give any third party, for a charge no more than your cost of physically performing source distribution, a complete machine-readable copy of the corresponding source code, to be distributed under the terms of Sections 1 and 2 above on a medium customarily used for software interchange; or,

    c) Accompany it with the information you received as to the offer to distribute corresponding source code. (This alternative is allowed only for noncommercial distribution and only if you received the program in object code or executable form with such an offer, in accord with Subsection b above.)

    The source code for a work means the preferred form of the work for making modifications to it. For an executable work, complete source code means all the source code for all modules it contains, plus any associated interface definition files, plus the scripts used to control compilation and installation of the executable. However, as a special exception, the source code distributed need not include anything that is normally distributed (in either source or binary form) with the major components (compiler, kernel, and so on) of the operating system on which the executable runs, unless that component itself accompanies the executable.

    If distribution of executable or object code is made by offering access to copy from a designated place, then offering equivalent access to copy the source code from the same place counts as distribution of the source code, even though third parties are not compelled to copy the source along with the object code.

4. You may not copy, modify, sublicense, or distribute the Program except as expressly provided under this License. Any attempt otherwise to copy, modify, sublicense or distribute the Program is void, and will automatically terminate your rights under this License. However, parties who have received copies, or rights, from you under this License will not have their licenses terminated so long as such parties remain in full compliance.

5. You are not required to accept this License, since you have not signed it. However, nothing else grants you permission to modify or distribute the Program or its derivative works. These actions are prohibited by law if you do not accept this License. Therefore, by modifying or distributing the Program (or any work based on the Program), you indicate your acceptance of this License to do so, and all its terms and conditions for copying, distributing or modifying the Program or works based on it.

6. Each time you redistribute the Program (or any work based on the Program), the recipient automatically receives a license from the original licensor to copy, distribute or modify the Program subject to these terms and conditions. You may not impose any further restrictions on the recipients' exercise of the rights granted herein. You are not responsible for enforcing compliance by third parties to this License.

7. If, as a consequence of a court judgment or allegation of patent infringement or for any other reason (not limited to patent issues), conditions are imposed on you (whether by court order, agreement or otherwise) that contradict the conditions of this License, they do not excuse you from the conditions of this License. If you cannot distribute so as to satisfy simultaneously your obligations under this License and any other pertinent obligations, then as a consequence you may not distribute the Program at all. For example, if a patent license would not permit royalty-free redistribution of the Program by all those who receive copies directly or indirectly through you, then the only way you could satisfy both it and this License would be to refrain entirely from distribution of the Program.

If any portion of this section is held invalid or unenforceable under any particular circumstance, the balance of the section is intended to apply and the section as a whole is intended to apply in other circumstances.

It is not the purpose of this section to induce you to infringe any patents or other property right claims or to contest validity of any such claims; this section has the sole purpose of protecting the integrity of the free software distribution system, which is implemented by public license practices. Many people have made generous contributions to the wide range of software distributed through that system in reliance on consistent application of that system; it is up to the author/donor to decide if he or she is willing to distribute software through any other system and a licensee cannot impose that choice.

This section is intended to make thoroughly clear what is believed to be a consequence of the rest of this License.

8. If the distribution and/or use of the Program is restricted in certain countries either by patents or by copyrighted interfaces, the original copyright holder who places the Program under this License may add an explicit geographical distribution limitation excluding those countries, so that distribution is permitted only in or among countries not thus excluded. In such case, this License incorporates the limitation as if written in the body of this License.

9. The Free Software Foundation may publish revised and/or new versions of the General Public License from time to time. Such new versions will be similar in spirit to the present version, but may differ in detail to address new problems or concerns.

Each version is given a distinguishing version number. If the Program specifies a version number of this License which applies to it and "any later version," you have the option of following the terms and conditions either of that version or of any later version published by the Free Software Foundation. If the Program does not specify a version number of this License, you may choose any version ever published by the Free Software Foundation.

10. If you wish to incorporate parts of the Program into other free programs whose distribution conditions are different, write to the author to ask for permission. For software which is copyrighted by the Free Software Foundation, write to the Free Software Foundation; we sometimes make exceptions for this. Our decision will be guided by the two goals of preserving the free status of all derivatives of our free software and of promoting the sharing and reuse of software generally.

NO WARRANTY

11. BECAUSE THE PROGRAM IS LICENSED FREE OF CHARGE, THERE IS NO WARRANTY FOR THE PROGRAM, TO THE EXTENT PERMITTED BY APPLICABLE LAW. EXCEPT WHEN OTHERWISE STATED IN WRITING THE COPYRIGHT HOLDERS AND/OR OTHER PARTIES PROVIDE THE PROGRAM "AS IS" WITHOUT WARRANTY OF ANY KIND, EITHER EXPRESSED OR IMPLIED, INCLUDING, BUT NOT LIMITED TO, THE IMPLIED WARRANTIES OF MERCHANTABILITY AND FITNESS FOR A PARTICULAR PURPOSE. THE ENTIRE RISK AS TO THE QUALITY AND PERFORMANCE OF THE PROGRAM IS WITH YOU. SHOULD THE PROGRAM PROVE DEFECTIVE, YOU ASSUME THE COST OF ALL NECESSARY SERVICING, REPAIR OR CORRECTION.

12. IN NO EVENT UNLESS REQUIRED BY APPLICABLE LAW OR AGREED TO IN WRITING WILL ANY COPYRIGHT HOLDER, OR ANY OTHER PARTY WHO MAY MODIFY AND/OR REDISTRIBUTE THE PROGRAM AS PERMITTED ABOVE, BE LIABLE TO YOU FOR DAMAGES, INCLUDING ANY GENERAL, SPECIAL, INCIDENTAL OR CONSEQUENTIAL DAMAGES ARISING OUT OF THE USE OR INABILITY TO USE THE PROGRAM (INCLUDING BUT NOT LIMITED TO LOSS OF DATA OR DATA BEING RENDERED INACCURATE OR LOSSES SUSTAINED BY YOU OR THIRD PARTIES OR A FAILURE OF THE PROGRAM TO OPERATE WITH ANY OTHER PROGRAMS), EVEN IF SUCH HOLDER OR OTHER PARTY HAS BEEN ADVISED OF THE POSSIBILITY OF SUCH DAMAGES.

END OF TERMS AND CONDITIONS

How to Apply These Terms to Your New Programs

If you develop a new program, and you want it to be of the greatest possible use to the public, the best way to achieve this is to make it free software which everyone can redistribute and change under these terms.

To do so, attach the following notices to the program. It is safest to attach them to the start of each source file to most effectively convey the exclusion of warranty; and each file should have at least the "copyright" line and a pointer to where the full notice is found.

<one line to give the program's name and a brief idea of what it does.>

Copyright © *<year> <name of author>*

This program is free software; you can redistribute it and/or modify it under the terms of the GNU General Public License as published by the Free Software Foundation; either version 2 of the License, or (at your option) any later version.

This program is distributed in the hope that it will be useful, but WITHOUT ANY WARRANTY; without even the implied warranty of MERCHANTABILITY or FITNESS FOR A PARTICULAR PURPOSE. See the GNU General Public License for more details.

You should have received a copy of the GNU General Public License along with this program; if not, write to the Free Software Foundation, Inc., 59 Temple Place, Suite 330, Boston, MA 02111-1307 USA.

Also add information on how to contact you by electronic and paper mail. If the program is interactive, make it output a short notice like this when it starts in an interactive mode:

Gnomovision version 69, Copyright © <year> <name of author>

Gnomovision comes with ABSOLUTELY NO WARRANTY; for details, type 'show w.'

This is free software, and you are welcome to redistribute it under certain conditions; type 'show c' for details.

The hypothetical commands 'show w' and 'show c' should show the appropriate parts of the General Public License. Of course, the commands you use may be called something other than `show w' and `show c'; they could even be mouse-clicks or menu items—whatever suits your program.

You should also get your employer (if you work as a programmer) or your school, if any, to sign a "copyright disclaimer" for the program, if necessary. Here is a sample; alter the names:

Yoyodyne, Inc., hereby disclaims all copyright interest in the program 'Gnomovision' (which makes passes at compilers) written by James Hacker.

<signature of Ty Coon>, 1 April 1989

Ty Coon, President of Vice

This General Public License does not permit incorporating your program into proprietary programs. If your program is a subroutine library, you may consider it more useful to permit linking proprietary applications with the library. If this is what you want to do, use the GNU Library General Public License instead of this License.